Problems of Democratisation in Indonesia

The **Research School of Pacific and Asian Studies (RSPAS)**, a part of the **ANU College of Asia and the Pacific** at **The Australian National University**, is home to **The Indonesia Project**, a major international centre, which supports research activities on the Indonesian economy and society. Established in 1965 in the School's Division of Economics, the Project is well known and respected in Indonesia and in other places where Indonesia attracts serious scholarly and official interest. Funded by the ANU and the Australian Agency for International Development (AusAID), the Indonesia Project monitors and analyses recent economic developments in Indonesia; informs Australian governments, business and the wider community about those developments and about future prospects; stimulates research on the Indonesian economy; and publishes the respected *Bulletin of Indonesian Economic Studies*.

The School's **Department of Political and Social Change** (PSC) focuses on domestic politics, social processes and state–society relationships in Asia and the Pacific, and has a long-established interest in Indonesia.

Together with PSC and RSPAS, the Project holds the annual Indonesia Update conference, which offers an overview of recent economic and political developments and devotes attention to a significant theme in Indonesia's development. The Project's *Bulletin of Indonesian Economic Studies* publishes the economic and political overviews, while the proceedings related to the theme of the conference are published in the Indonesia Update Series.

The **Institute of Southeast Asian Studies (ISEAS)** was established as an autonomous organization in 1968. It is a regional centre dedicated to the study of socio-political, security and economic trends and developments in Southeast Asia and its wider geostrategic and economic environment. The Institute's research programmes are the Regional Economic Studies (RES, including ASEAN and APEC), Regional Strategic and Political Studies (RSPS), and Regional Social and Cultural Studies (RSCS).

ISEAS Publishing, an established academic press, has issued more than 2,000 books and journals. It is the largest scholarly publisher of research about Southeast Asia from within the region. ISEAS Publishing works with many other academic and trade publishers and distributors to disseminate important research and analyses from and about Southeast Asia to the rest of the world.

Indonesia Update Series

Problems of Democratisation in Indonesia
Elections, Institutions and Society

EDITED BY
EDWARD ASPINALL AND **MARCUS MIETZNER**

LSEAS

INSTITUTE OF SOUTHEAST ASIAN STUDIES
Singapore

First published in Singapore in 2010 by
ISEAS Publishing
Institute of Southeast Asian Studies
30 Heng Mui Keng Terrace
Pasir Panjang
Singapore 119614

E-mail: publish@iseas.edu.sg
http://bookshop.iseas.edu.sg

ISEAS Library Cataloguing-in-Publication Data

Problems of democratisation in Indonesia : elections, institutions and society /
    edited by Edward Aspinall and Marcus Mietzner.
    (Indonesia update series)
    1.   Democratization — Indonesia — Congresses.
    2.   Elections — Indonesia — Congresses.
    3.   Decentralization in government — Indonesia — Congresses.
    4.   Women — Political activity — Indonesia — Congresses.
    5.   Indonesia — Politics and government — 1998 — Congresses.
    I.   Aspinall, Edward.
    II.   Mietzner, Marcus.
    III.   Australian National University. Indonesia Project.
    IV.   Indonesia Update Conference (2009 : Canberra, Australia)
DS644.4 I41 2009   2010

ISBN 978-981-4279-90-1 (soft cover)
ISBN 978-981-4279-89-5 (hard cover)
ISBN 978-981-4279-91-8 (E-book PDF)

Cover: Sarijo, a member of the Golkar party's security forces, is pictured here at a Golkar rally in Yogyakarta in the lead-up to the 2009 general election.
Photo courtesy of Emanuel Danu Primanto.

Edited and typeset by Beth Thomson, Japan Online, Canberra
Indexed by Angela Grant, Sydney
Printed in Singapore by Utopia Press Pte Ltd

CONTENTS

TABLES

MAPS AND FIGURES

MAPS

FIGURES

CONTRIBUTORS

Edward Aspinall
Senior Fellow, Department of Political and Social Change, School of International, Political and Strategic Studies, College of Asia and the Pacific, The Australian National University, Canberra

Sharon Bessell
Senior Lecturer, Crawford School of Economics and Government, College of Asia and the Pacific, The Australian National University, Canberra

Michael Buehler
Assistant Professor, Department of Political Science, Northern Illinois University

Richard Chauvel
Senior Lecturer, School of Social Sciences and Psychology, Victoria University, Melbourne

Larry Diamond
Senior Fellow, Hoover Institution, and Freeman Spogli Institute for International Studies, Stanford University; Director, Center on Democracy, Development, and the Rule of Law, Stanford University

Ariel Heryanto
Associate Professor of Indonesian Studies, School of Culture, History and Language, College of Asia and the Pacific, The Australian National University, Canberra

Sidney Jones
Senior Advisor, International Crisis Group, Southeast Asia Office, Jakarta

R. William Liddle
Professor of Political Science, Ohio State University, Columbus

Marcus Mietzner
Lecturer, School of Culture, History and Language, College of Asia and the Pacific, The Australian National University, Canberra

Saiful Mujani
Executive Director, Lembaga Survei Indonesia (Indonesian Survey Institute), Jakarta

Blair Palmer
Anthropologist, PhD dissertation submitted to The Australian National University, Canberra, in December 2009

Muhammad Qodari
Executive Director, Indo Barometer (IB), Jakarta

Hana A. Satriyo
Director, Gender and Women's Participation, The Asia Foundation, Jakarta

Stephen Sherlock
Consultant on Governance and Politics in Indonesia, Canberra and Jakarta

Adam Schmidt
Country Director, International Foundation for Electoral Systems (IFES), Jakarta

Rizal Sukma
Executive Director, Center for Strategic and International Studies (CSIS), Jakarta

Dirk Tomsa
Lecturer, School of Social Sciences, Politics and International Relations Program, La Trobe University, Melbourne

Ian Wilson
Lecturer, School of Social Sciences and Humanities, Murdoch University, Murdoch

ACKNOWLEDGMENTS

This book originated in a conference on the theme 'Democracy in practice' held at the Australian National University (ANU) in October 2009. Timed to reflect on the progress and problems of Indonesian democracy in a year of national elections, the conference was also the 27th annual Indonesia Update conference organised by the university's Indonesia Project. Attended by over 300 people, the conference was an occasion for focused analysis and lively debate on the state of Indonesian democracy. It was also a testament to the tremendous intellectual energy centred on Indonesia at the ANU, an environment in which both of us feel immensely privileged to work.

Our thanks go to the many ANU staff members and volunteers without whose assistance we would not have been able to hold such a successful conference. We are especially grateful to the administrative staff of the Indonesia Project, Cathy Haberle, Liz Drysdale and Trish van der Hoek, whose experience and sheer hard work were crucial to making such a complex event run so smoothly, and for the assistance of Allison Ley and Thuy Thu Pham of the Department of Political and Social Change. We are also thankful to the academic leaders of the Indonesia Project, in particular Chris Manning, Ross McLeod and Budy Resosudarmo, for giving us the opportunity to convene the conference and for supporting our plans for it. The principal sponsor of the Indonesia Project, and of the Indonesia Updates, is the Australian government's overseas development agency, AusAID. The agency has our sincere gratitude for making the conference possible and for assisting in the production of this book. AusAID's support for the Indonesia Project and Indonesia Updates over the years has added greatly to the depth and breadth of Indonesia expertise in Australia. In addition, we thank the ANU's Department of Political and Social Change for providing supplementary funding and the Asia Foundation for assisting several speakers and conference participants to come from Jakarta.

Of course, we are particularly grateful to the contributors to this volume. In planning the conference and this book, we aimed to bring together a group of leading analysts of distinct but complementary aspects of Indonesian politics and society, and of Indonesia in its broader global context. We hoped their combined contributions would provide both a level of detail and a comprehensiveness of scope that is sometimes lacking in discussions of Indonesian democracy. It is not for us to judge the success of our venture, but we were certainly impressed by, and appreciative of, the seriousness with which each of our authors went about grappling with the complexities of contemporary Indonesian democracy, and by the great knowledge and expertise they brought to bear on their topics. Twelve of the fifteen authors contributed papers to the conference and revised them for this book; we are grateful to them for devoting such a long period of creative intellectual work to this project. We also thank the three authors who did not present conference papers but agreed to contribute to the volume, putting aside other tasks in order to do so. All contributors deserve our special thanks for responding to a very tight editorial and production schedule.

Finally, we are grateful to those individuals who assisted in the production of the book. We depended upon Beth Thomson for her meticulous and professional copy-editing and typesetting. It was a pleasure to work with someone who has such exacting standards, such specialist knowledge and so much helpful advice. Staff at Cartographic & GIS Services at the ANU, in particular Jennifer Sheehan, prepared the maps, and impressed us with the care they took in researching recent boundary changes. Michael Cookson provided invaluable advice and assistance in helping us to establish those boundaries in Papua. Angela Grant produced the index. We are also grateful to Triena Ong and Rahilah Yusuf at the Institute of Southeast Asian Studies for their support in publishing this book, and for continuing to support the Indonesia Update series.

Edward Aspinall and Marcus Mietzner
Canberra
February 2010

GLOSSARY

abangan	term for nominal or less observant Muslims
adat	custom or tradition; customary or traditional law
aliran	'stream'; a term developed in 1950s anthropological research to distinguish between the various currents of Islam and their affiliated parties and oganisations
Apindo	Asosiasi Pengusaha Indonesia (Association of Indonesian Entrepreneurs)
ASEAN	Association of Southeast Asian Nations
bamus	*badan musyawarah* (steering committee)
Bappenas	Badan Perencanaan Pembangunan Nasional (National Development Planning Agency)
Bawaslu	Badan Pengawasan Pemilu (election supervisory body)
BKN	Badan Kepegawaian Negara (National Civil Service Agency)
BMI	Banteng Muda Indonesia (Indonesian Young Bulls)
BPK	Badan Pemeriksaan Keuangan (State Audit Agency)
BPS	Badan Pusat Statistik (Statistics Indonesia), the central statistics agency
Brigass	Brigade Siaga Satu (Alert One Brigade)
bupati	district head
CETRO	Centre for Electoral Reform
DPD	Dewan Perwakilan Daerah (Regional Representative Council)
DPR	Dewan Perwakilan Rakyat (People's Representative Council), the Indonesian parliament
DPRD	Dewan Perwakilan Rakyat Daerah (Regional People's Representative Council), regional legislature

DPRP	Dewan Perwakilan Rakyat Papua (Papuan People's Representative Council)
FBR	Forum Betawi Rempug (Betawi Brotherhood Forum)
Forkabi	Forum Komunikasi Anak Betawi (Children of Betawi Communication Forum)
Forkot	Forum Komunikasi Tabanan (Tabanan Communication Forum)
FPI	Front Pembela Islam (Defenders of Islam Front)
fraksi	political grouping within parliament, similar to a caucus
gali	*gabungan anak liar* (gangs of wild children)
GAM	Gerakan Aceh Merdeka (Free Aceh Movement)
Gerindra	Partai Gerakan Indonesia Raya (Greater Indonesia Movement Party)
Golkar	orig. Golongan Karya (the state political party under the New Order, and one of the major post-New Order parties)
gubernur	governor
Hanura	Partai Hati Nurani Rakyat (Peoples' Conscience Party)
haram	'forbidden' or prohibited under Islamic law
IFES	International Foundation for Electoral Systems
jago, jawara, jeger	local strongman
jasa	services
JPPR	Jaringan Pendidikan Pemilih untuk Rakyat (People's Voter Education Network)
kapubaten	district
KNPB	Komite Nasional Papua Barat (West Papua National Committee)
Kodam	Komando Daerah Militer (Military Area Command)
komisi	standing committee
Komnas Perempuan	Komisi Nasional Anti Kekerasan Terhadap Perempuan (National Commission on Violence Against Women)
Kopassus	Komando Pasukan Khusus (Special Forces)
kota	municipality
KPA	Komite Peralihan Aceh (Aceh Transitional Committee)
KPI	Koalisi Perempuan Indonesia (Indonesian Women's Coalition)
KPK	Komisi Pemberantasan Korupsi (Corruption Eradication Commission)

KPPI	Kaukus Perempuan Politik Indonesia (Indonesian Women's Political Caucus)
KPPOD	Komite Pemantauan Pelaksanaan Otonomi Daerah (Regional Autonomy Watch)
KPU	Komisi Pemilihan Umum (General Elections Commission)
KPUD	Komisi Pemilihan Umum Daerah (Regional General Elections Commission)
Lingkaran Survei Indonesia	Indonesian Survey Circle
LP3ES	Lembaga Penelitian, Pendidikan dan Penerangan Ekonomi dan Sosial (Institute for Social and Economic Research, Education and Information)
LSI	Lembaga Survei Indonesia (Indonesian Survey Institute)
Malari	Malapetaka Januari (January Disaster)
merdeka	freedom, independence
MOU	memorandum of understanding
MPR	Majelis Permusyawaratan Rakyat (Peoples' Consultative Assembly)
MRP	Majelis Rakyat Papua (Papuan People's Assembly)
Muhammadiyah	Indonesia's largest modernist Islamic organisation
MUI	Majelis Ulama Indonesia (Council of Islamic Scholars)
NU	Nahdlatul Ulama (Awakening of the Ulama), Indonesia's largest traditionalist Islamic organisation
OECD	Organisation for Economic Co-operation and Development
OPM	Organisasi Papua Merdeka (Free Papua Movement)
Opsus	Operasi Khusus (Special Operations)
ormas	*organisasi masyarakat* (social organisations)
PA	Partai Aceh (Aceh Party), a local Aceh party associated with former leaders of the separatist organisation GAM
PAN	Partai Amanat Nasional (National Mandate Party)
Pancasila	the five guiding principles of the Indonesian state (belief in God, humanitarianism, nationalism, democracy and social justice)
panja	*panitia kerja* (working committee)
pansus	*panitia khusus* (special committee)
Partai Patriot	Patriot Party
Partai Patriot Pancasila	Patriotic Pancasila Party

PBB	Partai Bulan Bintang (Crescent Moon and Star Party), an Islamic modernist political party
PBR	Partai Bintang Reformasi (Star Reformist Party), a splinter of PPP
PD	Partai Demokrat (Democratic Party), the party led by President Susilo Bambang Yudhoyono
PDA	Partai Daulat Aceh (Aceh Sovereignty Party), a local Aceh party
PDIP	Partai Demokrasi Indonesia Perjuangan (Indonesian Democratic Party of Struggle), the party led by former president Megawati Sukarnoputri
PDP	Presidium Dewan Papua (Papua Presidium Council)
PDS	Partai Damai Sejahtera (Prosperous Peace Party)
pecalang	'traditional' civilian security forces (Bali)
pemekaran	'blossoming', referring to the process of subdivision of administrative units
Pemuda Pancasila	Pancasila Youth
pilkada	*pemilihan kepala daerah* (direct elections of local government heads)
PKB	Partai Kebangkitan Bangsa (People's Awakening Party), a traditionalist Muslim party
PKI	Partai Komunis Indonesia (Indonesian Communist Party)
PKPI	Partai Keadilan dan Persatuan Indonesia (Indonesian Justice and Unity Party)
PKS	Partai Keadilan Sejahtera (Prosperous Justice Party), an Islamist party
PMB	Partai Matahari Bangsa (Sun of the Nation Party)
PNI	Partai Nasional Indonesia (Indonesian National Party), founded by former president Sukarno in the 1920s
PPP	Partai Persatuan Pembangunan (United Development Party), an Islamist party
PRA	Partai Rakyat Aceh (Aceh People's Party), a left-wing local Aceh party
preman	thug
PSHK	Pusat Studi Hukum dan Kebijakan (Centre for Indonesian Law and Policy Studies)
reformasi	'reform', the post-New Order period
santri	pious Muslims who seek to adhere strictly to the ritual and legal requirements of Islam
satgas	*satuan tugas* (task force)
SBY	Susilo Bambang Yudhoyono, Indonesia's president

SIRA	Sentral Informasi Referendum Aceh (Aceh Referendum Information Centre)
SPSI	Serikat Pekerja Seluruh Indonesia (All Indonesia Workers Union)
syari'ah	Islamic law
Tatib	*Peraturan Tata Tertib* [Rules of Procedure]
USAID	United States Agency for International Development
walikota	mayor

Currencies

$	US dollar
Rp	Indonesian rupiah

Map 1.1   Indonesia

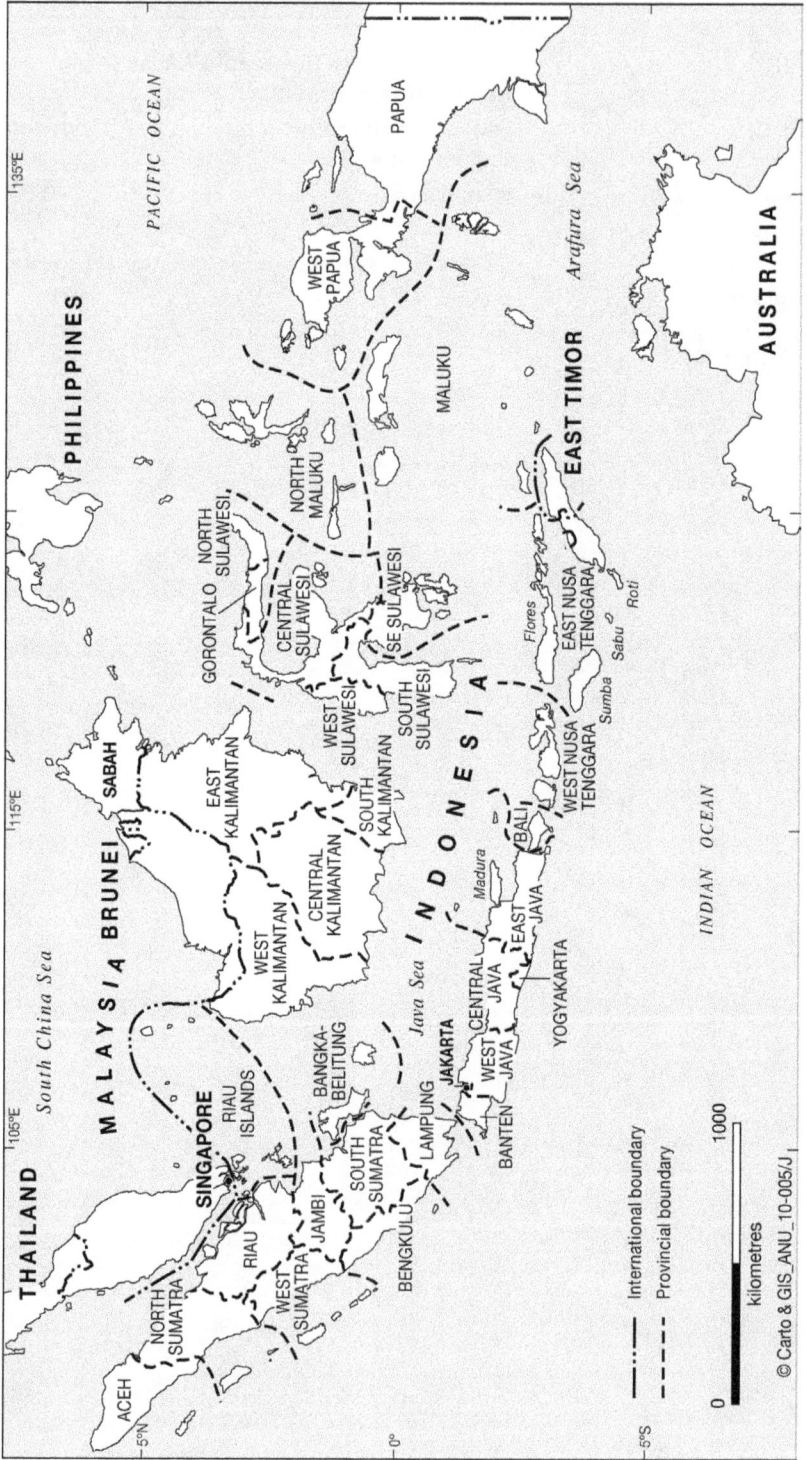

THAILAND

PHILIPPINES

South China Sea

PACIFIC OCEAN

MALAYSIA

BRUNEI

SABAH

SINGAPORE

RIAU
ISLANDS

ACEH

NORTH
SUMATRA

RIAU

WEST
SUMATRA

JAMBI

BENGKULU

SOUTH
SUMATRA

BANGKA-
BELITUNG

LAMPUNG

JAKARTA

BANTEN

WEST
JAVA

CENTRAL
JAVA

YOGYAKARTA

EAST
JAVA

Madura

WEST
KALIMANTAN

CENTRAL
KALIMANTAN

SOUTH
KALIMANTAN

EAST
KALIMANTAN

GORONTALO

NORTH
SULAWESI

CENTRAL
SULAWESI

WEST
SULAWESI

SOUTH
SULAWESI

SE SULAWESI

NORTH
MALUKU

MALUKU

WEST
PAPUA

PAPUA

INDONESIA

Java Sea

BALI

WEST NUSA
TENGGARA

EAST NUSA
TENGGARA

Flores

Sumba

Sabu

Roti

EAST TIMOR

Arafura Sea

INDIAN OCEAN

AUSTRALIA

5°N

0°

5°S

105°E

115°E

135°E

— ·· — International boundary

— — — Provincial boundary

0   1000

kilometres

© Carto & GIS_ANU_10-005/J

1 PROBLEMS OF DEMOCRATISATION IN INDONESIA: AN OVERVIEW

Marcus Mietzner and Edward Aspinall

Ever since the fall of Suharto's authoritarian New Order regime in 1998, analysts have struggled to understand the dynamics of the system that has taken its place. Unlike the New Order, whose centralised and static political system allowed scholars to make durable generalisations about Indonesian politics, the post-Suharto state has defied attempts to describe it in uniform and all-encompassing terms. The failure to define clearly what has emerged since 1998 is reflected in the absence of a widely accepted name for the new polity. While all other political regimes in Indonesia are known by standard labels—'parliamentary democracy' for the period between 1950 and 1957, 'Guided Democracy' for Sukarno's rule from 1959 to 1965 and the 'New Order' for Suharto's regime—scholars have yet to reach consensus on a term to describe the post-authoritarian regime. While they agree that the post-1998 political system has offered more freedom than previous regimes, there is disagreement about almost everything else. Even when authors describe Indonesia as a democracy, they usually qualify the noun with a variety of adjectives, such as 'collusive' or 'delegative' (Slater 2004), 'consolidated' but 'patrimonial' (Webber 2006), 'low quality' (Mietzner 2009a) or 'secular' (Mujani and Liddle 2009).

Yet amidst the diversity of views, it is possible to identify three broad schools of thought on post-New Order Indonesia. First, a significant number of scholars have maintained that despite important institutional reforms, democratic change has been superficial, with core structures of power remaining unchanged. In this perspective, the oligarchic elites who controlled the New Order have survived the 1998 regime change and continue to use the state for rent-seeking purposes (Robison and

Hadiz 2004; Boudreau 2009). Second, there are observers who believe that Indonesia has done exceptionally well in consolidating its democracy, especially from a comparative viewpoint (MacIntyre and Ramage 2008). Against the backdrop of the almost apocalyptic predictions for Indonesia in 1998, which saw the country following in the footsteps of the Soviet Union and Yugoslavia, these analysts point out that leading international thinktanks now acknowledge Indonesia as a functioning electoral democracy (Freedom House 2009). Moreover, this change occurred against a trend of democratic recession in the world more generally and Southeast Asia in particular. Third, some authors have taken the middle ground, emphasising that while Indonesia has made democratic progress, it remains crippled by severe structural problems, most notably corruption and weak law enforcement (Davidson 2009; Aspinall, forthcoming).

This volume on the inner workings of Indonesia's post-Suharto democracy mirrors the pluralism of opinions outlined above. It does not aim to present one dominant framework for interpreting Indonesian democracy and its successes or failures, but allows authors – distinguished experts in their fields – to develop their distinct views, analyses and theoretical approaches. Our objective is, however, to provide a level of detail on the inner workings and mechanics of Indonesia's democratic system that other works have often lacked. Using the 2009 national elections – the third since Indonesia's democratic transition began – as an entry point, the book's contributors focus on how exactly key democratic institutions and procedures have functioned since 1998. Looking beyond simplifying labels, the volume provides micro-analyses of important democratic processes and thus fills a significant gap in the literature on contemporary Indonesia. Students of Indonesia will find material in the volume that adds to existing knowledge on the country's politics and society. Comparativists, on the other hand, will be presented with reasons for paying more attention to the world's third-largest democracy.

In this overview of the volume, we introduce key debates on the post-New Order state and explain how the chapters fit into them. We begin by presenting a comparative perspective on Indonesia's democratisation. While most comparativists believe that Indonesia's post-1998 democracy has performed at least satisfactorily in the global scheme of things, they also insist that serious challenges remain. In the second section, we concentrate on the 2009 parliamentary and presidential elections, and what they say about Indonesia's democratic consolidation. In this section, we focus on the quality of electoral management, the drivers of voting behaviour and paradigmatic shifts in political power. Third, our discussion looks at two institutions of crucial importance for Indonesia's democracy: political parties and parliament. They have been among the most criticised institutions of the post-1998 period, and many key flaws of Indonesian democracy can be illustrated by studying them. In the fourth section, we turn to the influence of societal trends on electoral politics, highlighting the role of the entertainment industry and that of political thugs. In both cases, larger patterns prevalent in society have both affected democratic change and been remoulded by it. The fifth section analyses the participation of women in Indonesia's new democracy, pointing to some achievements but, above all, to the persistence of gender inequality as a major challenge. Finally, we evaluate the state of Indonesia's democracy at the local level, where most observers believe old power networks have been most enduring.

INDONESIA'S DEMOCRACY: A COMPARATIVE PERSPECTIVE

Despite the magnitude and importance of Indonesia's democratic transition, scholars of comparative political science initially showed little interest in it. While a large international conference in Jakarta in August 1998 – three months after Suharto's fall – brought together such prominent theorists of democratisation as Alfred Stepan, Juan Linz and Donald Horowitz, their attention quickly moved on to other places (Liddle 2001). Subsequently, the analysis of Indonesia's democratic reforms – as well as the social and political upheaval they triggered – was largely left to two distinct groups of scholars. First, there were the mainly junior comparativists who published insightful studies on Indonesia and other, mostly Southeast Asian, countries but lacked the clout to put Indonesia on the map of global political theory (Case 2002; Smith 2007; Slater 2008). The second group consisted of so-called 'Indonesianists', scholars with a longstanding research focus on the country. Even when grounded in theoretical discussions about democratisation and political change, their work on the post-Suharto polity mostly appeared in area studies journals on the Pacific, Asia or Southeast Asia, thus failing to influence larger debates on international political trends. Meanwhile, leading comparativists dealt with Indonesia only in a cursory fashion, integrating it into multi-country and quantitative studies (Diamond 2002) but rarely focusing on the country itself.

The lack of interest by senior comparativist scholars in Indonesia's democratisation is surprising, given that the country and its transition possess a multitude of striking features. First and foremost, as one of the most populous democracies in the world – only India and the United States are bigger – Indonesia could be viewed as one of the main 'laboratories' for political scientists interested in democratic transitions affecting large, heterogeneous states. Instead, most democratisation theorists have concentrated on the post-communist transitions in Eastern Europe and Central Asia, as well as the political transformation of Latin America. Similarly, as the state with the largest Muslim population in the world, Indonesia offered (and continues to offer) insights into the relationship between Islam, democracy and development. Most comparative political scientists, however, have derived their views on this topic by studying the Arab world and its democratic deficits (Stepan and Robertson 2004). Finally, Indonesia has implemented one of the world's biggest decentralisation programs, attracting the interest of development agencies and leading to a rich body of detailed local case studies (Aspinall and Fealy 2003; Schulte Nordholt and van Klinken 2007). But again, few comparativists paid attention. Indonesia, it appears, was too exceptional in religious, political and social terms for a comparison between it and other democratising states in Africa, Latin America or Eastern Europe to be deemed rewarding.

With senior comparative scholars largely disengaged, the task of locating Indonesia on the international map of democratisation fell to research and advocacy institutions such as Freedom House. In its annual reports, Freedom House measures the quality of political rights and civil liberties around the world. It is these reports that have made Indonesia's democratic development *vis-à-vis* other countries most evident. After having been ranked 'partly free' for much of its post-1998 transition, Indonesia was first considered 'free' in 2005, and has maintained that designation in subsequent years. At the same time, two other countries in Southeast Asia that were previously classed as 'free' — Thailand and the Philippines — lost that status in 2006 and 2007 respectively, and were downgraded to 'partly free'.

Arguably, the democracy indexes published by Freedom House and similar institutions were partly responsible for the renewed interest some senior comparativists began to take in Indonesia from the late 2000s. With democracy experiencing a global recession after 1999, Indonesia's apparent success in maintaining its democratic system stood out as an intriguing and encouraging counterexample. Suddenly, Indonesia's exceptionalism was no longer a disincentive to studying the country in a comparative framework, but an important reason for doing so. Alfred Stepan, for example, began to look at the interplay between religion and the state in Indonesia. According to Stepan, democracies have a better chance of surviving if they uphold 'twin tolerations', that is, if the state tolerates religious freedom and the faiths accept the sovereignty of the elected government. In addition to India and Senegal, he now views Indonesia as a state in which relatively consistent implementation of the twin tolerations has strengthened democracy. With a major international conference on Indonesia in March 2009 and a book soon to be published on the subject (Künkler and Stepan, forthcoming), Stepan has reinvigorated comparative interest in Indonesia.[1] As a result of this and other initiatives, the demarcation between comparative political science and Indonesianist scholarship has become increasingly blurred.

One comparative scholar who has deepened his engagement with Indonesia in recent years is Larry Diamond. In Chapter 2 of this volume, Diamond analyses the progress of Indonesia's democracy in the context of a global trend of stagnating or even receding democratisation. Using democracy indexes as well as survey data from Indonesia and comparable countries, Diamond argues that Indonesia has done better than expected – and also better than other countries at similar stages of democratic development. For example, survey data show that Indonesia has the highest percentage of what he labels 'Consistent Democrats' among the six leading East Asian democracies. But while such evidence contradicts claims that no genuine democratic change has taken place in Indonesia since 1998, Diamond also warns that the achievements are not irreversible. Indonesia still has considerable deficits in government effectiveness, upholding of the rule of law and corruption eradication. Without improvements in these areas, Indonesia's democratic achievements will remain vulnerable to backsliding. Nevertheless, Diamond's overall assessment of Indonesia's democracy is positive, echoing judgments by other comparativists who seem to have rediscovered Indonesia as a research topic.

ELECTIONS IN INDONESIA: COMPETITIVE BUT FLAWED

In evaluating the state of democracy in a particular country, analysts often use the openness, fairness and competiveness of its elections as a key indicator (Diamond and Morlino 2005). Generally, post-Suharto Indonesia has been rated highly in this regard, with Freedom House classifying the country as an 'electoral democracy' continuously since 1999. In order for Freedom House to grant this classification, a country has to meet four basic criteria. First, it must have 'a competitive, multiparty political system'. Second, it has to offer 'universal adult suffrage for all citizens'.[2] Third, it must hold 'regularly contested elections conducted in conditions of ballot secrecy, reasonable ballot security, and in the absence of massive voter fraud, and that yield results that are representative of the

---

1 Donald Horowitz has also continued to work on a book about 'the making of Indonesia's constitutional democracy'.
2 However, Freedom House tolerates 'exceptions for restrictions that states may legitimately place on citizens as sanctions for criminal offenses'.

public will'. And finally, there must be 'significant public access of major political parties to the electorate through the media and through generally open political campaigning' (Freedom House 2009). In 2009, Freedom House classified 119 out of 193 countries (62 per cent) as electoral democracies. It is important to note, however, that there is a significant difference between an 'electoral democracy' and a 'liberal democracy'. In electoral democracies, reasonably open elections can coexist with serious defects in the implementation of individual rights, the rule of law and other crucial preconditions for a free society. Liberal democracies, by contrast, enjoy not only free, fair and competitive elections, but also a large catalogue of civil liberties. According to Freedom House, only 89 of the 119 electoral democracies were liberal democracies in 2009. Interestingly, this also included Indonesia.

But not all analysts have shared such upbeat views on Indonesia's post-Suharto elections. In particular, some scholars do not even agree that Indonesia was an electoral democracy between 1998 and 2004. With the president still picked by the People's Consultative Assembly (Majelis Permusyawaratan Rakyat, MPR), these observers pointed out that there was no direct link between the outcome of the 1999 parliamentary elections and the selection of the highest office holder in the executive government. Although a majority of the MPR's 700 members were elected parliamentarians, the assembly also included 238 non-elected delegates, among them 38 from the armed forces. Indeed, the president elected by the MPR in October 1999, Abdurrahman Wahid, chaired a party that had obtained only 12 per cent of the vote in the legislative polls. In building the alliance that secured his election, Wahid made backroom deals with military leaders and others in order to defeat Megawati Sukarnoputri, whose party had won a large plurality in the legislative elections. Consequently, Diamond (2002: 22) classified Indonesia as a 'hybrid regime', at a time when Freedom House already viewed it as an electoral democracy (albeit not yet a liberal one).

Constitutional reform meant that from 2004 Indonesia's national parliament was fully elected and the president was directly elected by the population, removing some of the most serious objections to classifying Indonesia as an electoral democracy. Yet, as Indonesia's system became more structurally democratic, its democratic procedures showed signs of strain. One reason for the positive early evaluations of Indonesia's democracy (such as the Freedom House ratings) was the relatively clean, effective and peaceful implementation of national elections in 1999 and 2004. Defying predictions that these elections would be chaotic and violent, and their outcomes deeply contested, they were judged by observers to be free and fair, indeed, as being model transitional elections.

In this regard, however, the 2009 elections may present a worrying turning point, with a dramatic decline in the quality of electoral management. Apparently believing that the 2009 elections no longer needed the careful planning that the first two post-authoritarian ballots had naturally required, Indonesia's leaders (and officials of international development agencies) did not view the ballots as a policy priority. In Chapter 5 of this book, Adam Schmidt describes how short-sighted changes to the electoral laws and sloppy administration seriously undermined the effectiveness and credibility of the electoral process. Applying internationally used benchmarks to the 2009 elections, Schmidt concludes that Indonesia fell short in several important fields. In particular, deep-seated logistical problems produced faulty voter lists that led to the disenfranchisement of a considerable number of voters. Similarly, the failure of the election organisers to give voters consistent and comprehensive information on all aspects of the electoral process led to an unprecedented proportion of invalid votes. Had it not been for the magnitude of President Susilo Bambang Yudhoyono's victory (which was confirmed by independent pollsters), the 2009 election result could have been vulnerable to well-founded legal challenges.

Post-Suharto elections have been criticised not just for their procedural shortcomings, however. Even before the slide in the quality of electoral management that became visible in 2009, some scholars had questioned the depth of democratic participation in Indonesian elections. Many authors have described Indonesian ballots as elite-engineered affairs, with rich and powerful candidates either buying voters off or manipulating their religious or ethnic loyalties (Choi 2009; Indonesian Corruption Watch 2009). In this regard, observers of Indonesian elections have echoed a much wider body of comparative literature, especially in the Southeast Asian context, regarding the influence of political elites, patronage and 'money politics' in elections (Taylor 1996). Some chapters in this book tend to confirm the major thrust of that literature. For example, Blair Palmer's study of the 2009 legislative elections in Aceh argues that many citizens, especially in rural areas, view casting a vote for a party or candidate as something they will do in exchange for 'services' rendered to them (see Chapter 14). While 'services' can be interpreted in terms of government performance, all too often they refer to payments, gifts or other direct material benefits, leading to patronage-based voting.

Other contributions to this volume, however, provide a generally more optimistic view of the 2009 elections. Based on comprehensive survey data, Saiful Mujani and R. William Liddle maintain that the Indonesian voting public increasingly resembles the electorates of other, more mature democracies (see Chapter 4). Influenced by television advertisements, the state of the economy and the personal charisma of candidates,

Indonesian voters today do not seem to be much different from their counterparts in the United States, Europe or Australia. Similarly, in a case study of the presidential elections in Morotai (North Maluku), Sidney Jones finds that while some voters were vulnerable to money politics or intimidation, the majority still voted according to the opinions they had formed of the candidates (see Chapter 16). These opinions were, of course, shaped to a significant extent by an increasing army of political consultants and pollsters who worked around the clock to polish the images of the various nominees. Mohammad Qodari, a pollster himself, illustrates in Chapter 6 how the creation of a favourable reputation has become more important for Indonesian parties and candidates than the appeal to primordial sentiments or even material interests.

Despite the wide range of views on the quality of the elections, few credible observers would suggest that Indonesian polls have been systematically manipulated by the national government in order to stay in power. Unlike Singapore, Malaysia and Cambodia, which created electoral systems favouring their ruling regimes, Indonesia has provided a competitive arena for all major parties, including the opposition. In fact, Indonesian governments — both national and local — have faced serious problems in securing re-election. Ruling governments lost both the 1999 and 2004 elections, and the incumbency turnover in direct gubernatorial and district head elections has been hovering around 40 per cent (Erb and Sulistiyanto 2009). As Rizal Sukma explains in Chapter 3, the 2009 elections marked the first time in the post-Suharto era that an incumbent government was re-elected. However, this success was not rooted in electoral engineering but in Yudhoyono's unrivalled personal popularity. Riding on the president's high approval ratings, his Democratic Party (Partai Demokrat, PD) was able to emerge as Indonesia's largest political party, sidelining both Golkar and the Indonesian Democratic Party of Struggle (Partai Demokrasi Indonesia Perjuangan, PDIP). It is this constantly shifting and fiercely contested electoral landscape that above all else has motivated organisations such as Freedom House to view Indonesia as the only electoral democracy in ASEAN.

PARTIES AND PARLIAMENTS: WEAK PILLARS OF DEMOCRACY?

Whenever Indonesian media and civil society groups discuss the main sources of the country's problems, political parties and the national legislature are certain to feature at the top of the list. In editorials and on Jakarta's seminar circuit, these institutions are usually portrayed as corrupt, greedy, ineffective, self-absorbed, isolated from society and dominated by oligarchic elites.[3] Even more than the executive government, Indonesia's parliament and its parties have been identified as the ugly face of democracy. To be sure, they have done little to mitigate their negative image. High-profile arrests of legislators for corruption (with some accepting the services of prostitutes as bribes), the low quality of their legislative work, and ferocious factional infighting within parties and caucuses — all have contributed to the poor reputation of parties and parliament.

While much of the criticism is undoubtedly justified, a closer look produces a slightly more nuanced picture. To begin with, it should come as no surprise that party politicians and legislators rank very low on the hierarchy of respected professions in Indonesia. After all, this is a sentiment Indonesians share with almost every other nation. In a December 2009 Gallup poll, 55 per cent of Americans gave members of the US Congress 'low' or 'very low' ratings for honesty and ethical standards, making politics the least respected in a list of 22 professions.[4] In the same month, an opinion survey in Australia found that less than 0.5 per cent of respondents thought that becoming a politician was an honourable career choice.[5] But Indonesian editorials show little appreciation for the universal dimension of this problem, with most viewing it as an exclusively Indonesian concern. Similarly, Indonesian commentators have often chosen to overlook the country's progress in the fight against corruption. In 2001, Transparency International's Corruption Perception Index put Indonesia among the three most corrupt countries in the world. In 2009, by contrast, the index ranked Indonesia 111th out of 180 surveyed states, making it one of the fastest and most consistent climbers up the list.[6] Thus, while corruption in the political elite remains a major challenge, it is by no means unique to Indonesia, and the country has in fact recorded significant improvements.

Scholarly accounts of Indonesian parties and parliaments have been somewhat more generous than the popular commentaries. For example, while still critical of the parties' poor performance, academic observers have generally acknowledged the increased moderation in Indonesian party politics since 2003 and the positive effects this has had in steering

3 For a typical example, see 'Stop korupsi DPR, pangkas kewenangannya' [Stop the corruption in parliament, curtail its authority], *Kompas*, 7 July 2008.
4 'Health care workers are most trusted Americans, members of Congress are least trusted, says Gallup poll', *CNSNews.com*, 10 December 2009.
5 'Doctors, nurses most trusted professions', *WA Business News*, 18 December 2009.
6 'RI score improves in Corruption-Perception Index', *Jakarta Post*, 17 November 2009.

Indonesia away from the violent political conflict that haunted its early democratic transition (Johnson Tan 2006; Tomsa 2008). Unlike during the presidencies of Habibie (1998–99) and Abdurrahman Wahid (1999–2001), when parties tried to settle conflicts by mobilising their supporters at the grassroots, political leaders today mostly resort to negotiations, power sharing and peaceful dispute resolution in the courts. The passage of major constitutional amendments in 2002 marked the first time since the late 1940s that Indonesia had reorganised its political system without major intra-elite conflict. When a similar feat was attempted in the mid-1950s, negotiations became highly divisive and their breakdown led to four decades of authoritarian rule. While some authors have attributed the consensus among today's elite to the 'cartelisation' of Indonesian politics (Slater 2004; Ambardi 2009), a less disparaging reading would highlight the increasing maturity of the country's parties, and their healthy willingness to compromise.

In assessing the quality of party organisation and institutionalisation in Indonesia, the scholarly literature has thus produced more mixed findings than has the overwhelmingly negative domestic media. In Chapter 7 of this book, Dirk Tomsa points out that while most Indonesian parties still exhibit weak organisation, low discipline and programmatic superficiality, there have been exceptions. The Islamic Prosperous Justice Party (Partai Keadilan Sejahtera, PKS), for example, is marked by generally high organisational professionalism, consistent cadre development and ideological coherence. Although the party's puritanical image has suffered to some extent as a result of it being represented in most cabinets since 1999, PKS nevertheless increased its vote in the 2009 elections. Even parties that lost votes in 2009 have entrenched themselves more deeply in Indonesia's party system than sceptics had expected. While their share of the vote has declined markedly, the five largest parties in the 1999 parliament are still represented in 2009, despite the introduction of a parliamentary threshold and the emergence of new parties. Such party longevity has been rare in most East Asian democracies, with parties in South Korea, Thailand and the Philippines often disappearing after one or two elections. Most major Indonesian parties, in contrast, can still rely on core constituencies that provide them with sufficient support to retain an electoral presence (Ufen 2008).

While many of the structural problems afflicting Indonesian parties are rather common in contemporary democratic societies (low and falling memberships, lack of independent funding sources, weak programmatic distinctiveness), the post-Suharto parliament has acquired some features that set it apart from other legislatures in the world. Stephen Sherlock demonstrates in Chapter 8 of this book that power in the People's Representative Council (Dewan Perwakilan Rakyat, DPR) is centred in its legislative committees, rather than in the party-controlled caucuses that dominate conventional parliaments. Members of the DPR often identify more strongly with their committees than with their parties, making it difficult for the latter to control their parliamentary arms and ensure that party policies are distilled in legislation. On the one hand, this situation has ensured that legislators still scrutinise government legislation, programs and budgets critically even when their parties are represented in cabinet, as most of the major parties are. On the other hand, the excessive powers vested in the committees have led to a lack of transparency and accountability in these bodies and in the DPR as a whole. With committee members often operating behind the scenes, voters have struggled at the end of each DPR term to evaluate the performance of both individual legislators and the parties that nominated them.

The other distinctive feature of the DPR is its consensus-oriented decision-making process. Decisions are rarely made by majority vote; mostly, the DPR passes legislation, budgets and resolutions after intense internal negotiations. In these talks, all parties are expected to make concessions so that the final product can be presented as the result of a genuine agreement (*mufakat*). Once again, there have been advantages and disadvantages. On the upside, this approach has prevented the adoption of partisan and exclusivist policies and laws — an important precondition for social stability in an ethnically and religiously diverse nation like Indonesia. On the downside, it has made it more difficult for the parliament to pass coherent legislation, with laws often including contradictory or deliberately vague stipulations in order to please all those involved in the negotiations. At the same time, parliamentarians have frequently moved deliberations from the DPR building to more discreet venues such as hotels and resorts. There, parliamentary and party elites hammer out details of bills and key policies far away from public scrutiny, giving the media further material to depict Indonesia's parliament — whether fairly or not — as unaccountable and corrupt.

SOCIETY: CIVIL AND UNCIVIL INFLUENCES

It is conventional wisdom that the consolidation of young democracies requires more than just workable political institutions and procedures. Equally important are vibrant civil societies that monitor and criticise state institutions, identify socio-political problems, promote discussion about the future course of the country and stimulate the political awareness of citizens (Elliott 2003; Alagappa 2004). Civil society includes not only formal players such as the media, non-government organisations and religious bodies, but less organised groupings as well. However, it is well recognised that not all aspects of civil society activity are necessarily supportive of democratisation (Boyd 2004). Democratisation can also open space for intolerant, militant or illiberal actors that had previously been constrained by an authoritarian ruler, and which now aspire to challenge or undermine the emerging democratic system.

In Indonesia, civil society — and NGOs in particular — has been seen mostly as a catalyst for democratisation (Harney and Olivia 2003). Tens of thousands of NGOs across the country have run advocacy campaigns on issues ranging from political reform and anti-corruption programs to more technical matters such as water sanitation, health care and primary education. As pressure groups, they have been effective in scrutinising government budgets, uncovering corruption scandals and advocating urgently needed policies. Without this energetic civil society activism (which was strongly supported by the media), many of the key political reforms of the post-1998 period probably would not have materialised or would have been much weaker. In addition, major religious groups, notably the traditionalist Islamic organisation Nahdlatul Ulama and the modernist Muhammadiyah, have refrained from exclusivist demands that could have derailed Indonesia's democratisation (Bush 2009). Even if they were not the driving forces of democratic reform — as is sometimes claimed by foreign observers — they helped moderate communal tensions and assisted the post-Suharto state to develop the pluralist image necessary to accommodate Indonesia's non-Muslim minorities.

This does not mean, however, that societal influences on Indonesia's democratisation have been purely positive. In the media field, for example, the effects have been mixed. In general, the dramatic expansion of media freedom as well as the proliferation of television channels, radio stations and print media after 1998 are considered major achievements of Indonesia's democratisation, contributing to better societal control of government (Sen and Hill 2007). However, there have been unintended side-effects. Exposed to an incessant stream of broadcasts, citizens not only base their political choices on the media image of candidates but also struggle to distinguish between the virtual and real worlds. As Ariel Heryanto demonstrates in Chapter 9, Indonesians have increasingly looked to television celebrities for political leadership despite their lack of qualifications for political office. More fundamentally, Heryanto suggests that television and other electronic media are reshaping the everyday lives of ordinary Indonesians, and remoulding their political participation. Some have even come to view politics as an extension of the reality show *Indonesian Idol*, a popular singing contest in which anyone can participate. Enjoying the entertainment, and believing that they too can play a role in the 'show' of Indonesian politics, the masses are unaware that they — in Heryanto's view — are being politically 'domesticated'. In such a reading, the media is not merely an avenue of political participation and a bastion of the people's liberties (the conventional view), but also an agency that distances the population from politics.

Some sections of civil society have also undermined democratisation in more straightforward ways. For instance, a few radical groups at the fringes of Islamic politics have used the newly available freedom of expression to promote sectarian views. Since the late 1990s, militant bodies such as the Defenders of Islam Front (Front Pembela Islam, FPI) have campaigned for a more Islamic society and state, aiming to reduce the rights of religious minorities (Ahmad 2007). The authorities have often been reluctant to act against these groups and their violent methods (such as smashing up bars and gambling dens), fearing their political influence.

However, not all groups in the grey zone between lawfulness and illegality have been ideologically motivated. Despite claiming religious, ethnic or political motives, for some making money has been the primary goal. In Chapter 10 of this volume, Ian Wilson analyses the development of organised groups of *preman* ('thugs' or 'petty gangsters') in democratic Indonesia, focusing on their involvement in elite politics and elections. Especially during the early phase of the country's democratic transition, commentators noted the increased political role of *preman* (Hadiz 2003; Kristiansen 2003). Many of them organised militias and security forces for political parties, mobilising their followers on the streets and fighting for turf against rivals. Some *preman* leaders were even elected to political office. Wilson describes the political niche carved out by *preman*, but he also identifies a decline in their prominence as Indonesian democracy has consolidated.

In essence, Wilson argues that democratic politics have to a certain extent domesticated the *preman* – an analysis that resonates with Heryanto's view of the domestication of the masses. Both Heryanto and Wilson thus point, albeit in very different ways, not merely to the effects that society has on democratic institutions, but also to the effects of democratisation on society. They indicate that the taming or constraining of society's more raw political impulses – that is, the anarchic energy of the masses depicted by Heryanto and the thuggery of the *preman* described by Wilson – has been one important product of the growing institutionalisation of democratic politics. By pointing to a more politically domesticated society, they conjure an image that is very different from the highly vigilant civil society lauded in liberal theory on the one hand, and the much lamented 'uncivil society' on the other. From this perspective, democratisation has contributed both to the mitigation of society's violent potential *and* to the weakening of its inherently rebellious scepticism towards the ruling elite.

WOMEN IN POLITICS: PERSISTENT OBSTACLES

Like many other countries — whether democracies or authoritarian regimes — Indonesia has faced significant problems in expanding the participation of women in politics (Robinson 2008). Despite the country's rapid social modernisation since the 1980s, gender inequality remains deeply entrenched. Television advertisements continue to portray women as managers of the domestic sphere who ensure that the residence is clean and the food prepared when the money-earning husband returns home from work. In newspaper reports, wives of politicians are depicted as 'loyal companions' (*pendamping setia*) whose main task is to run the family effectively so that the husband can concentrate on important state business. Confronted with such prejudice, women active in politics have found it difficult to be taken seriously. In cabinet, women have customarily been given the post of state minister for women's empowerment, but denied key departments. In parliament, very few caucus leaders or committee chairpersons are women. In political parties, female cadres are expected to establish special women's organisations tasked with mobilising the female vote, but are generally kept out of senior leadership positions on the central board.

Nevertheless, some progress has occurred. In the cabinet appointed by Yudhoyono in 2009, five women hold portfolios — the highest number on record. Moreover, women now command some of the most important positions. Sri Mulyani Indrawati as finance minister has arguably been one of the most powerful politicians in Yudhoyono's government. Controlling the state budget and a huge administrative apparatus, Sri Mulyani has demonstrated that women can excel in one of the key departments — and, in fact, be more successful than most of the men who previously occupied that position. Her colleagues Mari Elka Pangestu, the trade minister, and Armida Alisjahbana, head of the National Development Planning Agency (Badan Perencanaan Pembangunan Nasional, Bappenas), also manage major departments traditionally dominated by men. With the number of women increasing from three in Megawati's cabinet (2001–2004) and four in Yudhoyono's first government (2004–2009) to five currently (in a cabinet with 34 members), female representation in the central executive has taken slow but detectable steps forward.

A similar picture of slow progress in the context of still-stark gender inequality is visible in Indonesia's legislatures. The proportion of women in the 2009 national parliament is the highest in Indonesian history. It increased from 10.8 per cent in the previous legislature to 17.8 per cent, bringing Indonesia close to the global average of 18.8 per cent. According to the Inter-Parliamentary Union, in 2009 Indonesia was placed 69th on a list of 187 countries surveyed for their level of female representation in parliament.[7] As Sharon Bessell explains in Chapter 11 of this book, the increased number of female legislators in Indonesia has partly been the result of a long campaign for affirmative action in elections. Yet as Bessell also stresses, the measures taken thus far have been weak, and the obstacles to gender equality in politics remain pervasive.

These obstacles are especially powerful in the regions. Hana Satriyo provides some disturbing figures in Chapter 12 of this volume. In 2009, only one of the 33 Indonesian governors was a woman — who, it should be noted, was also the representative of an entrenched political clan with questionable links to militias and other gangs. In the same vein, a mere seven (about 1.5 per cent) of around 500 district heads and mayors were female, suggesting that women at the grassroots have found it even harder than their colleagues in the centre to increase their political standing. In the national parliament, some of the women elected had formerly been television celebrities blessed with high name recognition and leagues of admirers (Mietzner 2009b) — an advantage rarely available to female nominees campaigning in the mundane world of district politics. Whatever the exact statistics and their causes, it is obvious that promoting gender parity in all strata of government will remain a central challenge for Indonesia's young democracy.

LOCAL POLITICS: DEMOCRACY OR ELITE CONTROL?

As the experience of women politicians indicates, many Indonesian regions appear as obdurate holdouts from the political and social reforms that have swept the country since 1998. This is ironic, because in many ways the regions have been the site of some of the most dramatic post-Suharto political restructuring, brought about by decentralisation policies. Yet, in many regions deeply entrenched elites have used the introduction of electoral democracy to secure executive and legislative positions for family members, cronies and loyalists. Far away from the capital, some local clans have turned provinces and districts into personal fiefdoms, as if to mock the promise of grassroots democracy that followed the fall of the New Order (Buehler and Johnson Tan 2007).

But if there is one thing we have learned about local politics in post-Suharto Indonesia, it is the difficulty of making generalisations: while some provinces and districts have indeed remained firmly in the grip of oligarchic cliques, others have seen reformist leaders emerge and run local government in relatively transparent and accountable ways (von

---

7 'Women in national parliaments: world classification', situation as of 31 December 2009, http://www.ipu.org/wmn-e/classif.htm.

Luebke 2009). This heterogeneity of political outcomes has itself been the result of the decentralisation program implemented since 2001, which shifted executive responsibilities and budgets from the centre to the districts. Consequently, Indonesia's polity was transformed from a centralistic state with uniform institutions and procedures into a highly diverse cosmos of districts with varying political cultures. In this situation, it has been difficult for scholars to offer analyses of local politics that go beyond anecdotes derived from individual cases.

Two broad observations can nevertheless be made. First, the concerns expressed by some Indonesian politicians that decentralisation would lead to territorial disintegration and administrative chaos have not materialised. If anything, the policy has helped to cool secessionist demands in resource-rich areas, by allowing local governments in such places to use more of their local income for the benefit of their own citizens. Similarly, there has been no breakdown of public services. Local governments have continued to function, with poorer territories receiving substantial financial support from the centre. Second, the quality of local government has not improved across the board either—despite this being the official rationale for decentralisation. In Chapter 13 of this book, Michael Buehler highlights the shortcomings of local administrations and legislatures, ranging from capacity problems to widespread corruption and rent seeking. As much of the government's budget was transferred from the centre to the regions, the 'corruption industry' apparently moved with it. Overall, decentralisation has massively transformed the face of Indonesia and its politics, but it has proven to be neither the nemesis feared by its critics nor the saviour anticipated by its advocates.

Some of the most substantial political change in regional Indonesia has occurred in the separatist regions of Aceh and Papua. Following a serious increase in violence after 1998, Aceh's rebels eventually ended their insurgency in 2005 (Aspinall 2009a). After being granted concessions that would previously have been unthinkable, the separatists dropped their demands for independence in exchange for full political participation. In Chapter 14, Blair Palmer discusses the integration of the former guerrillas into formal political processes, analysing in detail their involvement in Aceh's 2009 elections. He argues that the results represented a 'vote for peace'. To some extent, Aceh's ex-rebels have now become even more 'Indonesian' than political actors in other regions, perfecting the use of political patronage, grassroots networks and access to government for rent-seeking purposes (Aspinall 2009b). While this has raised eyebrows in circles concerned with clean governance, it was arguably an acceptable price to pay to resolve a conflict that had claimed over 10,000 lives since the 1970s.

Papua, on the other hand, has seen no formal peace agreement, but tensions in the province have also declined. While Papua is still 'not a happy place' (ICG 2006: 1), the systemic, deadly human rights violations of the past have now been replaced by 'chronic low-level abuse'. In Chapter 15, Richard Chauvel illustrates the changes that have taken place in Papua, focusing on the 2009 elections in the province. He argues that there are two distinct realms of politics in Papua: the first, the realm of electoral politics, is open and competitive; the second, that of the pro-independence movement, is repressed and clandestine. Some issues that motivate pro-independence sentiment—such as migration by non-Papuan settlers into the territory—find expression in the electoral realm, but mostly the realms remain separate. The restrictions on free expression and organisation used to suppress pro-independence sentiment, Chauvel argues, make Papua a significant holdout from the Indonesian democratic norm.

PROBLEMS OF DEMOCRATISATION IN INDONESIA

As the above discussion demonstrates, the evaluation of Indonesia's democratisation depends largely on the particular viewpoint from which the observer begins. Seen in isolation (especially from an activist or Indonesianist perspective), many of the institutions and policy areas discussed in this volume appear to be riddled with deep-seated structural defects. Whether it is the conduct of elections, the roles of parliament, parties and civil society, the engagement of women in politics or regional political dynamics—in all these important fields, a host of problems has prevented Indonesia's democracy from consolidating fully and delivering tangible benefits to ordinary citizens. Once viewed through a comparative lens, however, these issues look much less exceptional. Indeed, if measured against other countries at comparable stages of democratisation, Indonesia starts to look like an impressive example of a successful transition to democracy in the contemporary period.

This volume leaves it to individual readers to select for themselves the perspective they deem most useful for evaluating Indonesia's democratic development since 1998. In our view, trying to impose a uniform framework of interpretation on the chapters in this book would divert from the productive pluralism that has been one of the strongest features of scholarly debate on Indonesia's democratisation. Instead, we hope that this book will help to provide readers with an overview of the discussions that have shaped political science research on the post-Suharto polity, both in Indonesia and abroad.

REFERENCES

Ahmad, Munawar (2007), 'Faith and violence', *Inside Indonesia* 89(January–March), http://www.insideindonesia.org/.

Alagappa, Muthiah (ed.) (2004), *Civil Society and Political Change in Asia: Expanding and Contracting Democratic Space*, Stanford University Press, Stanford CA.

Ambardi, Kuskridho (2009), *Mengungkap Politik Kartel: Studi Tentang Sistem Kepartaian di Indonesia Era Reformasi* [Uncovering the Political Cartel: A Study of the Party System in Indonesia's Era of Reform], Lembaga Survei Indonesia, Jakarta.

Aspinall, Edward (2009a), *Islam and Nation: Separatist Rebellion in Aceh, Indonesia*, Stanford University Press, Stanford CA.

Aspinall, Edward (2009b), 'Combatants to contractors: the political economy of peace in Aceh', *Indonesia* 87(April): 1–34.

Aspinall, Edward (forthcoming), '"Indonesia: the irony of success', *Journal of Democracy*, 21(2).

Aspinall, Edward and Greg Fealy (eds) (2003), *Local Power and Politics in Indonesia: Decentralisation and Democratisation*, Institute of Southeast Asian Studies, Singapore.

Boudreau, Vincent (2009), 'Elections, repression and authoritarian survival in post-transition Indonesia and the Philippines', *Pacific Review* 22(2): 233–53.

Boyd, Richard (2004), *Uncivil Society: The Perils of Pluralism and the Making of Modern Liberalism*, Rowman & Littlefield/Lexington Books, Lanham MD.

Buehler, Michael and Paige Johnson Tan (2007), 'Party–candidate relationships in Indonesian local politics: a case study of the 2005 regional elections in Gowa, South Sulawesi province', *Indonesia* 84(October): 41–69.

Bush, Robin (2009), *Nahdlatul Ulama and the Struggle for Power within Islam and Politics in Indonesia*, Institute of Southeast Asian Studies, Singapore.

Case, William (2002), *Politics in Southeast Asia: Democracy or Less*, Curzon, Richmond.

Choi, Nankyung (2009), 'Democracy and patrimonial politics in local Indonesia', *Indonesia* 88(October): 131–64.

Davidson, Jamie S. (2009), 'Dilemmas of democratic consolidation in Indonesia', *Pacific Review* 22(3): 293–310.

Diamond, Larry (2002), 'Thinking about hybrid regimes', *Journal of Democracy* 13(2): 21–35.

Diamond, Larry and Leonardo Morlino (eds) (2005), *Assessing the Quality of Democracy*, Johns Hopkins University Press, Baltimore MD.

Elliott, Carolyn M. (2003), *Civil Society and Democracy: A Reader*, Oxford University Press, New Delhi.

Erb, Maribeth, and Priyambudi Sulistiyanto (eds) (2009), *Deepening Democracy in Indonesia? Direct Elections for Local Leaders (Pilkada)*, Institute of Southeast Asian Studies, Singapore.

Freedom House (2009), *Freedom in the World 2009*, Freedom House, Washington DC.

Hadiz, Vedi R. (2003), 'Power and politics in North Sumatra: the uncompleted *reformasi*', in E. Aspinall and G. Fealy (eds), *Local Power and Politics in Indonesia: Decentralisation and Democratisation*, Institute of Southeast Asian Studies, Singapore, pp. 119–31.

Harney, Stefano, and Rita Olivia (2003), *Civil Society and Civil Society Organizations in Indonesia*, International Labour Office, Geneva.

ICG (International Crisis Group) (2006), 'Papua: answers to frequently asked questions', Asia Briefing No. 53, ICG, 5 September.

Indonesian Corruption Watch (2009), 'Purchasing power', *Inside Indonesia* 97(July–September), http://www.insideindonesia.org/.

Johnson Tan, Paige (2006), 'Indonesia seven years after Suharto: party system institutionalization in a new democracy', *Contemporary Southeast Asia* 28(1): 484–508.

Kristiansen, Stein (2003), 'Violent youth groups in Indonesia: the cases of Yogyakarta and Nusa Tenggara Barat', *Sojourn: Journal of Social Issues in Southeast Asia* 18(1): 110–38.

Künkler, Mirjam and Alfred Stepan (eds) (forthcoming), *Indonesia, Islam, and Democratic Consolidation* [working title], Columbia University Press, New York NY.

Liddle, R. William (ed.) (2001), *Crafting Indonesian Democracy*, Mizan, Bandung.

MacIntyre, Andrew and Douglas Ramage (2008), *Seeing Indonesia as a Normal Country: Implications for Australia*, Australian Strategic Policy Institute, Canberra.

Mietzner, Marcus (2009a), 'Indonesia and the pitfalls of low-quality democracy: a case study of the gubernatorial elections in North Sulawesi', in A. Ufen and M. Bünte (eds), *Democratization in Post-Suharto Indonesia*, Routledge, London and New York, pp. 124–49.

Mietzner, Marcus (2009b), 'Indonesia's 2009 elections: populism, dynasties and the consolidation of the party system', *Analysis*, Lowy Institute for International Policy, Sydney, May.

Mujani, Saiful and R. William Liddle (2009), 'Muslim Indonesia's secular democracy', *Asian Survey* 49(4): 575–90.

Robinson, Kathryn (2008), *Gender, Islam and Democracy in Indonesia*, Routledge, London and New York.

Robison, Richard and Vedi R. Hadiz (2004), *Reorganising Power in Indonesia: The Politics of Oligarchy in an Age of Markets*, Routledge, London and New York.

Schulte Nordholt, Henk and Gerry van Klinken (2007), *Renegotiating Boundaries: Local Politics in Post-Suharto Indonesia*, KITLV Press, Leiden.

Sen, Krishna and David T. Hill (2007), *Media, Culture and Politics in Indonesia*, Equinox, Jakarta.

Slater, Dan (2004), 'Indonesia's accountability trap: party cartels and presidential power after democratic transition', *Indonesia* 78(October): 61–92.

Slater, Dan (2008), 'Democracies and dictatorships do not float freely: structural sources of political regimes in Southeast Asia', in E. Martinez Kuhonta, D. Slater and Tuong Vu (eds), *Southeast Asia in Political Science: Theory, Region, and Qualitative Analysis*, Stanford University Press, Stanford CA, pp. 55–79.

Smith, Benjamin (2007), *Hard Times in the Lands of Plenty: Oil Politics in Iran and Indonesia*, Cornell University Press, Ithaca NY.

Stepan, Alfred and Graeme B. Robertson (2004), 'Arab, not Muslim, exceptionalism', *Journal of Democracy* 15(4): 140–46.

Taylor, R.H. (ed.) (1996), *The Politics of Elections in Southeast Asia*, Cambridge University Press, Cambridge.

Tomsa, Dirk (2008), *Party Politics and Democratization in Indonesia: Golkar in the Post-Suharto Era*, Routledge, London and New York.

Ufen, Andreas (2008), 'Political party and party system institutionalisation in Southeast Asia: lessons for democratic consolidation in Indonesia, the Philippines and Thailand', *Pacific Review* 21(3): 327–50.

von Luebke, Christian (2009), 'The political economy of local governance: findings from an Indonesian field study', *Bulletin of Indonesian Economic Studies* 45(2): 201–30.

Webber, Douglas (2006), 'A consolidated patrimonial democracy? Democratization in post-Suharto Indonesia', *Democratization* 13(3): 396–420.

2 INDONESIA'S PLACE IN GLOBAL DEMOCRACY

Larry Diamond *

Indonesia has been a latecomer to democracy during the historic 'third wave' of global democratisation. It was not until a quarter-century into this wave – in 1999 – that Indonesia became an electoral democracy. By then the third wave of democracy had already crested, though levels of freedom in the world continued to improve for some years thereafter. The democratic transformation of East Asia had already largely occurred. The Philippine transition took place in 1986, South Korea's in 1987 and Taiwan's during the period from 1987 to 1996. Mongolia also became a democracy in the early 1990s after the collapse of communism. By 1995, three-fifths of all the states in the world were electoral democracies – in the sense that they could choose and replace their leaders in free, fair and meaningful (multi-party) elections (see Table 2.1). The wave of democracy that began in the 1970s in southern Europe and then spread to Latin America had by the mid-1990s gone well beyond East Asia to incorporate most of Central and Eastern Europe, some of the former Soviet Union and, surprisingly, much of sub-Saharan Africa – by the count of Freedom House, fully half of the 48 states in that region.[1] At that moment in the mid-1990s when the third wave essentially crested, Indonesia seemed as stably authoritarian as it had ever been during the three-decade period of Suharto's authoritarian 'New Order'.

---

* I am very grateful to Aayush Man Sakya for his outstanding research assistance in preparing most of the tables and figures for this paper.
1 See Freedom House's website (http://www.freedomhouse.org/), and especially its flagship publication *Freedom in the World* (Freedom House, various years), for more information on the trends and statistics referred to in this chapter.

Table 2.1   The growth of electoral democracy, 1973–2006

Year	No. of democracies	No. of countries	Democracies as a % of all countries	Rate of increase in democracies (% p.a.)
1973	40	150	26.7	
1980	54	163	33.1	
1984	60	166	36.1	
1987	65	166	39.2	
1988	67	166	40.4	3.1
1990	76	165	46.1	
1991	91	183	49.7	19.7
1992	99	186	53.2	8.1
1993	108	190	56.8	8.3
1994	114	191	59.7	5.3
1995	117	191	61.3	2.6
1996	118	191	61.8	0.9
1997	117	191	61.3	−0.9
1998	117	191	61.3	0.0
1999	120	192	62.5	2.6
2000	119	192	62.0	−0.8
2001	120	192	62.5	0.8
2002	120	192	62.5	0.0
2003	115	192	59.8	−4.2
2004	117	192	60.9	1.7
2005	120	192	62.5	2.6
2006	121	193	62.6	0.8
2007	120	193	62.2	−0.8
2008	119	193	61.6	−0.8
2009	116	193	60.1	−2.5

Source: The figures for 1973–88 reflect my own scoring. Those for 1990–2008 are from the annual *Freedom in the World* surveys by Freedom House, with the exception of the following, which Freedom House rates as democracies and I rate as non-democracies: Russia 2000–2003, Nigeria 2003–2005, Venezuela 2004–2006 and the Central African Republic 2005–2007. Closer inspection of a few smaller countries classified as democracies by Freedom House could also lead to their reclassification as non-democracies.

Observers did not realise it at the time (and many still do not), but the scope of democratic expansion in the world essentially came to a halt in the latter half of the 1990s. Since 1995, the extent of democracies (both in number and as a proportion of all the world's states) has been in an equilibrium. Some transitions to democracy have occurred in the decade-plus since then, but they have largely been offset by transitions away from democracy, back to authoritarian rule, in other countries. As a result, there has been only very modest oscillation in the overall number of democracies, and since 2006 the number of democracies has been steadily (albeit modestly) in decline.

Oddly, it has been in this period that Indonesia has emerged and developed as a democracy. As the remainder of this chapter shows, Indonesia in this period — its first full decade of democracy — has become in many ways a surprising political success story. While in recent years democracy has gradually been receding in the world (including in Southeast Asia), Indonesia's democracy has not only survived but improved. It is not only a reasonably stable democracy — with no obvious threats or potent anti-democratic challengers on the horizon — but it is even in some respects a relatively liberal democracy, with reasonably fair elections and extensive freedoms of press and association. It remains, as it has been for decades, in the bottom half of countries on all measures of the quality of governance, but it has made significant improvements on most of these in the last decade. And its public exhibits one of the most robust profiles of support for democracy and liberal values, and trust in public institutions, of any East Asian democracy. This, I argue, is an impressive record of progress, but still only a partial one. If Indonesia's democracy is to become truly 'consolidated', and hence stable for the long run, it must become a higher-quality democracy, in particular one that makes much more dramatic progress in reducing corruption, providing a rule of law, and modernising and professionalising the overall architecture of the state.

This chapter proceeds as follows. First I consider in greater depth the global context in which Indonesia's democracy has been emerging in the last decade, a context of a gathering democratic recession and increasing democratic vulnerability. Next I evaluate Indonesian democracy's relative performance in socio-economic development during its first decade, then its political performance on indicators of democracy and governance. The penultimate section looks in depth at public opinion data from the Asian Barometer survey to compare Indonesians' attitudes and values towards democracy with those of publics from the other emerging democracies of East and Southeast Asia (Korea, Taiwan, the Philippines, Thailand and Mongolia). Finally, I weigh the meaning of these levels and trends (and related ones) for the future of democracy in Indonesia.

INDONESIA, THE THIRD WAVE OF DEMOCRATISATION AND ITS RECESSION

It is hard to overstate the rather exceptional nature of the timing and trajectory of Indonesia's democratic emergence. By the mid-1990s, the big and strategically important countries that were going to democratise any time soon already had. I have identified elsewhere 23 'strategic swing states' outside the industrialised democratic West (Diamond 2008: 63, Table 3.2). Only two of these — India and Venezuela — were democracies when the third wave began in 1974. Twelve of them (Argentina, Brazil, Turkey, the Philippines, Korea, Taiwan, Thailand, Pakistan, Bangladesh, Poland, Russia and South Africa) became democracies between 1980 and 1996. Only four others democratised subsequently: Mexico, Nigeria, Indonesia and Ukraine. (And only five — China, Vietnam, Egypt, Iran and Saudi Arabia — remained authoritarian throughout.) But here is the interesting thing: of the 18 'swing' states that were or became democracies in this period, seven — Russia, Nigeria, Venezuela, the Philippines, Thailand, Pakistan and Bangladesh — have suffered breakdowns of democracy (and only Bangladesh has really returned to democracy). Several others of these democracies — such as Argentina, South Africa and Ukraine — are struggling with serious problems of governance performance and public confidence. Korea and Taiwan suffer chronically polarised politics with high levels of public distrust and disillusionment. As I will explain at great length, Indonesia's 10-year democratic performance looks, by contrast, pretty good.

There is a broader irony to Indonesia's democratic emergence during this last decade. The very year that Indonesia became a democracy, 1999, marked the beginning of what I believe has become a significant democratic recession in the world, though not yet (fortunately) a full 'reverse wave of democracy', which Samuel Huntington (1991) defines as a period of time in which the reversals of democracy significantly outpace the transitions to democracy. The critical event in this regard was the October military coup that ended the raucous, corrupt and increasingly illiberal electoral democracy in Pakistan. Since then there have been 17 more reversals of democracy in the world, in the very decade when democracy was settling in Indonesia (against many expectations of fragility). In fact, 60 per cent of all 30 democratic reversals that have occurred during the 35 years of the third wave have occurred in this past decade, and eight just in the years 2007–2009. If we count not only blatant reversals of democracy — by either military or executive coup — but also incremental degradations of the democratic process that eventually drag a system below the threshold of electoral democracy, then by my count (which is very close to that of Freedom House), one of every five democracies that has existed during the third wave has been reversed. And of course the incidence of reversal is much higher in countries (like Indonesia) with below middle-income status.

Another indicator suggesting a global democratic recession is that the level of freedom in the world, as measured by Freedom House, declined in each of the four years from 2006 to 2009. For many years after 1995, levels of civil and political freedom (as measured annually by Freedom House) continued to expand, even as the number of electoral democracies levelled off. In every year except one between 1996 and 2005, the number of countries improving their freedom scores (on either political rights or civil liberties or both) exceeded the number of countries declining in freedom — usually by a large margin. The years 2006–2009 were the first consecutive years since the end of the Cold War in which the number of countries declining in freedom exceeded the number gaining. Nearly four times as many countries declined as improved in freedom in 2007, and in 2008 well over twice as many declined as improved.

Of course, the declines in democracy and freedom are related. First, obviously, when democracy is lost, freedom levels decline. But there is also the fact that a number of countries still listed by Freedom House as democracies have relatively poor and declining freedom scores, at or around the mid-point on its seven-point scales of political rights and civil liberties, and with very bad governance scores as measured by the World Bank.[2] If we were to compile a list of today's 'at-risk' democracies — such as Bangladesh, Bolivia, Burundi, Guatemala, Haiti, Malawi, Moldova, Nicaragua, Senegal and Sri Lanka — we would see a significant correlation between the quality of democracy and the political stability, legitimacy and progress towards consolidation of democracy. It is striking that none of the at-risk democracies are liberal democracies — which I define empirically as political systems that obtain a score of 1 or 2 on each of the twin scales of political rights and civil liberties (where 1 indicates most free and 7 least free). Most vulnerable democracies rate no better than middling scores, though a few do have political rights and civil liberty scores somewhat about the mid-point. And as we see in Table 2.2, all of the democracies that have broken down since 1999 were also illiberal, and a number of them had gradually been getting more so over time.

It is worth bearing these problems in mind as we think about the character, degree and performance of democracy in Indonesia, and its future. The troubled and failed democracies of the third wave have shared a few key characteristics. First, with a few exceptions, such as Russia, Venezuela and Thailand, they tend to be poor or lower-middle income, with per capita incomes (in purchasing power parity dollars) under $5,000. Indonesia falls into this category, but it is a diverse group with many democracies that are also doing better or at least not in grave danger. Second, they are poorly governed. Most of the at-risk democracies fall

---

2 The six governance measures that make up the World Bank's Worldwide Governance Indicators are described in Kaufmann, Kraay and Mastruzzi (2009), and can be viewed interactively at http://info.worldbank.org/governance/wgi/index.asp.

Table 2.2   Cases of loss of democracy, 1999–2009

Country	Freedom scores in year before democratic reversal[a]	Per capita GNP in year of reversal (PPP$)[b]
Pakistan, 1999	4,5	1,960
Russia, 2000	4,5	8,030
Nepal, 2002	3,4	1,420
Nigeria, 2003	4,5	900
Venezuela, 2005	3,4	6,440
Thailand, 2006	3,3	8,440
Philippines, 2007	3,3	3,730
Kenya, 2007	3,3	1,540
Georgia, 2008	4,4	4,850
Mauritania, 2008	4,4	2,000
Central African Republic, 2008	5,5	730
Honduras, 2009	3,3	3,880
Madagascar, 2009	4,3	1,040
Niger, 2009	3,4	680

a   Based on a score of 1 (most free) to 7 (least free). The first figure is the country's score on political rights; the second is its score on civil liberties.
b   In some cases the figures are off by one year.
Source: Freedom House (various years); World Bank, *World Development Report*, various years.

into the bottom third of all the world's states in controlling corruption (as measured annually by the World Bank); Indonesia, even with its improvements in the last decade, is still barely in this bottom third.[3] In addition, their governments are not very effective in terms of the quality and independence of the civil service, and of public services and policy formulation and implementation more generally, where again they tend to cluster in the bottom third or quartile of states in the world.[4] Here, fortunately, Indonesia does better, and has again improved markedly in the past decade. Third, they are politically unstable, with significant levels of politically motivated violence or a recent history of such that has not been put to rest, or a more general diffuse sense that the government is frag-

---

3   Some of the worst performers among democracies in controlling corruption are Haiti with a percentile score of 6.8, Guinea-Bissau (8.2), Bangladesh (10.6), Sierra Leone (12.6), Burundi (15.9), East Timor (19.3) and Nicaragua (21.3).
4   An explanation of these measures can be found in Kaufmann, Kraay and Mastruzzi (2009).

ile and could be overthrown. Indonesia has improved here as well but suffers vulnerability and at least perceptions, as measured by the World Bank, of political fragility and risk.[5] Fourth, they are deeply polarised on class, ethnic or other lines of cleavage (sometimes deeply rooted in enmity between parties, as in Bangladesh), which is one reason why they suffer civil wars and high levels of political violence. Early in Indonesia's democratic transition, the country looked to be seriously endangered by ethnic and separatist violence, but its decentralisation reforms have helped to contain this. Fifth, executive power is seriously abused. Executive abuse of power has been the key factor in the demise of democracy in places like Russia, Venezuela, Nigeria and the Philippines. Several of the at-risk countries have presidents with grandiose political projects that they believe require them to concentrate and aggrandise power. For Evo Morales in Bolivia and Rafael Correa in Ecuador, it is to remake the country along populist-left policy lines while redistributing wealth and power to the countries' historically dispossessed indigenous majorities (and to themselves and their supporters). For their fellow leftist Daniel Ortega in Nicaragua, it seems to be to restore the dominance of the Sandinista party and movement, as well as his own revolutionary authority and legacy — while digging into the same national trough of corruption at which previous presidents of the country have fed. For Abdoulaye Wade in Senegal, it is to dominate the country's institutions and pass power on to his son. In Sri Lanka, having finally defeated the Tamil Tigers in a civil war, Mahinda Rajapaksa seems determined to promote an ethnic chauvinist agenda for Sinhalese dominance, which would squander the opportunity provided by the end of the war to forge reconciliation and establish a more enduring basis for peace. Set not only against the very low standard of these extreme examples of abuse, but also against higher standards, Indonesia has had decent and relatively restrained presidential leadership during its first decade.

THE RELATIVE PERFORMANCE OF INDONESIAN DEMOCRACY: SOCIO-ECONOMIC DEVELOPMENT

How has Indonesia's democracy done in its first decade? Let us now take a comparative look, not by assessing Indonesia against the lowest

---

5 Indonesia's percentile score (15.8) on this measure of political stability appears to many observers to be inexplicably low. I fail to fully comprehend the reasons for the country's extremely low scores, but it should be noted that this measure relies more heavily on information and perceptions from commercial firms than any of the other five governance measures used by the World Bank.

standard — democracies that have broken down or seem at imminent risk
of doing so — but rather by comparing it with two sets of reference groups.
One is a set of other large and significant emerging market democracies
outside East Asia: Argentina, Bangladesh, Brazil, Ghana, India, Mexico,
South Africa and Turkey. The list is somewhat arbitrary but captures
size and strategic importance (or, in the case of Ghana, the best performance among the new democracies in Africa). The second set is the other
five countries in East Asia that are (or were until recently) democracies:
Korea, Taiwan, Thailand, the Philippines and Mongolia. One way to
judge how Indonesia's democracy has done in the last decade is to compare its performance on a number of measures of development, governance and democracy with that of these two reference groups. I do not
suggest that this even begins to be an adequate means of assessment, but
without a comparative perspective it is difficult to get a fully meaningful sense of how Indonesian democracy has done in its first decade and
where it stands today.

On the measures of social and economic development, Indonesia's
performance in the decade 1999–2008 was reasonably good relative to
other emerging market democracies around the world. Its average GDP
growth rate for the period (4.8 per cent) was better than all its peers in
Figure 2.1a (save India and Bangladesh, which were starting from much
lower levels) and on a par with most of its East Asian peers in Figure 2.1b.
During the decade 1995–2006 (admittedly, not fully overlapping with
the era of democracy), it recorded around a 10 per cent improvement
in its Human Development Index score, quite respectable in comparative terms (see Figure 2.2). Its annual population growth rate during the
2000–2007 period (1.4 per cent) was at a level reflective of an economy
and society where improved health and education and more job opportunities for women were reducing fertility. Its adult literacy rate of 91 per
cent was well above the average of 79.6 per cent for the emerging market
set, and even slightly exceeded that for much richer democracies like Brazil (89.6 per cent), South Africa (87.6 per cent) and Turkey (88.1 per cent).
In the mortality rate for children under five years of age, Indonesia, with
a figure in 2000 of 31 deaths per 1,000 births, outperformed much richer
Mexico with a rate of 35 deaths per 1,000 deaths, let alone poorer countries like India (72) and Bangladesh (61).

Underlying such positive social outcomes is the fact that Indonesia
has a much better income distribution than all its richer peers among
emerging market democracies, with a Gini coefficient well below those
of Argentina, Brazil, Mexico, South Africa and Turkey. Some of this is a
legacy of the authoritarian period, but it does appear that socio-economic
progress has continued during the period of democracy — which, after
all, inherited an economy that had been badly shocked by the 1997
financial crisis. Of course, if we compare within East Asia, Indonesia's

Figure 2.1 Average GDP growth in Indonesia and other emerging democracies, 1999–2008 (% p.a.)

(a) Emerging democracies outside East Asia

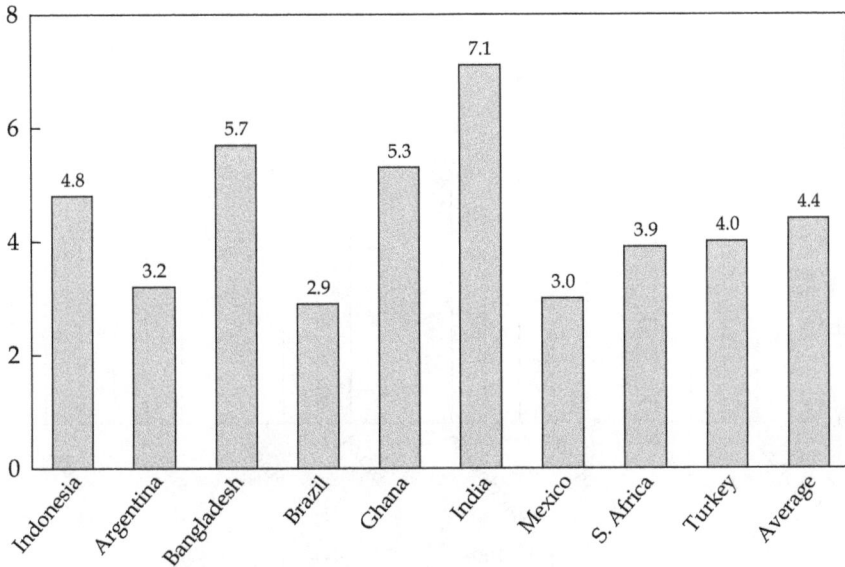

(b) Emerging democracies within East Asia

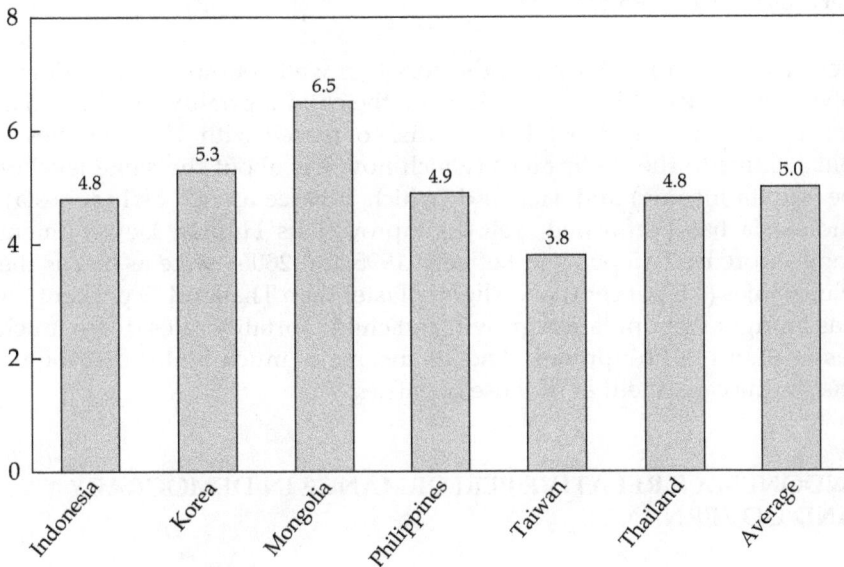

Source: International Monetary Fund, World Economic Outlook Database, October 2009, http://www.imf.org/external/pubs/ft/weo/2009/02/weodata/weoselgr.aspx.

Figure 2.2   Scores on Human Development Index of Indonesia and other emerging democracies, 1995 and 2006

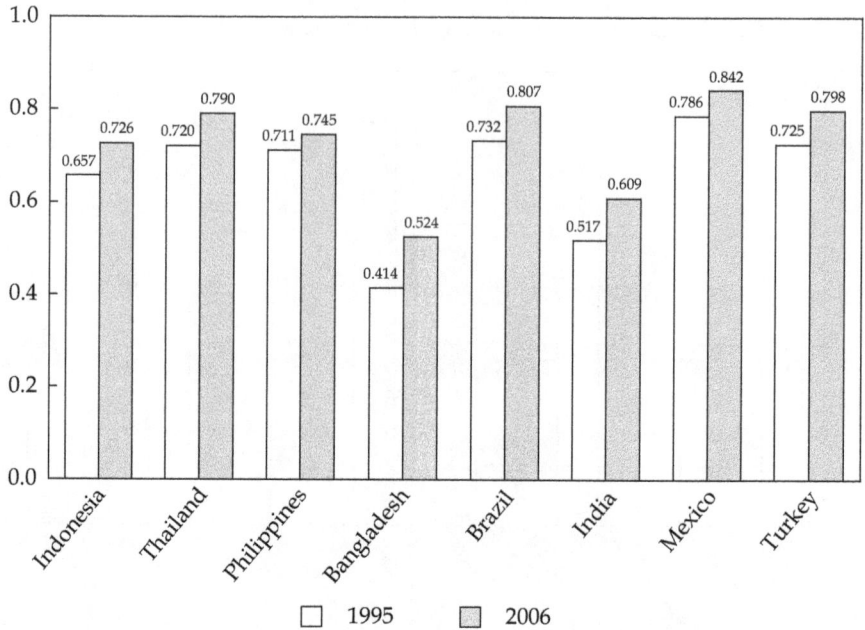

Source: United Nations Development Programme, *Human Development Report 2009*, http:// hdr.undp.org/en/statistics/data/.

performance on most social indicators lags well behind the now developed economies of Korea and Taiwan; the child mortality rate in Korea, for instance, is only 5 per 1,000 births, compared with 31 in Indonesia. But relative to the Philippines (which now has about the same level of per capita income) and Thailand (which is twice as rich as Indonesia), Indonesia has performed well. It improved its Human Development Index score by 10.5 per cent between 1995 and 2006, twice as fast as the Philippines (4.8 per cent) and slightly faster than Thailand (9 per cent). It has brought its population growth and child mortality rates down much faster than the Philippines. And its income is much better distributed than is the case in either of those countries.

INDONESIA'S RELATIVE PERFORMANCE IN DEMOCRACY AND GOVERNANCE

Indonesia has also done surprisingly well in terms of democracy and governance. Let us examine first its scores on political rights and civil lib-

Table 2.3   Trends in Indonesia's scores on political rights and civil liberties, 1997–2009[a]

	1997	1998	1999	2000–2005	2006–2009
Political rights, civil liberties	7,5	6,4	4,4	3,4	2,3

a Based on a score of 1 (most free) to 7 (least free). The first figure is the score on political rights; the second is the score on civil liberties.

Source: Freedom House (various years).

erties, as measured annually by Freedom House, which awards a score of 1 for most free and 7 for least free on each scale.[6] Indonesia's freedom scores have steadily improved over time, from a score of 6 on political rights and 4 on civil liberties during the 1998 transitional year to 4,4 in 1999, 3,4 in 2000–2005 and 2,3 in 2006–2009 (see Table 2.3). This reflects significant improvements in the climate of freedom, rule of law and political competition, even during the early years of Indonesia's democratic decade, and in essence confirms other assessments that democracy has moved forward politically under the presidency of Susilo Bambang Yudhoyono. As a result, Indonesia has been rated a 'free' country since 2006.

As we see in Table 2.4, in 2008 Indonesia's freedom scores were on a par with those of India and Mexico, and better than Turkey's. And its democratic progress stands in stark contrast to the Philippines and Thailand, where freedom (and democracy) deteriorated sharply during the decade. In terms of democratic vitality and quality, and on some more general measures of governance as well, Indonesia has 'traded places' with these two Southeast Asian countries, an outcome that few if any observers of the region anticipated during the early to mid 1990s.

Yet on other measures of governance, Indonesia still has a way to go, and outstripping countries like Bangladesh and the Philippines is not exactly cause for celebration. The remaining rows in Table 2.4 examine Indonesia's performance on several other dimensions of governance

---

6 The annual Freedom House scores on political rights and civil liberties are aggregate measures of a larger number of scores on different categories of questions (for example, on civil rights, freedom of expression and belief, associational rights, rule of law, and personal autonomy and individual rights). The full checklist of questions for the survey is extremely detailed and may be viewed at http://www.freedomhouse.org/template.cfm?page=351&ana_page=341&year=2008. Although the scores are derived from the assessments of observers based mainly in the United States, most of them are experts on the countries and regions who follow events closely and who have been trained by Freedom House to apply the standardised methodology.

Table 2.4 *Comparative measures of democracy and governance in emerging democracies, 1998 and 2008*[a]

Measure	Indo-nesia	Thai-land	Philip-pines	India	Bangla-desh	Argen-tina	Brazil	Mexico	South Africa	Turkey
Political rights, civil liberties[b]										
1998	6,4	3,3	2,3	2,4	2,4	2,3	3,4	3,4	1,2	4,5
2008	2,3	6,4	4,3	2,3	5,4	2,2	2,2	2,3	2,2	3,3
Voice & accountability										
1998	16.3	61.1	60.6	58.2	41.8	55.3	55.8	47.1	73.6	29.8
2008	44.2	32.2	41.3	58.7	30.8	57.2	61.1	50.5	67.8	41.8
State quality: average government effectiveness & regulatory quality										
1998	29.2	57.7	54.9	43.2	27.6	66.4	57.0	64.5	70.3	59.8
2008	46.4	59.4	53.4	50.3	21.8	38.4	56.3	63.2	73.5	60.8
Rule of law										
1998	23.8	65.7	52.9	60.5	21.9	57.1	46.2	37.1	58.1	53.8
2008	28.7	54.1	39.7	56.5	27.3	32.1	46.4	29.7	56.0	55.5
Control of corruption										
1998	9.2	57.8	41.3	45.6	25.2	53.9	58.7	35.9	71.8	51.0
2008	31.4	43.0	26.1	44.4	10.6	40.1	58.5	49.8	65.2	60.4

a Political rights and civil liberties are measured on a scale of 1 to 7; all other figures are percentile scores.
b The first figure is the country's score on political rights; the second is its score on civil liberties.

Source: Political rights and civil liberties: Freedom House (1999, 2009); all others: World Bank (2009).

as measured annually by the World Bank. (I have combined two of the measures, government effectiveness and regulatory quality, into a single average measure of 'state quality'.) These measures are compiled quite differently from those of Freedom House, even for the dimension of 'voice and accountability', a composite measure of freedom to participate in selecting the government, and freedom of expression, association and media. Rather than using one set of expert assessments, as Freedom House does, the World Bank governance indicators take the average of a number of different sources: various expert ratings (including those of Freedom House for the 'voice and accountability' measure), political risk analyses, surveys of domestic firms, public opinion surveys and the perceptions of country analysts at the major multilateral development banks (Kaufmann, Kraay and Mastruzzi 2009: 7). By these more complex measures, the quality of political development in Indonesia has not progressed to nearly as high a level as the Freedom House ratings of political rights and civil liberties would suggest. Indonesia's percentile score on voice and accountability stood at only 44.2 in 2008 — better than Turkey, the Philippines, Thailand and Bangladesh, but well behind the other emerging market democracies, whose scores ranged from 51 to 68.

The next rows in Table 2.4 assess state quality, as an average of two percentile scores: government effectiveness (the quality of public services and policy formulation, and the independence and capacity of the civil service) and regulatory quality ('the ability of the government to provide sound policies and regulations that ... promote private sector development'). Here as on other items, Indonesia has improved considerably since its transition to democracy. Whereas it was just about at the bottom of this set of emerging market democracies in 1998, by 2008 it was at least doing more respectably, close to India, and better than Bangladesh and Argentina.

It is on the rule of law (which measures not only the independence and effectiveness of the police and courts but also the quality of contract enforcement and property rights) that Indonesia still lags furthest behind. Its percentile score has improved little since 1998, and trails very far behind even some other emerging market countries that either are poorer (Ghana, not shown here, and India) or face horrible legacies of crime and state violence (South Africa). On rule of law, even the Philippines (39.7) and Thailand (54.1) score well ahead of Indonesia (28.7).

In 1998, Indonesia was in the bottom 10 per cent of countries in the world in its effectiveness in controlling corruption, with a score of 9.2. None of Indonesia's peers among emerging market democracies scored nearly so miserably then on this measure. A decade later, Indonesia is still — according to this compilation of measures — very corrupt, as anyone who reads the almost daily revelations in Indonesia's press about new corruption scandals involving parliamentarians, police officers, prosecutors and other senior officials would know. It has at least escaped the bottom quartile of countries (scoring now at 31.4), but it still lags behind the other emerging market democracies in Table 2.4, except for Bangladesh and the Philippines.

The picture presented above of Indonesia's political progress in the past decade is a mixed one. The country has taken long strides towards freedom in the judgment of Freedom House, but less impressive ones by the World Bank's methods. Its level of state capacity in economic and administrative affairs is now about middling, but it is still plagued by extensive corruption and a weak rule of law. Yet, when we look at change over time, the picture improves. According to the World Bank, Indonesia has made significant progress since 1998 on virtually every one of its six indicators of governance. On voice and accountability, for example, its score jumped from 16.3 in 1998 to 44.2 in 2008, on government effectiveness it jumped from 19.4 to 47.4, on control of corruption it rose from 9.2 to 31.4 and even on rule of law it increased from 23.8 to 28.7. In some cases progress was steady; in others there was significant progress only after a dip in performance between 1998 and 2003, reflecting some of the drift and even chaos of the early transition period.[7] These positive changes doubtless reflect the institutional reforms undertaken by Indonesia during its first decade of democratic transition, and the establishment of new government bodies designed to improve governance, such as the powerful Corruption Eradication Commission (Komisi Pemberantasan Korupsi, KPK).

The picture becomes rather more dramatic, and more positive, when we compare Indonesia's progress on some of the governance scores with that of other countries around the world. On voice and accountability, Indonesia's improvement between 1998 and 2008 (of 0.9 points on a scale ranging from 2.5 to –2.5) was one of the top five records of improvement in the world, trailing only Ghana, Niger, Sierra Leone and Serbia (Kaufmann, Kraay and Mastruzzi 2009: 33, Table 5).[8] On government effectiveness, Indonesia's gain during the decade (0.56 points) placed it thirteenth in the world in terms of improvement. And on control of corruption, Indonesia's improvement (0.51 points) was eighth best in the world. Also striking about this record of globally pace-setting improve-

---

7   Note that Indonesia's score on the World Bank's political stability measure fell from 10.1 in 1998 to 3.8 in 2003, making it one of the most unstable places in the world on this measure. But it has since climbed back up from that brink, and in 2008 its score stood at 15.8.

8   The authors also note that we may have considerable confidence in the reliability of this verdict of improvement, since almost all of the component measures point in the same direction.

ment on three of the six governance indicators is that Indonesia is one of the few 'normal' countries to appear repeatedly on these lists of 'most improved' countries. Generally, the ones that show up frequently are the states that are recovering from violent conflict, civil war or state collapse — places like Serbia, Iraq, Rwanda, Liberia and Sierra Leone. These war-torn states started with more extreme levels of bad governance in 1998, which made dramatic improvement 'easier' to achieve in the sense that coming up to merely poor levels would constitute a sharp gain. In fact, the only other country not recovering from war to improve so dramatically on as many as three of the six governance indicators was Albania (which had the powerful motivation, like Serbia, of wanting to integrate into the European Union). Figure 2.3, which illustrates Indonesia's progress in reducing corruption in comparison with the other emerging market democracies and its East Asian democratic peers, shows that the country has been doing very well in comparative terms. Similarly strong relative performance is visible in the other fields of governance measured by the World Bank, except political stability. In most of these areas Indonesia improved its percentile rank more than most of its emerging market peers, which either improved more modestly, remained at roughly their previous levels or declined.

In sum, Indonesia has made quite significant progress in democracy and governance over the last decade. Not only is it a much freer country than it was in 1998, or even than in its very early years of democracy, but it is also at least a somewhat better-governed country on every one of the World Bank's measures of governance. Few countries have made more progress in improving the quality of governance in the past decade than Indonesia (and most of the others were previously completely failed states). Yet much remains to be done, if the expert ratings behind these statistics are to be believed. Indonesia remains in the bottom third of countries in the world in terms of both corruption and rule of law, and its average level of state quality, while having improved a lot, is still in the bottom half. If Indonesia is to institutionalise liberal democracy, and probably if it is to launch into the higher rates of economic growth of which it is capable, it will have to do much more to improve the quality of its governance.

HOW INDONESIANS AND OTHER EAST ASIANS VIEW DEMOCRACY

Rather surprisingly, the state of democracy in Indonesia today becomes more hopeful if we examine what its people actually think. Doing so is in fact vital to understanding the depth and durability of democracy

Figure 2.3   Control of corruption in Indonesia and other emerging democracies, 1998 and 2008 (%)

(a) Emerging democracies outside East Asia

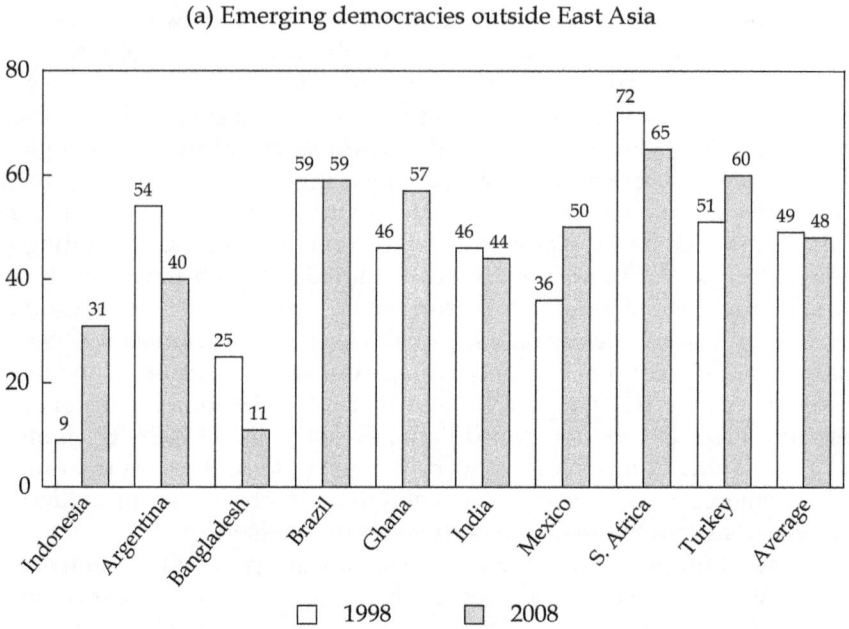

□ 1998   ▨ 2008

(b) Emerging democracies within East Asia

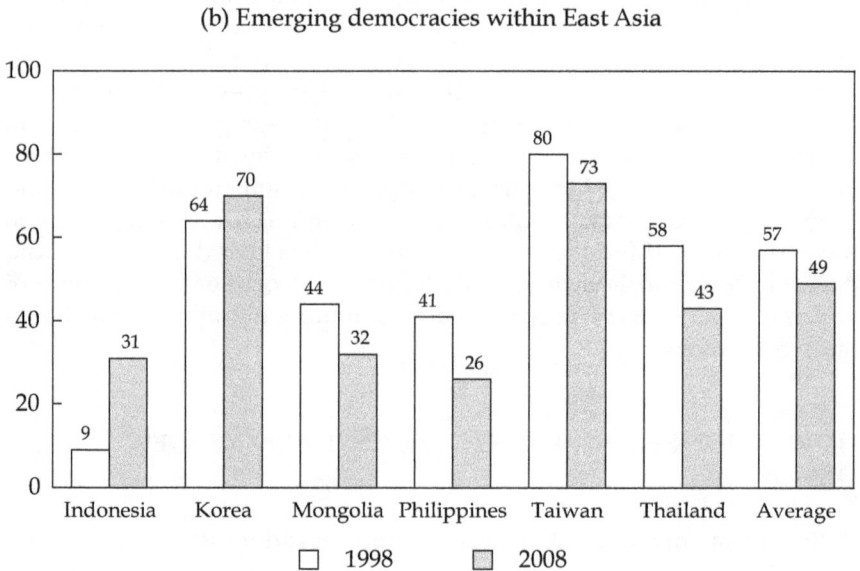

□ 1998   ▨ 2008

Source: World Bank.

in Indonesia, for two reasons. First, democracy is about popular sovereignty, and one cannot gain an adequate purchase on the quality of democracy without knowing how a country's people evaluate the extent and performance of its democracy. And second, democratic stability depends heavily on robust public support for democracy. To measure progress towards the consolidation of democracy, we must know the extent to which its citizens regard it as legitimate—as a better form of government than any other they can imagine.

The only way we can know the extent to which people value and support their democratic institutions (or even perceive them as democratic) is to ask them, through the scientific instrument of a public opinion survey of a representative sample of the voting-age public. This is what the Asian Barometer does. Indonesia was one of six emerging East Asian democracies it surveyed systematically during 2006.[9] Drawing national random samples of the voting-age population, the Asian Barometer asked a large number of standardised questions about people's attitudes and values towards democracy and their evaluations of their own governments, enabling meaningful and revealing comparisons among these countries.

Let us first examine how East Asians evaluate the extent of democracy in their country and the degree to which they want their country to be democratic. Each of these questions was evaluated on a 10-point scale, with 1 being the least democratic and 10 the most democratic. Relative to other East Asians, Indonesians evaluated their democracy quite highly, at an average level of 7.0 on the 10-point scale (Table 2.5). Only Thais placed their democracy higher, at 7.5. (Ironically, their democracy was displaced by a military coup in September 2006, about four months after the survey was conducted.) Indonesians also said they wanted a strongly democratic country, with an average level of desire of 8.5, as high as Korea, higher than Taiwan and slightly outpaced again by Thailand. (Here, though, Mongolia was off the charts as number 1.)

More demanding and complex measures of support for democracy show a similar depth and vigour of democratic attitudes in Indonesia. The Asian Barometer constructed a scale of five individual measures of support for democracy.[10] In Figure 2.4, I present the mean levels of

9 Indonesia was surveyed in November 2006, the Philippines actually in November–December 2005 and the other four countries in the year between. See http://www.asianbarometer.org/newenglish/Introduction/Surveytime table.htm and, more generally, Chu and Huang (2009).

10 These items were: (1) desire for democracy (again on a 10-point scale, but here simply the percentage of the public picking a figure of 6 or higher); (2) the belief that 'democracy is suitable for our country' (again as measured by a score of 6 or higher on the 10-point scale); (3) an affirmative answer to the question of whether the respondent believes democracy can be effective in

Table 2.5   Perceived extent of and desire for democracy among emerging democracies, 2006

	Indonesia	Korea	Taiwan	Thailand	Philip-pines	Mongolia
Perceived extent of democracy	7.0	6.7	7.0	7.5	5.6	6.7
Desire for democracy	8.5	8.5	8.1	8.8	7.4	9.5

Source: Asian Barometer, Wave 2.

agreement with these five items (summarised as 'support for democracy'), together with the overall levels of satisfaction with democracy. Interestingly, the emerging democracies, Indonesia, Thailand and Mongolia (but not the Philippines), demonstrated higher levels of support for democracy on the measures used by the Asian Barometer than did Korea and Taiwan. As we will see, the picture changes when we measure democratic tendencies differently, but this is nevertheless a striking difference.[11] Indonesians showed robust levels of support for democracy on four of the five measures. Only when democracy was pitted against economic development as a choice or priority did Indonesians waiver in large numbers, with only 21 per cent saying they believed that democracy was as important as or more important than democracy (but similarly low figures were found almost everywhere in the region).

Indonesians are (or at least were in 2006) also reasonably satisfied with 'the way democracy is working in our country' (Figure 2.4). Nearly three in five Indonesians expressed strong or at least some satisfaction, again exceeded only by Thailand and Mongolia. This is encouraging, because democratic satisfaction may help to sustain higher levels of support for democracy and discourage the temptation to search for authoritarian alternatives. It is a sign of 'performance' legitimacy, and democracy is probably on its strongest legs when it enjoys support both

---

'solving the problems of the country'; (4) the belief that 'democracy is always preferable' (in contrast to two other options – that 'sometimes authoritarian rule can be preferable' or that 'it doesn't matter'); and (5) the response that democracy is either 'more important' than or 'equally important' to economic development when asked to choose between the two goals.

11 The difference may be due to two factors: citizens in the more highly educated democracies of East Asia are more critical of their democracies because of their higher levels of knowledge and information; and respondents compared their current democracies to previous authoritarian regimes that were quite successful in delivering economic development.

*Figure 2.4   Support for and satisfaction with democracy in Indonesia and
other East Asian emerging democracies, 2006 (%)[a]*

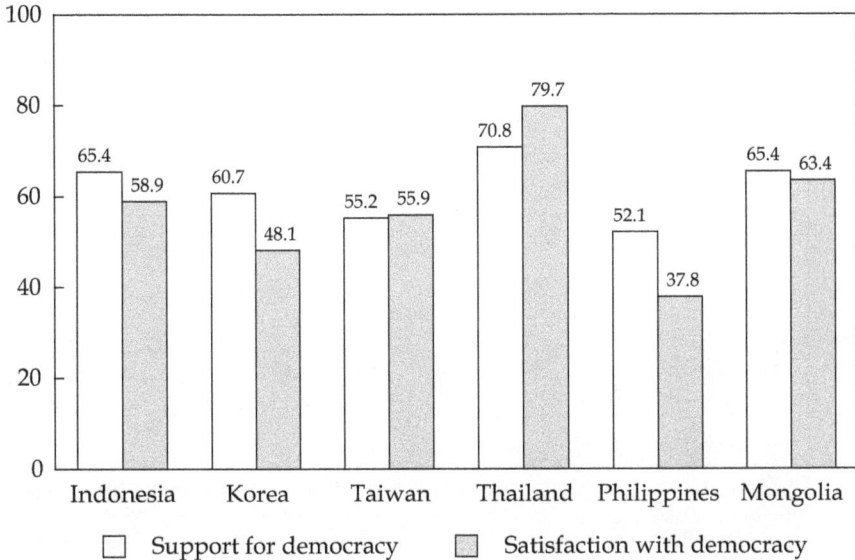

☐ Support for democracy   ▨ Satisfaction with democracy

a   Support for democracy is the average level of pro-democratic response on five questions of democratic support (see footnote 10). Satisfaction with democracy is the percentage of respondents saying they are satisfied or very satisfied with the way democracy is working in their country.

Source: Asian Barometer, Wave 2.

as an intrinsic value and instrumentally, based on what is judged to be
good performance.

The problem with the notion of support for democracy is that it is
not clear what people have in mind when the word 'democracy' is mentioned. And in this day and age, there is a certain general social desirability attached to the word. Thus, the Asian Barometer also sought to get
at the depth of democratic commitment in two other ways. One was to
pose authoritarian alternatives and see how consistently citizens rejected
them. Respondents were asked whether they agreed or disagreed with
each of three statements: that the army should come in to govern the
country; that only one political party should be allowed to contest and
hold office; and that 'We should get rid of parliament and elections and
have a strong leader decide things'. After a dozen years of examining
public opinion survey data in new democracies, I have come to believe
that the percentage of the population rejecting all three of these alternatives is one of the most important indicators of the depth of commitment
to democracy. And here, not surprisingly, we see something of a reverse
pattern: the strongest levels of democratic support were in Korea and

Figure 2.5   Rejection of authoritarianism in Indonesia and other East Asian
                 emerging democracies, 2006 (%)[a]

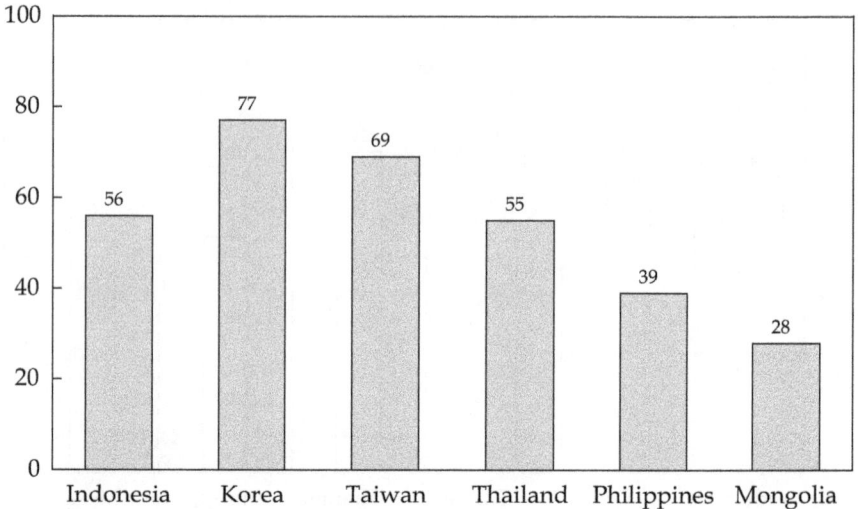

a   Figures represent the percentage of the public disagreeing with all three of the following
    options: (1) one-party rule, (2) military rule and (3) 'get rid of parliament and elections
    and have a strong leader decide things'.
Source: Asian Barometer, Wave 2.

Taiwan, where 77 and 69 per cent of the samples respectively rejected
all three authoritarian options. But a majority also did so in Indonesia
(56 per cent), compared with much lower levels in the Philippines and
Mongolia (see Figure 2.5).

The other way to examine the depth of democratic commitment is
to pose a series of questions that test support for liberal values like civic
pluralism, freedom of speech, judicial independence, popular sovereignty, and checks and balances. The Asian Barometer has constructed
and tested a seven-item scale of liberal values that performs well in scale
tests of coherence and reliability. It asks respondents to agree or disagree with statements such as 'Government leaders are like the head of a
family; we should all follow their decisions'; 'If the government is constantly checked [that is, monitored and supervised] by the legislature, it
cannot possibly accomplish great things'; and 'If people have too many
ways of thinking, society will be chaotic'.[12] This is a high bar for exhibit-

---

12 The other statements are: 'Government should decide whether certain ideas
    should be allowed to be discussed in society'; 'Harmony of the community
    will be disrupted if people organize into lots of groups'; 'When judges decide
    important cases, they should accept the view of the executive branches'; and

Figure 2.6   *Support for liberal values in Indonesia and other East Asian*
emerging democracies, 2006 (%)

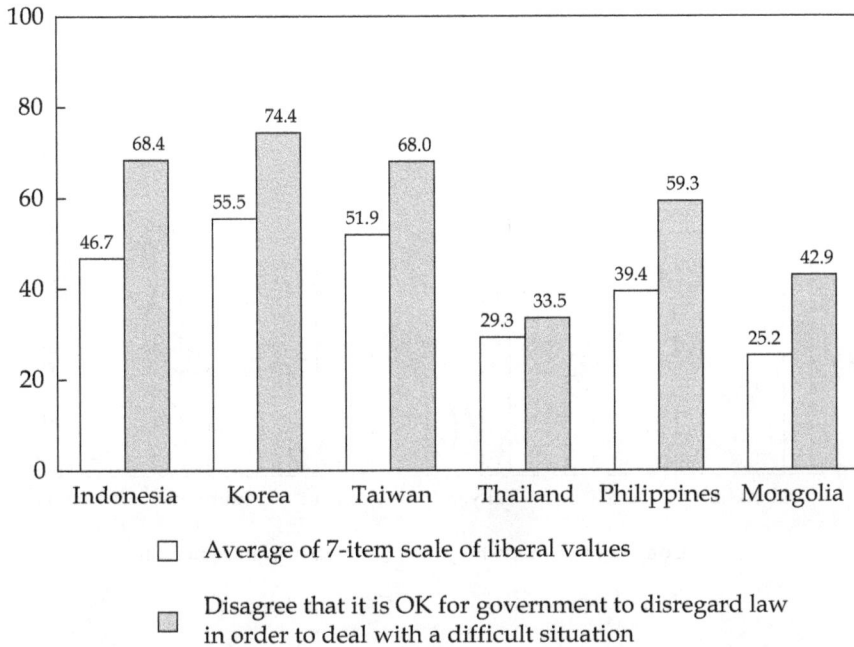

☐   Average of 7-item scale of liberal values

▨   Disagree that it is OK for government to disregard law
in order to deal with a difficult situation

Source: Asian Barometer, Wave 2.

ing democratic commitment, because a liberal orientation requires disagreeing with each of the seven statements posed.[13] Nevertheless, the
average level of support for liberal values in Indonesia was 47 per cent
(Figure 2.6).

I regard this as the single most striking comparative statistic in this
discussion, because support in Indonesia was not much lower than in
Taiwan and Korea (52 and 56 per cent respectively), which have much
more developed, educated and globally integrated societies. Thailand,
the Philippines and Mongolia all showed much lower average levels of

---

'If we have political leaders who are morally upright, we can let them decide
everything'.

13 Public opinion survey researchers have long noted a somewhat greater tendency for respondents to agree than disagree with any random statement,
perhaps because some respondents instinctively want to be polite or agree-
able in response to the researcher, even though the instructions stress that
there is no 'right' answer to any question. Thus, posing illiberal statements
that respondents must disagree with represents a strong test of liberal values.

Figure 2.7   Categories of democrats in Indonesia and other East Asian emerging democracies, 2006 (%)

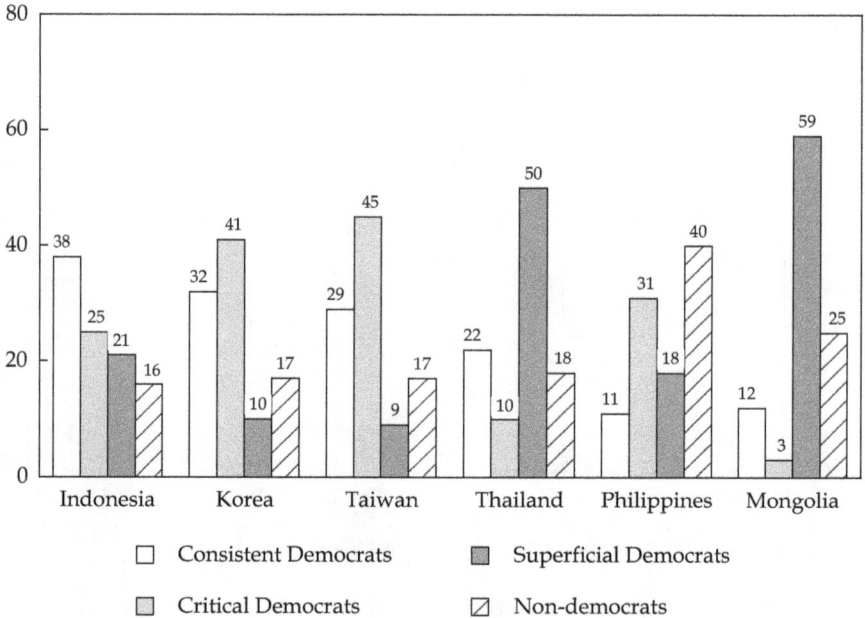

Source: Asian Barometer, Wave 2.

support for liberal values, none over 40 per cent. Clearly, Indonesians are not just supporting democracy out of some vague preference for elections or popular government. For example, 57 per cent of Indonesians disagreed with the statement that judges should accept the view of the executive branch when deciding important cases, and 52 per cent disagreed with the view that if the society has morally upright leaders 'we can let them decide everything'. In addition, though it is not technically part of the 'liberal values' battery, 68 per cent of Indonesians disagreed that it is alright for the government 'to disregard the law in order to deal with a difficult situation'. This is the same solid majority as in Taiwan and much higher than in Thailand and Mongolia.

To complete the portrait of public support for liberal democracy, the Asian Barometer assembled the respondents from each country into four groups based on their levels of support for democracy and for liberal values (Figure 2.7). Consistent Democrats are above the mean for East Asia in levels of support both for democracy and for liberal values. Critical Democrats support liberal values but are below the mean on support for democracy. Superficial Democrats support democracy but are below the mean on liberal values. And Non-democrats are below the mean on both scales.[14] It will come as a surprise to many readers (as it did to many of us in the Asian Barometer project) that Indonesia has the highest percentage of Consistent Democrats (38 per cent) of *any* of the six East Asian democracies (or quasi-democracies). Only Korea is also over 30 per cent. In Korea and Taiwan, where highly educated publics reject authoritarian options but are more wary of democracy and democratic parties and politicians, the modal category is Critical Democrats (who represent 41 per cent and 45 per cent of each sample). Superficial Democrats are the modal category in Thailand and Mongolia (50 per cent and 59 per cent respectively), while Non-democrats are the modal category in the Philippines (40 per cent), showing how far that society has fallen in democratic practice and spirit.

If one were to imagine an ideal step pattern in the categories, the largest category would be Consistent Democrats, followed by Critical Democrats, Superficial Democrats and then Non-democrats (ideally at a fairly low level). Only Indonesia among the six countries exhibits precisely this pattern, as is apparent in the figure. While further research is clearly needed to explore the underlying correlates and causal dynamics of these attitudinal and value patterns in Indonesia, and to determine their evolution and resilience over time, it appears that there is a broad normative foundation in society for the progress that Indonesia's democracy has made in the last decade. Whether this is a response to democratic improvement, or a cause of it, is not clear, and we should be wary of inferring too much from one survey. But the picture that emerges is certainly an encouraging one.

Finally, let us examine comparative levels of trust in political institutions. Asian Barometer asked respondents how much trust they had in a variety of political and state institutions: a great deal, quite a lot, not very much or none at all. Those answering 'a great deal' or 'quite a lot' were counted as trusting a particular institution. It should by now not be surprising that none of the six East Asian countries exhibited higher levels of trust in political institutions, on average, than Indonesia, at 62 per cent (Figure 2.8).[15] Save for Thailand, average levels of trust in political and government institutions were much lower in the other countries, and only about half or less in Korea and Taiwan — where the public tends to be liberal but also deeply sceptical and rather disaffected. In much of the rest of the democratic world, particularly in Latin America and the post-

---

14 This framework, a significant conceptual and methodological advance in the study of democratic legitimacy, was developed by Chu and Huang (2009).

15 Thailand, at 63 per cent, effectively tied with Indonesia, but in the wake of the coup and the intense polarisation of Thai politics, the figure has probably declined sharply.

Figure 2.8   Trust in state institutions in Indonesia and other East Asian emerging democracies, 2006 (%)

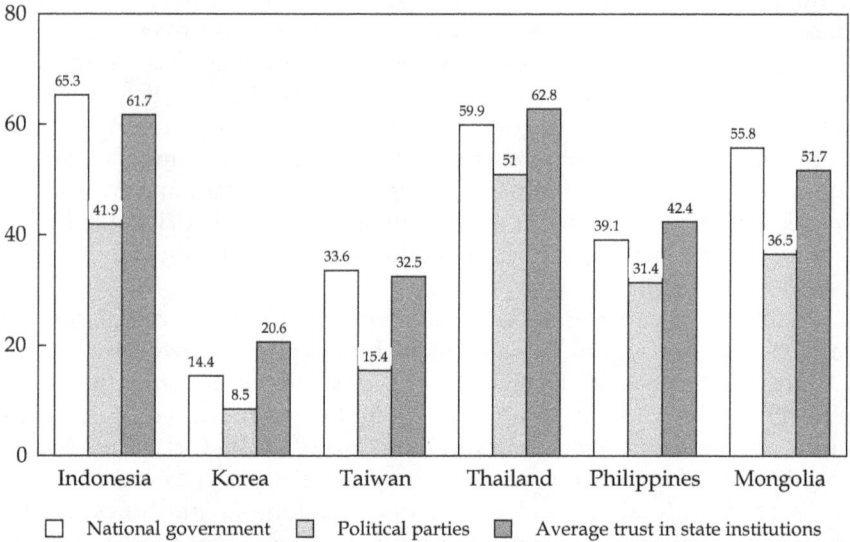

Source: Asian Barometer, Wave 2.

communist countries, as well as Korea and Taiwan, one is hard-pressed to find even a quarter of the public saying that they trust political parties and parliament. In Indonesia, however, 42 per cent said they trusted parties and 59 per cent parliament.[16] About two-thirds of Indonesians said they trusted the national government – the highest figure among the East Asian countries, and perhaps one advance indicator of why Yudhoyono stood such a good chance of being re-elected as president in 2009 on the first ballot.

To summarise, then, not only are Indonesians superficially supportive of 'democracy', but they manifest support for liberal values to a degree that we would not predict from the country's level of economic development. Indonesians' strong support for democracy *and* for liberal democratic values powerfully contradicts arguments that posit a fundamental contradiction between Islam and democracy, or between Islam and values such as tolerance, due process and individual rights. Indonesians show quite a lot of trust in the political and administrative institutions of their democracy, and they judge their political system already to be fairly democratic. Thus, they are more satisfied with the way democracy

---

16   It should be noted that surveys conducted by some domestic polling organisations in Indonesia show widely varying results on similar questions.

is working in their country than are most of the publics in East Asia or elsewhere in the developing world.

To widen the comparative optic, we can briefly compare a few of the attitudes and values expressed in Indonesia in 2006 with the responses to identical questions asked in Latin America and sub-Saharan Africa in 2008. In Latin America in 2008, on average only 37 per cent (and about the same proportion in Brazil) said they were satisfied with the way democracy was working.[17] In Mexico the figure was 23 per cent—compared to 59 per cent in Indonesia in 2006. While Indonesians rated their democracy at 7.0 on the 10-point scale, on average Latin Americans put theirs at only 5.8 (in Brazil the average was 6.0). While 64 per cent of Indonesians said democracy was preferable to any other form of government, only 57 per cent of all Latin Americans (and 47 per cent of Brazilians) said this. Only 30 per cent of Latin Americans trusted parties and 32 per cent parliament in 2008, compared to 42 per cent and 59 per cent respectively in Indonesia in 2006.

In the most recent Afrobarometer, conducted in 2008, the average level of preference for democracy was significantly higher than in Indonesia (70 per cent compared to 64 per cent).[18] But Indonesia's level was not much lower than South Africa's (67 per cent), and the average level of satisfaction with democracy in Indonesia, 59 per cent, was substantially higher than the level in Africa on average (49 per cent, the same as for South Africa), though Ghana's was much higher (80 per cent). Indonesians were also slightly more inclined to reject military rule (62 per cent) than Africans overall (despite having gotten rapid economic development during most of the period they lived under it), but less likely than in South Africa (67 per cent) or Ghana (78 per cent). The case of Ghana shows that levels of democratic support and satisfaction can realistically range higher than they do in Indonesia, even (or perhaps especially) in a country with lower levels of income and education.

Overall, these levels of public attitudes and values towards democracy in Indonesia appear encouraging not only in isolation, but even more so when compared with a variety of relevant reference groups. But more detailed analysis is needed to determine which Indonesians (in terms of class, regional and religious characteristics) support democracy and which are ambivalent towards or rejecting of it. And much more time is needed to determine how resilient these orientations will be, and how much they depend on the relatively good performance, economi-

---

17   The figures I report here for Latin America are the average of the mean percentage levels in each country. The country scores may be found in Latinobarómetro (2008).

18   See http://www.afrobarometer.org/newsupdates.html.

cally and politically, of Indonesia's democracy, especially (so far) under the presidency of Yudhoyono.

CONCLUSION: IS INDONESIAN DEMOCRACY CONSOLIDATING OR CONSOLIDATED?

This chapter has given a largely encouraging portrait of Indonesia's democratic growth and performance in its first decade. Between 1998 and 2009 Indonesia became a relatively free country and a more vigorous, stable and legitimate democracy than most sympathetic observers probably dared to hope when the decades-old autocracy came crashing down in 1998. As we have seen, Indonesia made appreciable progress on a large number of governance and socio-economic development measures during its first full decade of democracy. Moreover, its people seem to recognise and appreciate that performance; they are by and large satisfied with the way democracy is working in their country and they are trusting and supportive of its institutions. In a comparative context, Indonesia still lags well behind the more democratically institutionalised and economically developed emerging market countries in the quality of its governance, but it has improved faster than most, and has levels of support for democracy and liberal democratic values that compare favourably with those in most of its East Asian peers.

It is comforting to know that the quality of democracy in Indonesia, and public support for it, is improving more quickly, and in some respects appears more resilient, than in other developing countries to which Indonesia might be compared. But in the end, Indonesian democracy will succeed or fail on its own terms, not simply because it is not doing as badly as some other emerging market democracies. The most important question is whether democracy in Indonesia is really here to stay. Is it consolidated? Has democracy so clearly become 'the only game in town' that its reversal is unthinkable?

Despite clear progress over the last decade, democracy in Indonesia still appears vulnerable to reversal. It is possible, as Liddle and Mujani (forthcoming) have done, to apply the three-dimensional typology of Juan Linz and Alfred Stepan—encompassing behaviour, attitudes and constitutional commitment—and conclude that Indonesian democracy is essentially consolidated because: (1) 'No significant political group currently threatens to overthrow democracy or to separate from the Indonesian nation-state'[19] (the behavioural dimension); (2) there is, attitudinally,

---

19   The quotation is from page 5 of the original 2009 manuscript. I am grateful to Professor Liddle for providing me with a copy.

pretty substantial and steady mass support for democracy as the best form of government; and (3) key political and social actors are committed to solving their disputes and pursuing their interests non-violently, through the constitutional process (Liddle and Mujani, forthcoming: 9). But as the authors note, there remain significant (and not fully known or understood) levels of political violence in Indonesia, and it is not clear to what extent Islamist parties and movements that favour a *syari'ah* state fully accept the democratic constitutional order, even though both Islamist violence and support for a *syari'ah* state are currently in decline. While the share of the parliamentary vote of 'the largest self-declared Islamist party', the United Development Party (Partai Persatuan Pembangunan, PPP), declined from 11 per cent in 1999 to 8 per cent in 2004 to 5 per cent in 2009, the share of the more militant Prosperous Justice Party (Partai Keadilan Sejahtera, PKS) improved from 2 per cent to 7 per cent to 8 per cent during the course of Indonesia's three democratic national elections.[20] Yet encouragingly, their combined support has remained stable at 13–15 per cent, and PKS has yet to top 10 per cent. Moreover there is a live debate about the extent to which PKS is adapting to, and being domesticated by, democratic politics (see Bubalo, Fealy and Mason 2008).

More worrisome may be the level of behavioural, attitudinal and constitutional commitment to democracy among key elites who retain the ability to diminish or reverse democracy in Indonesia. This could still be the case with the military – although its prerogatives and political role have clearly been diluted over the course of Indonesia's democratic transition – and with former high-ranking military officers such as the two unsuccessful vice-presidential candidates in 2009, Prabowo Subianto (PDIP) and Wiranto (Golkar).[21] A democracy has not really crossed the threshold of consolidation until it has become *enduringly* 'the only game in town'. For this to happen, commitments to democratic norms and behaviours must not only reach a high critical mass among the public at large, they must also encompass all elites and organisations that have the potential to disrupt the system. This means that powerful actors must become either unconditionally committed to democracy and its rules and restraints, or so marginal that they can no longer threaten the system. While the evidence of the five years to 2009 is encouraging, we cannot really assess these trends without the passage of more time, and especially without knowing the extent to which democratic progress has been dependent on a skilful and restrained leader like Yudhoyono

20 See Liddle and Mujani (forthcoming: 6) and, for the full electoral trends, Mujani and Liddle in this volume.
21 For the role of the military in the democratic transition – and the continuing obstacles to military reform – see Mietzner (2009).

and can carry on without him. It will also be important to track public opinion and value indicators over time to assess the resilience of the results. I have argued elsewhere that at the level of mass public support, 70 per cent seems to be a critical threshold of democratic consolidation (Diamond 1999: Ch. 5). Ideally, this should be assessed not by a single indicator but by multiple ones, perhaps especially rejection of all authoritarian alternatives.

In my previous work, I have argued that there is a strong causal association between the quality of democracy and the stability or consolidation of democracy (Diamond 1999: Ch. 3). During Yudhoyono's first presidential term, 2004–2009, Indonesia improved its performance on a number of indicators of governance. However, its poor performance on corruption and rule of law remain an obstacle to genuine consolidation.

The consolidation of democracy overall tends also to be associated with the consolidation of specific democratic institutions, not least the party system. Here one could see hope in the growth of Yudhoyono's Democratic Party (Partai Demokrat, PD) to become the largest party in parliament, but still it has only a quarter of the seats, while seven other parties have at least 5 per cent. Comparative experience tells us that the combination of presidentialism and such a high number of relevant parties (due to a purely proportional representation electoral system) is an unstable one for democracy. Further aggregation of the party system, perhaps by adopting a mixed electoral system (in which, for example, half the seats would be filled from single-member districts), would contribute to democratic consolidation, as would the internal democratisation of parties. It would help as well if Indonesian parties were to deepen their popular roots and develop some stable institutional bases of support in society, beyond the individual personalities and networks of their leaders.[22] But around the world, this is not an easy thing for democratic parties to do when they are born into a media-saturated age. On the other hand, the country is now largely free of one of the most common sources of destabilising political polarisation, in that 'most Indonesian voters do not give high priority to the demands of religious and ethnic groups' (Mujani and Liddle, this volume, page 95).

The most formidable challenge for consolidating democracy involves the rule of law. Levels of corruption must continue to be brought down. The independence, capacity and integrity of the judiciary must be strengthened. The nascent anti-corruption institutions, particularly the KPK, must be defended against the inevitable assaults on their vitality

---

22 In the judgment of Mujani and Liddle (this volume) this is not happening; they believe that electoral volatility remains high and the roots of parties shallow.

and efficacy by vested interests who feel threatened by any serious pursuit of public integrity. Access to justice by ordinary Indonesians must be improved. The capacity, professionalism and political neutrality of the police and security forces must be enhanced. Levels of political violence should diminish even further if these things happen.

To conclude, if we apply absolute (theoretically derived) standards, rather than merely 'grade on a curve' comparatively, Indonesian democracy is progressing, but not nearly as well as the comparative data sometimes suggest. If democracy is really to become 'the only game in town', it must continue to become a better — a more accountable, transparent, lawful, inclusive, fair and responsive — democracy for ordinary Indonesians.

REFERENCES

Bubalo, Anthony, Greg Fealy and Whit Mason (2008), 'Zealous democrats: Islamism and democracy in Egypt, Indonesia and Turkey', Lowy Institute Paper No. 25, Lowy Institute for International Policy, Sydney.

Chu, Yun-han and Min-hua Huang (2009), 'A typological analysis of democratic legitimacy', Asian Barometer Working Paper Series No. 48, International Political Science Association, Santiago, http://www.asianbarometer.org/newenglish/publications/workingpapers/no.48.pdf.

Diamond, Larry (1999), *Developing Democracy: Toward Consolidation*, Johns Hopkins University Press, Baltimore MD.

Diamond, Larry (2008), *The Spirit of Democracy: The Struggle to Build Free Societies throughout the World*, Times Books, New York NY.

Freedom House (various years), *Freedom in the World*, Freedom House, Washington DC, http://www.freedomhouse.org/template.cfm?page=15.

Huntington, Samuel P. (1991), *The Third Wave: Global Democratization in the Late Twentieth Century*, University of Oklahoma Press, Norman OK.

Kaufmann, Daniel, Aart Kraay and Massimo Mastruzzi (2009), 'Governance matters VIII: aggregate and individual governance indicators, 1996–2008', World Bank Policy Research Working Paper No. 4978, 29 June, http://ssrn.com/abstract=1424591.

Latinobarómetro Corporation (2008), *Annual Report 2008*, English edition, www.latinobarometro.org.

Liddle, R. William and Saiful Mujani (forthcoming), 'Indonesian democracy: from transition to consolidation', in M. Kuenkler and A. Stepan (eds), *Indonesia, Islam, and Democratic Consolidation*.

Mietzner, Marcus (2009), *Military Politics, Islam and the State in Indonesia: From Turbulent Transition to Democratic Consolidation*, Institute of Southeast Asian Studies, Singapore.

World Bank (2009), 'Governance matters 2009: Worldwide Governance Indicators, 1996–2008', http://info.worldbank.org/governance/wgi/index.asp, interactive website, accessed September 2009.

PART I

Managing Democracy

3 INDONESIA'S 2009 ELECTIONS: DEFECTIVE SYSTEM, RESILIENT DEMOCRACY

*Rizal Sukma**

In 2009, Indonesia held its third set of nationwide democratic elections since the end of Suharto's authoritarian New Order regime in 1998. Surprising many observers, the elections were marred by far worse administrative and technical defects than any previous post-Suharto election, pointing to significant underlying problems in Indonesian democracy. At the same time, the elections were generally agreed to be free and fair, they produced renewed democratic legitimacy for government institutions, and they confirmed or modified, rather than overturned, most of the broad patterns of political alignment established over the preceding decade. Overall, the elections thus point to a high degree of stability and resilience in Indonesia's new democracy, despite the problems.

The elections were held in two rounds. On 9 April 2009 legislative elections determined the membership of national and regional parliaments. The results confirmed a slow but steady change in Indonesia's electoral politics, with some parties gaining significantly in support and others declining, but with the overall pattern of a fragmented multi-party system remaining intact. On 8 July 2009, the first round of direct presidential elections was held, the second such elections since Suharto's fall in 1998. A second-round presidential election, planned for September, proved unnecessary because of a landslide victory by President Susilo Bambang Yudhoyono in the first round, in which he won 60.8 per cent of the vote.

---

* An earlier version of this article appeared in the *Bulletin of Indonesian Economic Studies* in 2009; see Sukma (2009).

The magnitude of this victory points to relatively high popular satisfaction with government, more than 10 years into Indonesia's democratic transition. Yet the achievements of these elections in consolidating Indonesian democracy were significantly undermined by serious technical flaws that marked a worrying decline in the professionalism of Indonesia's electoral management, and which may be viewed as emblematic of wider problems of governance that still bedevil Indonesian democracy.

This chapter examines key developments related to the election cycle of 2009 and their implications for Indonesian democracy. It is divided into five sections. The first discusses the legislative elections, which continued a slow but important change in Indonesia's electoral politics. The second section analyses the July presidential election, which favoured the candidate best able to navigate a political battleground characterised by the overriding importance of personality and image. The third looks at the influence of political Islam, whose relatively poor performance in 2009 confirms Islam's struggle to remain relevant in a formal political life dominated by non-theocratic forces. The fourth section examines the formation of Yudhoyono's cabinet immediately after the elections, and what this indicates about patterns of coalition building and power sharing. The fifth and final section considers the prospects for Indonesia's democratic resilience in light of the trends and dynamics revealed by its third post-Suharto national elections.

THE LEGISLATIVE ELECTIONS

Parliaments and parliamentary elections have been central institutions in Indonesian democratisation from the start of the post-Suharto period. Using a system of proportional representation, in the first democratic elections of the new era, in 1999, Indonesians voted to produce a national parliament (Dewan Perwakilan Rakyat, DPR) that was not dominated by one or two large parties, but instead contained a multiplicity of medium-sized and small ones. The DPR then became the major locus of political bargaining and negotiation in establishing the main structures of Indonesian democracy, and in determining the rise and fall of Indonesia's first democratically elected presidents. Although the powers and independence of the president have been strengthened since the introduction of direct presidential elections in 2004, parliaments at the national and regional levels still retain crucial law-making and budgetary powers and thus remain a crucial focus of political contestation, as in most democracies. As a result, the president still needs to take account of the composition of the DPR, and the balance of the main parties within it, in order to achieve his or her legislative goals and maintain a stable cabinet. Signifi-

cantly, it is also in the legislative elections that Indonesia's societal pluralism is most fully reflected in the formal political system: the contestants
have included a range of parties associated with differing societal constituencies and representing varying positions on contentious issues like
the place that Islam should occupy in social and political affairs.

But parliamentary elections also pose significant technical challenges
in a country as large as Indonesia. In 2009, a main task of the General
Elections Commission (Komisi Pemilihan Umum, KPU) was to administer the elections in 77 electoral districts for the national parliament and in
33 provinces for the Regional Representative Council (Dewan Perwakilan Daerah, DPD), with a total of around 171.3 million eligible voters.
At the same time, the KPU had to administer elections for the local legislatures (Dewan Perwakilan Rakyat Daerah, DPRD), at both the provincial (*propinsi*) and district/municipality (*kabupaten/kota*) levels. At the
national level alone, 11,301 candidates from 38 national political parties
competed for 560 seats in the DPR; another 1,116 candidates competed
for 128 seats in the DPD and 278,851 candidates competed for seats in
the local legislatures. With a total of 528,217 polling stations to be staffed
and more than 700 million ballots to be printed, the KPU faced severe
logistical challenges.

In contrast to the 2004 elections, when the KPU coped relatively well,
the team responsible for administering the 2009 elections was hampered
by its own incompetence. The selection process for membership of the
commission was dogged by public criticism from the outset. Many well-
known figures, including former KPU members such as Ramlan Surbakti
and Valina Singka Subekti, were excluded. The preliminary selection
committee at the Ministry of Home Affairs, which required candidates
to pass a 'psychological test' before their names were passed to a parliamentary selection committee, was accused by many people of using
subjective methods of selection. The public was also shocked by the
DPR's decision to exclude from the final selection process the respected
chair of the Centre for Electoral Reform (CETRO), Hadar Gumay. None
of the newly appointed members had served on the commission previously. Public doubts about their capacity and expertise were expressed
immediately after their appointment. Even though some had served previously in various regional KPU offices, it was not clear that they had the
capacity to organise national elections or were well versed in electoral
management. President Yudhoyono even had to postpone the swearing-
in of one member because corruption charges had been laid against him.

From the beginning, preparations for the elections were hampered by
tremendous technical and logistical problems. Some ballots were incor-
rectly printed, some were in short supply, and some were sent to the
wrong provinces and districts. Uncertain campaign schedules, problems

Table 3.1   Results of the 2009 legislative elections[a]

Political party	2004		2009	
	Votes (%)	Seats (no.)	Votes (%)	Seats (no.)
Partai Demokrat (PD)	7.5	55	20.9	148
Golkar	21.6	129	14.5	106
Partai Demokrasi Indonesia Perjuangan (PDIP)	18.5	109	14.0	94
Partai Keadilan Sejahtera (PKS)	7.3	45	7.9	57
Partai Amanat Nasional (PAN)	6.4	53	6.0	45
Partai Persatuan Pembangunan (PPP)	8.2	58	5.3	38
Partai Kebangkitan Bangsa (PKB)	10.6	52	4.9	28
Gerindra (Partai Gerakan Indonesia Raya)	–	–	4.5	26
Hanura (Partai Hati Nurani Rakyat)	–	–	3.8	18
Total	**80.1**	**501**	**81.8**	**560**

a   The figures shown represent valid votes for parties that gained seats in the DPR.
Source: KPU (2009).

with the transport of election materials, a lack of experienced staff and many other problems served to underline the KPU's incompetence. The worst problems related to the fixed voter list (*daftar pemilih tetap*, DPT); they included the absence from the list of millions of eligible voters, the presence of large numbers of fictitious voters, the registration of some voters at two or even three polling stations, and the inclusion of active members of the armed forces (who do not have the right to vote) and deceased persons.[1] All of this generated accusations of attempted manipulation by the KPU, triggering doubts about the fairness and legitimacy of the elections.

Despite these problems, the parliamentary elections passed without major violence, confirming Indonesia's good record of peaceful post-transitional elections. The results pointed to significant changes in the distribution of votes among parties and in the allocation of seats in the DPR (Table 3.1). First, the Democratic Party (Partai Demokrat, PD), established by Yudhoyono as his 2004 electoral vehicle, emerged as the most successful party, outpolling the more established Golkar party led

---

1   For a comprehensive discussion of Indonesia's election management problems, see Schmidt's chapter in this volume.

by Vice-President Jusuf Kalla and the Indonesian Democratic Party of Struggle (Partai Demokrasi Indonesia Perjuangan, PDIP) led by former president Megawati Sukarnoputri. Second, the electoral strength of Golkar and PDIP continued to decline, with their share of the vote falling by as much as 25 per cent. Third, only nine of the 38 parties contesting the national election passed the electoral threshold of 2.5 per cent that would make them eligible to be represented in the DPR, a significant reduction from the 16 parties in the 2004–2009 parliament. Fourth, the Islamic and Muslim-based parties fared poorly relative to 2004, with the Prosperous Justice Party (Partai Keadilan Sejahtera, PKS) the only one to achieve a (small) increase. Fifth, the results of the elections brought two newcomers to the political scene: the Greater Indonesia Movement Party (Partai Gerakan Rakyat Indonesia Raya, Gerindra), established by retired general Prabowo Subianto, and the People's Conscience Party (Partai Hati Nurani Rakyat, Hanura), established by retired general Wiranto.

PD experienced an almost threefold increase over its 2004 result, from just 7.5 per cent to 20.9 per cent, securing 148 DPR seats (up from just 55 in 2004). For a party established only in September 2001 this was a remarkable achievement. PD benefited immensely from the popularity of the president himself. Mietzner (2009: 5) argues, for example, that 'PD's level of support is more a reflection of Yudhoyono's popularity and the performance of his government than the result of organisational success'. Many Indonesians admired Yudhoyono for his personal qualities, seeing him as polite, wise, fatherly, well mannered and calm. His personal popularity was amplified by the perceived achievements of his government, including political stability, social welfare initiatives such as a cash hand-out program, improved economic performance and successes in combating corruption. Thus, a survey by the Indonesian Survey Institute (Lembaga Survei Indonesia, LSI) in February 2009 found that around 70 per cent of respondents were satisfied with Yudhoyono's leadership (LSI 2009).

For both Golkar and PDIP, the disappointing election results triggered internal debate. One important factor was the ability of Gerindra and Hanura to capture the votes of Golkar's traditional supporters.[2] Golkar's role as junior partner in the first Yudhoyono administration had hampered the party's ability to take credit for government successes, which were instead attributed to Yudhoyono and PD. Golkar's losses were also due partly to the lack of any charismatic figure who could rival Yud-

---

2 Golkar's secretary general, Soemarsono, admitted that many of the party's supporters had shifted their allegiance to new parties established by former Golkar politicians. See 'Apa yang menyebabkan Golkar kalah telak?' [What caused Golkar's terrible loss?], *Kompas*, 13 April 2009.

hoyono in popularity. For PDIP, the elitist nature of the party's leadership, dominated by Megawati family members, may have contributed to its electoral decline (Mietzner 2009: 10). Voters had seemingly become disenchanted with Megawati's aloofness, hardly an asset in an intrinsically populist party. The party was also beset by internal problems that resulted in the departure of key cadres and loyalists. Moreover, the public's positive perceptions of the Yudhoyono government made it difficult for PDIP to erase voters' memories of the weaknesses of the earlier Megawati presidency.

Four Islamic and Muslim-based parties — the National Mandate Party (Partai Amanat Nasional, PAN), the United Development Party (Partai Persatuan Pembangunan, PPP), the People's Awakening Party (Partai Kebangkitan Bangsa, PKB) and the Crescent Moon and Star Party (Partai Bulan Bintang, PBB) — did not perform well. PAN, which had presented itself as a true reformist party in the early post-Suharto years, lost much of its appeal following the resignation of its founder, Amien Rais, as chair in 2005. Indonesia's second-largest mass Islamic organisation, Muhammadiyah, which had served as the party's main power base, became disillusioned with PAN's leaders because of their tendency to dissociate the party from the organisation, and advised its members not to feel obliged to vote for PAN. PPP was hampered by internal conflict and a need for regeneration, while PKB's loss of support was caused primarily by internal conflict generated by the erratic manoeuvring of the party's founder, former president Abdurrahman Wahid. Disappointed by his inability to dismiss the current chair, Muhamin Iskandar, Wahid went so far as to campaign against PKB in the 2009 elections, calling on his supporters to vote for PDIP or Gerindra instead.

Apart from PD, the only parties that gained new support were the Islamist PKS and the two newcomers led by retired generals, Gerindra and Hanura. Nevertheless, Gerindra managed to gain only 4.5 per cent of the vote and Hanura just 3.8 per cent. The leaders of both were disappointed by the results, given the billions of rupiahs they had spent on aggressive advertising and campaigning. Meanwhile, PKS, despite its tireless efforts over the preceding five years, managed to garner only 7.9 per cent of the vote—a slight increase over its 7.3 per cent in 2004, but far below the ambitious 20 per cent target the party had set for itself. Not only was PKS unable to expand its support base but it also failed to capitalise on the steady decline of the other Islamic parties, whose former supporters seem to have moved to secular parties instead.

In addition to the shifts in the fortunes of individual parties, the 2009 parliamentary elections served as a 'killing ground' for national politicians who failed to make it back into parliament. In December 2008, the Constitutional Court decided that the semi-open proportional list system provided for in Law No. 10/2008 on General Elections contravened the constitution; it therefore ruled that seats won by parties would be allocated to their candidates in the order of votes they had won as individuals, rather than in the order of candidates' names on the party list. This decision, which heightened competition between individual candidates even within the same party, proved to be a major stumbling block for many incumbent DPR members. Several well-known individuals failed to gain enough votes to be re-elected, losing out to more popular 'celebrity' candidates or to politicians with genuine grassroots support. For example, House speaker Agung Laksono, Golkar members Ferry Mursidan Baldan and Happy Bone Zulkarnaen and PAN figures Abdillah Toha, Didiek Rachbini and Dedy Djamaludin Malik all failed to be re-elected. The consequences of the court's decision for the shape of the new parliament were significant: around 70 per cent of the seats were filled by new members (Sulaiman 2009).

As predicted, the election results were challenged by a number of parties, and post-election disputes simmered. Two potential candidates for president, Megawati and Wiranto, complained that the legislative elections had been a fraud and threatened to boycott the presidential election. Large parties, including PDIP and Golkar, threatened to sue the KPU and the government over what they claimed were fraud-ridden elections, and there were even calls for a re-run. The Constitutional Court received 722 formal complaints following these elections, with the majority disputing the validity of the vote count.[3] Of 44 political parties (including six local parties in Aceh province), only two did *not* file any dispute (Faiz 2009). NGOs criticised the KPU for various shortcomings in the electoral process and filed a citizens' lawsuit against it. The KPU's lack of professionalism was further exposed when the Constitutional Court's chair, Mahfud M.D., complained that the electoral body was not serious in responding to the cases brought against it by the political parties.[4]

To make matters worse, vote counting and seat allocation dragged on for far too long. After spending billions of rupiah on an electronic vote-counting system, the KPU was forced to terminate its implementation because staff could not update the results as counting progressed, and

---

3 'Hanura klaim rebut satu kursi DPR Partai Golkar' [Hanura claims it has taken one DPR seat from Golkar], *Hukumonline*, 22 June, http://www.hukum online.com/berita/baca/hol22367/hanura-klaim-rebut-satu-kursi-dpr-partai-golkar.

4 'Ketua MK: KPU tak hadiri 11 sidang gugatan' [Constitutional Court chair: KPU failed to attend 11 court sittings], *Vivanews*, 19 May 2009, http://politik. vivanews.com/news/read/59006-ketua_MK_KPU_tak_hadiri_150_sidang_gugatan.

had to revert to the old manual system. The allocation of parliamentary seats was postponed several times, and changed twice — first on 14 May, then on 2 September — before the KPU was able to announce the final allocation on 17 September. Given all these problems, there is no doubt that the quality of electoral management of the 2009 legislative elections was far below that of the 2004 elections. Despite warnings from civil society organisations and political parties long before election day, the KPU failed to improve its performance. The same serious electoral management problems marred the presidential election in July, and the outcome was again challenged as a result.

THE PRESIDENTIAL ELECTION

One of the major changes made to Indonesia's political architecture after the first years of the democratic transition was the introduction of direct elections for heads of executive government both at the centre and in the regions. In the first direct presidential elections in 2004, Susilo Bambang Yudhoyono proved to be the national politician most adept at taking advantage of this change. Lacking a substantial political machinery of his own, he was able to sponsor the formation of a party, PD, which secured enough votes to form the foundation of a presidential campaign. Taking advantage of the profile he had built up during his previous years of service in the cabinet, and relying on the politics of image building and media management, he was able to secure a comfortable second-round victory and defeat the incumbent, Megawati. In the succeeding years Yudhoyono has proven to be a capable if unexciting president, but one who is forever conscious of maintaining his public image and approval ratings, and forever hesitant to take actions that might damage his reputation in the eyes of the voters. In this sense he is arguably Indonesia's first truly modern politician, well adapted to a contemporary political landscape dominated by the electronic media.

In 2004 Yudhoyono had organised a partnership with Jusuf Kalla relatively early in the electoral cycle. At that time, with only a small and untested party to back him and with victory far from certain, Yudhoyono had badly wanted the added electoral security provided by the Golkar party machine and by Kalla's personal riches. In the succeeding years of government, the relationship between the two men was often tense. Vice-President Kalla was seen as making decisions that were not always in line with President Yudhoyono's preferences. He was also accused of interfering in policy making and of setting the government's agenda to an extent that far surpassed the role conventionally expected of a vice-president. For his part, Kalla was often irritated by what he and many others perceived as Yudhoyono's indecisiveness in making important decisions.

Given this background, it is not surprising that the partnership was not renewed in 2009. As various polls began to suggest that PD would come first in the legislative elections — with a forecast vote of more than 20 per cent — Yudhoyono avoided nominating his running mate early in the game. When the president still did not announce his choice at PD's national convention in early February, it was taken by many as an indication that he did not want to continue his partnership with Kalla. Speculation strengthened when PD's deputy chair, Ahmad Mubarok, remarked that Golkar might get only 2.5 per cent of the vote in the legislative elections, angering many of that party's leaders. Some of Kalla's supporters within Golkar began to urge him to run for the presidency himself, and eventually he began to signal that he might indeed challenge Yudhoyono.

After the legislative election, although Yudhoyono formed a coalition with four Islamic and Muslim-based parties (PKS, PAN, PPP and PKB) in his bid for a second presidential term, PD's stunning performance gave him greater freedom to choose his running mate. In late April, Golkar took the initiative and decided to nominate Kalla as its presidential candidate. However, its share of the vote in the legislative elections did not allow it to meet either of the requirements for nominating a presidential candidate — namely, at least 20 per cent of seats in the DPR or 25 per cent of the popular vote — so Kalla had to form a coalition, and chose Wiranto of Hanura as his running mate. Meanwhile, Yudhoyono named as his running mate the governor of the central bank, Boediono, a respected economist and former coordinating minister for economic affairs. PDIP, which had nominated Megawati, found itself in tough negotiations with Prabowo of Gerindra, who also wanted to run for the presidency. After intense talks, Prabowo finally accepted Megawati's invitation to become her vice-presidential candidate.

As the election drew closer, the position of the Yudhoyono–Boediono pairing became virtually unassailable. Various polls showed them consistently in the lead. The polls were confirmed by the results on election day itself: when the KPU announced the official results, the Yudhoyono–Boediono ticket had won a clear majority with 60.8 per cent of the vote. Megawati–Prabowo took second place with 26.8 per cent and, to their surprise, Kalla–Wiranto came a distant third with only 12.4 per cent of the vote. Thus, in contrast to the first direct presidential elections in 2004, when Yudhoyono had to face Megawati in a run-off, this time he won clearly in the first round.

The reasons for Yudhoyono's landslide victory were much the same as those for PD's win in the legislative elections. The 2009 presidential elections can be characterised as a 'beauty contest' in which popularity was determined largely by personal qualities rather than policies,[5] and it is clear that, for most voters, Yudhoyono was preferred because of his perceived personal traits. An exit poll conducted by the Institute for Social and Economic Research, Education and Information (Lembaga Penelitian, Pendidikan dan Penerangan Ekonomi dan Sosial, LP3ES), for example, found that 27.5 per cent of the voters chose Yudhoyono because they perceived him as 'charismatic and wise'. The same poll showed that he scored far above Megawati and Kalla on 'honesty' and 'experience'.[6] Yudhoyono's personal popularity was reinforced by general public satisfaction with his policies — especially the cash hand-out program, the lowering of fuel prices (following large increases not long before), the operational assistance for schools and the vigorous anti-corruption drive — as well as by the effectiveness of his campaign and his political advertising. Whatever the factors in play, the results clearly represented a significant vote of confidence in Yudhoyono's ability to govern, and reflected voters' preference for continuity.

As with the legislative elections, the results of the presidential election were contested. Both Megawati and Kalla complained that the election had been marred by 'massive and systematic fraud', and challenged the result in the Constitutional Court. Megawati's legal team alleged that the KPU had awarded around 28.6 million votes to Yudhoyono that 'came from voters registered more than once, underage voters and even dead voters'. They insisted that they had 'evidence' that Yudhoyono and Boediono had received only 48.7 per cent of the total vote, and demanded that the KPU hold a run-off vote between Yudhoyono and Megawati. Kalla's legal team also alleged that there had been widespread irregularities in the voting and vote counting. Like Megawati's team, they presented 'evidence' showing that Kalla had taken second place, with 39 million votes (well over twice the official figure). They too demanded that a run-off election be held — in this case between Yudhoyono and Kalla. In its decision on 18 August, the court rejected both of these pleas. It found that neither candidate had provided the court with substantial evidence to support their respective cases, and declared the results of the election based on the KPU's decision to be valid.[7]

The incompetence of the KPU, rather than any demonstrated systematic fraud or manipulation, had once again provided the basis for

---

5 A survey conducted by *Kompas* in June 2008 showed that 49.3 per cent of respondents would vote on the basis of a candidate's personal charisma (Margaretha 2009: 2).

6 'Sihir dari Cikeas' [Magic from Cikeas], *Tempo*, 20–26 July 2009.

7 'Megawati and Kalla jockey for slim chance at runoff', *Jakarta Post*, 5 August 2009.

contestation of the election results. The administrative and logistical problems that engulfed the parliamentary elections had continued unabated throughout the presidential election period. The main problems still centred on the defective list of voters. One week before election day, the KPU had not yet been able to update the list, allegedly leaving millions of eligible voters unregistered. The list still included more than 10 million voters who had been registered more than once.[8] The KPU stubbornly refused demands by Megawati and Kalla for unregistered voters to be given access to the polling stations simply by showing their identity cards. Political tensions escalated rapidly when Kalla and Megawati met to discuss the problem on 5 July, demanding that the KPU revise the list. There were calls for the postponement of the election, and even threats to boycott or withdraw from the presidential race.

These tensions quickly subsided when, on 6 July, the Constitutional Court ruled that unregistered voters could cast a ballot by showing their identity cards. The court took the opportunity to criticise the KPU for its unprofessional conduct and incompetence. All of this brought the KPU under fire, with members of the DPR, NGOs and election watchdogs increasingly calling for its commissioners to step down and be put on trial, even though the general public largely perceived the presidential election to be free and fair.[9] The terms of the current KPU commissioners do not expire until 2012, so the same team will administer hundreds of local elections until then. It is likely, therefore, that electoral management problems will continue to undermine the quality of Indonesia's democracy.

THE ISLAMIC FACTOR

One important feature of Indonesian politics since 1998 has been the return of Islam as a potent political force. However, analysts also point to the fall in the Islamic and Muslim-based parties' share of the vote as evidence of the declining significance of the Islamic factor. It has been argued, for example, that 'the parliamentary elections in the largest Muslim-majority [country,] Indonesia, have reaffirmed the appeal of broad-based secular parties over Islamic-oriented rivals' (Rashid 2009). This

---

8 'Ada 11.2 juta data pemilih ganda' [There are 11.2 million double voters], *Kompas*, 8 July 2009.

9 In a nationwide survey conducted by LSI on 8 July, 33 per cent of respondents said that the election was 'very' fair and clean, and 59 per cent that it was 'sufficiently' fair and clean. See 'Voters, elites at odds over election fairness', *Jakarta Post*, 17 July 2009.

is seen as a trend that began soon after the opening of political space in 1998, with the combined vote of Islamic and Muslim-based parties declining from 37 per cent in the first democratic elections in 1999 to around 24 per cent in 2009. Moreover, in the 2004 presidential election, Indonesian voters — the majority of whom are Muslim — voted for Yudhoyono rather than Amien Rais or Hamzah Haz, two prominent Muslim leaders who ran on opposing tickets. In 2009, none of the presidential or vice-presidential candidates had backgrounds as leaders of Islamic parties or organisations.

Moreover, Islamic parties played little role in shaping the presidential race. Despite repeated calls from veteran Muslim politicians for the Islamic parties to form their own coalition and nominate their own candidates in 2009, the responses were typically guided by a strong dose of pragmatism and realism. For example, the deputy chair of PPP, Emron Pangkapi, stated that his party would not question whether a presidential candidate was from the nationalist or the religious camp. 'What matters', he said, 'is whether the person can win the election or not'. The deputy chair of PKS, Mahfudz Siddiq, also stated that Islamic parties had no choice but to form coalitions with nationalist parties, because it would be difficult for them to find a candidate who could compete with Yudhoyono or Megawati.[10] This pragmatic line of reasoning drove the Islamic parties to back Yudhoyono's bid for re-election.

Yet the Islamic parties had limited influence as coalition partners, a weakness highlighted by the marginal role they played in influencing the choice of vice-presidential candidate. Despite their objections, Yudhoyono stuck to the choice of Boediono as his running mate. The chair of PKS, Tifatul Sembiring, questioned Boediono's Islamic credentials, while other PKS leaders even threatened to quit the coalition with PD in protest against Yudhoyono's choice.[11] Amien Rais, chief patron of PAN, also objected to the president's decision and stated openly that the Yudhoyono–Boediono pairing lacked Islamic credentials.[12] Yudhoyono's Islamic coalition partners complained that they were not being given a sufficiently prominent role in the organisation and conduct of the presidential campaign. Instead, that role was occupied largely by professional consultants such as Fox Indonesia, and by Yudhoyono's own supporters, who typically had military backgrounds.[13]

---

10 'Parpol Islam jangan jadi pengekor' [Islamic parties should not just be followers], *Republika*, 17 April 2009.

11 'PKS questions Boediono's faith', *Jakarta Post*, 15 May 2009.

12 'Dukungan PAN: beda sikap dengan partai bukan pengkhianat' [PAN's support: disagreeing with the party is not treacherous], *Kompas*, 28 May 2009.

13 'Partai koalisi SBY banyak nganggurnya' [SBY's coalition partners are often idle], *Republika Online*, 30 June 2009, http://www.republika.co.id/.

The limited role of the Islamic factor was again demonstrated by Jusuf Kalla's presidential bid. The leaders of the two largest non-political Islamic organisations, Nahdlatul Ulama (NU) and Muhammadiyah, bestowed their support and blessing on Kalla.[14] There was an effort on the part of some within the Kalla–Wiranto camp to have the pair project a more overtly Islamic image. Members of the campaign team often emphasised the fact that both Kalla's and Wiranto's wives wore the *jilbab* (headscarf), unlike the wives of Yudhoyono and Boediono. Despite these efforts, and the seemingly crucial support of NU and Muhammadiyah, Kalla came last in the election.

Yet despite the apparent decline in importance of Islamic parties in electoral politics, it would be premature to conclude that political Islam has lost its appeal. Two other factors contributed to the poor performance of Islamic parties in the 2009 elections. First, internal rifts and disunity damaged the image of Islamic parties. Second, they lacked credible leaders. As argued by Effendy (2009a), the fact that 'none of the existing Islamic parties had experienced, strong, and respected leaders ... made constituents turn their heads to Susilo Bambang Yudhoyono or even Megawati Soekarnoputri'. Given that the Islamic community still constitutes a very sizeable voting bloc, a future revival of Islamic parties is not out of the question. Fealy (2009) notes that Islamic parties could recover their influence, provided they can address the problem of leadership and combine Islamic ideas with a commitment to economic prosperity.[15] He also argues that since Yudhoyono and Megawati are likely to retire from politics in 2014, the 'strength of two of the main non-Islamic parties, PD and PDIP, may not last until the next election'.

Moreover, despite waning influence in the formal political process, the importance of Islam in daily political life cannot be overlooked. What has transpired in the formal electoral process reflects the growing irrelevance of the *santri–abangan*[16] divide in Indonesia's polity rather than the end of the influence of Islam per se. The dichotomy has become increasingly blurred as parties from both camps move to the centre and adopt similar 'nationalist–religious' platforms (Platzdasch 2009). Islam is thus in the process of being 'mainstreamed' into the heart of Indonesia's politics. The Islamist PKS, for example, has continued its efforts to project an image as an 'open' party, and has downplayed its exclusively Islamic

---

14 'Tim JK–Win garap semua elemen' [JK–Win team woos all elements], *Kompas*, 3 June 2009; 'Sesepuh Golkar turun untuk JK–Wiranto' [Golkar elders support JK–Wiranto team], *Kompas*, 11 June 2009.

15 See also 'Partai politik Islam akan segera bangkit' [Islamic parties will soon awaken], *Republika*, 20 March 2009.

16 *Abangan* refers to nominal or non-practising Muslims. *Santri* refers to pious Muslims.

identity. Similar efforts have been made by PAN, PKB and PPP. Meanwhile, PD, which fits loosely into the camp of secular nationalist parties, is trying to project an image of being a nationalist party accommodative of Islamic interests. Golkar has been treading the same path. Even PDIP persuaded itself that it needed to improve its image in the eyes of Muslim constituents and established its own Islamic organisations, such as Baitul Muslimin (House of Muslims). The 2009 elections further reinforced the process of nationalisation of Islamic politics and Islamisation of national politics.

The process of Islamic mainstreaming also reflects a broader trend within the polity, in which the preferences of the majority of voters are no longer based exclusively on the official religious or ideological positions advocated by political parties or presidential candidates. Thus, it has been pointed out that

> ... many Muslim voters now appear to believe that their religious interests can be sufficiently represented by the pluralist Muslim parties PKB and PAN or ... by the nationalist parties [such as] the Democrat Party, Golkar, and even PDI-P (Platzdasch 2009).

The same can be said of voters' attitudes to presidential candidates. A survey by the Centre for Strategic and International Studies (CSIS) in June 2009, for example, revealed that 51.9 per cent of respondents thought that Yudhoyono represented Muslim interests (and only 20.7 per cent viewed Kalla in the same light) (CSIS 2009). However, the Islamic mainstreaming process does not mean that Indonesia is about to move towards a theocratic form of politics. Platzdasch (2009) argues that 'the trend of convergence towards an ideological middle-ground is without doubt positive, as it contributes to political stability'.

The importance of Islam as a factor in Indonesia's day-to-day politics is also reflected in the tendency among nationalist parties and leaders to avoid being seen as unfriendly to Muslim voters' aspirations. As Platzdasch (2009) argues, 'political parties of all stripes can no longer afford to be seen as neutral or indifferent towards Islamic interests'. Party responses to four controversial issues illustrate this point well. First, except for PDIP, the nationalist parties, including PD, endorsed the controversial PKS-initiated law on pornography, which was seen by many as undermining Indonesia's freedom of expression and cultural pluralism. Second, the government's semi-ban on the Ahmadiyah sect was endorsed by all nationalist parties, despite protests by human rights groups and civil society that it jeopardised religious freedom.[17] Third, none of the nationalist parties openly opposed the 2009 introduction

---

17 For a brief discussion of the case of Ahmadiyah, see van Klinken (2008).

of a bylaw on stoning for adultery in the province of Aceh. Finally, on the more general question of state identity, no politician in Indonesia would dare to proclaim openly that he or she would turn Indonesia into a purely secular state.[18] All these responses clearly suggest that no one is prepared to take measures deemed unfriendly to the aspirations of the broad Muslim constituency. In other words, despite the declining significance of Islamic and Muslim-based parties, the Islamic factor remains very important in Indonesia's day-to-day political life.

THE SECOND YUDHOYONO CABINET: PATTERNS OF POWER SHARING

The political dynamics in the immediate post-election period created a strong sense of *déjà vu*. As in the 2004 post-election period, political antagonism during the campaign did not prevent rival political parties from seeking to form a coalition with, and become a part of, the new government established by the victor.[19] Indeed, the formation of broad and inclusive 'rainbow cabinets' containing all or most of the major political parties represented in national parliament has become a consistent pattern in post-Suharto political life. From the perspective of the president in power, inviting major political parties into government provides a degree of political stability and support in the parliament. Parties that choose to participate in cabinet in turn receive access not only to the levers of policy making but also to the state resources and patronage that come with government office.

The results of the elections significantly changed the configuration of power in the DPR. PD, which had only 55 seats in the 2004–2009 DPR, became the largest party with 148 seats, and the PD-led campaign-period coalition secured 316 of the 560 seats in the new parliament. Yudhoyono himself received a strong mandate by virtue of his clear first-round victory. The election results therefore gave the president the opportunity to build his second term on a much stronger foundation than his first. However, it was not immediately obvious that his abundance of political capital would make Yudhoyono's second administration very different from the first.

Instead, post-election political developments suggested that old habits die hard. Yudhoyono soon began preparing the groundwork for an

---

18 The reverse is also true: no religious-based parties or politicians would proclaim openly that they would turn Indonesia into a theocratic state.

19 On coalition building in the aftermath of the 2004 elections, see Aspinall (2005: 17–18).

expansion of his support base among rival parties, by calling for all political forces to be part of, and 'work in harmony with', his second administration. While stating that his original coalition partners would have
the inside running in the allocation of cabinet positions, the president
also indicated that 'there will always be room for wider togetherness',
implying that parties outside PD's campaign coalition could be included
(Maulia 2009). Some of his aides indicated that he would welcome the
participation of leading figures from rival parties still outside the coalition, including Golkar, PDIP and even Gerindra. PD's deputy chair, Ach-
mad Mubarok, for example, stated that Yudhoyono would be 'willing
to accept Golkar back into his political circle and give some ministerial
posts to a number of Golkar executives'.[20]

It was of course perfectly legitimate for Yudhoyono to forge a broad
coalition to support his government. In order to rule effectively, he
needed to minimise the kinds of difficulties his government encountered
during its first five years. During that period his room to manoeuvre had
been constrained by the fact that his party held only a small proportion of
seats in the DPR, and his government had often faced difficult challenges
on legislative and policy issues. To cite just one example, his government
had to back down and withdraw from the Defence Cooperation Agreement with Singapore after strong pressure from the DPR. Moreover, a
coalition restricted solely to PD and the Islamic parties might not have
created a stronger presidency. As the PD deputy chair acknowledged,
bringing Golkar into the coalition would lessen Yudhoyono's depend-
ence on his Islamic coalition partners, especially PKS.[21]

The implications of bringing all parties into the government were
nevertheless problematic for Indonesia's young democracy. While strong
government might be more likely under a grand coalition scenario, critics
argued that it was not good for Indonesia's democracy, since a well-functioning democracy required the parliament to play an effective 'checks
and balances' role. If most or all parties joined a governing coalition, it
would be unrealistic to expect the DPR to function effectively as a check
on executive power.

In fact, it was by no means certain that a grand coalition would make
Yudhoyono's second term more effective than the previous one. Indonesian politics often defies conventional political norms, and there is
no guarantee that government parties in the DPR will consistently support the government. Forces in the DPR often pursue their own logic

---

20 'SBY likely to embrace Golkar's return', *Jakarta Post*, 13 July 2009.
21 'Pendekatan PD ke PDIP untuk tekan partai koalisi' [PD's approach to
    PDIP is to put pressure on coalition parties], *Republika Online*, http://www.
    republika.co.id/.

and interests when it comes to their stance *vis-à-vis* government policies. Members do not always follow their party leaders' directions, and the 'party line' is often absent in the DPR, where consensus decision making and cross-party committees are all-important (see the chapter by Sherlock in this volume). In other words, a government functioning effectively with the full support of the DPR might still not be possible under a grand coalition. At the same time, a coalition that included too many parties would bring its own risks and problems, including a cumbersome cabinet decision-making process, with the president continually needing to work at maintaining a broad consensus. It was also likely that such a government would become less effective well in advance of the 2014 elections as coalition members repositioned themselves to compete against each other.

As Yudhoyono's victory became imminent, party elites engaged in frantic attempts to join the winning camp. Whether to be inside or outside the government was particularly divisive for Golkar and PDIP. Important segments of both parties manoeuvred to bring themselves into the governing coalition while others opposed such moves. Golkar had been the governing party of the New Order regime, and most of its leaders viewed it as a natural party of government and thus found it hard to conceive of Golkar playing a purely oppositional role. Jusuf Kalla's decision to run against Yudhoyono in the presidential election, however, had effectively placed the party in an oppositional position. This situation was soon remedied by the election of Aburizal Bakrie, a close ally of Yudhoyono, as the new chair of Golkar in early October 2009. One of Indonesia's richest businessmen and a former minister, Bakrie quickly made it clear that Golkar would join the coalition government. Within PDIP, the strongest proponent of participation in the Yudhoyono government was none other than Megawati's husband, Taufik Kiemas. Despite his election as speaker of the People's Consultative Assembly (Majelis Permusyawaratan Rakyat, MPR) with the support of PD, Megawati herself continued to object to any suggestion that PDIP should join the government, and her recalcitrance eventually won out.

In the end, the cabinet formed by Yudhoyono in late October 2009 reflected his decision to opt for a wide but not all-inclusive coalition: the four Islamic coalition partners and Golkar were represented but PDIP, Gerindra and Hanura were not. As in the previous cabinet, the appointment of some ministers — especially from the coalition parties — reflected Yudhoyono's preference for political compromise rather than expertise.

Such a majority coalition will not necessarily ensure that Yudhoyono's second term is more effective than his first, and there is no guarantee that pro-government factions in the DPR will consistently support the government. Indeed, the fragility and fluidity of coalition politics in

Indonesia was immediately demonstrated in the aftermath of the formation of the cabinet by a DPR investigation into a highly contentious government bailout of a private bank, Bank Century. The Yudhoyono government suddenly faced a serious challenge from its own coalition partners, who were now putting pressure on the minister of finance, Sri Mulyani Indrawati, and Vice-President Boediono by investigating the circumstances surrounding the Bank Century rescue. Sri Mulyani accused the new Golkar chair, Aburizal Bakrie, of instigating the investigations because some of her decisions as minister had disadvantaged his companies.[22] Other analysts suspected some coalition parties of eyeing Boediono and Sri Mulyani's posts. Not only did the inquiry point to continuing fractiousness within the governing coalition, it also affected the ability of the government to function effectively.

This early fracture in the coalition overshadowed earlier signs that Yudhoyono's second term would herald the possibility of change. Previously, the president had largely been perceived as an indecisive leader prone to giving in to political pressure, but his decision to select Boediono as his running mate, overriding the objections of coalition partners, seemed to point towards him becoming more assertive. It was also argued at the time that the choice of Boediono 'reflects SBY's new priority once he gets re-elected: to have a strong presidency, one that will not be dogged by rivalries with his VP' (Bayuni 2009). However, the extent to which that promise could be fulfilled always depended on Yudhoyono's ability to resist pressures from his coalition partners. The shape of his new cabinet and the political dynamics during the first months of his second term pointed towards greater continuity than change in the president's approach.

CONCLUSION: PROSPECTS FOR DEMOCRATIC RESILIENCE

In many respects the 2009 elections were another sign of Indonesia's continuing progress in democratisation. Despite the chaotic administration and post-election disputation, the polls were implemented without significant violent incidents. All post-election disputes were resolved through the Constitutional Court. The maturity of citizens in exercising their democratic rights and responsibilities was clearly demonstrated when all parties accepted the court's decisions. Indeed, willingness on the part of participants to abide by the rules of the game and resolve disputes through the courts has been evident since the 2004 elections. Thus, we may conclude that Indonesia has come a long way towards institu-

---

22 'Jakarta official defends bailout', *Wall Street Journal*, 10 December 2009.

tionalising two important aspects of democracy: the function of elections as the only legitimate mechanism of political succession, and the use of peaceful mechanisms for dispute settlement.

The outcome of the elections also reflected the continuing diminution of traditional authority in democratic politics, and the rise of voter autonomy. The influence of traditional community leaders such as clerics in shaping people's election preferences is fast eroding. Syafiq Hasyim of the International Centre for Islam and Pluralism (ICIP) argues, for example, that political involvement has reduced the standing of clerics in the eyes of society because 'what [is] happening now in Indonesia is that clerics are being viewed as mere tools to garner votes, particularly during elections'.[23] Yudhoyono's victory and Kalla's defeat clearly demonstrate this. Although NU and Muhammadiyah leaders had called on their followers to support Kalla, an exit poll after the presidential election showed that 60 per cent of NU and 59 per cent of Muhammadiyah votes went to Yudhoyono, and only 16 per cent and 19 per cent respectively to Kalla (Effendy 2009b). In other words, both NU and Muhammadiyah voters have become more independent of traditional sources of authority in casting their ballots.

The trend towards growing autonomy among voters is not confined to NU and Muhammadiyah. In fact, there is evidence to suggest that since the 2004 elections Indonesian electoral politics has increasingly been shaped by the rising proportion of autonomous voters who play an important role as 'swing voters'. PKS and PD owed their rise in 2004 to this group. Most of these swing votes have come from the urban middle class and from young voters. Autonomous voters, especially the younger ones, transcend traditional ideological and religious politics and are not constrained by emotional allegiance to parties and individual leaders. Their numbers are significant. A survey by CSIS in September 2008 showed that 'swing' and undecided voters constituted 30 per cent of all eligible voters (CSIS 2008). According to Indonesia's central statistics agency, around 95.7 million (61.5 per cent) of the country's 189 million eligible voters were under 40 years old. Of this group, 19.8 per cent were first-time voters in the 2009 elections, and 22.3 per cent were 22–29 years old.[24] These voters have demonstrated their ability to reward and punish politicians through the electoral process. The emergence of autonomous voters is a healthy development in Indonesia's journey towards becoming a well-functioning, modern democracy.

---

23 'Clerics fast losing clout as democracy gains ground', *Jakarta Post*, 28 July 2009.

24 Quoted in 'Pemilih muda dan perubahan' [Young voters and change], http://perubahanuntukrakyat.com/2009/03/24/pemilih-muda-dan-perubahan/.

The elections also showed a positive trend towards further consolidation of support for democracy itself. It has been argued that democracy's survival depends on the preferences and perceptions of the political elite and citizens, whose support for democracy 'constitutes the most important, and even defining element of democratic consolidation' (Schedler 2001: 75). An examination of the Indonesian case suggests that there has been increasing commitment to, and support for, democracy on the part of the people. Though their motives for supporting it might vary, the political elites have also accepted that democracy is 'the only game in town'. But the most significant support for democracy in Indonesia, support that will guarantee the survival of the system, has come from the mainstream Muslim community and its leaders. Both NU and Muhammadiyah, which respectively claim around 35 million and 30 million supporters, have supported democracy and have participated in preserving and consolidating the democratisation process.

The 2009 elections also provided further confirmation of the military's commitment to remain neutral in the electoral process, and thus in politics. The process of reforming the military is far from complete; in fact, the current pace of reform is much slower than in the early years of the post-Suharto era, especially between 2000 and 2002. Some even contend that military reform stalled during Yudhoyono's first administration. However, this does not negate the fact that the military's role in politics has waned further since 2004.

Despite all the problems, Indonesian politics has displayed a considerable degree of democratic resilience. The electoral cycle of 2009 confirmed this trend, serving as an important step towards further consolidation of democracy. Indonesia's ability to address the problems and challenges it faces will determine the future quality of its democracy. For a democracy to be regarded as 'consolidated' requires not only that the state has the capacity to enforce the law and deliver policies (Wanandi 2002: 135), but also that a strong democratic culture exists within the society (International IDEA 2000: 13). This can be attained only through the institutionalisation of good governance and the creation of an open, tolerant and pluralist society. In the first five years of Yudhoyono's democratically elected government, Indonesia struggled to address those problems. Now the president has been given an even stronger five-year mandate to tackle them.

REFERENCES

Aspinall, Edward (2005), 'Politics: Indonesia's year of elections and the end of the political transition', in B.P. Resosudarmo (ed.), *The Politics and Economics of Indonesia's Natural Resources*, Institute of Southeast Asian Studies, Singapore, pp. 13–30.

Bayuni, Endy M. (2009), 'Boediono for running mate? What was behind the choice?', *Jakarta Post*, 15 May.

CSIS (Centre for Strategic and International Studies) (2008), 'Mesin partai Golkar menjelang pemilu 2009' [The machinery of the Golkar party in the run-up to the 2009 elections], unpublished survey report, CSIS, Jakarta, October.

CSIS (Centre for Strategic and International Studies) (2009), 'Efek kampanye dalam pilpres' [Effects of the campaign on the presidential elections], survey report, CSIS, Jakarta, July.

Effendy, Bahtiar (2009a), 'Islamic parties have long been at an impasse', *Jakarta Post*, 17 April.

Effendy, Bahtiar (2009b), 'The fluidity of Islam and Yudhoyono's presidential triumph', *Jakarta Post*, 11 July.

Faiz, Pan Mohamad (2009), 'Sengketa antar caleg' [Disputes among the candidates for parliament], 30 June, http://panmohamadfaiz.com/2009/06/30/sengketa-antarcaleg/.

Fealy, Greg (2009), 'Indonesia's Islamic parties in decline', *Inside Story*, 11 May, http://inside.org.au/indonesia%E2%80%99s-islamic-parties-in-decline/.

International IDEA (International Institute for Democracy and Electoral Assistance) (2000), *Democratization in Indonesia: An Assessment*, International IDEA, Stockholm.

KPU (Komisi Pemilihan Umum) (2009) 'Hasil penghitungan suara sah partai politik peserta pemilu dalam pemilu anggota DPR, DPD dan DPRD, tahun 2009' [Results of the counting of valid votes for political parties participating in the 2009 general elections for the People's Representative Council, the Regional Representative Council and the Regional People's Representative Assemblies], http://mediacenter.kpu.go.id/images/mediacenter/berita/SUARA_KPU/HASIL_PENGHITUNGAN_SUARA_SAH.pdf.

LSI (Lembaga Survei Indonesia) (2009), 'Efek calon terhadap perolehan suara partai menjelang pemilu 2009' [Candidates' effects on votes for political parties in the run-up to the 2009 elections], LSI, Jakarta, February, http://www.lsi.or.id/riset/356/efek-caleg-pada-pemilu-legislatif-2009.

Margaretha, Hazelia (2009), 'Indonesia's 2009 legislative elections: the emerging danger of charismatic politics', *RSIS Commentaries*, 19 January, http://www.rsis.edu.sg/publications/Perspective/RSIS0072009.pdf.

Maulia, Erwida (2009), 'SBY to fill cabinet only with coalition partners', *Jakarta Post*, 5 August.

Mietzner, Marcus (2009), 'Indonesia's 2009 elections: populism, dynasties and the consolidation of the party system', *Analysis*, Lowy Institute for International Policy, Sydney, May.

Platzdasch, Bernhard (2009), 'Down but not out: Islamic political parties did not do well, but Islamic politics are going mainstream', *Inside Indonesia* 97(July–September), http://insideindonesia.org.

Rashid, Harun ur (2009), 'Indonesians reject Islamic parties at polls', *Jakarta Post*, 2 May.

Schedler, Andreas (2001), 'Measuring democratic consolidation', *Studies in Comparative International Development* 36(1): 66–92.

Sukma, Rizal (2009), '*Indonesian politics in 2009: defective elections, resilient democracy*', *Bulletin of Indonesian Economic Studies* 45(3): 317–36.

Sulaiman, Yohanes (2009), 'Indonesian parliament in SBY's second term', *Jakarta Post*, 24 August.

van Klinken, Gerry (2008), 'Indonesian politics in 2008: the ambiguities of democratic change', *Bulletin of Indonesian Economic Studies* 44(3): 368–70.

Wanandi, Jusuf (2002), 'Indonesia: a failed state?' *Washington Quarterly* 25(3): 135–46.

4 VOTERS AND THE NEW INDONESIAN DEMOCRACY

*Saiful Mujani and R. William Liddle**

The study of voting behaviour in democratic Indonesia has become one of the most contested areas in the scholarly debate on the shape and character of the post-Suharto polity. In particular, analysts of Indonesian politics have focused on two main questions. First, why have Indonesian citizens voted as they have for parties and presidential/vice-presidential candidates in the post-authoritarian national elections that have now been held three times since the 1998 democratic transition? And second, what are the implications of this behaviour for the quality of current and future Indonesian democratic life?

In a series of studies based on our own national political opinion surveys since Suharto's fall, we have tried to find comprehensive answers to these questions. In our first major discussion of the subject, we argued that leadership or candidate appeal and self-identification with a political party ('party ID' in the voting behaviour literature) were the most important factors shaping individual partisan and candidate choices in the 1999 and 2004 elections.[1] With this conclusion, we rejected an alternative interpretation that had been held by most scholars since the earliest democratic elections in 1955. According to these scholars, sociological or cultural factors — most notably religious affinities, but also region,

---

* The authors would like to thank Djayadi Hanan for valuable research assistance.
1 For further information about the 1999 and 2004 surveys, see Liddle and Mujani (2007). The 2009 surveys were carried out by the Indonesia Survey Institute (Lembaga Survey Indonesia, LSI), and involved 1,800 respondents in April and 1,200 in July. More details on the research methodology are available from the authors.

ethnicity and social class — were the principal determinant of Indonesian voting behaviour.[2]

In our 2009 surveys, we found strong continuities but also striking shifts in the factors shaping voter choice. These new findings are based on two national opinion polls that we conducted just after the parliamentary and presidential elections in April and July. Party leader or candidate appeal remains the most important factor, but party and presidential/vice-presidential media campaigns, especially on television, have become powerful forces in their own right. At the same time, party ID has weakened, though it remains influential in explaining individual votes for some parties and candidates. However, the most remarkable finding of our new research is the prominence of voter perceptions of the national economic condition, a factor that was not significant in 1999 and 2004. Also newly significant is voter evaluation of the economic and other policies of incumbent president Susilo Bambang Yudhoyono, factors introduced into our 2009 surveys for the first time. As in 1999 and 2004, we found little evidence that voters were influenced by religious, ethnic, regional or social class identities and affiliations.

This chapter presents the key results of our surveys in two main steps. First, we discuss the reasons for partisan and presidential choice in the 2009 ballots. We begin with sociological factors, which according to academic and journalistic conventional wisdom are still the most important drivers of voting behaviour. Subsequently, we turn to the appeal of leaders and candidates and party ID, the predominant factors in our 1999 and 2004 surveys. This is followed by our findings on the role of media campaigns and the incumbent's performance, both factors closely connected to leadership. We then explain the results of our multivariate analysis, in which all of these factors are directly compared with each other. Before concluding, the second major section of the chapter discusses some implications of our empirical findings for the present and future of Indonesian democracy.

EXPLAINING PARTISAN AND PRESIDENTIAL CHOICE

The 2009 parliamentary and presidential elections in Indonesia have been the focus of much controversial debate, for a number of reasons. To begin with, the ballots marked the first time in Indonesian history that an

---

2 The classic political science study of the 1955 election is Feith (1957). See also Lev (1967), Liddle (1970) and Emmerson (1976). Analyses of the 1999 and 2004 elections emphasising the role of religion include King (2003), Baswedan (2004) and Baswedan (2007).

incumbent government was democratically re-elected. They also marked the introduction of a new open party list system, which made Indonesia's legislative polls one of the most complex and competitive in the world. There were also a host of administrative problems, and the elections witnessed the increasing dominance of the entertainment industry in campaigns. These issues are discussed comprehensively in other chapters in this volume (see, for instance, Sukma, Schmidt and Heryanto). In the framework of our analysis of voting behaviour, this section presents the main factors motivating voters when going to the ballot box in 2009.

Sociological factors

In the 1999 and 2004 elections, according to the findings of our previous surveys, sociological factors were not important determinants of voting behaviour. Most strikingly, adherence to a particular world religion or *aliran* did not have a significant direct influence on voters. *Aliran* is a term referring to the clusters of parties and affiliated organisations asserted to represent Islamic subgroups in 1950s anthropological research (Geertz 1960). Differences in regional residence, specifically the frequently discussed gulf between residents of Java and inhabitants of other islands, were also generally not significant as an influence on voting behaviour.

As stated in the introduction, these findings contradicted previous political science claims that *aliran* or region were major determinants of Indonesian voting behaviour. The relevance of religion — operationalised as a division between orthodox (*santri*) and syncretist (*abangan*) — was only apparent in a comparison of voters for the People's Awakening Party (Partai Kebangkitan Bangsa, PKB), a party founded by the traditionalist orthodox social and educational organisation Nahdlatul Ulama (NU), and voters for the Indonesian Democratic Party of Struggle (Partai Demokrasi Indonesia Perjuangan, PDIP), the party historically most closely associated with secular nationalism and syncretism in religion.[3] Our 2009 election survey confirmed, indeed deepened, this finding. There was no consistent or solid evidence of voter polarisation based on *aliran* or Muslim religiosity in either the legislative or presidential

3 In our previous study, *aliran* was defined as an index of Muslim religiosity constructed from a number of indicators of intensity of practising Muslim religious rituals, both mandatory (the five daily prayers and fasting during the month of Ramadhan) and suggested (reciting the Qur'an, participating in religious studies or attending religious lectures). This measure was again used in our 2009 study, which showed only slight changes over time. For example, in 2009, 55.2 per cent of respondents said they 'always/regularly' carried out the required daily prayers, whereas the proportion was 58.1 per cent in 2004 and 53 per cent in 1999.

elections. Even the 1999 and 2004 influence of *aliran* in the competition between PDIP and PKB had vanished. This finding probably indicates that a greater number of orthodox Muslims voted for PDIP in 2009 than in previous elections, making it less distinguishable from parties with historic or other ties to Islam.

The lack of significance of religious factors was particularly evident in the 2009 presidential election. In that campaign, vice-presidential candidate Wiranto's team tried to position him and his presidential running mate, Jusuf Kalla, as more religiously orthodox than the team of Yudhoyono and his running mate, Boediono. In campaign speeches Wiranto emphasised that his and Kalla's wives both wore the Islamic headscarf (*jilbab*).[4] In the same vein, rumours were spread that Boediono was a practitioner of *kejawen*, Javanese mysticism, and that his wife was Catholic.[5] Despite the prominence of this theme in the Kalla–Wiranto campaign, we found no evidence that it had any impact on orthodox Muslim voters.

A similar trend could be detected as far as regional residency is concerned. In 1999 and 2004, a regional effect was measurable when we compared voters for PDIP and PKB (more of whom lived on Java) with voters for Golkar (who tended to be spread more widely outside Java and Bali). This effect weakened in 2009 because of the levelling impact of the massive regional shifts in the parliamentary vote. The number of Golkar voters dropped sharply throughout the outer islands, much more than in Java. As a result, the regional profile of Golkar voters no longer differs much from that of other parties, especially the Democratic Party (Partai Demokrat, PD), the United Development Party (Partai Persatuan Pembangunan, PPP), the Prosperous Justice Party (Partai Keadilan Sejahtera, PKS) and the National Mandate Party (Partai Amanat Nasional, PAN). PD is a personal electoral vehicle created in 2002 by the now incumbent President Yudhoyono. PPP and PKS are Islamist parties, while PAN is a secular nationalist party founded by leaders of Muhammadiyah, Indonesia's largest modernist Islamic organisation.

Second, PD's spectacular increase in votes — about 200 per cent above its 2004 share — was spread remarkably evenly across the country. Many regions outside Java controlled by Golkar in 2004, especially on Sumatra, are now dominated by PD. In the electoral districts of Kalimantan, Sulawesi, Nusa Tenggara, Maluku and Papua, which were dominated by Golkar in 2004, PD's 2009 votes were roughly equal to those achieved by Suharto's former electoral machine. Yudhoyono's party also grew sig-

---

4 'Istri berjilbab bukan bagian dari kampanye JK–Win' [Wives wearing headscarves are not part of the Kalla–Wiranto campaign], *Kompas*, 27 May 2009.
5 'Apa masalahnya kalau istri Boediono Katolik?' [What's the problem if Boediono's wife is Catholic?], *Kupang Pos*, 25 June 2009.

nificantly on Java, its base in 2004. Consequently, PD has now become the most national of the Indonesian parties.

The absence of a regional effect was also apparent in the presidential election. The Kalla–Wiranto team tried hard to identify itself as more representative of the outer islands than Yudhoyono–Boediono, whom it labelled the 'Mataram' or 'Majapahit' candidates, references to early Javanese kingdoms.[6] Both Yudhoyono and Boediono are from East Java, born in Pacitan and Blitar respectively. Kalla and Wiranto, from Sulawesi and Java, were a more typical combination, one candidate representing Java and the other the outer islands. Voters were obviously unaffected by this campaign, however, since the Yudhoyono–Boediono pair came first in all provinces except South Sulawesi, Jusuf Kalla's home, and Bali, a stronghold of former president Megawati Sukarnoputri, the third candidate in the presidential contest.

After religion and regionalism, social class is often claimed to play an important role in shaping partisan choice. In the Indonesian case, the Indonesian Communist Party (Partai Komunis Indonesia, PKI), supported by urban and plantation workers and landless peasants, won 16 per cent of the 1955 vote, making it the fourth-largest party in Indonesia's only democratic election before 1999 (Feith 1957; Liddle 1970). PKI was destroyed in 1965–66, but observers ever since, beginning with Wertheim (1966), have been expecting the return of class politics. So far, however, this has not occurred. In today's democracy, social class—at least as defined by level of education, income and type of employment—is becoming less, not more, important to voter choice. In the 1999 and 2004 parliamentary elections, voters for PAN, PKS and PD tended to come from a more educated, higher-income, white-collar middle class. In the 2009 election, by contrast, all parties tended to represent all social classes. PD, in particular, but also PAN and PKS, now reach lower as well as middle and upper-class voters.

The same effect could be observed in the presidential election. Since its formation in the late 1990s, PDIP has positioned itself as the party of the 'little people'. Its leaders appropriately claim continuity with the Indonesian National Party (Partai Nasional Indonesia, PNI) founded by Megawati's (and Indonesia's founding) father Sukarno in the 1920s. In the 2009 campaigns, Megawati and her vice-presidential running mate Prabowo Subianto, head of the new Greater Indonesia Movement Party (Partai Gerakan Indonesia Raya, Gerindra), defended the interests of small farmers, fishers and petty traders. Prabowo in particular attacked the Yudhoyono government's alleged support for big business and

---

6 This campaign was supported by the fact that Yudhoyono had named his first grandchild, born in 2008, after a queen of the Majapahit kingdom; see 'SBY names 1st grandchild', *Jakarta Post*, 19 August 2008.

*Figure 4.1   Mean score for likeability of party leader
(1 = least liked, 10 = most liked)*

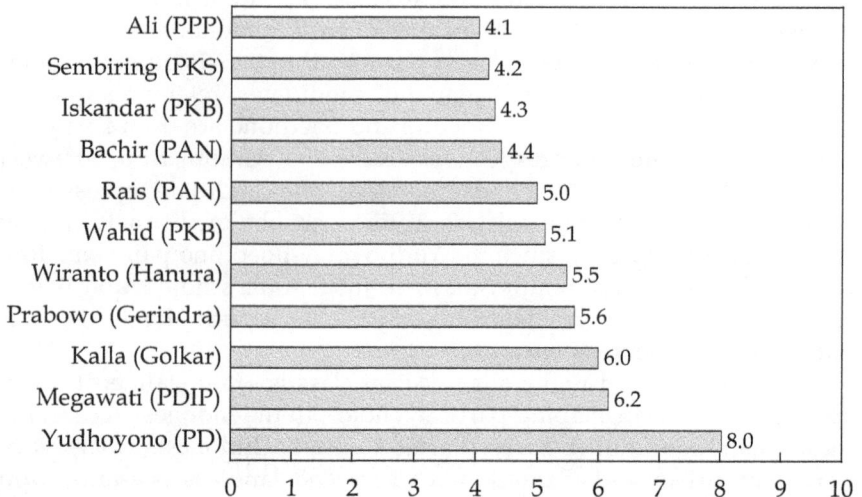

Leader	Score
Ali (PPP)	4.1
Sembiring (PKS)	4.2
Iskandar (PKB)	4.3
Bachir (PAN)	4.4
Rais (PAN)	5.0
Wahid (PKB)	5.1
Wiranto (Hanura)	5.5
Prabowo (Gerindra)	5.6
Kalla (Golkar)	6.0
Megawati (PDIP)	6.2
Yudhoyono (PD)	8.0

foreign economic interests. This issue — more than any other — stoked the fears of Yudhoyono supporters and fuelled the hopes of the opposition. In the polling booth, however, voters of whatever social class, and in large numbers, preferred PD over PDIP and Gerindra, and Yudhoyono–Boediono over Megawati–Prabowo.

Leaders and candidates

In our previous study, party leadership was the factor most strongly associated with the choice of a political party in 1999 and 2004 and also in the presidential election in 2004. The likeability of a party leader had a very strong effect on the choice of that leader's party in the parliamentary elections and in the presidential election as well.

In the 1999 and 2004 study, likeability was measured by asking respondents to choose the party leader they liked the most (*paling disukai*). In 2009, to get greater variation, respondents were asked to rate the likeability of leaders on a scale of 1 to 10. Among the listed leaders, the most liked was Yudhoyono and the least liked was Suryadarma Ali of PPP (Figure 4.1). These numbers show that the electoral success of PD and the re-election of President Yudhoyono in 2009 were clearly connected to the positive evaluations of Yudhoyono as a leader. Moreover, Yudhoyono's status as the leader most liked by voters is a finding with powerful implications for voting for PD. It must, however, be combined with other factors, as we discuss below in our multivariate analysis.

Figure 4.2 *Mean score for feeling close to a particular party*
(1 = not close at all, 4 = very close)

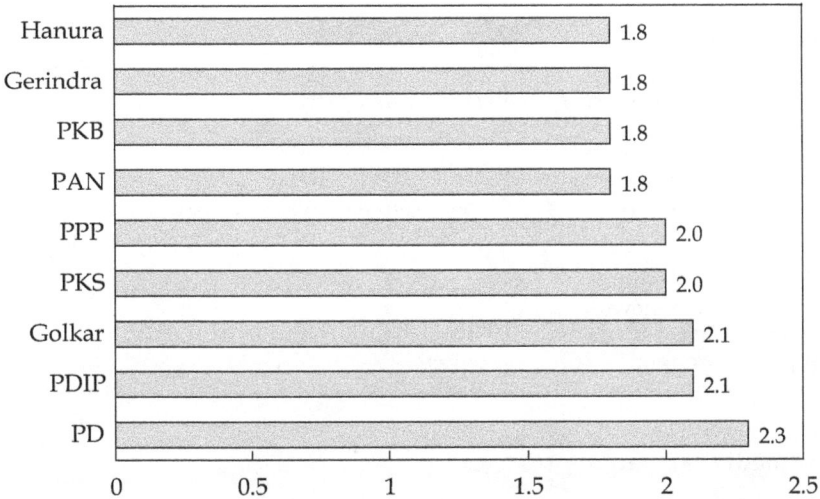

Party ID

Indonesian political parties no longer appear to have deep psychological roots in the electorate. As recently as August 2004, nearly 60 per cent of Indonesian voters stated that they felt close to a certain party. This figure declined steadily until March 2006 and has since remained at a low level, averaging 22 per cent in our two 2009 surveys. In 2009, voters who identified with a party were further asked whether they felt very close (4), close (3), somewhat close (2) or not close at all (1) to that party. The responses registered a mean score of between 1.8 for Hanura and 2.3 for PD, suggesting that even the one-fifth of voters who identify today with a party do so only weakly (Figure 4.2). The low level of party ID in the surveys is certainly mirrored in a large body of critical commentary on political parties in the Indonesian media and popular discussions, with parties generally accused of self-absorption, social isolation and massive corruption (see Tomsa in this volume).

Despite these caveats and other factors — for example, a high incidence of swing voting (voters shifting their party choice) in 2004 and 2009 — we nonetheless find that party ID remains strongly associated with partisan choice. Party ID can of course explain why some old parties (such as Golkar, PPP and PDIP, which were all active in the Suharto era) are still in the game. It cannot explain, however, why between 2004 and 2009 one party increased its vote sharply (PD), some remained relatively stable (PKS and PAN) and several others declined significantly (PDIP, Golkar, PKB and PPP).

Table 4.1   Exposure to voter mobilisation through direct contact and the mass media, April 2009

Form of contact	Actor/media	%
Ever contacted by another person directly (face to face or by telephone, text message or other means) to choose a certain party	Person from a party	6.5
	Prominent citizen/local civil society organisation	2.1
	Person from the village or urban ward	1.3
Ever, at least once, followed social, political and government news during a political campaign through:	TV	88.8
	Newspaper	34.9
	Radio	30.0
	Internet	4.3

The media campaign

In 2009, we asked voters a series of questions about sources of political information and mobilisation, including direct contact with party representatives or their intermediaries and exposure to the mass media. We then connected these findings to partisan and presidential choice. The results showed that very few voters had ever been contacted directly by parties, village officials or religious leaders. Parties using traditional networks such as local government bureaucracies, religious social organisations like NU and Muhammadiyah, and networks of Islamic scholars (*ulama*) are evidently having difficulty reaching voters. Against this background, it should come as no surprise that Islamic parties like PPP and PKB have lost votes in recent elections.

In contrast, almost all Indonesian voters in 2009 were reached by the mass media, especially television. A vast majority of voters (88.8 per cent) reported having seen political or governmental news on TV during an election campaign, while 34.9 per cent had read election-related news in a newspaper and 30 per cent had listened to it on the radio. Internet use, on the other hand, was still very limited (Table 4.1).

In our survey, respondents were asked to name the parties and candidates whose campaign information and advertisements they had most often seen on TV, read in the newspapers or heard on the radio. Table 4.2 shows that the advertisements of PD, then Gerindra and Golkar, were most often viewed by voters. PD also headed the lists of voters who had read newspapers and listened to the radio. In the presidential race, voters paid far more attention to Yudhoyono–Boediono advertisements than those of their opponents (Figure 4.3). Obviously, the frequency with

Table 4.2   Campaign exposure and party advertisements most often seen, read or listened to, April 2009 (%)

Party	TV	Newspaper	Radio
Partai Demokrat (PD)	34.3	7.9	6.7
Gerindra (Partai Gerakan Indonesia Raya)	24.8	2.7	2.6
Golkar	10.8	5.1	3.9
Partai Demokrasi Indonesia Perjuangan (PDIP)	5.5	1.9	2.1
Partai Keadilan Sejahtera (PKS)	2.6	1.2	0.9
Partai Persatuan Pembangunan (PPP)	1.0	0.1	0.3
Partai Amanat Nasional (PAN)	0.9	0.6	0.7
Hanura (Partai Hati Nurani Rakyat)	0.5	0.2	0.8
Partai Kebangkitan Bangsa (PKB)	0.3	0.1	0.2
Other parties/none	19.3	80.2	81.8

which voters took notice of advertisements closely corresponded with the campaign spending of the various parties. Between January and late March 2009, PD was the party with the largest expenditure on television advertisements (Rp 51 billion, or $5.1 million), followed by Golkar with Rp 48 billion ($4.8 million) and Gerindra with Rp 45 billion ($4.4 million).[7]

While this research cannot, of course, confirm a causal relationship between exposure to advertisements and voting for a party or candidate, it does demonstrate that the relationship is a close one. This is especially the case for PKB, where 66.7 per cent of voters who most often watched PKB's TV campaign advertisements voted for that party, PKS (54.5 per cent), PAN (50 per cent), and PDIP (44.8 per cent). The very high figure for PKB mirrors the fact that only a few survey respondents (0.3 per cent) claimed to have watched PKB advertisements most often. The lower but still substantial figure for PD (32 per cent) partly reflects that party's media saturation, which meant that almost all voters were exposed to its advertisements. In addition, it is worth noting that exposure to the TV campaigns and advertisements of Gerindra was much higher than the comparable figures for Golkar or PDIP (Table 4.2), but the association with voting was much less strong (Figure 4.4). Twenty-five per cent of survey respondents claimed to have watched Gerindra campaigning and advertisements most often, but the party won only 4.5 per cent of the national vote. This may partly have been due to the very fierce — and

---

7   'Media panen iklan parpol' [Political party ads a media harvest], *BBC Indonesia*, 31 March 2009.

Figure 4.3   Campaign exposure and candidate advertisements most often seen, read or listened to, July 2009 (%)

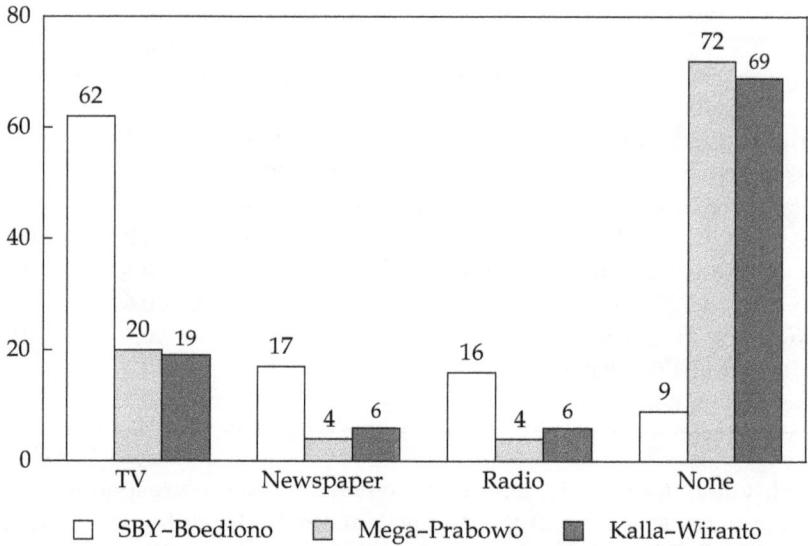

Legend: □ SBY–Boediono   ▨ Mega–Prabowo   ▦ Kalla–Wiranto

Figure 4.4   Association between campaign and party advertisements viewed most often on TV and voting for that party, April 2009 (%)

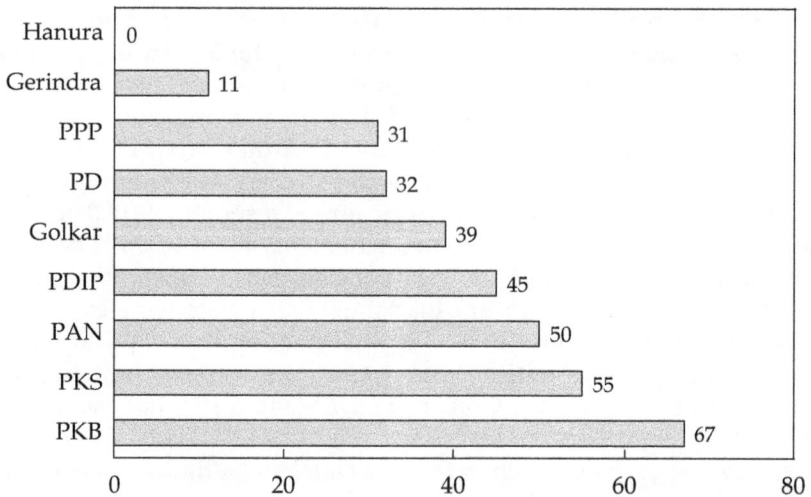

very public—campaign against Prabowo by former activists who have not forgiven him for his behaviour towards them in 1998, when troops under his command kidnapped and tortured anti-Suharto student leaders. Despite the negative campaigning, Gerindra emerged as the largest

Figure 4.5   *Association between candidate advertisements viewed most often on TV and voting for those candidates, July 2009 (%)*

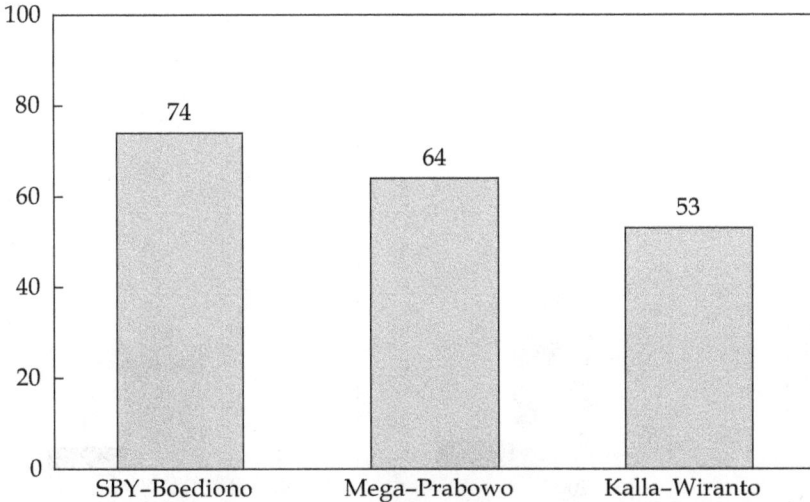

new party in 2009. In the presidential election, the relationship between exposure to advertisements and voting for a candidate was again close (Figure 4.5).

Media campaigns and advertisements reflect not only frequency and intensity of exposure but also content and substance. From August 2008, PD's advertisements in the media emphasised the achievements of the Yudhoyono government, particularly in the field of economic stability and the fight against corruption. Naturally, opposition parties such as PDIP and Gerindra attacked PD's claims. In their view, the government had failed in many political and economic areas, including in its attempts to increase the prosperity of farmers and other lower-class groups in society. Golkar's position, by contrast, was ambivalent. It could not attack the government directly because Jusuf Kalla was the incumbent vice-president, but nonetheless asserted that if Golkar won the country would be better off.

The incumbent's performance

Given the huge differences in how the government and the opposition depicted the state of the economy under Yudhoyono, it was clear that the outcome of the elections would be heavily influenced by voters' evaluations of their own and the national economic condition. In the 1999 and 2004 elections, the direct effects of voters' evaluations on the electoral prospects of the government were not visible because the difference

*Figure 4.6   Voters' evaluation of the national economic condition in 2009
            compared to the previous year (%)*

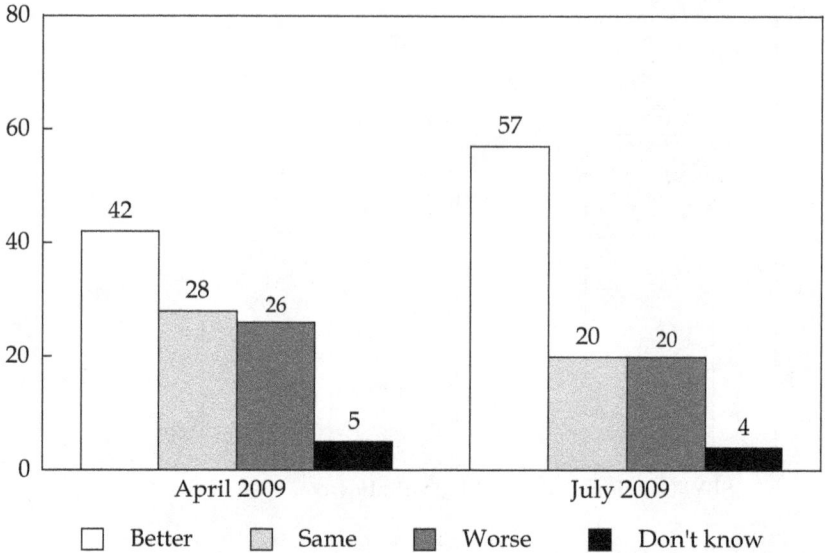

between the incumbent party and president on the one hand and their
challengers on the other was obscure. In 1999, there was a largely new
party system and even Golkar, the old state party under the authoritarian
Suharto, had repositioned itself as a democratic party. In the 2004 election, the line separating opposition and incumbent forces — most parties,
including Golkar, were in Megawati's government — was again opaque.
In 2009, however, President Yudhoyono and PD were the clear incumbents and Megawati and PDIP the clear challengers.

    In our April and July 2009 surveys, we asked respondents to evaluate
the economic condition of their household and the national economy in
2009 compared with the previous year, assessing whether it had become
much better, better, worse or much worse, or had remained unchanged.
Significantly, in both surveys more respondents had a favourable than
unfavourable view of their household's and the nation's economic condition (Figure 4.6).

    The relatively high levels of satisfaction with economic conditions
appear paradoxical, given that 2009 was a year of global financial crisis
which saw economic growth in Indonesia decline from about 6 per cent
in 2008 to about 4 per cent in 2009. There are two probable answers to
this puzzle. First, Indonesia was much less affected by the crisis than its
Southeast Asian neighbours, particularly Thailand and Malaysia. Second,
the effects of the crisis were more than mitigated by the massive welfare
programs implemented and promoted heavily by the government dur-

Figure 4.7   *Association between voters' evaluation of the national economic condition and voting for incumbent (PD) and opposition (PDIP/Gerindra) parties (%)*

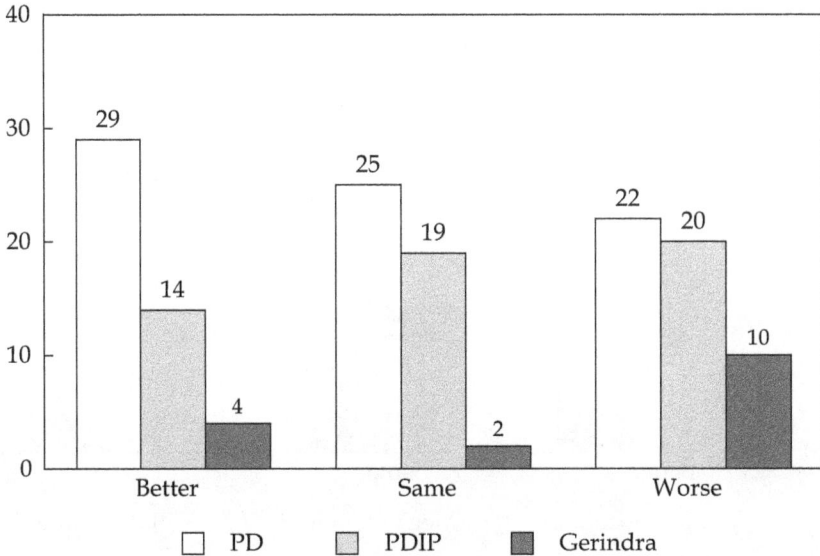

ing the previous few years. For example, budgetary spending on poverty alleviation measures increased by 283 per cent between 2005 and 2008 (Kuncoro, Widodo and McLeod 2009: 166). All of these programs were known to voters and evaluated positively by them. Moreover, fuel prices, always highly sensitive politically, fell in 2009. In addition, employment figures rose and the percentage of Indonesians living below the poverty line fell. Inflation was also very low at the time of the elections, after a sharp increase in living costs in the previous year.

Evaluations of both the household and national economic condition were closely correlated with partisan and presidential choice, but more strongly with the latter. This confirms the finding of many studies in the political economy literature that evaluations of the national economic condition are more important in determining electoral behaviour than evaluations of household economic condition (Kiewiet 1983). For example, Figure 4.7 shows a significant divergence between PD voters on the one hand and PDIP and Gerindra voters on the other in the relationship between evaluation of national economic condition and partisan choice.[8] The more favourable the evaluation, the more likely voters were

---

8   In the two cross-tab analyses, the five ordinal scales were simplified into three categories: 'better' (formerly much better and better), 'the same' and 'worse' (formerly worse and much worse).

Figure 4.8   Association between voters' evaluation of the national economic condition and voting for the president/vice-president

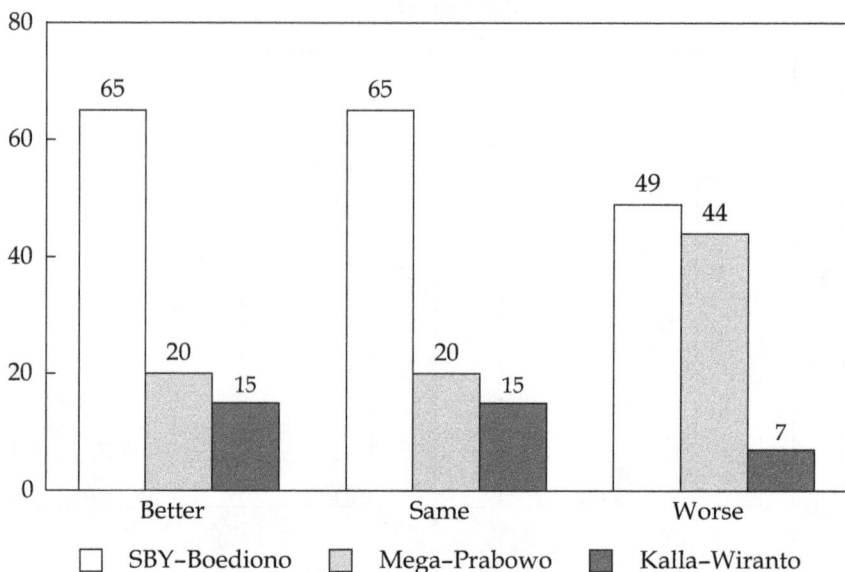

☐ SBY–Boediono   ▨ Mega–Prabowo   ▪ Kalla–Wiranto

to support PD; conversely, the less favourable the evaluation, the more likely voters were to vote for PDIP or Gerindra. There are no such comparable patterns for other parties.

This finding underscores the reality of the election campaign: in the eyes of the voters, only PDIP and Gerindra were opposition parties. All the large parties, except PDIP, had been Yudhoyono allies in the parliament and the government between 2004 and 2009. Gerindra alone appeared to be a force that could strengthen the PDIP-led opposition. Again, this reflected the dynamics of Gerindra's campaign, which openly opposed government economic policies. It was hardly surprising, then, that the pattern of correlation between assessment of the economy and electoral choice continued through the presidential campaign (Figure 4.8). The more positive the comparative evaluation of the national economic condition, the stronger the tendency to choose incumbent over challenger. At the same time, there was no significant differentiation between Yudhoyono–Boediono and Kalla–Wiranto. As the sitting vice-president but not Yudhoyono's running mate, Kalla profited somewhat from the generally positive evaluations of the economy, but not enough to make him electorally competitive. In part, this was the result of his ambiguous role as neither a clear incumbent nor a clear representative of the opposition.

Table 4.3   Government performance in selected socio-economic areas (%)

	Very good	Good	Bad	Very bad	Don't know
Reducing poverty					
April 2009	3.9	48.4	39.2	5.0	3.5
July 2009	3.0	54.1	34.5	4.7	2.7
Reducing unemployment					
April 2009	2.6	41.1	46.3	6.0	4.1
July 2009	3.1	51.3	37.7	5.3	2.6
Stabilising prices of basic commodities					
April 2009	4.7	59.2	31.8	2.9	1.3
July 2009	7.2	61.4	26.9	3.3	1.2
Health					
April 2009	7.4	78.2	11.2	0.6	2.5
July 2009	6.6	77.9	12.7	1.5	1.3
Education					
April 2009	9.0	78.1	9.1	0.2	3.7
July 2009	8.8	77.7	11.2	0.7	1.6

The association between evaluation of the national economic condition and voting behaviour becomes stronger when that evaluation is connected to more specific areas of government performance in the socio-economic sector. We made this connection in our 2009 surveys (Table 4.3). Nonetheless, we still need to determine whether the political economy effect remains significant regardless of the impact of political leadership and party ID. The last part of our analysis will address this issue.

Multivariate analysis

When subjected to multivariate analysis, leadership appeal, campaign advertising and political economy emerge as the factors that most help to explain the 2009 parliamentary vote (Table 4.4). In our analysis, the dependent variable is a pair of parties (for example PD voters versus Golkar voters) and the independent variables are our hypothesised explanatory factors, from religious affiliation to perceived national economic condition. The strength of multivariate analysis is that it allows us to compare simultaneously the effect of all the independent variables on partisan choice, as expressed in the preference for one party over another. Significant associations are marked by asterisks, depending on the level of probability, with three asterisks indicating the strongest association.[9]

The results presented in Table 4.4 demonstrate that President Yudhoyono's likeability is most strongly associated with a vote for PD versus PDIP, PAN, PPP and Hanura, and less strongly but still significantly associated with a vote for PD versus PKB and Gerindra. These findings reflect recent developments in leadership competition and party politics. For almost five years, Yudhoyono was under a strong public spotlight. During most of this time, and especially after mid-2008, he enjoyed relatively high approval ratings. During this same period, most of the other parties retained their old leaders, despite their defeats in 2004 and their poor performance in opinion polls before the 2009 ballot. Abdurrahman Wahid, for example, a former Indonesian president (1999–2001) and PKB's patron, refused to leave the political stage despite severe illnesses and fierce intra-party conflicts. In such a situation, Yudhoyono's likeability was a factor in the president being able to attract large numbers of voters from outside the immediate PD constituency.

Unlike leader appeal, the direct effect of media campaigns loses significance in most paired party comparisons after political economy and leader likeability are included in the analysis.[10] We interpret this finding to mean that media campaigns and leader likeability, and also media campaigns and political economy, are closely connected. Since PD's campaign themes were built around Yudhoyono's personality and the government's socio-economic policies, both implemented and promised, the closeness of this relationship was clearly identifiable during the parliamentary ballot.

A different pattern emerges in the multivariate analysis of the effect of media campaigns on the presidential election (Table 4.5). Here the

---

9   As the number of parties analysed here is nine (the parties that have seats in the 2009–2014 parliament), the pairs of dependent variables are eight times nine, or 72. For reasons of space, in Table 4.4 we display only eight results of the analysis, with PD as a reference category. All of the tables are available from the authors.

10 In this analysis, the media advertisements index was built from three items: party advertisements seen most often on TV, heard most often on radio and read most often in the newspaper. In constructing this index, answers concerning PD advertisements were coded 1 and all others were coded 0. The three items were then summed to constitute a PD advertisement index with a scale of 1–3. For the likeability index, the scores of parties with two leaders (for example, Amien Rais and Sustrisno Bachir in PAN) were summed to produce a single index for each party. The political economy variable combined assessments of the national economy with the closely associated evaluations of governmental performance.

effect is significant regardless of leader likeability, party ID and political economy. Presumably this is because the presidential election campaign was marked by strong disputes over issues and programs, making the effect of the advertising itself still visible. In its strategies and advertisements, Yudhoyono's media team focused on welfare programs, not the president's personal qualities. By contrast, the media campaign for the legislative election a few months earlier had mainly identified the party with its leader. It proclaimed, for example, that 'Partai Demokrat is SBY's party', using the president's familiar initials to tie him to the institutionally underdeveloped party.

Finally, some demographic factors were also important in both the parliamentary and presidential elections, though less so than in 1999 and 2004. In voting for parties, Muslim religiosity is still statistically significant as an explanation of voting for PKB relative to PD and PDIP. Region also plays a role in explaining voting for Golkar relative to PD, PKB and PDIP, but to a lesser extent than in the earlier elections. In the presidential election, age, the urban–rural cleavage and gender had independent effects on voting for Yudhoyono relative to Kalla. Younger, rural males were more likely to vote for Kalla. During the presidential election campaign, Kalla presented himself as more spontaneous and open and frequently attacked Yudhoyono – a stylistic difference that may have appealed to younger male voters. Yudhoyono, in turn, was more popular among urban than village voters, perhaps because of the greater stability of village voters' partisan connections and their relative lack of exposure to the Yudhoyono–Boediono-dominated mass media.

IMPLICATIONS FOR THE QUALITY OF INDONESIAN DEMOCRACY

What is the relevance of our findings for the quality of democracy in today's Indonesia? The survey data suggest several direct implications. First, on the positive side, perhaps the most important is that Indonesian voters have become increasingly rational. From previous surveys, we know that they have identified a set of priority goals: economic growth, general prosperity, national unity, education, rule of law. They turn to individual leaders rather than political parties to achieve those goals, and they set standards for those leaders: personal integrity, social empathy, professional competence (Mujani and Liddle 2009). In 2004, they elected Susilo Bambang Yudhoyono president because they thought he was the most promising of the nominated candidates. Five years later, they gave him a second term because they perceived him to have performed well enough to merit re-election. In 2014, we expect most voters

Table 4.4 Multinomial logistic regression analysis of voting for parties, with Partai Demokrat (PD) as the reference category

	Golkar	Standard error	PDIP	Standard error	PKS	Standard error	PAN	Standard error
Education	0.010	0.158	-0.094	0.223	0.103	0.183	-0.376	0.251
Media campaign: SBY	-0.668	0.573	-0.918	0.778	-2.233**	0.738	-0.532	0.862
Likeability								
SBY	0.395***	0.091	-0.449***	0.106	-0.164	0.118	-0.487***	0.126
Sukarnoputri	-0.015	0.079	0.450***	0.112	-0.048	0.101	0.322**	0.119
Kalla	0.203*	0.091	0.038	0.109	-0.055	0.106	-0.201	0.128
Prabowo	0.017	0.109	0.134	0.143	0.225	0.143	0.108	0.164
Wiranto	0.045	0.111	-0.005	0.150	-0.158	0.155	-0.160	0.170
Iskandar	-0.145	0.141	0.506**	0.187	0.171	0.166	0.210	0.177
Ali	0.100	0.153	-0.138	0.195	-0.335*	0.169	-0.631**	0.213
Rais + Bachir	-0.019	0.121	-0.364*	0.161	0.025	0.147	0.270	0.162
Wahid + Sembiring	-0.005	0.124	-0.202	0.185	0.349**	0.129	0.223	0.189
Political economy	-0.213	0.158	-0.438*	0.198	-0.370*	0.193	0.073	0.246
Santri	0.487	0.288	0.224	0.354	-0.239	0.339	-0.423	0.429
Party ID								
PD	-1.399***	0.270	-2.659***	0.448	-1.762***	0.376	-1.689***	0.476
PDIP	0.078	0.340	2.478***	0.405	0.090	0.421	-0.009	0.448
Golkar	2.195***	0.295	0.422	0.429	0.270	0.387	0.525	0.497
PKS	-0.290	0.443	0.687	0.528	3.034***	0.399	1.370*	0.526
PAN	-0.943	0.565	0.999	0.561	0.157	0.503	3.134***	0.523
PKB	0.750	0.470	-1.917**	0.664	-0.038	0.564	-1.939**	0.674
PPP	-0.484	0.490	0.742	0.617	-0.221	0.516	0.253	0.589
Gerindra	-0.144	0.559	-0.144	0.618	-0.054	0.623	-0.979	0.720
Hamura	-0.387	0.618	-0.772	0.720	-1.241	0.673	-0.400	0.754
Rural area	0.082	0.317	0.712	0.411	-0.088	0.393	0.061	0.479
Region: Java	-0.773*	0.316	-0.112	0.419	-0.403	0.395	-0.508	0.479

Table 4.4 (continued)

	PPP	Standard error	PKB	Standard error	Gerindra	Standard error	Hanura	Standard error
Education	-0.485	0.307	-0.391	0.317	0.699**	0.242	0.476*	0.247
Media campaign: SBY	0.849	0.959	-1.162	1.111	-1.005	0.913	-2.223*	1.105
Likeability								
SBY	-0.500***	0.121	-0.293*	0.146	-0.319*	0.134	-0.610***	0.127
Sukarnoputri	0.033	0.123	-0.120	0.157	-0.199	0.140	0.056	0.132
Kalla	-0.187	0.141	0.132	0.164	0.034	0.138	0.089	0.134
Prabowo	-0.205	0.200	-0.037	0.210	0.103	0.173	-0.425*	0.185
Wiranto	0.033	0.212	0.304	0.210	-0.026	0.180	0.772***	0.183
Iskandar	-0.803**	0.235	0.370	0.198	-0.184	0.223	0.206	0.265
Ali	0.745**	0.254	-0.066	0.227	0.508*	0.231	0.153	0.251
Rais + Bachir	0.410	0.220	-0.226	0.258	0.306	0.195	-0.135	0.222
Wahid + Sembiring	-0.175	0.225	-0.189	0.213	-0.274	0.195	-0.266	0.224
Political economy	-0.292	0.277	-0.637*	0.288	-0.711**	0.252	-0.264	0.265
Santri	0.906	0.609	1.363*	0.663	0.708	0.508	0.653	0.495
Party ID								
PD	-2.045***	0.472	-2.824***	0.549	-2.650***	0.503	-1.008*	0.436
PDIP	-1.246*	0.598	-1.162	0.674	0.599	0.549	-0.199	0.568
Golkar	1.211**	0.426	-0.101	0.618	0.884*	0.452	0.687	0.513
PKS	-2.585**	0.857	-0.975	0.927	0.673	0.537	1.508**	0.492
PAN	-0.706	0.785	-0.454	0.879	-0.629	0.601	-1.020	0.639
PKB	1.607*	0.663	4.731***	0.657	2.119**	0.676	-0.551	0.758
PPP	3.630***	0.568	0.655	0.723	-1.190	0.728	0.386	0.608
Gerindra	-1.197	1.041	0.166	1.001	3.638***	0.619	-1.791*	0.705
Hanura	0.089	0.894	-0.275	0.868	-3.472***	0.780	3.038***	0.700
Rural area	0.959	0.548	0.357	0.562	0.505	0.490	1.049	0.572
Region: Java	0.092	0.659	0.804	0.777	-0.593	0.521	-0.132	0.534

*** = P < 0.001; ** = P < 0.01; * = P < 0.05.

Table 4.5   Multivariate analysis of presidential/vice-presidential election (multinomial logistic regression)

Parameter	B	Standard error
Mega–Prabowo/SBY–Boediono		
Intercept	1.149	2.026
Likeability:		
SBY	–1.194***	0.160
Megawati	1.373***	0.180
Kalla	–0.171	0.116
Age	0.219	0.175
Education	0.376	0.220
Religion: *santri*	–0.003	0.264
Party ID		
PD	–1.939***	0.406
PDIP	1.715***	0.352
Golkar	0.026	0.345
Political economy	–0.918*	0.468
SBY campaign	–0.765**	0.232
Male	0.485	0.375
Rural area	1.069**	0.410
Region: Java	0.460	0.415
JK–Wiranto/SBY–Boediono		
Intercept	–1.345	1.935
Likeability:		
SBY	–0.957***	0.128
Megawati	–0.274**	0.091
Kalla	1.141***	0.128
Age	–0.369*	0.157
Education	0.239	0.175
Religion: *santri*	–0.166	0.259
Party ID		
PD	–0.374	0.287
PDIP	–0.423	0.323
Golkar	0.863**	0.265
Political economy	0.644	0.439
SBY campaign	–0.785***	0.194
Male	1.294***	0.352
Rural area	0.707*	0.363
Region: Java	–0.249	0.336

B = logistic regression coefficient. *** = $P < 0.001$; ** = $P < 0.01$; * = $P < 0.05$.

to engage in similar calculations, though of course without the term-limited Yudhoyono.

From the perspective of democratic consolidation, a second and related positive finding is that most Indonesian voters do not give high priority to the demands of religious and ethnic groups and are therefore not attracted to parties based on religious and ethnic identities. In multi-ethnic, multi-religious Indonesia, this reduces the probability of conflict based on primordial tensions and gives elected officials considerable political capital. When tensions rise and hopefully before violent conflict breaks out, officials can legitimately claim that most Indonesians want the issues resolved as quickly and peacefully as possible. During the first Yudhoyono government, Vice-President Jusuf Kalla played this role successfully on several occasions, especially when managing the fragile peace in post-Helsinki Aceh.

There are also findings with less clear implications for Indonesia's democratisation, however. For instance, the irrelevance of social class divisions for partisan choice can be interpreted in highly divergent ways. In most modern democracies, divisions of economic interest—if not class in a Marxian sense—provide the most important basis of partisan differences. In such societies, parties and their leaders take political power in order to implement economic policies and programs rooted in broader conceptions or ideologies about the relative weight to be allotted to market freedoms versus state intervention in the economy. Perhaps the reluctance of Indonesians to form left–right parties is constrained by the horrific memories on both sides of a large and growing communist party that was violently destroyed in 1965–66. Alternatively, it may be that Indonesian voters, in a high-information, TV-driven era, are simply short-cutting the old ideological differences and making their own direct assessments of elected officials' policies and programs.

The independent impact of television campaigns, especially on the presidential vote, also has mixed implications for democratic quality. In Indonesia—as in most other countries—TV news, talk shows and political commercials give citizens access to valuable information and commentary on politics and government. Indeed, modern democratic life in large, complex societies is inconceivable without the media, especially TV. On the other hand, the information transmitted by TV is distorted and biased in many ways. In the Indonesian case, perhaps the biggest failing is the absence of balance and transparency in the funding of political commercials during campaigns. A few candidates and parties have huge budgets for TV advertisements, while most have none. Moreover, voters have no way of finding out who finances the advertisements.

Arguably, the weakening of voters' identification with political parties is the most important of the findings with mainly negative implications. This is the other side of the coin of reliance on individual leaders, and is thus to some extent ineluctable. In democratic theory, political parties are based on long-lasting economic and social interests that provide relatively permanent links between government policy makers on the one hand and voters on the other (Lipset and Rokkan 1967). In Indonesia, however, many parties (including of course Yudhoyono's PD) are little more than extensions of the personality of a single leader at the top. In the 2009 elections, only two new parties passed the 2.5 per cent threshold for parliamentary seats. Not coincidentally, both are personal vehicles of wealthy, well-networked retired army officers, Prabowo Subianto in the case of Gerindra and Wiranto in the case of Hanura.

High party system volatility is a direct consequence of the identification of parties with single leaders. PDIP, for example, won an extraordinary 34 per cent of parliamentary seats in 1999 because it was identified with Megawati Sukarnoputri, daughter of Indonesia's founding president and standard bearer of the opposition to President Suharto's authoritarian New Order throughout the 1990s. Subsequently, the party's support plummeted by more than 15 points in 2004 because of a loss of confidence in then incumbent president Megawati. When she leaves politics, the party will probably shrink further or even break apart. Similarly, PD won an impressive 7 per cent of parliamentary seats in 2004 (despite having been founded only two years earlier), mainly on the strength of the leadership image projected by Susilo Bambang Yudhoyono, a retired army general and one-time member of Megawati's cabinet. While Yudhoyono's perceived success as president explains the 2009 jump to 21 per cent of the vote, the party still lacks a strong nationwide organisation and is jokingly referred to as 'SBY's fan club'. Without Yudhoyono at the head of the ticket in 2014, the party may well lose many votes.

Finally, Indonesian political parties have a reputation for excessive control from the top, meaning that local party branches and ordinary members have little influence on internal party policies or leadership or candidate selection. Even worse, there is no tradition or culture of party accountability to an electorate. Elected members of both local and national legislatures often regard voters and interest groups as supplicants, not citizens with the right to demand responsiveness and accountability (Antlöv and Cederroth 2004). The decline in party ID in our surveys may reflect in part growing voter dissatisfaction with these distant party leaders and organisations.

CONCLUSION

We now return to the two questions asked at the beginning of this chapter: why have Indonesians voted as they have in the three national democratic elections since 1999, and what are the broader implications of this behaviour for the quality of Indonesian democracy? The answer to the first question is relatively straightforward. In 1999 and 2004, Indonesian voters were motivated primarily by their support for particular leaders and the strength of their identification with political parties. In 2009, voters were influenced in addition by the media campaigns of parties and presidential candidates, by their perceptions of the state of the national economy and by their evaluations of governmental performance. Millions of Indonesians who evaluated the national economy positively voted for PD in the parliamentary election and to re-elect Susilo Bambang Yudhoyono in the presidential election. Religion, regionalism and social class, on the other hand, did not play a major role in shaping electoral behaviour in any of those years.

The answer to the second question is more complex. On the positive side, there appears to be a close alignment between voter preferences, election results and governmental policy outcomes, particularly with regard to presidential politics. Voters want to be governed by a president who can stimulate the economy, promote general prosperity, defend national unity, fight corruption and improve the quality of education and health care. In that regard, most voters perceived that Yudhoyono had performed well enough in those areas to merit re-election. In addition to the voters' increased attention to performance indicators, the low priority most Indonesians gave to religious or ethnic factors is another positive sign of growing rationality in the electorate.

On the negative side, Indonesians voted to perpetuate an ineffectual party system characterised by too much fragmentation (nine parties with more than 3 per cent of the vote in 2009), too much volatility (from PDIP as the largest party with 34 per cent in 1999 to PD as the largest with 21 per cent today), too little internal party democracy, too much personalistic leadership and, perhaps most important, too little responsiveness to the electorate. We recognise, of course, that the instability of the party system is the mirror image of a much better-functioning presidency. While this combination of a strong presidency and a frail party system is certainly not without problems, Indonesia's polity is likely to remain stable in the short term. The president has ample support from the parties in his pre-presidential election coalition, much more than he had at the beginning of his first term. Furthermore, since Yudhoyono's inauguration in October 2009, Golkar has joined the cabinet as well.

Such a grand governing coalition will have both advantages and drawbacks. Arguably, Yudhoyono will have the political resources to govern more effectively than in his first term. But he will not have the checks on his personal power that opposition parties provide in many democracies, and that have been conspicuously lacking in democratic

Indonesia since 1999 (Slater 2004; Ambardi 2008). Fighting corruption, for example, may turn out to be harder or less attractive when a large majority of the political parties represented in parliament are also in government.

The worst disadvantage may not appear until 2014, however, at the end of Yudhoyono's second and final term. It may then become clear that Indonesian democracy as a whole is too dependent on the vagaries of presidential recruitment without a solid base in a well-functioning party system. The voters were lucky to get Yudhoyono in 2004, and lucky again in 2009 to be able to re-elect a president who has been both responsive and responsible. If they are not equally lucky in 2014, they will be at the mercy of a party system with all the deficiencies we have described.

REFERENCES

Ambardi, Kuskridho (2008), 'The making of the Indonesian multiparty system: a cartelized party system and its origin', PhD thesis, Ohio State University, Columbus OH.

Antlöv, Hans and Sven Cederroth (eds) (2004), *Elections in Indonesia: The New Order and Beyond*, RoutledgeCurzon, London.

Baswedan, Anies (2004), 'Sirkulasi suara dalam pemilu 2004' [Circulation of votes in the 2004 election], unpublished paper, Northern Illinois University, DeKalb IL.

Baswedan, Anies (2007), 'Indonesian politics in 2007: the presidency, local elections and the future of democracy', *Bulletin of Indonesian Economic Studies* 43(3): 323–40.

Emmerson, Donald (1976), *Indonesia's Elite: Political Culture and Cultural Politics*, Cornell University Press, Ithaca NY.

Feith, Herbert (1957), *The Indonesian Elections of 1955*, Cornell Modern Indonesia Project, Cornell University Press, Ithaca NY.

Geertz, Clifford (1960), *The Religion of Java*, Free Press, New York NY.

Kiewiet, D.R. (1983), *Macroeconomics and Micropolitics: The Electoral Effects of Economic Issues*, University of Chicago Press, Chicago IL.

King, Dwight (2003), *Half-hearted Reform: Electoral Institutions and the Struggle for Democracy in Indonesia*, Praeger, New York NY.

Kuncoro, Mudrajad, Tri Widodo and Ross H. McLeod (2009), 'Survey of recent developments', *Bulletin of Indonesian Economic Studies* 45(2): 151–76.

Lev, Daniel (1967), 'Political parties in Indonesia', *Journal of Southeast Asian History*, Special Issue: 52–67.

Liddle, R. William (1970), *Ethnicity, Party and National Integration: An Indonesian Case Study*, Yale University Press, New Haven CT.

Liddle, R. William and Saiful Mujani (2007), 'Leadership, party, and religion: explaining voting behavior in Indonesia', *Comparative Political Studies* 40(7): 832–57.

Lipset, Seymour Martin and Stein Rokkan (1967), *Party Systems and Voter Alignments: Cross-national Perspectives*, Free Press, New York NY.

Mujani, Saiful and R. William Liddle (2009), 'Voter preferences for presidential/vice-presidential candidates: public opinion trends', Lembaga Survei Indonesia, Jakarta, 25–30 May.

Slater, Dan (2004), 'Indonesia's accountability trap: party cartels and presidential power after democratic transition', *Indonesia* 78(October): 61–92.

Wertheim, W.F. (1966), 'Indonesia before and after the Untung coup', *Pacific Affairs* 39(1–2): 115–27.

5 INDONESIA'S 2009 ELECTIONS: PERFORMANCE CHALLENGES AND NEGATIVE PRECEDENTS

*Adam Schmidt**

In the run-up to Indonesia's 2009 legislative and presidential elections, very few international observers believed that the polls would pose a serious challenge to the country's continuing process of democratisation. Successful national elections had been held in 1999 and 2004, and Indonesia had conducted around 500 direct local ballots without significant problems since 2005. The expectation, therefore, was that the third post-authoritarian elections would be a routine affair.

But while the 2009 ballots did have a successful political outcome, they were in fact surprisingly chaotic. The conduct of the elections fell short of important basic standards of democratic electoral performance and they were organised in an ad hoc manner. The accessibility and quality of the electoral process varied widely across the country. A delayed and poorly crafted legal framework, a lack of resources and a dysfunctional voter registry all contributed to the difficulties experienced in 2009, demonstrating that Indonesia's election management processes had performed far less well than what could reasonably have been expected based on past performance. If it had not been for the convincing margin of victory achieved by President Susilo Bambang Yudhoyono and his Democratic Party (Partai Demokrat, PD) in both the legislative and presidential elections, the poor management of the elections could easily have become a catalyst for more serious political disagreements. As it was, the Constitutional Court played an extraordinary role in averting a last-minute boycott of the presidential election by the opposition

---

* The views expressed in this chapter are those of the author and do not necessarily reflect those of the institution for which he works.

candidates. Its transparent adjudication of results-related disputes after both the April and July elections was the main reason that a potentially damaging period of political paralysis was averted.

This chapter discusses the quality of management of the 2009 polls in four steps. The first section provides some background on the importance of elections for democratic consolidation, discusses Indonesia's electoral experience since 1998 and describes the main problems besetting the 2009 ballots. The second section looks at one of the chief reasons for the decline in the quality of election administration in 2009: the weakened capacity of the General Elections Commission (Komisi Pemilihan Umum, KPU) following considerable changes to Indonesia's electoral laws. The third part begins by assessing the areas of electoral organisation in which Indonesia performed satisfactorily in 2009: political parties were able to exercise freedom of expression; media reporting was balanced; the elections were conducted peacefully; and procedures for post-election dispute resolution were effective. It then describes the areas where performance was *not* satisfactory, paying particular attention to the problems with the voter registry. The conclusion reviews Indonesia's overall progress in holding elections. Although the country has achieved remarkable political stability since 1998, I argue that the current quality of electoral management may not be sufficient to deal with the closer election outcomes anticipated in the post-Yudhoyono polity after 2014.

ELECTIONS IN INDONESIA

Effective election administration and organisation is a distinct indicator of a country's democratic health and political stability (Guess and Gueorguieva 2008: 2). Scholar Jørgen Elklit surmises that 'a truly independent, impartial, and dedicated electoral commission is instrumental for achieving an electoral outcome which at the end of the day is acceptable to most contestants' (Elklit 1999: 17). As the United Nations' Declaration of Principles for International Election Observation (2005) notes, there is substantial evidence that for 'governments legitimized through genuine democratic elections, the scope for non-democratic challenges to power is reduced'.[1] The ability of a state to manage its electoral processes effectively is therefore a precondition for the establishment of public confidence in the wider democratic process.

Individual and collective rights to participate in elections are codified in the United Nations' Universal Declaration of Human Rights (1948), which states that

---

1 See http://www.accessdemocracy.org/files/1923_declaration_102705_0.pdf.

... the will of the people shall be the basis of the authority of government; this shall be expressed in periodic and genuine elections which shall be by universal and equal suffrage and shall be held by secret vote or by equivalent free voting procedures (article 21).[2]

This principle is further defined in the International Covenant on Civil and Political Rights (1966), which states that every eligible citizen should have the 'right and opportunity' to participate and compete in regularly scheduled elections (article 25).[3] Most countries have adopted these international legal instruments through national laws that establish a legal framework to regulate the electoral system and political behaviour.

The broad features of Indonesia's current electoral framework were determined by constitutional amendments carried out by the People's Consultative Assembly (Majelis Permusyawaratan Rakyat, MPR) between 1999 and 2002. These changes provided for the direct election of the president and vice-president and the establishment of a permanent, independent general elections commission. Previously, the president had been elected by the MPR. It had a significant number of appointed members who could be relied upon to vote in accordance with the wishes of the president, supported by elected members who sat in the chamber by virtue of engineered elections. During the New Order era (1966–98), this mechanism was misused to elect Suharto to the presidency seven consecutive times. Following the first post-authoritarian elections in 1999, the proportion of democratically elected members in the MPR increased, but some appointees remained. Thus, the country's electoral process and management practice were still not completely independent, with political masters and partisan objectives continuing to guide the administration and implementation of elections. With the constitutional amendments carried out between 1999 and 2002, Indonesia joined an international trend, particularly among countries undergoing democratic transition, to place election administration responsibilities under the purview of an independent election management body (Lopez-Pintor 2000: 12). This important legal change fulfilled the constitutional stipulation for Indonesia's general elections to be 'organized by a general elections commission of a national, permanent and independent character'.[4]

Under the requirements of the Universal Declaration of Human Rights and the International Covenant on Civil and Political Rights, democratic states are committed to ensuring inclusive and widely accessible electoral processes. A country's election management body carries the chief responsibility for putting these principles into practice. Ideally

---

2 See http://www.un.org/en/documents/udhr/.
3 See http://www2.ohchr.org/english/law/ccpr.htm.
4 Constitution of the Republic of Indonesia, Chapter VIIB, article 22E.

it does this by providing equitable, uniform and standardised operating procedures for elections and by ensuring that all eligible citizens have the opportunity both to run for office and to vote. Against this background, analysts such as Patrick Merloe (2008: 30) have characterised the 'impartiality and effectiveness of electoral management bodies as a threshold matter for democratic elections'. In countries where either the competency or the neutrality of the election organisers is not assured, corrosive doubts about the legitimacy of the electoral process and the results are likely to arise among the public and political actors alike. The responsibilities of an independent election commission are therefore not unlike those of a referee: to master the rules of the game and to exercise complete independence in the implementation of those regulations. If it does not, then the credibility of the results will suffer accordingly.

Despite Indonesia's long and difficult legacy of engineered elections under Suharto, the first two national elections held after 1998 were widely considered organisational and political successes. In 1999, the KPU was made up of representatives of all participating political parties and could not be regarded as independent. Nevertheless, the results of the polls were seen as highly credible. The commissioners running the KPU in 2004 had no formal ties with any of the parties and so could be considered independent of the political process. Although some were later tried for corruption, the elections themselves again enjoyed strong legitimacy.

Given these impressive successes, most political observers assumed that the organisational accomplishments of the past would necessarily predict similar outcomes in the future. In this view, the post-2004 challenge for Indonesia was simply to sustain and slightly professionalise the election administration process. But this proved much more difficult than most Indonesians or international analysts had imagined. Without doubt, the quality and credibility of the 2009 general elections fell well short of the standards set by their 1999 and 2004 predecessors. It became clear that the financial investments and policy decisions needed to sustain the country's formerly positive electoral performance had not been made. This was most apparent in the failure of the KPU to develop into a professional, fully institutionalised election management body.

Candidates, leaders of political parties and civil society activists have all called the April 2009 legislative elections the 'worst' in the post-Suharto era.[5] They certainly have a point. Systemic problems with the voter lists, for instance, denied many eligible voters their civic right to participate in the elections. Far from being a capstone in Indonesia's democratic consolidation as some had predicted, the 2009 elections exposed an unsteady

---

5   '"Fraud" in Indonesia elections: political leaders', *Agence France Press*, 14 April 2009.

electoral process weakened by a new legal framework.[6] The new set of laws removed many of the features that had allowed the KPU to perform its functions professionally and independently in 2004, instead creating new operational dependencies that the commission would find difficult to overcome. This was further compounded by the selection of new commissioners who were relatively inexperienced in election administration and thus struggled to navigate the legal and structural impediments created by the revised legal framework. Some of the main problems associated with the legal framework for the 2009 elections are described in the next section.

THE 2009 ELECTORAL FRAMEWORK

The neutrality and professional capacity of a country's election management body is a primary prerequisite for democratic elections (Lopez-Pintor 2000: 14). The responsibilities and resources given to the KPU have thus been a major focus of the debate on Indonesia's post-Suharto elections. Reflecting the success of the 2004 elections, in a global survey of election management bodies conducted in 2006, Indonesia's model of electoral management was among those categorized as independent (International IDEA 2006: 312). Clearly Indonesia had made substantial strides towards setting an achievable standard of impartial electoral organisation through a non-political commission.

Significantly, the 2004 KPU was given the appropriate resources and management tools necessary to implement the elections without having to rely on other government institutions. Moreover, it was the beneficiary of substantial levels of international technical assistance and support in areas such as voter education and the provision of public information. But although the law governing the 2004 general elections had turned the KPU into a powerful and independent institution, the commission's image was soon to be severely compromised by a corruption scandal that engulfed almost all of its members together with many top staff in the KPU secretariat.

With the head of the KPU and other senior officials sentenced to several years in prison for illicit procurement practices, it was only to be expected that Indonesia's lawmakers would review the powers of the agency ahead of the 2009 polls. The scandal also had very practical

---

6 The legal framework for the 2009 elections was based on four key laws: Law No. 22/2007 on the Organisation of General Elections; Law No. 2/2008 on Political Parties; Law No. 10/2008 on General Elections; and Law No. 42/2008 on Presidential Elections.

consequences for the KPU's capacity to operate effectively during the remainder of its term, which ended in 2007 and thus covered part of the period needed to prepare for the next elections. With many of its key management staff in jail or under suspicion, the internal management structure of the commission was reduced to a minimum, undercutting its capacity to develop as an institution at a time when this had the best prospects for success.[7] The KPU was essentially paralysed until a new set of commissioners was appointed in November 2007. But the new commissioners had very little election-related experience and inherited substantial human resource and technical challenges. In addition, they had to deal with a new law that greatly reduced the KPU's authority.

Law No. 22/2007 on the Organisation of General Elections

Law No. 22/2007 on the Organisation of General Elections came into force in April 2007. Its purpose was to bring clarity to the roles of the various agencies responsible for managing and supervising elections. Primarily this meant the election management body (the KPU and its regional offices), which was responsible for managing the elections and implementing election management procedures, and the election supervisory body (Badan Pengawasan Pemilu, Bawaslu, and its affiliated offices), which was responsible for supervising the KPU and the electoral process.

But although the law was intended to improve administrative procedures in 2009, it in fact turned out to be a severe impediment to the KPU's proper functioning. Rather than reinforcing the commission's authority as the paramount manager of the full spectrum of election administration tasks, Law No. 22/2007 instead created new and unexpected dependencies for it in the performance of its mandate. This stood in stark contrast to the intent of the law's initiators — politicians and activists who wanted to change the KPU's structure to better meet the needs of the organisation. As far back as 2002, commentators had suggested that the commission's structure should be more closely linked to its strategic planning objectives — that it should be more service delivery focused, more transparent in its operations and more capable of setting reasonable performance expectations. Changes had been made to the KPU's structure in 2003 under Presidential Decree No. 54/2003, but these were only minor, and following the arrest of its senior officials the calls for structural changes intensified.

---

7 ACE Encyclopaedia, 'Effective electoral assistance: the electoral cycle approach', http://aceproject.org/ace-en/focus/focus-on-effective-electoral-assistance/the-electoral-cycle-approach.

Not surprisingly, the corruption scandal provided the main impetus for the deliberations on Law No. 22/2007. Although the KPU had delivered highly credible elections in 2004 in the face of remarkable organisational and logistical challenges, the greed of its members had undermined the KPU's long-term legacy and triggered public demands for its powers to be curtailed. In reaction to the corruption in the KPU, it was understandable that Indonesia's policy makers would attempt to deliver structural reform in the areas of procurement and financial management. However, the provisions in Law No. 22/2007 that were supposed to achieve this had undesired consequences for the quality of election administration in 2009. Most importantly, the restrictions on the authority of the KPU to manage resources and projects reflected strict and 'idealistic' anti-corruption guidelines, but failed to take into account the practical and often unorthodox problems of on-the-ground election management and implementation.

The KPU's ability to move funds quickly to support its operations was greatly inhibited by the new rules on financial disbursement. Under the new guidelines, the commission was treated like any other government agency, despite being required to meet fixed deadlines set by a rigid calendar of electoral events. Without flexible and sufficient access to funds, it found itself incapable at times of meeting its operational mandates. This was particularly evident during the voter registry update process, when the KPU and its affiliated offices were unable to guarantee timely access to the funds needed to support the large number of staff involved in the exercise. As a result, national surveys indicated that only 50 per cent of provincial and district KPU offices were able to complete the voter update process in the prescribed manner (Khalik 2008). According to regional KPU commissioners, the 'normal' financial procedures applied by local governments were not sufficiently responsive to the rigid electoral timeline dictated by Law No. 10/2008 on General Elections, forcing some regional offices to miss key markers on the electoral calendar and to skip some aspects of the electoral process altogether.

Law No. 10/2008 on General Elections

Also limiting the authority of the KPU in the area of voter registration was the requirement in Law No. 10/2008 on General Elections for the commission to base its voter lists on population data compiled by the Ministry of Home Affairs, rather than the more accurate census data, as in 2004. Thus, although the commission and its field offices were to be responsible for updating the voter lists, the baseline quality of those lists would be determined primarily by the quality of the underlying population data provided by the Ministry of Home Affairs. The process of updating the lists was further complicated by a mismatch between the

KPU's data requirements and the ministry's data management systems. In April 2008, the ministry delivered its village and community-level population data to the KPU in the form of approximately 80,000 Excel files. Confronted with this huge number of files, the KPU had to develop a data conversion program to create temporary lists of voters. It also identified serious problems with the data, but was unable to do much about it because of budget constraints and the limited time available to update the lists. Finally, the quality of the data and the ability of the KPU to readily correct it was undermined by changes to the data update process, which no longer relied on door-to-door visits as it had in 2004, but rather on passive office-based procedures.

To add to the KPU's difficulties, the 2008 General Elections Law and other statutes regulating the legislative and presidential elections were passed only in the second half of 2008, giving it very little time to study the changes to the electoral system. Law No. 10/2008 altered the system in a number of important ways (see Table 5.1). It reduced the number of seats per electoral district from a maximum of 12 in 2004 to a maximum of 10 in 2009, thereby strengthening the larger parties at the expense of the medium-sized and smaller ones. It also introduced a new parliamentary threshold of 2.5 per cent of the national vote for parties to be able to take up seats in the People's Representative Council (Dewan Perwakilan Rakyat, DPR). Again, this had the effect of preventing small or minor parties with inconsequential national support from obtaining seats in parliament. The new regulation replaced the system practised in the 1999 and 2004 elections whereby parties that failed to meet a prescribed threshold were forced to disband but successful candidates from those parties were nevertheless allowed to take up their seats in the DPR. This system had proven unworkable, because many parties that failed to exceed the threshold did not disband, but simply renamed themselves and continued to contest elections under their new names.

Constitutional Court rulings added a new layer of complexity to the preparations for the April parliamentary elections and the July presidential election. In December 2008, for instance, the court annulled article 214 of Law No. 10/2008. The verdict effectively abolished the system whereby candidates were elected in the order in which they were ranked on a party's list of candidates, regardless of the number of votes they themselves had received. Instead, the court ruled that seats were to be allocated on the basis of the number of votes for the individual nominee. Moreover, on 6 July — only two days before the presidential election — the court ruled that, owing to deficiencies in the voter registry, eligible voters would be allowed to confirm their eligibility to vote by presenting their national ID cards and other documents at the polling station on election day (Tedjasukmana 2009).

Table 5.1   Main changes to the electoral system introduced by Law No. 10/2008 on General Elections

	2004 elections	2009 elections
Size of national assembly (DPR)	550 members	560 members
Number of electoral districts nationwide	69 electoral districts	77 electoral districts
Number of seats per district	3 to 12 seats	3 to 10 seats
Electoral threshold for parties to take up seats in the DPR	None	2.5 per cent of the valid national vote
Electoral formula	Hare quota	Hare quota with multi-stage iteration
Structure of ballot (parties versus individual candidates)	Semi-open party list system with individual candidates needing to exceed 100 per cent of a pre-defined quota in order to win a seat on the basis of the individual's personal vote rather than his/her position on the party list	Semi-open party list system with individual candidates needing to exceed 30 per cent of a pre-defined quota in order to win a seat on the basis of the individual's personal vote rather than his/her position on the party list[a]

a   The Constitutional Court struck out article 214 of the law in December 2008, effectively abolishing the party list system altogether (see text).

While these were both progressive rulings that supported a citizen's right to participate in elections, they had significant operational implications for election organisers. Coming a little over four months before the legislative election in the case of the open list ruling and only 36 hours before the presidential election in the case of the ID card verdict, the court's decisions forced the KPU to make last-minute changes to an already rushed electoral process.

By placing unworkable restrictions on the KPU's financial and administrative authority, the new electoral framework unwittingly ensured that the commission would struggle to meet its timeline and other basic enfranchisement expectations for the 2009 polls. In combination with the new selection process for KPU commissioners, which led to the appointment of individuals with little previous experience in managing national elections, the introduction of these operational dependencies deeply disrupted the prospects for smooth elections in 2009.

Table 5.2   Internationally accepted criteria for electoral performance and Indonesia's electoral performance in 2009

Performance criteria	Achieved?
1 Freedom of expression by political parties	Yes
2 Media balance in reporting on parties and candidates	Yes
3 Informed electorate	No
4 Well-trained permanent and ad hoc staff in the election management body	No
5 Peaceful conduct of polling	Yes
6 Civil society involved in all aspects of the electoral process	No
7 Transparent vote-counting process	No
8 Auditable publication of results	No
9 Accurate voter lists	No
10 Well-functioning dispute resolution process	Yes

Source of performance criteria: ACE Electoral Knowledge Network; Inter-Parliamentary Union's Declaration on Free and Fair Elections; Organization for Security and Co-operation in Europe's International Election Observation Standards.

EVALUATING THE 2009 ELECTIONS: SUCCESSES AND FAILURES

While conducted within a complex domestic framework, Indonesia's 2009 legislative and presidential elections should be evaluated through the lens of general international election standards.[8] These are the standards typically used by international observer groups, practitioners and governments to evaluate the credibility and legitimacy of electoral processes. In this section, I focus on what I believe to be the most important criteria for assessing electoral performance (see Table 5.2). The list I have compiled is neither comprehensive nor scientific, but it should capture the most vital areas of performance.

In general, substandard performance or outright failure in any of the areas listed in Table 5.2 may compromise the legitimacy and credibility of the overall electoral process. In evaluating Indonesia's 2009 elections against the criteria listed in the table (based on data from technical assistance organisations as well as media and observer reports), I found strong

---

8 The standards assembled for this study were guided by the ACE Electoral Knowledge Network, the Inter-Parliamentary Union's Declaration on Free and Fair Elections and the Organization for Security and Co-operation in Europe's International Election Observation Standards.

indications that the polls did not achieve high standards of performance. Worse, the analysis finds that Indonesia's electoral performance actually deteriorated between 2004 and 2009. When a country performs badly in multiple areas, as Indonesia did in 2009, it is a clear sign that its elections lack the procedural integrity to be considered credible and legitimate. The 2009 elections also provide evidence for the general rule that failure in multiple areas adds credence to damaging claims of fraud, which in turn have the potential to contribute to an erosion of confidence in the overall electoral process.

Successes

Freedom of expression by political parties

By and large, the political parties and candidates participating in the 2009 elections were able to practise their right to speak freely, distribute literature and perform other campaign-related activities. With 38 political parties competing at the national level and an additional six local parties competing in Aceh, Indonesian voters enjoyed a multitude of choices. Political parties and their candidates presented the public with a range of agendas, platforms and objectives, even if these were widely criticised for their vagueness and lack of distinctiveness. Very few parties complained that they had been prevented from expressing their political views. Indeed, the only documented exceptions to this were reports of intimidation by supporters of Partai Aceh—the party representing the interests of the former rebel movement in Aceh—who were accused of trying to prevent other parties from campaigning openly in the party's strongholds. To be fair, however, Partai Aceh also claimed to have been the target of similar forms of electoral intimidation in areas outside its strongholds (see Palmer in this volume).[9]

If anything, the quantity of the campaign material provided by the numerous political parties and candidates participating in the four separate legislative elections held in April 2009—national, regional,[10] provincial and district/municipality—could be considered too overwhelming for the individual voter to digest properly in the time available. The Constitutional Court's ruling on open party lists encouraged candidates to compete more vigorously than ever against candidates from other—and their own—parties. The result was an intense and often vivid display

---

9   'Terror and threats still rife on Aceh campaign trail', *Jakarta Globe*, 29 March 2009.

10   The Regional Representative Council (Dewan Perwakilan Daerah, DPD) is elected to represent regional interests in Jakarta. It is permitted to draft laws on regional issues for consideration by the DPR and the government.

of Indonesia's dynamic electoral competition. On the whole, then, Indonesia's 2009 elections deserved very high marks when evaluated on the criterion of freedom of expression.

Balanced media reporting

Indonesia's election laws require the media to provide equitable and unbiased coverage of the full range of certified political parties for the legislative elections and of the primary candidates for the presidential election. As Indonesians received the vast majority of their news and political reporting from non-government media — 90 per cent of citizens cited television as their main source of information (IFES and KPU 2008) — the non-state broadcasters and print organs were the most powerful medium in shaping political views. In 2009, two of the leading private television networks, MetroTV and TVOne, dedicated substantial programming time to the elections, marketing themselves as the 2009 election channels. Both are owned by leading members of the Golkar party — MetroTV by Surya Paloh and TVOne by Aburizal Bakrie — creating some concerns about their neutrality. However, the two men were known to be bitter rivals who had fought each other for the Golkar leadership, and they supported different presidential candidates. Despite the concerns, during the elections their channels presented a wide variety of views.

Overall, Indonesia's highly dynamic media landscape gave voters ample opportunity to access non-biased information. Around a dozen national television channels covered the elections, reporting on both the government and opposition parties. The incumbent naturally enjoyed an advantage in that the media continued to report on official state events and government members' activities throughout the campaign period. But this is a phenomenon common to all democratic states, including the consolidated democracies in the West.

Peaceful conduct of polling

As part of the 2005 Helsinki peace agreement for Aceh, local Acehnese parties were given permission to participate in the provincial and district-level legislative elections, despite the requirement under Indonesian law that parties must have a nationwide structure (see Palmer in this volume). Before the elections, many had feared that the contest between the national and local parties would stir up old tensions, causing civic discord. But although there was an up-tick in campaign-related violence and intimidation before the elections, on election day itself voters cast their ballots without major interruption. Indeed, the only notable cases of violence on polling day took place in Papua, where electoral tensions turned ugly, disrupting voting in parts of Jayapura. In most other parts of Papua, however, polling was conducted in an orderly fashion.

Across Indonesia, peace and security largely prevailed on election day in both April and July, and there was no repeat of the Papua incidents during the July presidential election. Those who wished to vote could do so in a peaceful and secure environment. The fact that the elections took place in such a stable environment was testament to the civic nature of the event and the effectiveness of Indonesia's police and security forces in maintaining security. Given the unstable democratic transition Indonesia had experienced in the early years of the post-Suharto era, the peacefulness of the 2009 elections—and of its predecessors in 1999 and 2004—must be viewed as a considerable achievement for both the government and society.

Well-functioning dispute resolution process

In Indonesia, the jurisdiction to rule on electoral disputes rests with the Constitutional Court. During the 2009 legislative elections, the court proved to be an impartial and professional adjudicator of such disputes. In cases where the evidence suggested substantial fraud or deviation from due electoral process, the court did not hesitate to annul the results and order a rerun in the affected areas (Pasandaran 2009). When the constitutional right of citizens to participate in the elections was threatened by flawed voter lists, leading the opposing presidential candidates to threaten to boycott the July election, the court intervened to ensure that all eligible voters were able to participate, thereby averting a potential constitutional crisis. Undoubtedly the role of the Constitutional Court in settling electoral disputes was instrumental in ensuring that political parties and candidates accepted the final, albeit flawed, election results.

The professionalism and independence of the Constitutional Court stood in stark contrast to the performance of the KPU and Bawaslu, both of which were beset by regulatory and capacity weaknesses. Bawaslu in particular was widely described as a 'paper tiger', because although it collected data and complaints, it had no means of resolving the disputes between electoral participants.

Failures

Informed electorate

For voters to engage effectively with the electoral process, they need to be well informed about electoral rules and procedures. In 2009, however, the KPU faced significant funding shortages for the development and

Figure 5.1   *Adequacy of information on 2009 elections, September 2008 and March 2009*

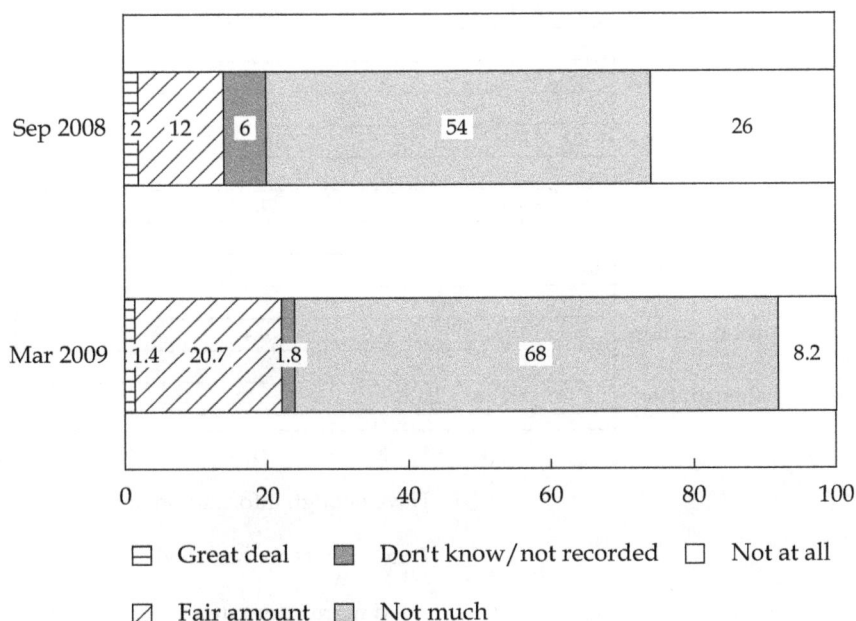

Source: IFES and KPU (2008, 2009).

dissemination of public information, leading to strikingly low levels of knowledge among voters about specific aspects of the electoral process.

In a survey conducted in September 2008, just a few months before the April 2009 elections, the KPU and the International Foundation for Electoral Systems (IFES) found that 54 per cent of respondents claimed to have been given very little information about the elections and 26 per cent no information at all (see Figure 5.1). Only 12 per cent of respondents said they had received a fair amount of information, and just 2 per cent a great deal. A follow-up survey conducted in March 2009 found that some advances had been made in increasing the levels of awareness: the proportion of respondents claiming to have received a fair amount or a great deal of information about the 2009 elections had increased to 22 per cent, while the proportion saying they had received no information at all had fallen to 8 per cent. On the other hand, the proportion responding 'not much' had increased from 54 to 68 per cent (see IFES and KPU 2008, 2009).

Most respondents felt they needed more information than they had been given on various facets of the election process: 83 per cent said they wanted more information on vote-counting procedures; 80 per cent on

Figure 5.2   Knowledge of election process and voting procedures, March 2009

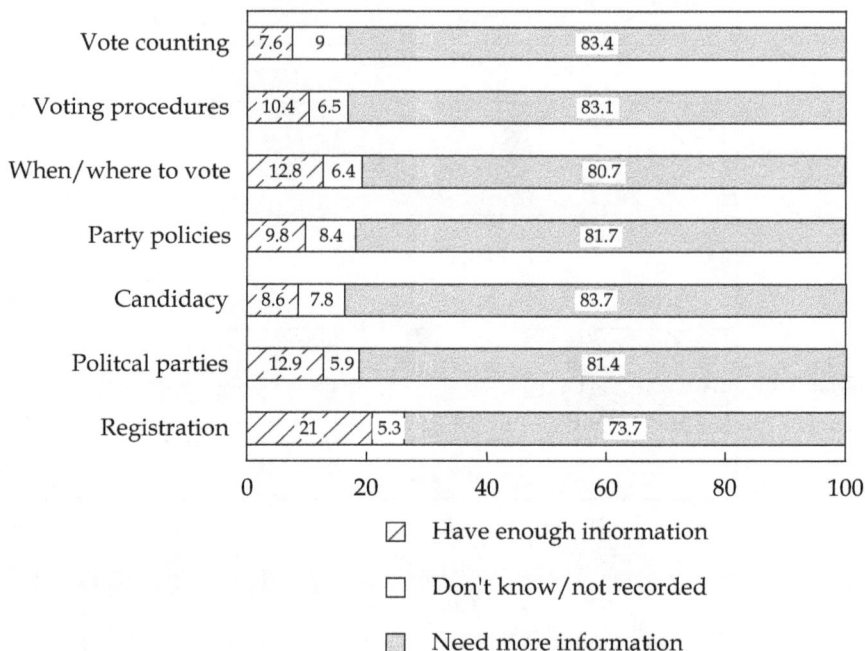

Vote counting	7.6 | 9 | 83.4
Voting procedures	10.4 | 6.5 | 83.1
When/where to vote	12.8 | 6.4 | 80.7
Party policies	9.8 | 8.4 | 81.7
Candidacy	8.6 | 7.8 | 83.7
Politcal parties	12.9 | 5.9 | 81.4
Registration	21 | 5.3 | 73.7

0   20   40   60   80   100

▨ Have enough information

☐ Don't know/not recorded

▨ Need more information

Source: IFES and KPU (2008, 2009).

when and where to vote; 84 per cent on candidacy requirements; 81 per cent on the participating political parties; and 74 per cent on voter registration (see Figure 5.2). These figures reflect an abysmal performance by the election administration in the area of informing the voting public of its rights and responsibilities to participate in the electoral process.

While voters were generally lacking in knowledge about the elections, one issue in particular created confusion. In 2009, for the first time in the history of Indonesian elections, voters were asked to express their preference by marking the ballot paper with a pen (*mencontreng*) rather than punching a hole in the ballot paper (*mencoblos*). Although a relatively minor change, the implementation of the new method was complicated by the manner in which it was written into law as well as by the KPU's interpretation and regulatory implementation of the law. The KPU chose to maintain a rigid interpretation of voter intent that allowed very little variation in the way voters could mark the ballot paper. But because it did not explain the new procedure to the public well in advance of the elections, many voters ended up casting invalid votes on election day. Remarkably, the proportion of invalid votes totalled 14.4 per cent of all votes cast during the April elections, outnumbering the votes received

Table 5.3   Votes for the three highest-ranking parties versus invalid votes,
April 2009 (%)

Party	Share of vote
Partai Demokrat (PD)	20.85
Golkar	14.45
Invalid (*suara tidak sah*)	14.38
Partai Demokrasi Indonesia Perjuangan (PDIP)	14.03

Source: General Elections Commission (KPU).

by the third highest-ranking party, and only slightly below the votes cast for the second-placed party (see Table 5.3). These figures provide a clear indication that the Indonesian electorate did not have all the information it needed to participate successfully in the elections in 2009.

Well-trained staff

To ensure that election performance standards are maintained throughout the country, election management bodies must receive adequate training. Unlike in 2004, however, Indonesia did not implement a standardised training program for electoral staff before the 2009 legislative or presidential elections, because of delays both in the development of electoral regulations and in the production of training manuals. The success or failure of the elections was therefore dependent on the creative capacity and past experience of the regional KPU commissioners and their staff. While the enthusiasm and flexibility of local staff did help to prevent a complete breakdown of the electoral process, the lack of clear standards had severe consequences for the quality of the elections, particularly the counting and reporting of results. For example, the new form developed to report the results — the 'C1' form — proved difficult to fill out and was thus a source of many accounting errors after the elections. This was exacerbated by poor staff training, which not only opened the way for an increase in administrative mistakes but also diluted the integrity of the process as a whole. On the crucial criterion of well-trained electoral staff, therefore, Indonesia did not achieve an adequate standard of performance in 2009, and again performed less well than it had in 2004.

Civil society involvement

One of the most critical features underpinning the integrity of elections is the active and unfettered involvement of civil society organisations in the electoral process. They are able to make an important contribution to a whole range of election administration tasks. The mobilisation of civil society networks to conduct voter education activities at the grassroots level is an effective way to increase public awareness about when, where and how to vote. Civil society networks also fulfil an important observation function. Where civic networks are actively engaged in observing all stages of an election, the administration's efforts to ensure a transparent and credible electoral process will be complemented and reinforced.

But while civil society groups in Indonesia are generally vibrant and vocal, the element of election monitoring by NGOs was largely missing from the 2009 general elections. There were some examples of civil society mobilising to observe elections, but the numbers of volunteers were limited to perhaps a few thousand overall. This was in stark contrast to the situation in 2004, when hundreds of thousands of well-trained domestic observers were deployed throughout Indonesia to ensure the integrity of the electoral process. In 2009, no funding was made available to help NGOs mobilise a domestic observation effort. Based on the experience in 2004, international donors and state actors had assumed that civil society would be capable of performing these functions without external assistance and that there would be no need to support the sector. This turned out to be a huge miscalculation, with NGOs unable to cover the costs of logistical support and human resources. Beyond the funding issue, however, the KPU missed many opportunities to engage more actively with civil society actors to enhance the integrity of the 2009 elections. The lack of formal involvement of civil society in most stages of the electoral process stood out as one of the most consequential failures of Indonesia's electoral performance in 2009.

Transparent vote-counting process

A transparent vote-counting process is indispensable for an election to be called professional and credible. Although vote-counting procedures performed adequately on election day at the polling station level, the process by which the results were physically tabulated on the C1 forms and transmitted to the next administrative level was very opaque. In the case of the legislative elections, the large number of political parties and candidates participating in the elections led to a cumbersome C1 form that was prone to transcription and other administrative errors. Based on the author's own observations on election day, the results entered on many of the forms had been crossed out and re-entered at various stages of the administrative process. This threw the accuracy of the tabulation into question, opening the way for manipulation at various levels of the counting process. Consequently, the legislative elections generated many complaints from winning and losing candidates alike who complained that the final tabulation did not reflect their actual results as reported by the polling stations on election day.

Moreover, the KPU failed to adequately test and deliver a method of obtaining a 'quick count' at each polling station, to provide a separate trail of the results that could be compared with the final tabulation. Without this important feature, there could be no centralised cross-checking of the lower-level results. Instead, the KPU left it to independent polling institutes to conduct and publish their own quick counts. Luckily for the commission, their figures turned out to be very close to the official ones. Nevertheless, the lack of transparency and auditing features in the tabulation process constituted a failure of the 2009 elections and led to an erosion of public confidence in the electoral process.

Auditable publication of results

In line with the very low level of transparency in vote-counting procedures, by early 2010 the KPU had not yet made an auditable set of results available for either the legislative or presidential elections. It is almost without precedent for the election administration body in an electoral democracy not to publish the final results down to the lowest polling-district level — it is, after all, the body tasked with ensuring the credibility and integrity of the elections. It is standard practice in other democratic states — even those with less electoral experience than Indonesia — to publish the results so that they may can be subjected to a rigorous process of audit and review by the political parties, candidates and interested members of the public. In 2004, the KPU had made the election results more widely available, so once again it appears that Indonesia took a step backward in 2009 in this regard.

Accurate voter lists

In a democracy, all eligible citizens must be given a genuine opportunity to register to vote — including the chance to review and inspect the lists of voters. In essence, the registry of voters is the foundation document for electoral administration. It tells the administrators who is qualified to vote by virtue of having fulfilled residency, age and other requirements, and which citizens are eligible to run as candidates. The election administration body has the critical role of ensuring that voter registration is professionally managed, well understood and conducted in a transparent manner that is open to public observation.

The suspect management of the voter registry was the single most contentious issue during the 2009 elections in Indonesia. The wide-scale omission of eligible voters from the lists and the inaccurate recording of details severely hampered Indonesians in their attempts to exercise their fundamental right to participate in the elections. Estimates of the number of Indonesians disenfranchised by the substandard updating and management of the lists range from hundreds of thousands to tens of millions (Rondonuwu and Creagh 2009), although the true number cannot be quantified without a proper auditing of the data. The poor quality of the voter registry became the basis for complaints by the losing presidential and vice-presidential candidates, Megawati Sukarnoputri–Prabowo Subianto and Jusuf Kalla–Wiranto, who asked the Constitutional Court to order a rerun or second round of elections. Ultimately the petitioners were unable to convince the court that the wide margin of victory of the Yudhoyono–Boediono team was due to errors in the voter registry. However, if the result had been closer, Indonesia's electoral dispute resolution system could well have come under greater pressure, leading to larger, more serious demonstrations by supporters of the unsuccessful candidates.

The KPU was only partly to blame for the flawed voter lists, however. As discussed earlier, it was required to base its lists on population data constructed by the Ministry of Home Affairs. An analysis of sample data conducted by the KPU as well as a subsequent audit of the temporary voter lists by two independent organisations — the Institute for Social and Economic Research, Education and Information (Lembaga Penelitian, Pendidikan dan Penerangan Ekonomi dan Sosial, LP3ES) and the National Democratic Institute for International Affairs (NDI) — uncovered systemic weaknesses in the collection and management of the population data from the civil registry (Khalik 2008).

But although the KPU had to work with poorly assembled baseline data, its own deficiencies were also apparent in the quality of the lists. Reflecting its lack of resources and specialist skills, the lists it compiled were both inaccurate and incomplete. The KPU's capacity to update and manage the lists was further compromised by an inadequate period prescribed by the 2008 General Elections Law for the updating and public review of the temporary voter lists. Moreover, the KPU conducted only a very limited public information campaign to inform voters of the need to review the lists before the elections to make sure they were accurate.

The accuracy and reach of the 2009 voter registry cannot be known in the absence of up-to-date population data and a comprehensive quantitative analysis of the voter lists compiled across the country's approximatly 470 districts and municipalities. With central guidance by the KPU to its provincial and district-level offices scarce or nonexistent, the coding, electronic format and final form of the lists lacked uniformity. Local KPU offices often decided for themselves how and in what form to design the lists. This constituted a serious deviation from international election administration norms, which seek to ensure standard data collection and management processes. The purpose of such standards is to ensure that consistent procedures are used throughout the country, guaranteeing all citizens equal rights to the electoral franchise. The fact that Indonesia was unable to meet this basic condition in 2009 seriously undermined the professionalism and credibility of its electoral process.

CONCLUSION

This chapter has highlighted the mixed record of Indonesia's election administration in 2009. On the positive side, there can be no doubt that Indonesia continued to make substantial progress in its relatively rapid transition to democracy since 1998. With hundreds of thousands of candidates standing for election and voter turnout at internationally competitive levels, the 2009 elections again reflected the health and vibrancy of the democratic dialogue that prevails in contemporary Indonesia. The elections were conducted in a stable and secure environment, and where there were disputes, all contenders accepted the decisions of the Constitutional Court. Compared with the tumultuous and deeply flawed elections in other nominal democracies in Southeast Asia, particularly Thailand and the Philippines, Indonesia performed well in 2009. But as the only country in ASEAN classified by Freedom House as an electoral democracy in 2009,[11] Indonesia should maintain higher electoral standards than its troubled neighbours. Measured against internationally accepted standards, the 2009 elections did not fulfil this expectation.

Overall, the legitimacy and credibility of the 2009 elections were significantly reduced by a flawed electoral framework, substandard implementation of administrative processes, severe information deficits and a discredited voter registry. It deserves to be reiterated that one of the primary objectives of a properly functioning electoral process is to ensure equitable enfranchisement opportunities for all citizens of voting age. The international electoral norms listed in the International Covenant on Civil and Political Rights state that 'every citizen shall have the right to vote and to be elected at genuine periodic elections'. But for reasons both within and outside its control, the KPU was unable to ensure that all eligible Indonesian voters had the necessary information, access and enfranchisement opportunities to participate in the 2009 elections.

The fact that potentially millions of eligible voters may have been left off the voter registry suggests a dysfunctional administration and a

---

11   See http://www.freedomhouse.org/template.cfm?page=477&year=2009.

flawed implementation of the 2009 electoral process. Accordingly, Indonesia will be hard-pressed to restore its democratic electoral practice to the levels experienced in 2004. In preparation for the 2014 elections, the independent executive authority of the KPU should be reinforced to ensure neutrality in the future management of the electoral process. Similarly, Indonesians must be informed of their rights and responsibilities through a coordinated public information and education campaign that corresponds both to the electoral process and to key election events.

The failure of Indonesia's policy makers, bureaucracy and election administrators to protect basic electoral rights in 2009 must not be repeated if the country wishes to maintain public confidence in its democracy. Indonesia was fortunate that, in the July presidential election, the incumbent's margin of victory was outside both the margin of error and any conceivable margin of fraud or disenfranchisement. With Yudhoyono retiring in 2014 and no clear front-runner in sight to take his place, Indonesia may not be so lucky next time round. In a more competitive political environment, opportunists may seek to take advantage of the weakened electoral process or to delegitimise the polls by unsubstantiated claims of fraud. In this context, Indonesia should examine the case of Kenya's 2007 presidential election. In this previously stable electoral democracy, the vote-counting and reporting process failed to produce a transparent result in a very close race, leading to disputes that degenerated into severe electoral violence and to a prolonged constitutional crisis.

Indonesia should not rely on the intervention of the Constitutional Court alone to resolve its underlying election administration weaknesses, as it did in 2009. With around 550 direct local elections scheduled between 2010 and 2014 and the next national ballots due in 2014, the electoral process needs to be improved immediately if Indonesia's democracy is to consolidate further.

REFERENCES

Elklit, Jørgen (1999), 'Electoral institutional change and democratic transition: you can bring a horse to water, but you can't make it drink', *Democratization* 6(4): 28–51.

Guess, George M. and Vassia Gueorguieva (2008), *Dysfunctional Decentralization: Election Management in Theory and Practice*, Center for Democracy and Election Management, American University, Washington DC.

IFES and KPU (International Foundation for Electoral Systems and Komisi Pemilihan Umum) (2008), 'National survey to track voter awareness', IFES and KPU, Jakarta, September, www.ifes.or.id.

IFES and KPU (International Foundation for Electoral Systems and Komisi Pemilihan Umum) (2009), 'National survey to track voter awareness', IFES and KPU, Jakarta, March, www.ifes.or.id.

International IDEA (International Institute for Democracy and Electoral Assistance) (2006), *Electoral Management Design: The International IDEA Handbook*, International IDEA, Stockholm.

Khalik, Abdul (2008), 'Most voter lists remain invalid: survey', *Jakarta Post*, 14 August.

Lopez-Pintor, Rafael (2000), *Electoral Management Bodies as Institutions of Governance*, United Nations Development Programme, New York NY.

Merloe, Patrick (2008), 'Human rights: the basis for inclusiveness, transparency, accountability and public confidence in elections', in National Democratic Institute for International Affairs (NDI) (ed.), *Promoting Legal Frameworks for Democratic Elections*, NDI, Washington DC.

Pasandaran, Camelia (2009), 'Court orders election rerun in South Nias district', *Jakarta Globe*, 9 June.

Rondonuwu, Olivia and Sunanda Creagh (2009), 'Voter row dogs final hours before Indonesia election', *Reuters*, 7 July.

Tedjasukmana, Jason (2009), 'Indonesia gets ready for round one at polls', *Time Magazine*, 7 July.

6 THE PROFESSIONALISATION OF POLITICS: THE GROWING ROLE OF POLLING ORGANISATIONS AND POLITICAL CONSULTANTS

Muhammad Qodari

The 2009 elections marked a new stage in Indonesian electoral politics. For the first time voters were able to elect directly members of the legislatures, because of the introduction of an open party list system. In the past, political parties were the key to political success: voters simply chose the party they preferred and it was a candidate's place on the party list that determined whether or not that person was elected. Now, if a party gains enough votes in a particular electoral district to win a seat, it is the candidate from that party with the highest number of individual votes who gets the seat. This system continues a trend that began with the introduction of direct presidential elections in 2004 and then of direct elections for heads of local government in 2005. The introduction of direct elections has caused dramatic changes in electioneering and campaign strategies, throwing the political spotlight onto individual candidates in campaigning at all levels. The mass media and image building by candidates have become all-important.

Before the introduction of direct elections, the most important actors in election campaigns were the party machines, which had organisations that stretched down to the grassroots. The chief method of communicating with voters was face-to-face. In direct elections, by contrast, victory is determined not by how a candidate reaches out to potential voters through a party machine, but by how issues are framed and an image built in the media. Victory is determined by the candidate's performance, the issues he or she raises, and how the person looks in advertisements

(Nimmo 1976). As a result, the role of the mass media and advertising in Indonesian elections has increased massively. In the 1999 elections, parties spent Rp 97.2 billion (about $10 million) on advertising. After 10 years this sum had gone up tenfold. During the recent legislative elections, total expenditure on advertising by the parties was Rp 1.1 trillion ($117 million) (AGB Nielsen Media Research 2009).

This new media-driven political landscape has given birth to important new categories of political actors in Indonesia: polling organisations and political consultants. Direct elections call for experts who can map voter preferences, understand the strengths and weaknesses of a candidate, create and package issues, build an attractive image, and understand what strategies will persuade voters. Political parties lack this kind of expertise, but polling organisations and political consultants have it. In 2009, as I will argue in this chapter, they came into their own as important players, influencing campaigning and helping to set the country's political direction.

In this chapter I examine the roles played by survey organisations and political consultants in contemporary Indonesia. I first discuss the rise of polling organisations, tracing their shift from marginal research bodies to players at the centre of power. I then consider the debates about whether the publication of polling results affects election outcomes, and about the ethics of polling. Next, I turn my attention to the role of political consultants, a breed of political actor that offers all-encompassing campaign services to candidates, covering everything from the design of grand campaign themes down to the nitty-gritty of organisational details. After describing the emergence of contemporary political consultants from the space occupied by advertising agencies in the 1999 elections, I provide some concrete examples of how consultants go about supporting and advising their clients in local elections. I conclude that, unlike in some Western countries where consultants are seen as complementing political parties, in Indonesia there is evidence to suggest that they are displacing them as the central locomotive of election campaigning. Overall, the analysis suggests that a new breed of political advisers and consultants is not only professionalising Indonesian politics, but also becoming increasingly influential within it.

When reading this chapter, readers should note that it draws heavily on my personal experience and observations as a pollster. I joined the Indonesian Survey Institute (Lembaga Survei Indonesia, LSI) as research director when it was established around June 2003, moved to the Indonesian Survey Circle (Lingkaran Survei Indonesia) in 2005 as deputy executive director, and established my own polling organisation, Indo Barometer, at the end of 2006. It is thus possible that an element of subjectivity may affect my arguments and conclusions. Nevertheless, I hope they will help spur further research on the topic.[1]

THE RISE OF POLLING AND SURVEY ORGANISATIONS

In the New Order period (1966–98), it was virtually impossible to conduct surveys on political topics. The regime did not like criticism and it did not approve of any activity that involved the probing of public opinion. Moreover, political surveys would have been pointless when elections did not really reflect voters' aspirations. Voting patterns were determined by systematic pressure from the government, not by free choice.

Political polling thus gathered steam only during the 1999 elections, after the fall of the New Order. Most early organisers of polling were NGOs funded by foreign agencies or the mass media. Polls by LP3ES,[2] a pioneer in political surveys, were mostly funded by the United States Agency for International Development (USAID) and the Ford Foundation. According to Mietzner (2009), between 1999 and 2004 Indonesian polling became more sophisticated, but 'Indonesia's political elite remained sceptical of its strategic significance' (p. 101). In the 2004 elections, more organisations carried out polling, including the research and development division of *Kompas* newspaper and LSI.[3] Political parties also started to show more interest in polling. Nevertheless, party leaders ignored polls showing that the retired general and former minister Susilo Bambang Yudhoyono was ahead in the direct presidential election to be held that year, because they 'expected that once their dominant party machines began campaigning for their nominees, the tide would turn in their favour' (Mietzner 2009: 102). They were shocked when the polls turned out to be right and Yudhoyono won the election. Despite this lesson, survey agencies began to grow rapidly only after the impetus of the introduction of direct elections for local heads of government in 2005. They continued to expand their role in the 2009 general election. Important pollsters now include Lingkaran Survei Indonesia, Indo Barometer, CIRRUS Surveyor Group and others.

---

1   It should be noted that mine is not the first publication on this topic. See in particular Mietzner (2009).
2   Institute for Social and Economic Research, Education and Information (Lembaga Penelitian, Pendidikan dan Penerangan Ekonomi dan Sosial).
3   Like LP3ES, LSI was an NGO that received funding from foreign agencies (initially the Japan International Cooperation Agency).

Strikingly, at the same time that survey organisations have mush-roomed, their surveys have become increasingly accurate. Across the 1999, 2004 and 2009 elections for the national legislature, survey organi-sations predicted the victors with successively greater precision. In 1999, the average gap between survey predictions and party results was 5 per cent, but in 2004 it fell to 2 per cent and in 2009 it was below 2 per cent. Sample sizes also became progressively smaller, making surveys much less costly. In 1999, survey organisations sampled on average 5,000 respondents to measure national voter preferences. This figure fell to 2,500 in 2004 and 1,200 in 2009, yet was accompanied by an *increase* in predictive accuracy. These outcomes have boosted the credibility of poll-ing organisations, made the media more interested in publishing their surveys and increased the demand from parties and candidates for their services.

Polling, which used to be viewed as just a method of scientific research, is now seen as a tool for gaining political power. This develop-ment was not intended, planned or even anticipated by pollsters, but instead resulted from the changing electoral landscape. The introduction of direct elections in presidential, local executive and now even legis-lative polls means that candidates rather than party machines are the key to political success. Previously, for example, local government lead-ers (governors, district heads and mayors) were elected by members of the local legislative body (Dewan Perwakilan Rakyat Daerah, DPRD). They did not need to be popular or likeable; as long as they had strong networks, lobbying power and funds, they stood a good chance of win-ning over enough DPRD members to gain power. It was the same with candidates for local or national legislatures. Popular candidates were not guaranteed a seat, because seats were determined by the ranking of candidates on the party list. Candidates with a high ranking would win even if they were virtually unknown to the public. Direct elections have changed all that. Local government leaders are now elected by popular vote, and in legislative elections, popular candidates can defeat those who are listed higher on the party list. To win, all candidates now need to strive to be popular with voters.

The leaders of the big parties realised this only after they experienced major losses in the local executive elections held in June 2005. Of 160 elections conducted at that time, only 60 were won by candidates from parties that dominated the local legislatures in the regions concerned. Candidates from the big parties even lost in regions they had tradition-ally dominated. To cite just two examples, the PDIP candidate in the dis-trict of Bangli in Bali, where PDIP had won an absolute majority of votes (54 per cent) in the local legislative elections, was defeated by a margin of 70 per cent to 30 per cent; and in the district of Gorontalo in northern

Sulawesi, the Golkar candidate was defeated by a margin of 64 per cent to 36 per cent, despite the party previously having won 58 per cent of the legislative vote in that district (Eriyanto 2007). Results like these made the June 2005 round of local executive elections look like doomsday for the big political parties. Overconfident, they still relied on the networks and party infrastructure they had used in the old system of party-based elections. They often nominated their own leaders as candidates, even though they were not popular with voters. They learned the hard way that, in direct elections, a candidate's popularity and likeability is what determines victory, not party strength.

After June 2005, many parties changed their approach. Whether they liked it or not, to win they had to support candidates who were popular and likeable. In order to identify such people, they turned to public opinion surveys. At this point polling became a determinant of political power.

The changes Golkar made to the way it selects its candidates for regional government elections provide an illustrative case study.[4] Before the June 2005 local executive elections, the party had an internal regulation (Juklak 01/DPD/Golkar/II/2005) setting out the following process for selecting candidates: the provincial party branch would elicit names of potential candidates from the public and pick three; these three names would then be reported to the national party board, but the final choice would be made by the local branch. In September 2005, the party revised its guidelines. Under the new system, the local branch would still recruit potential candidates and send the list to the central board in Jakarta. However, five months before the election, Golkar would appoint an independent survey organisation to measure the popularity of each potential candidate. The central board would also have a say in deciding which of the top-ranking candidates would be chosen as the party's definitive candidate. The change not only made polling an integral element in the selection process, it also increased the role of central party leaders in selecting truly popular candidates. As a result, the party now tends to nominate people who are not local party leaders and often are not even party members.

Following Golkar, other major parties—notably the Indonesian Democratic Party of Struggle (Partai Demokrasi Indonesia Perjuangan, PDIP), the Democratic Party (Partai Demokrat, PD), the Prosperous Justice Party (Partai Keadilan Sejahtera, PKS) and the National Mandate Party (Partai Amanat Nasional, PAN)—are also relying more heavily on surveys when selecting candidates for local government office. Political surveys have thus dramatically changed how individuals gain power in

---

4   See Eriyanto, Wardoyo and Sudirman (2007) and Nyarwi and Eriyanto (2007).

regional Indonesia. In the past, if somebody wanted to become a local government leader, that person had to concentrate on building support among local party leaders. Now, one has to show strong survey results to get party support.[5] Arguably, survey organisations have become more important than local party branches.

The use of survey methods carried through to the national legislative and presidential elections. In the 2009 legislative elections, many candidates used survey organisations to measure their popularity and support. Surveys were even more important in the presidential elections. Susilo Bambang Yudhoyono secured the biggest coalition of political parties in the lead-up to the July 2009 election, largely because the parties were aware of reliable survey findings saying that he was by far the most popular candidate. Similarly, Yudhoyono still picked Boediono as his running mate despite the economist's low popularity, because surveys showed that the president was so popular he could run with practically anybody and still win.[6]

POLLING AS AN INSTRUMENT OF MOBILISATION?

As well as being a neutral way to measure people's opinions, many Indonesian politicians believe that polling can be an instrument of mobilisation: that polling not only measures but also *influences* opinion. This resonates with a broader debate: the comparative literature distinguishes between the direct and indirect effects of polling (Lang and Lang 1984; Henshel and Johnston 1987). The former refer to the direct effects of the publication of polling results on how voters decide to cast their votes; the latter refer to how leading candidates might benefit by way of greater media coverage, increased donations and other indirect benefits. There are three main positions articulated by experts who debate the direct effects of polling. First, some scholars suggest that polling has no discernible impact and that voters do not use polling results when deciding how to vote (West 1991; Price and Stroud 2005). A second view is that polls have a 'bandwagon' effect, with voters tending to choose candidates or parties that are predicted to win (Skalaban 1988; Ansolabehere and

---

5 There are credible rumours of candidates trying to manipulate this process. For example, many stories have circulated of candidates trying to bribe or otherwise persuade field surveyors to change their survey results. Another tactic is for individual candidates to conduct their own surveys before the formal party-commissioned surveys, and leak the results to the media in the hope of influencing the party's central leaders.

6 'Panggung kecil untuk orang besar' [A small stage for a big man], *Tempo*, 18 May 2009; 'Sihir dari Cikeas' [Magic from Cikeas], *Tempo*, 20 July 2009.

Iyenger 1994). A third position is that polling has an 'underdog' effect, with voters tending to choose candidates or parties that seem likely to lose (Fleitas 1971; Ceci and Kain 1982).

Conventional wisdom in Indonesia holds strongly to the bandwagon effect position. Most political actors believe that candidates or parties who lead in the published polls will find it easier to attract support and win elections. As a result, some parties and candidates use polling not only to measure public support but also to persuade the public and gain elite backing. Candidates tend to publish polling they have commissioned if it shows them leading, but to suppress it if it shows them losing.[7] It is not uncommon for candidates to try to intervene in the polling process to produce a favourable result, with the intervention typically coming either before the survey is conducted, when the client requests a positive finding, or after the survey shows a poor result, when the client asks for the results to be suppressed or manipulated. In wanting to have positive survey results published, candidates seek both indirect and direct benefits: they may want to gain the endorsement of a political party or attract financial support from sponsors, or they may simply want to be seen as strong by voters. Professional survey organisations reject such interventions. But there are undoubtedly some organisations that manipulate polling results for financial reward, endangering the credibility of the survey industry as a whole.

In fact, more research is needed to show, empirically, whether or not the publication of polling results has a significant direct effect on Indonesian voters. One study (Eriyanto 2009) suggests that it has minimal impact, despite politicians' assumptions. But this study did not look at the indirect impacts on party leaders, campaign sponsors, businesspeople and other elite groups. My own feeling is that polling in Indonesia has little direct impact on voters, but a significant indirect impact on such elites. As a result, favourable poll results can produce very positive effects for candidates, as indicated by the many instances when party elites use such polls to make decisions about which candidates to endorse. Businesspeople and sponsors also use polling data when mak-

---

7   One interesting example occurred in the Central Java gubernatorial election in 2008, in which Golkar candidate Bambang Sadono finished second. Before the election, a number of survey organisations had predicted that Sadono would win. He then ran advertisements in the mass media highlighting his lead in the polls, and produced hundreds of banners carrying the same message, in an attempt to win over undecided voters. This belief in the efficacy of surveys can have unhealthy effects, such as when candidates or parties commission surveys that do not use credible methodologies in order to show a lead, and publish the results. In some regions, this has led to a 'war' of surveys, with different organisations publishing starkly differing results.

ing decisions, preferring to finance candidates who are predicted to win. As Fahmi Idris, a Golkar politician and member of the 2009 'success team' of unsuccessful presidential candidate Jusuf Kalla put it:

> So the pattern of donations [for businesspeople] is more or less like this. For instance, let's say they give 10 per cent to one pair of candidates, and 5 per cent to a second pair. Then where does the remaining 85 per cent go? Obviously it goes to the candidate with the biggest chance of winning.[8]

In Indonesia, big donors tend to be fluid and pragmatic in their preferences. In such circumstances, polling can have real impacts on election outcomes by skewing fundraising patterns, which in turn affects media campaigns.

ETHICS AND THE REGULATION OF POLLING ORGANISATIONS

The emergence of a new political market, and the growth of polling organisations to service it, has not been accompanied by the emergence of widely agreed and strong standards of ethical conduct. The polling industry currently resembles the mass media during the boom years after 1998, when the collapse of the Suharto regime's repressive controls suddenly freed up the media market and practically anybody could publish a newspaper. Some who did so created quality products, but many simply pandered to the market for sex and violence.

Similarly, at present, anyone can establish a survey organisation. Some are highly professional but others are questionable. The good ones understand survey methods, know how to conduct scientific surveys and are independent. Others lack these characteristics. Eventually, a process of natural selection should mean that those organisations with good standards and ethics survive while the others lose public trust and vanish. The problem, however, is that few people in both the general public and the political parties understand what goes into producing a high-quality survey. Many believe that all organisations have similar standards, presenting a barrier to the natural selection process.

To make matters worse, there is no agreement about a code of ethics for the profession. Many democratic countries have authoritative associations of polling organisations that produce codes of ethics for their members, establish standards, conduct training and capacity-building programs, evaluate polling activities and apply sanctions when ethi-

---

8 'Wawancara khusus Fahmi Idris: mesin Golkar tak bergerak dukung JK, saya syok' [Fahmi Idris special interview: Golkar political machine didn't work to support JK, I was shocked], *Tempo*, 20 July 2009.

cal breaches occur. In Indonesia there are two national associations, the Indonesian Association for Public Opinion Research (Asosiasi Riset Opini Publik Indonesia, AROPI) and the Indonesian Association for Public Opinion Surveys (Perhimpunan Survei Opini Publik Indonesia, PERSEPI). Each has its own code of ethics, adapted from the code of conduct of the World Association for Public Opinion Research. However, not all polling organisations are members of these associations and agreement has not been reached on some ethical issues.

Several issues that were clarified long ago in countries like the United States are still being debated in Indonesia. One such issue concerns transparency. The American Association for Public Opinion Research (AAPOR) holds that at least two matters must be declared when a polling organisation publishes a survey: the survey's method (sample size, data collection method, accuracy of results and so on), and the identity of the sponsor financing it. Almost all polling organisations in Indonesia declare their methods but only a few declare their sponsors. A second issue concerns how to decide which surveys can be published and which cannot. In the United States and some European countries, a clear distinction is drawn between private and public surveys. Public surveys are generally financed by the polling organisation itself, or by a sponsor such as a funding agency or social body where there can be no suggestion of a conflict of interest. Private surveys are commissioned by clients who then have exclusive rights to the results.

During the 2009 elections in Indonesia, many organisations conducted private surveys (on behalf of candidates or parties), but then published the results, generating a debate about ethics. For example, LSI routinely publicised its surveys, despite the fact that they were funded by Fox Indonesia, the campaign consultant of PD and Susilo Bambang Yudhoyono.[9] These surveys always put PD and Yudhoyono in first place. Other parties denounced this practice as unethical, declaring that privately commissioned polling should never be published. LSI defended itself by saying there was no ethical problem with publishing the survey results because it had used correct methods, and had declared the identity of the sponsor.

THE RISE OF CONSULTANTS AS A POLITICAL FORCE

The changed political landscape has also given rise to a new class of political consultant. In established democracies, consultants play an important

---

9 'LSI disewa tim sukses SBY–Boediono' [LSI hired by SBY–Boediono campaign team], *Republika*, 4 June 2009.

role in elections. In the United States, for example, they first appeared in the 1930s (Sabato 1981) and their influence has grown along with the influence of money, media and individual candidates — as opposed to party machines — in elections (Petracca 1989; Sabato 1989; Dulio 2001). In Indonesia, too, the rise of political consultants has largely been a result of the introduction of candidate-centred elections, and the increasing importance of the mass media during elections.

During the New Order era there were no political consultants in Indonesia, because the minor parties lacked the funds and the conviction even to try to design winning strategies against the Golkar juggernaut. But in 1999, in the first post-Suharto legislative elections, campaign consultants began to play a role. At that time, advertising agencies were the key players. They helped to design parties' mass media campaigns, particularly television advertisements, and even helped to design party logos. With 100 million voters spread across the 2 million square kilometres of the Indonesian archipelago, and with little time to establish themselves, the parties had little alternative but to use advertising and the mass media to reach out to the electorate.

In the 2004 elections, advertising agencies again played an important role as campaign consultants. They helped parties and presidential candidates to design their campaign messages, produce commercials and decide on media placement. Media campaigns now took the place of mass street campaigns, which had been the dominant mode of campaigning during the New Order era (see Heryanto in this volume). One agency that played an important role in 2004 was Hotline Advertising, which helped design Golkar's campaign for the legislative elections as well as that of Susilo Bambang Yudhoyono in the presidential race.

As already noted, changes in electioneering style became especially marked with the introduction of direct elections for local government positions in 2005. With the exception of the 2004 presidential poll, political parties and candidates had no experience of this kind of election, where voters would choose individual candidates directly. Candidates now had to be individually popular with the public if they wanted to succeed, and to achieve this they had to introduce themselves on a massive scale to voters. This imperative made media campaigns crucial, because it was only through the media and advertising that candidates could hope to be recognised by large numbers of voters within a very short time period. And recognition was not enough; candidates also needed to persuade the public that they were likeable and competent.

Lingkaran Survei Indonesia, established by Denny J.A. as a split from LSI, can be considered the first organisation to position itself as a political consultancy in Indonesia. Before this there had been persons or organisations helping the 'success' teams of candidates, but they did not call themselves professional political consultants. Other organisations have followed, including Indo Barometer, Fox Indonesia, Charta Politika, Suara Indonesia and Final Point. Unlike the consultants in the 2004 elections, who generally came from commercial advertising agencies like Hotline Advertising and Matahari Advertising, the new consultants specialised in providing broad political consulting services, not just advertisements and image building. They offered the full range of services needed to secure the victory of a candidate — from strategic planning to conceptualising a candidate's 'vision and mission', from campaigning door to door and designing and organising media campaigns to providing poll monitors on election day.

By the time of the 2009 elections, consultants offering comprehensive campaign packages had become extremely influential. All the big parties and presidential candidates were assisted by such consultants, as were many of the candidates for legislative bodies such as the national parliament (Dewan Perwakilan Rakyat, DPR). The trend is for such consultants to handle virtually all aspects of the campaigns on which they work. This was the case, for example, when Lingkaran Survei Indonesia and Indo Barometer were engaged as campaign consultants in the local leadership elections. It was the same with Fox Indonesia during the legislative and presidential elections in 2009.

Unlike in the United States, where there has long been a trend towards specialisation among political consultants (De Vries 1989; Petracca 1989), in Indonesia most consultants are generalists and do all of the jobs that were traditionally handled by parties. This partly reflects the preferences of candidates. Now that individual popularity is a key determinant of electoral success, many candidates are not party cadres, even though they are nominated for political office by one of the parties. Instead, they have diverse backgrounds in the business community, academia, the NGO world and the like. Their non-party backgrounds often make them more comfortable working outside party structures, which they view as bureaucratic and slow. At least in local government elections, they tend to see the party as providing just a nomination — a ticket to run on — and nothing else.

HOW DO CONSULTANTS HELP CANDIDATES WIN?

It is worth pausing to consider in more detail what political consultants actually do to help their candidates win, and I offer the following observations based largely on personal experience. A key starting point here is to recognise that candidates are most likely to win if they possess two attributes: high *name recognition* (when asked whether they know of the

Table 6.1   Four possible conditions for a candidate's name recognition and likeability

Condition	Name recognition	Likeability
1	Low	Low
2	High	Low
3	Low	High
4	High	High

candidate, a high proportion of voters answer in the affirmative) and high *likeability* (when asked whether they approve of the candidate, a high proportion say yes). Together, these two factors tend to translate into high *electability* (measured in polls by voters indicating that they will vote for the candidate). So the main task of a campaign consultant is to package and promote the candidate to the public in such a way that his or her name recognition and likeability will increase. This can be done in various ways, starting from improving the candidate's physical appearance, enhancing his or her public speaking ability, constructing an appealing program and designing visually appealing campaign materials. Promotion of the candidate can be done through mass rallies or other direct meetings between the candidate and communities, through the use of outdoor media such as banners and posters, and through newspaper, radio, television and internet advertisements.

The first step, however, is always to conduct research to map the strengths and weaknesses of the client compared to rivals. Several kinds of research can be done, but two are most important. First is analysis of existing data, such as demographic data and the results of previous elections in the locality. Second is local public opinion surveys, which can be used to gain a lot of information on, for example, the client's level of name recognition and likeability, the public's evaluation of the incumbent's record and the issues of most significance to voters. Surveys can also be used to map the candidate's strength among various demographics. Using local surveys, campaign consultants can acquire a picture of the problems faced by the client, and his or her strengths and weaknesses compared to competitors. The position of the client in relation to competitors determines the strategy the consultant will employ. Generally, there are four possible conditions a client may experience. These are summarised in Table 6.1.

If the unfortunate client finds him or herself in condition 1 (both name recognition and likeability are low), it becomes imperative to boost the candidate's profile as quickly as possible. One way to do that is to pick a popular, widely known running mate. Another is to provide information about the candidate extensively to voters using advertisements and door-to-door campaigning. Despite the difficulties, both approaches can be successful. Thus, during the 2008 gubernatorial election in Central Java, the successful candidate, Bibit Waluyo (supported by PDIP), was initially relatively unknown and had very low electability. His popularity and electability were increased by partnering him with a well-known candidate, the head of Kebumen district, Rustriningsih, as his deputy gubernatorial candidate. In the 2008 North Sumatra election, the victory of Samsul Arifin, who was initially little known beyond Langkat where he was district head, was made possible by a massive promotional campaign that increased his name recognition in all regions of the province.

In condition 2 (high name recognition, low approval), the client does not need to make him or herself better known to the public. Instead, the campaign consultant needs to change how the public evaluates the client, by improving the capability and competence of the candidate in the eyes of voters. This is done by selecting issues that will resonate with the public, and which are then 'attached' to the candidate's campaign and promoted massively among voters. The victory of Eko Maulana Ali in the 2007 Bangka Belitung provincial election is an example. Maulana Ali's name recognition was high when he began the race, but his approval ratings were below those of the incumbent, Hudarni Rani. To overcome this hurdle, Maulana Ali's campaign focused heavily on popular issues such as free education and health care, dramatically increasing his electability.

Candidates are in condition 3 if they have low name recognition but high approval among the voters who do know of them. Here the approach is simply to promote the candidate to the voters as much as possible, of course stressing his or her capability. An illustration is the victory of Syahrul Yasin Limpo as governor in the 2008 South Sulawesi election. Before the election, he was far less well known than Amin Syam, the incumbent governor. But Yasin Limpo had the potential to achieve high electability. He was young and energetic, and he had the advantage of voters' disappointment with the incumbent. A campaign of advertisements and other electoral mobilisation increased Yasin Limpo's name recognition, thus boosting his electability.

A political consultant's job is easiest when a candidate is in condition 4 (high name recognition and high approval). In such circumstances the candidate will already be in a leading position, being both well known and well liked by voters. The strategy here is simply to maintain voter support and minimise the possibility of voters shifting to competitors.

The strategy political consultants use will also depend on whether or not the client is an incumbent. Incumbency confers definite advantages: incumbents are typically better known by the public and they have

Table 6.2   Three possible positions for an incumbent seeking re-election

Position of incumbent	Satisfaction with past work	Voters' stated intention to re-elect incumbent
Strong	High (>70%)	High (>70%)
Moderate	Moderate (50–70%)	Moderate (50–70%)
Weak	Low (<50%)	Low (<50%)

access to resources such as political networks, funding and the bureaucracy. However, incumbency can also confer disadvantages: incumbents are often the target of public criticism and negative campaigns, particularly if they have not performed strongly in office, as is often the case.

Table 6.2 illustrates three possible positions incumbents may find themselves in when seeking re-election, and which will determine the strategy their consultants choose. First, if the incumbent is in a strong position—more than 70 per cent of voters are satisfied with the incumbent's past work—and there is no rival figure who can match the person in capacity, then the desire of the voters to re-elect the incumbent will be very high. In such a situation, the consultant just needs to maintain or even increase the candidate's popularity by communicating his or her achievements to the voters. There are many examples of victories by incumbent governors in this situation in recent years, including those of Ismeth Abdullah (Riau Islands), Fadel Muhammad (Gorontalo), Zulkifli Nurdin (Jambi) and Rusli Zaenal (Riau). Most voters were satisfied with their work, and they did not face strong competitors.

An incumbent with a satisfaction rating of between 50 and 70 per cent will be in a moderate position. In such circumstances the most important factor is the strength of the rival candidates. The incumbent will be in a difficult position if there is a strong rival who is able to attract dissatisfied voters. The strategy used by campaign consultants here is to guide incumbents to improve their performance in government and then communicate their achievements, and to try to convince voters that the incumbent is still the best choice available. One good example is the 2006 re-election of Ratu Atut Chosiyah as governor of Banten. Voter satisfaction with the governor was not high but she was helped by a lack of strong competitors. In the end, voters still considered her the best among the available choices to lead the province.

An incumbent's position is weak if voter satisfaction and voters' stated intention to re-elect the individual are both below 50 per cent. In such circumstances, a campaign consultant will try to improve the incumbent's performance during the remainder of his or her tenure and then publicise those achievements, with a promise of even better results in the future. One example is the 2007 victory of Thaib Armaiyn as governor of North Maluku, despite low voter satisfaction and the emergence of a very strong competitor (Abdul Gafur).

To summarise, campaign consultants carry out work on behalf of their clients in two phases. In the first phase they identify a client's strong and weak points, in relation to those of competitors, by means of surveys. In the next stage, the survey results are used to help design a winning political strategy. Each client will have a different set of strengths and weaknesses and a different mix of name recognition, likeability and electability, and these will inform the campaign strategy, but a set of tried and tested formulas for every situation is already beginning to emerge.

CONSULTANTS: CHALLENGING THE POLITICAL PARTIES?

Not surprisingly, many political party activists are alarmed by the growing prominence of consultants. They say, rightly, that consultants are impinging on, or even taking over, many jobs that were previously done by the parties: candidate recruitment, campaign theme development, advertisement production, door-to-door campaigning, fundraising and so on. Some party officials say that by doing these things consultants are weakening the parties. For example, in 2009 there was open conflict between Fox Indonesia, the consultant running the Yudhoyono–Boediono campaign, and the party that had nominated the pair, PD. Fox Indonesia took on a large number of key campaign tasks, including preparing the candidates for the televised debates, organising campaign events, and coordinating and designing campaign advertising, messages and slogans. The scale of the work done by Fox Indonesia created envy and complaints among PD leaders, who felt they had been sidelined.[10]

In the United States, there is a long-running debate about the relationship between the rise of consultants and the decline of parties. Some analysts see the expanding role of political consultants as the cause of the decline (Sabato 1981; Medvic and Lenart 1997). Others disagree (Kolodny and Logan 1998; Dulio 2001) and view the rise of political consultants rather as a natural effect of candidate-centred elections. These analysts say that campaigns that focus on image, advertising and the media need

---

10 'Elektabilitas SBY anjlok, dominasi Fox bikin kesal partai pendukung' [SBY's electability drops, SBY's coalition party protests Fox's dominant role], *detikNews*, 29 June 2009; 'Fox diprotes, kader parpol mulai nggak nyaman' [Protest against Fox, party officials begin to feel uneasy], *Rakyat Merdeka*, 30 June 2009.

specialist expertise, which is lacking in parties, and that political parties realise this fact and therefore welcome political consultants. In this view, consultants and parties complement rather than conflict with each other.

Despite the differences in opinion, most experts agree that, overall, political consultants are crucial in helping parties secure electoral victory (Thurber 1998: 147), and that they are not entirely eliminating the role of the parties. Four arguments are usually put forward to sustain this position. First, scholars such as Dulio (2001) argue that parties realise that the new style of elections requires special expertise and therefore delegate election-related work to consultants. Even so, they point out, there is constant interaction and communication between consultants and the parties, and consultants' decisions are always discussed with party leaders. Second, scholars note that most consultants in the United States have backgrounds as party members, and have typically worked as party organisers or volunteers before switching to the consulting profession. They never become entirely detached from their original parties, and much political consultancy work remains highly partisan. Third, the tendency towards specialisation among political consultants (De Vries 1989: 21) creates a proliferation of small consultancies, each with a unique skill set, with the result that individually these organisations remain much weaker than the large and powerful party organisations. Fourth, party infrastructure continues to be important for securing electoral victories. Consultants may plan strategies, but the support of the party machine is usually critical to provide the funds, networks of volunteers and voter profiles that candidates need in order to win (Herrnson 1992; Cantor and Herrnson 1997).

The trends in Indonesia are precisely the opposite of these developments in the United States. Rather than having party backgrounds, for example, most political consultants in Indonesia are independent and unaffiliated. They are mostly political experts (Denny J.A., Muhammad Qodari, Rizal Malarangeng), academics (Bima Arya Sugiarto, Effendi Ghazali, Sukardi Rinakit) or advertising or public relations professionals (Subijakto, Miranti Abidin, Ipang Wahdi). Their non-party backgrounds make it easy for them to work with any party or candidate. In one local election they may support a candidate from Golkar, and in the next support one from PDIP. In the legislative election they may work for PDIP, but in the presidential election in the same year support the PD candidate, and so on. This elasticity naturally creates suspicion among party members.

Moreover, political consultancy organisations in Indonesia are generalists, and they are usually big. Most do all campaign-related jobs for a candidate, from advertisement production to campaign scheduling, from debate preparation to devising vision and mission statements, from door-to-door campaigning to fundraising. This is different from the United States, where candidates usually hire a number of specialists to do different jobs. In Indonesia most candidates hire only one consultant, giving that consultant great influence over the campaign. At the same time, political consultants are reluctant to use party infrastructure, distrusting its professionalism and seeing little of value in it. Instead, they build their own infrastructure and networks and recruit their own volunteers.

Although it is much too early to argue that consultants are displacing the parties in Indonesia, they are nevertheless taking over some significant functions that used to be performed by the parties, rather than being merely complementary to them. Sometimes the consultant has a position and status that is above the party, especially if the candidate trusts the consultant more than the party (as was apparently the case with Yudhoyono and his preference for Fox Indonesia over PD in 2009). Not surprisingly, such developments create tensions and conflicts between consultants and the political parties.

CONCLUSION

In pointing to the rise of survey organisations and consultants as influential players in the new political landscape in Indonesia, I have emphasised the influence of the new system of direct, candidate-focused elections. By shifting the focus from party machines to individuals, direct elections have elevated the role of the mass media, advertising, news management, public relations and similar campaign techniques. This change in turn has propelled survey organisations and consultants to the centre of political life. The new system demands special expertise in such fields as mapping voter preferences through surveys, producing slick advertisements that resonate with popular opinion, and building effective and appealing public images for candidates. Such expertise is lacking within the parties, which in Indonesia have trained people in the techniques of political mobilisation and networking rather than managing public opinion. Though the political parties are still the crucial building blocks of Indonesian politics, their role in designing and managing political campaigns is increasingly being overshadowed by the new class of political professionals.

It is possible to debate critically the implications of the rise of professional pollsters and consultants for Indonesian democracy, and we can find similar debates in many democratic countries. Some people may see their rise as involving not merely the professionalisation of politics but also its depoliticisation, with the new emphasis on slick campaign management and the individual making politics more superficial, elevating image over content, and marginalising the role of ideology, a factor that was once crucial in Indonesian politics. Others may say that the growing influence of a small group of highly trained professionals shuts the door even more firmly on political participation by ordinary citizens, who are normally recruited into political life through the political parties. In response, other people—and I count myself among their number— believe that the increased professionalisation of campaigns is in fact making Indonesian politics *more* responsive to the views and aspirations of ordinary citizens. Indonesian polling organisations and consultants invest great expertise and effort in investigating the views and political preferences of the population, and in encouraging politicians to respond accordingly. What could be more democratic than that?

The growing influence of this new political class does not mean, how-ever, that there are no challenges ahead. The biggest challenge for survey organisations and political consultants in Indonesia is to improve their professionalism. Survey organisations must be able to deal definitively with the accusations of unethical conduct that have dogged the industry for several years; political consultants need to achieve a new, balanced working relationship with parties. Dealing with such problems will be crucial for the political professionals if they want to become a respected part of Indonesia's new political landscape. If they fail, they may still end up undermining the credibility of Indonesian democracy rather than enhancing it.

REFERENCES

AGB Nielsen Media Research (2009), 'Pemilu mengangkat popularitas berita' [Election raises popularity of news], *AGB Nielsen Media Research* 34, June.
Ansolabehere, Stephen and Shanto Iyenger (1994), 'Of horseshoes and horse races: experimental studies of the impact of poll results on electoral behav-ior', *Political Communication* 11: 413–30.
Cantor, David M. and Paul S. Herrnson (1997), 'Party campaign activity and party unity in the U.S. House of Representatives', *Legislative Studies Quarterly* 22(3): 393–415.
Ceci, Stephen J. and Edward L. Kain (1982), 'Jumping on the bandwagon with the underdog: the impact of attitude polls on polling behavior', *Public Opinion Quarterly* 46: 228–42.
De Vries, Walter (1989), 'American campaign consulting; trends and concerns', *PS: Political Science and Politics* 22(1): 21–5.
Dulio, David A. (2001), 'For better or worse? How political consultants are chang-ing elections in the United States', PhD thesis, Faculty of the School of Public Affairs, American University, Washington DC.
Eriyanto (2007), 'Pilkada dan penguasaan partai politik' [Local elections and political parties' control], *Kajian Bulanan Lingkaran Survei Indonesia* 3(July): 1–16.

Eriyanto (2009), 'Efek polling pada pemilih; studi eksprerimental publikasi hasil polling pada perilaku pemilih pada pilkada dan pemilu presiden' [The impact of polling on voters: an experimental study of polling results and voter behaviour in the local and presidential elections], MA thesis, Department of Communication, Faculty of Social and Political Science, University of Indonesia, Jakarta, August.

Eriyanto, Emanuel Lalang Wardoyo and Aa Sudirman (2007), 'Strategi aktor pro demokrasi dalam pilkada: studi pencalonan dan pertarungan kandidat dalam pilkada Manggarai, Belitung Timur dan Serdang Bedagai' [The strategies of pro-democracy actors in local elections: a study of candidate recruitment and competition in the Manggarai, East Belitung and Serdang Bedagai local elections], research report, DEMOS, Jakarta.

Fleitas, Daniel (1971), 'Bandwagon and underdog effects in minimal-information elections', *American Political Science Review* 65: 434–8.

Henshel, Richard L. and William Johnston (1987), 'The emergence of bandwagon effects: a theory', *Sociological Quarterly* 28: 493–511.

Herrnson, Paul S. (1992), 'Campaign professionalism and fundraising in congressional elections', *Journal of Politics* 54(3): 859–70.

Kolodny, Robin and Angela Logan (1998), 'Political consultants and the extension of party goals', *PS: Political Science and Politics* 31(2): 155–9.

Lang, Kurt and Gladys Lang (1984), 'The impact of polls on public opinion', *Annals of the American Academy of Political and Social Science* 472: 129–41.

Medvic, Stephen and Silvo Lenart (1997), 'The influence of political consultants in the 1992 congressional elections', *Legislative Studies Quarterly* 22(1): 61–77.

Mietzner, Marcus (2009), 'Political opinion polling in post-authoritarian Indonesia: catalyst or obstacle to democratic consolidation?', *Bijdragen tot de Taal-, Land- en Volkenkunde* 165(1): 95–126.

Nimmo, Dan (1976), 'Political image makers and the mass media', *Annals of the American Academy of Political and Social Science* 427: 33–44.

Nyarwi, Ahmad and Eriyanto (2007), 'Siasat partai politik dan strategi pencalonan' [Political parties' tactics and strategies for nomination], *Kajian Bulanan Lingkaran Survei Indonesia* 3(July): 17–24.

Petracca, Mark (1989), 'Political consultants and democratic governance', *PS: Political Science and Politics* 22(1): 11–14.

Price, Vincent and Natalie Jomini Stroud (2005), 'Public attitudes toward polls: evidence from the 2000 U.S. presidential election', *International Journal of Public Opinion Research* 18: 393–421.

Sabato, Larry J. (1981), *The Rise of Political Consultants: New Ways of Winning Elections*, Basic Books, New York NY.

Sabato, Larry J. (1989), 'Political influence, the news media and campaign consultants', *PS: Political Science and Politics* 22(1): 15–17.

Skalaban, Andrew (1988), 'Do the polls affect elections? Some 1980 evidence', *Political Behavior* 10: 136–50.

Thurber, James A. (1998), 'The study of campaign consultants: a subfield in search of theory', *PS: Political Science and Politics* 31(2): 145–9.

West, Darrell (1991), 'Polling effects in election campaigns', *Political Behavior* 13: 151–63.

7 THE INDONESIAN PARTY SYSTEM AFTER THE 2009 ELECTIONS: TOWARDS STABILITY?

Dirk Tomsa

When Indonesia's long-time ruler Suharto fell in 1998, very few observers expected that the country would be able to build a stable democracy. Most predictions for Indonesia at the time were gloomy, ranging from a quick return to military dictatorship and continued paralysis to the complete break-up of the state. Yet in 2009, just a little over 10 years later, Indonesia stood out as the most democratic country in Southeast Asia (Freedom House 2009). Despite the persistence of some severe democratic deficits — including widespread corruption and continuing limitations in the application of the rule of law (Davidson 2009) — the world's most populous Muslim state has reached a number of remarkable democratic milestones since 1998, especially with regard to what the World Bank calls 'voice and accountability'.[1] Perhaps most strikingly, elections have been widely accepted as the only legitimate means to distribute formal political power, even in those parts of the country that experienced separatist or communal violence in the early years of the transition (Tomsa 2009a; Palmer in this volume).

---

1 'Voice and accountability' is one of six indicators used by the World Bank in its Worldwide Governance Indicators (WGI) project to evaluate the socio-political and economic progress of states. According to the WGI website (http://info. worldbank.org/governance/wgi/), this particular indicator measures 'the extent to which a country's citizens are able to participate in selecting their government, as well as freedom of expression, freedom of association, and a free media'. See Diamond in this volume for more details.

The successful entrenchment of elections, however, has somewhat distracted from the poor performance of the political parties that contest them. Not many scholarly analyses of Indonesian party politics have been published so far, but the few available works have been mostly unfavourable, to say the least. One of the first sustained critiques came from Vedi Hadiz (2004: 619), whose neo-Marxist analysis of post-New Order Indonesia described political parties as little more than 'expressions of shifting alliances of predatory interests'. Others have used institutionalisation theory to explore the weaknesses of the parties and the party system (Johnson Tan 2002, 2006; Tomsa 2008). The negative views of Indonesian parties were perhaps best summed up by Carothers (2006: 175), who asserted that:

> Indonesia's main political parties remain almost archetypical embodiments of the standard lament about parties—they are intensely leader-centric organizations dominated by a small circle of elite politicians who hold onto their positions atop parties seemingly indefinitely, are immersed in patronage politics, and who are far more devoted to political intrigues in the capital than the prosaic work of trying to listen to and represent a base of constituents.

More recently, however, some scholars have sought to counter or at least modify the prevailing consensus on the poor state of Indonesia's political parties. Mietzner (2008a), for example, has highlighted the centripetal tendencies in the party system, arguing that the lack of ideological polarisation among Indonesian parties has facilitated the stabilisation of the overall political system. Similarly, Ufen (2008a: 342) in his comparative study of party and party system institutionalisation in Indonesia, Thailand and the Philippines concluded that 'a fair degree of party and party system institutionalisation has been achieved in Indonesia', although he cautioned against too much optimism. Both Mietzner and Ufen have argued that analyses of Indonesia's parties and party system cannot be conducted effectively (and realistically) without measuring them against comparable countries in the Southeast Asian region; in that comparison, they argue, Indonesia's party politics have fared rather well.

Against this background, the 2009 parliamentary and presidential elections have delivered mixed messages for analysts of Indonesian party politics. On the one hand, parties like those founded by controversial former generals Prabowo Subianto and Wiranto failed to attract widespread support, and the stability of the overall party system seems to have increased (Mietzner 2009a; Sherlock 2009). On the other hand, the results of the elections also showed that almost all of the established major parties—that is, those represented in parliament since the first post-Suharto elections in 1999—have continued to lose votes, thereby further reaffirming the ongoing dissatisfaction with many of the main parties among large parts of the population. As a consequence of these two somewhat antagonistic trends, contemporary Indonesian party politics seems to represent a paradox: while the party system has apparently become stronger, most of the parties that constitute the system have become weaker.

This chapter seeks to explain the dynamics behind this paradoxical situation. It discusses the state of Indonesian party politics in five sections. The first provides a brief overview of the 2009 parliamentary election results and evaluates their impact on Indonesia's party system. The discussion emphasises that the apparent party system stability reflected in the election results was not achieved through greater party institutionalisation, but first and foremost through institutional engineering. The second section of the chapter reviews the reasons for the decline of Indonesia's 'core parties', that is, the six parties that have been represented in all post-1999 parliaments. In almost all of these parties, internal frictions, programmatic shallowness, corrupt behaviour and an increasing tendency towards 'presidentialisation' have undermined the effectiveness of party organisation. The third section highlights how the Prosperous Justice Party (Partai Keadilan Sejahtera, PKS) has so far been able to buck the trend followed by the other core parties. However, while arguably still the best institutionalised of the Indonesian parties, even PKS has not been entirely immune to some of the damaging features that have characterised its more conventional counterparts. The fourth section of the chapter assesses whether an institutionalised party system can be based on poorly institutionalised parties. The final section presents an outlook for the prospects of party and party system institutionalisation in the years ahead, suggesting that unless the parties develop stronger organisational roots, the party system will remain volatile.

THE 2009 ELECTIONS: CONSOLIDATING THE PARTY SYSTEM?

Indonesia's third legislative election after the end of the New Order was held in April 2009. It was organised far less professionally than the two previous polls in 1999 and 2004 (see Schmidt in this volume), but overall it still fulfilled most of the criteria for a free and fair election, and was widely regarded as a genuine reflection of the political preferences of the people. Two changes to the electoral rules had major ramifications for the outcome of the poll. First, the switch from a partially open party list system to a fully open party list system, mandated by the Constitutional Court in 2008, paved the way for unprecedented levels of intra-party competition, as legislative candidates placed lower on the party lists sud-

Table 7.1   Legislative election results, 2009

Party	Share of vote (%)	Seats in the DPR (no.)	Share of seats (%)
Partai Demokrat (PD)	20.8	148	26.4
Golkar	14.4	106	18.9
Partai Demokrasi Indonesia Perjuangan (PDIP)	14.0	94	16.8
Partai Keadilan Sejahtera (PKS)	7.9	57	10.2
Partai Amanat Nasional (PAN)	6.0	46	8.2
Partai Persatuan Pembangunan (PPP)	5.3	38	6.8
Partai Kebangkitan Bangsa (PKB)	4.9	28	5.0
Partai Gerakan Indonesia Raya (Gerindra)	4.5	26	4.6
Partai Hati Nurani Rakyat (Hanura)	3.8	17	3.0
Other	18.4	0	0.0
Total	**100.0**	**560**	**100.0**

Source: Data from the General Elections Commission (Komisi Pemilihan Umum, KPU).

denly stood a genuine chance of being elected.[2] Second, a parliamentary threshold was introduced for the first time, barring all parties that failed to reach 2.5 per cent of the vote from winning seats in parliament. The effects of this reform in particular were immediately visible in the election result. Of the 38 parties that contested the 560 seats in the House of Representatives (Dewan Perwakilan Rakyat, DPR), only nine were successful in their bids for seats in parliament (see Table 7.1).

In one of the first scholarly assessments of the ballots, Mietzner (2009a: 17) has pointed out that 'while the 2009 parliamentary elections have led to some significant changes in the strength of the various parties, the party system as such has remained remarkably stable'. In other words, volatility in the party system—that is, the degree of change in support for each party from one election to the next—has remained high,[3] but voters have mostly switched between the major parties rather

---

2 It should be noted, however, that in the end very few low-ranked candidates managed to capitalise on this reform and actually win seats. Overall, only 30 of the 560 elected candidates won their seats from a list place lower than fourth.

3 Volatility is commonly calculated 'by adding the net change in percentage of seats or votes gained or lost by each party from one election to the next, then

than giving their support to a completely new party. Coupled with the effects of the new threshold regulation, this has led to an 'institutionally induced concentration in the party system' (Mietzner 2009a: 8). Indeed, compared to the 2004–2009 period, the absolute number of parties represented in parliament shrank from 17 to 9, while the effective number of parties fell from 8.6 to 6.2.[4] Perhaps even more significantly, there is now a 'discernible core' of six parties—Golkar, the Indonesian Democratic Party of Struggle (Partai Demokrasi Indonesia Perjuangan, PDIP), the United Development Party (Partai Persatuan Pembangunan, PPP), the National Mandate Party (Partai Amanat Nasional, PAN), the People's Awakening Party (Partai Kebangkitan Bangsa, PKB) and PKS—that have been continuously represented in the Indonesian parliament since the first post-Suharto election in 1999.[5] According to Stephen Wolinetz (2006), the existence of such a 'discernible core' may already be sufficient for a party system to be regarded as institutionalised so long as the parties interact with each other on a regular basis.

There is little doubt that Indonesia's major post-Suharto parties have indeed interacted regularly.[6] It is less clear, however, whether these parties possess the institutional capacity to sustain the stability of the party system in the long term. A closer look at the election results of the six core parties over the 10 years from 1999 to 2009 illustrates that, with the exception of PKS, all have consistently lost votes since 1999 (see Table 7.2). Most dramatically, PDIP, PPP and PKB saw their shares of the overall vote more than halve over the course of the three elections, while the share of Golkar remained fairly stable between 1999 and 2004 but slumped below 15 per cent in 2009. PAN's decline has been the most moderate, but it also started from the lowest support base in 1999.

REASONS FOR THE DECLINE OF THE CORE PARTIES

The reasons for the decline in support for all core parties except PKS are manifold and of course differ from party to party. Nevertheless, a few common features can be identified as key explanatory variables for these

---

dividing by two' (Mainwaring and Scully 1995: 6). In Indonesia, volatility stands at just under 30 for the change that occurred between the 2004 and 2009 elections. This is slightly higher than for the 1999–2004 period.

4 The effective number of parties is calculated by squaring each party's share of seats or votes, adding all of these squares, and then dividing 1.00 by this number. See Laakso and Taagepera (1979) for details.

5 In 1999, PKS ran under the name Partai Keadilan (Justice Party).

6 In fact, many observers have expressed concern that this interaction may be too regular and too close (see below).

Table 7.2   Election results of the six core parties, 1999–2009 (%)

Party	1999	2004	2009
Golkar	22.4	21.6	14.4
Partai Demokrasi Indonesia Perjuangan (PDIP)	33.7	18.5	14.0
Partai Keadilan Sejahtera (PKS)	1.4	7.3	7.9
Partai Amanat Nasional (PAN)	7.1	6.4	6.0
Partai Persatuan Pembangunan (PPP)	10.7	8.2	5.3
Partai Kebangkitan Bangsa (PKB)	12.6	10.6	4.9

Source: Tomsa (2008: 14); Mietzner (2009a: 8); data from the General Elections Commission (Komisi Pemilihan Umum, KPU).

parties' deteriorating performance at the ballot box. Among the most prominent are a lack of organisational coherence and programmatic distinctiveness, repeated involvement in corruption and money politics, and the ever-growing personalisation of politics in Indonesia. In addition, the parties' poor public image is further shaped and reinforced by an often sensationalist media that seems keen to incessantly highlight all of the above-mentioned problems.

De-alignment: internal frictions and programmatic shallowness

First, all five parties have failed to capitalise on the favourable starting conditions they enjoyed shortly after Suharto's fall to build strong party organisations with easily identifiable core values. As a result, there have been clearly discernible signs of de-alignment, that is, a process in which voters detach themselves from their partisan choices without defining new preferences (Ufen 2008b). Back in 1999, parties like PDIP, PKB and PAN may have been new legal entities, but they all could rely on established organisational infrastructures. They had either inherited old party networks from the New Order and previous regimes (as in the case of PDIP) or were able to mobilise support through the religious mass organisations with which they were affiliated — PKB, for example, was effectively the political arm of Nahdlatul Ulama (NU) and PAN had close ties with Muhammadiyah. Due to these historical connections, they also represented distinct socio-political values like secular nationalism (PDIP), traditionalist Islam (PKB) and modernist Islam (PAN). Similarly, Golkar and PPP could fall back on institutional and semi-ideological foundations set during the New Order that provided them with important if somewhat artificial roots in society.

But following the 1999 election, in which these five parties alone won a combined share of the vote of more than 86 per cent, opportunities to build on existing strengths were squandered as factionalism and ineffective leadership gradually eroded the solidity of the parties. In 2004, many voters responded to the parties' problems by switching to the Democratic Party (Partai Demokrat, PD) and to PKS (Tomsa 2008: 152 ff.), but the leaders of the core parties largely ignored these early warning signs and initiated very little change. Indeed, in the run-up to the 2009 elections, all five parties were still — or again — beset by virtually the same troubles as in 2004. While Golkar and PAN tussled over the best strategy for nominating a presidential or vice-presidential candidate, PPP remained split between traditionalists and modernists, and PKB was embroiled in yet another power struggle between supporters of the party's founder Abdurrahman Wahid and his rivals, this time successfully led by his own nephew, Muhaimin Iskandar.

In view of these internal problems, it is hardly surprising that the parties spent little time sharpening their programmatic profiles. Even though Golkar and PDIP have conventionally been described as secular, and PPP, PAN and PKB as Islamic (to varying degrees), none of these parties have maintained a clearly identifiable corporate identity beyond these labels. Instead, all parties seem to have embraced — either explicitly or implicitly — the new catchphrase of being 'religious–nationalist' (see Platzdasch 2009). Political values derived from long-existing social cleavages, which were still somewhat discernible in 1999, have been diluted over the years, particularly because of the inclusion of nearly all parties in the various multi-party coalition cabinets since 1999. In the run-up to the 2009 elections, campaign strategists found it practically impossible to position their parties against their competitors, as all except PDIP were represented in Susilo Bambang Yudhoyono's first United Indonesia Cabinet. As a consequence, during the 2009 election campaign the majority of parties were essentially indistinguishable in their promises to voters. Tellingly, the only party that did remain outside cabinet, PDIP, tried hard to capitalise on its perceived 'opposition' status but failed to do so. This was partly due to the popularity of many government policies, but also because PDIP failed to advance credible alternative policy suggestions.

Corruption and money politics

The core parties have also done themselves no favours by repeatedly getting involved in corruption scandals. Unable to raise funds through regular means, Indonesian parties have routinely engaged in a plethora of illicit fundraising activities to improve their financial situations (Mietzner 2008b). The prevalence of such corrupt practices has been a recurrent theme since the early days of the post-Suharto era, but the problems became particularly apparent after the Corruption Eradication Commission (Komisi Pemberantasan Korupsi, KPK) began to specifically target bribery cases in parliament as Yudhoyono's first term drew to a close. Between May 2008 and October 2009, several lawmakers were convicted and sentenced to jail terms for their involvement in corruption. And while there is a general consensus that corruption in the DPR is systemic and affects all parties, it is perhaps no coincidence that the majority of politicians found guilty in 2008 and 2009 were members of the established core parties. Among them were Saleh Djasit, Anthony Zeidra Abidin and Hamka Yandhu from Golkar, Noor Adenan Razak and Abdul Hadi Djamal from PAN, Al-Amin Nasution from PPP and Yusuf Erwin Faishal from PKB.

Its bold investigations have earned the KPK a lot of respect among the Indonesian public and foreign observers, but the parties have increasingly viewed it as a major threat to their vested interests. Their representatives in parliament have sought to weaken the commission by delaying budget approvals and sponsoring new, less effective, legislation for an Anti-Corruption Court. Moreover, when in late 2009 two deputy chairs of the commission became the targets of a dubious police investigation, party politicians were accused of siding with the police against the KPK.[7] This further reinforced the widely held opinion that, in the fight against corruption, political parties are primarily part of the problem rather than part of the solution.

Closely related to the perpetual problem of corruption is the increasing commercialisation of electoral politics. This trend has not only affected the image of Indonesia's parties, but also transformed the role they play in the recruitment of political leaders. The need to mobilise huge amounts of money in order to run for parliament or local executive posts such as governor, mayor or district head has made it ever more difficult for ordinary citizens to become involved in politics. Accordingly, more and more wealthy entrepreneurs have entered party politics in recent years, often at the expense of more professional and committed, but less well-off, party cadres. At the national level, businesspeople have dominated the corridors of power in parliament and have taken over the chairs of major parties such as Golkar and PAN. At the local level, this process has been accentuated further by the introduction in 2005 of direct local elections, which have frequently been won by entrepreneurs and entrenched bureaucrats. As a result, the widespread public impression of parties as mere vehicles for power-hungry and self-interested elites

---

7　See, for example, 'Lawmakers seen on the side of police in KPK conflict', *Jakarta Globe*, 6 November 2009.

has been further reinforced, as can be seen from the results of numerous public opinion surveys.[8]

The presidentialisation of party politics and the rise of personalistic parties

A third major factor in the decline of the core parties is what Ufen (2008b) has called the 'presidentialisation' of Indonesian parties. The term refers to the increasing personalisation of Indonesian politics, which has complemented the process of de-alignment described above. Even though charismatic leaders already played an important role in the 1999 election, the importance of personalistic politics was taken to a new level with the introduction of direct presidential elections in 2004 and the subsequent extension of direct elections to governors, mayors and district heads in the following year (Mujani and Liddle 2007).

Ironically, the institutional changes that stimulated this process of presidentialisation were crafted by the very parties that are now suffering the worst damage from this development. Golkar and PPP, for example, were heavily involved in negotiating the presidential election bill in 2003, but these parties never had charismatic leaders and consequently failed to capitalise on the presidentialisation trend. To some extent, they believed that voters could still be mobilised easily through party machines. However, Golkar in particular learned that this was a serious miscalculation when its candidates were roundly defeated in the 2004 and 2009 presidential elections. In contrast to Golkar and PPP, parties like PDIP, PAN and PKB seemed reasonably well positioned for direct elections, as they were initially dominated by strong charismatic leaders with fairly large pools of loyal supporters. But by 2009 these leaders had either retired from politics (Amien Rais), estranged themselves from their parties and their former followers (Abdurrahman Wahid) or simply lost much of their mass appeal (Megawati Sukarnoputri). Struggling to compensate for the loss of their leaders, these three parties—just like Golkar and PPP—had difficulty coming to terms with the new electoral dynamics.

Where the core parties failed, others stepped in. PD led the way in 2004, demonstrating that it was possible to create a party from scratch without paying much attention to organisational structures or political ideas. From the beginning the party's identity was intrinsically tied to the presidential ambitions of Yudhoyono, and its huge gains in 2009 were

---

8   In a survey conducted in November 2008, more than half of the respondents (58 per cent) said that no Indonesian party was free of corruption, and 38 per cent opined that no party paid attention to the people's needs (LSI 2008).

much more a reflection of the president's popularity than the performance of the party as such.[9] Inspired by PD's successes, others were quick to follow. Shortly after the 2004 elections, two controversial former generals, Wiranto and Prabowo Subianto, founded their own parties, the People's Conscience Party (Partai Hati Nurani Rakyat, Hanura) and the Greater Indonesia Movement Party (Partai Gerakan Indonesia Raya, Gerindra). The only function of these parties was to provide a political vehicle for their ambitious leaders, both former Suharto protégés. Despite immense financial investments by the two ex-generals, however, the two new parties could not emulate PD's achievements. While PD easily won the 2009 elections with more than 20 per cent of the vote, Gerindra and Hanura each had to make do with less than 5 per cent.

There were many reasons for the relatively feeble performance of the two newcomers. Most importantly, their populist campaign slogans — which echoed anti-capitalist and anti-globalisation themes — were no match for PD's main drawcard: the government's timely provision of direct cash payouts to the poor shortly before the election. Since PD was largely synonymous with the government, the popularity of the cash payments won over voters who might otherwise have been attracted to Gerindra (Tomsa 2009b). But even though the election results of Gerindra and Hanura were major disappointments for Prabowo and Wiranto, the fact that the two parties did pass the electoral threshold pointed to the continued strength of the trend towards presidentialisation.

The emergence of presidentialised parties in Indonesia's post-1998 polity is closely linked to the ever-growing importance of political consultancies and the mass media, especially television. Professional consultants were basically unheard-of during the 1999 campaign, but have been omnipresent in all national and local elections since 2004 (Mietzner 2009b; Qodari, this volume). While some old party stalwarts from the established core parties seem to remain suspicious of the usefulness of such consultants, parties like PD and Gerindra have fully embraced them and used their services extensively in the 2009 campaign. The spin doctors, some of whom were hired from abroad, communicated their carefully crafted messages through thousands of political advertisements in the media. In the first quarter of 2009 alone, the media research institute ACNielsen documented more than 20,000 party advertisements spread over 19 different television channels,[10] a massive increase from the 2004 campaign. More than half of these were PD and Golkar spots,

---

9   Survey data have shown a strong correlation between levels of support for Yudhoyono and support for PD. See Mujani and Liddle in this volume.

10   'Demokrat dominasi iklan TV, Golkar di koran' [PD dominates advertisements on TV, Golkar in the newspapers], *Vivanews*, 28 April 2009.

but Gerindra also spent big on its media campaign. According to ACN-ielsen estimates, the three top spenders in that period paid about Rp 185 billion ($18.5 million, Golkar), Rp 123 billion ($12.3 million, PD) and Rp 66 billion ($6.6 million, Gerindra) for their advertisements in print and electronic media outlets.[11] Unsurprisingly, the advertisements of PD and Gerindra focused almost exclusively on their leaders, Yudhoyono and Prabowo. Thus, the new style of presidentialised campaigning has fed further into the growing commercialisation of party politics, with significant implications for all Indonesian parties.

STILL THE ODD ONE OUT? PKS AND THE CHALLENGES OF INSTITUTIONALISATION

One party that has faced particularly vexing challenges in view of these new developments is the puritan Islamic party PKS. Even though PKS is one of the six core parties that has won seats in every legislative election since 1999, it has always been somewhat different from the rest. Having grown from the small university-based *tarbiyah* (lit. 'education') movement of the 1980s into Indonesia's strongest Islamic party in just over two decades, PKS has demonstrated that it is indeed possible for an Indonesian party to win votes through organisational and programmatic discipline rather than charismatic leaders or money politics. In contrast to all its electoral rivals, PKS has not only upheld decent levels of accountability in its internal affairs but also implemented strict recruitment guidelines for new cadres. In addition, it has espoused strong socio-political values based on a fairly orthodox interpretation of Islam. Personal piety, modesty and moral discipline as well as egalitarianism and social justice are all important components of the PKS ideology, and its members are expected to abide by these principles. In short, within the spectrum of Indonesian parties, PKS has been unusually well institutionalised (Heilmann 2008; Hasan 2009).

Since the 2004 elections, however, the party has struggled to maintain its high standards. If in the early days of its development PKS was seen as uncompromisingly committed to its campaign slogan *bersih dan peduli* (clean and caring), the party has more recently come under increasing scrutiny for some questionable political manoeuvres, ideological

---

11 'Belanja iklan partai politik mencapai Rp. 1 triliun' [Expenditure on party advertising reaches Rp 1 trillion], *Tempointeraktif*, 28 April 2009. Taken together, expenses for all political advertisements in the first quarter of 2009 exceeded Rp 1 trillion ($100 million), already far more than the estimated Rp 494 billion ($49.4 million) parties had spent on the entire campaign in 2004 (Hicks 2009).

inconsistencies and disciplinary transgressions of individual members. Particularly damaging to the reputation of PKS were reports of party members' involvement in corruption scandals and money politics as well as the dubious pro-Suharto campaign in late 2008 in which the party hailed the former authoritarian ruler as a national hero.[12]

These incidents occurred against the backdrop of a controversial and not always linear shift away from the party's Islamist origins towards a more pragmatic orientation (Bubalo, Fealy and Mason 2008: Ch. 2). While Islam was retained as the party's ideological foundation in the 2009 campaign, PKS leaders have, since around 2006, repeatedly sought to showcase the party's commitment to pluralism and democracy. From alliances with non-Muslims in local elections and continuous support for the Yudhoyono-led coalition government to the organisation in 2008 of a major party event in Hindu-dominated Bali, PKS has tried hard to demonstrate that it is not out to transform Indonesia into an Islamic state. In explaining the decision to hold the event in Bali, for instance, the party's deputy secretary general, Fahri Hamzah, stressed that PKS wanted to make it clear to everyone that the party acknowledged pluralism and the nation's religious, ethnic and cultural diversity.[13]

Interestingly, Greg Fealy (2009) has identified this shift as one of the reasons for the stagnation of PKS's electoral support in 2009. According to Fealy, 'It appears likely that the party's compromises were met either with scepticism or disapproval by many of the electors whom it was hoping to attract'. Indeed, there are widespread doubts about whether the party's declared intention to become more pluralistic is genuine. Critics have pointed out that the alleged ideological shift has been largely pragmatic in nature, and does not reflect a deep doctrinal transformation of its leaders and members. On the other hand, its more conservative supporters have expressed concern that the party has gradually abandoned its previous Islamist agenda, forcing PKS to launch frequent initiatives to reassure its core base. In parliament, for example, the party was a driving force behind the controversial anti-pornography bill, which was passed into law in October 2008. Moreover, in the same year PKS fuelled heated debate on religious freedom when it joined calls for the disbandment of the Ahmadiyah sect, which many Muslim Indonesians view as deviant (Hasan 2009: 11).

The ongoing process of reorientation has triggered divisive debates within the PKS leadership as well as the party's rank and file. Many

---

12 'PKS continues promoting Soeharto', *Tempointeractive*, 20 November 2008.
13 'PKS gelar mukernas di Bali' [PKS holds national working meeting in Bali], 1 February 2008, http://www.pk-sejahtera.org.uk/index. php?Itemid=46&id=109&option=com_content&task=view.

members and supporters have been outspoken in the view that after accepting positions in Yudhoyono's first and second cabinets, PKS has lost its ideological, political and moral purity. They have criticised the party not only for making too many compromises in inter-elite negotiations, but also for the significant number of leaders who have become rather wealthy through this wheeling and dealing, something that was frowned upon during the party's formative years. The pragmatic faction in the PKS elite, by contrast, has maintained that the only way for PKS to grow into a large party in the future is to throw its ideological ballast overboard and seek to participate in government. Only through executive and legislative power, they have argued, will PKS be able to collect the funds necessary to expand the party's infrastructure and support base. This paradigmatic debate is likely to mark the party's internal development under the second Yudhoyono government. It is already obvious, however, that the days of PKS as a small anti-establishment party have come to an end.

POORLY INSTITUTIONALISED PARTIES, INSTITUTIONALISED PARTY SYSTEM?

The discussion so far has shown that the concentration in the Indonesian party system has *not* been the result of greater party institutionalisation. With the partial exception of PKS, parties have not strengthened their organisational apparatuses, deepened their roots in society or developed into autonomous political actors. On the contrary, if anything the established core parties have become further de-institutionalised, while newer parties like PD, Gerindra and Hanura have not even begun to establish comprehensive and effective party structures. It should therefore come as no surprise that, despite the healthy concentration in the number of parties that made it into parliament, volatility in the party system remains fairly high. While the post-Suharto polity has never had a single dominant party (with the possible exception of PDIP in 1999), the trend towards a cluster of small and medium-sized parties became particularly evident in 2009. As Table 7.3 demonstrates, the vote was spread more evenly among the major parties in 2009 than in previous years, highlighting the continuing fragmentation in the party system.

Another instructive indicator of the continued party system fragmentation despite the threshold-induced concentration in the DPR is the map of seat distributions in regional parliaments. With the introduction of an electoral threshold for provincial and district legislatures postponed to 2014 and 2019 respectively, there were very few signs in 2009 of concentration or stabilisation of the party system at the local level. Several of the

*Table 7.3   Fragmentation of the Indonesian party system: biggest parties'
share of the vote, 1999–2009 (%)*

	1999	2004	2009
Share of four biggest parties	79.5	58.8	57.3
Share of five biggest parties	86.6	66.3	63.3
Share of six biggest parties	88.6	73.6	68.6
Share of seven biggest parties	89.9	80.1	73.5

Source: Tomsa (2008: 187); data from the General Elections Commission (Komisi Pemilihan Umum, KPU).

tiny parties that failed to take the national 2.5 per cent hurdle managed to win seats in the regions. At the provincial level, for example, an average of 12.9 parties secured parliamentary representation, with particularly heavy fragmentation in several provinces in eastern Indonesia as well as the provinces of North Sumatra, Bengkulu and Banten (see Table 7.4).

The figures in Tables 7.3 and 7.4 illustrate that, in spite of the greater concentration at the national level, the Indonesian party system is not genuinely institutionalised. Indeed, most scholars regard party system institutionalisation as a multi-dimensional process that entails more than just stability and continuity. Two other necessary elements often raised by scholars are the nature of inter-party competition and the overall legitimacy of the party system as expressed in levels of public appreciation of the parties and the system in which they operate (Mainwaring and Scully 1995; Randall and Svasand 2001). In both of these dimensions, the record of Indonesia's party system is mixed at best, making its institutionalisation even more difficult.

To begin with, the nature of inter-party competition in Indonesia has often been criticised as rife with collusion (Slater 2004; Ambardi 2008). Indeed, all governments since Abdurrahman Wahid's first cabinet in 1999 have been multi-party coalitions in which power sharing appears to be more common than competing for power. Yudhoyono's second United Indonesia Cabinet, which includes representatives of six of the nine parties in parliament (PD, Golkar, PKS, PKB, PAN and PPP), has continued this tradition, further heightening concerns about the lack of transparency and accountability in the system. But on the other hand, Indonesian party politics is also highly competitive — so much so, in fact, that there has long been a tendency for politicians not to acknowledge defeat at the ballot box. Throughout the post-Suharto era, election results at both the national and local levels have continually been contested by one party or another. Significantly, the main motivation for parties to complain about electoral results has not been genuine concern for the quality of democ-

Table 7.4   Party fragmentation at the provincial level: number of parties in provincial parliaments, 2009

Province	No. of parties	Province	No. of parties	Province	No. of parties
Aceh	11	Banten	16	E. Nusa Tenggara	18
North Sumatra	16	West Java	9	South Sulawesi	16
West Sumatra	10	Central Java	10	West Sulawesi	17
Riau	11	Yogyakarta	10	Central Sulawesi	15
Jambi	11	East Java	12	S.E. Sulawesi	14
South Sumatra	13	Bali	10	North Sulawesi	12
Bengkulu	16	West Kalimantan	13	Gorontalo	12
Lampung	11	Central Kalimantan	11	Maluku	16
Kepulauan Riau	14	East Kalimantan	12	North Maluku	15
Bangka Belitung	9	South Kalimantan	11	Papua	18
Jakarta	10	W. Nusa Tenggara	15	West Papua	n.a.

Source: Compiled from provincial election commissions and local newspapers.

racy, but rather fear of being excluded from the corridors of power. Certainly, such fears have not always been unjustified. Particularly at the local level, the redistribution of power in the aftermath of executive elections can often lead to major disruptions of existing patronage networks.

The good news is that Indonesian parties have sought largely nonviolent ways to express their dissatisfaction with election results. Despite the plentiful logistical and organisational flaws in the 2009 elections, for example, electoral losers limited their protests to complaints filed with the Constitutional Court. Most importantly, all parties involved accepted the verdicts of the court. It is also noteworthy that, despite the high stakes during electoral contests, Indonesian parties have rarely engaged in violence or intimidation before or during campaigns (Buehler 2009). In contrast to parties in neighbouring countries like Thailand or the Philippines where election-related violence is still fairly common,[14] Indonesian parties seem to have internalised peaceful electoral competition as the only legitimate means to distribute formal political power. Given the developments in other Southeast Asian countries since 2005, this in itself is an achievement that should not be taken for granted.

---

14   One of the more extreme cases of such violence occurred in the Philippines' Maguindanao province on 23 October 2009 when at least 57 people were killed during an escalating feud between two rival political clans. See 'Philippines "poll-related" deaths reach 57', http://news.bbc.co.uk/2/hi/asia-pacific/8377875.stm.

Finally, the level of public acceptance and appreciation of the democratic system and the parties operating within it can be measured by looking at the voter turnout in the last three elections. In spite of a continuous decline since 1999, voter participation in elections in Indonesia has remained fairly high by international standards, suggesting generally strong support for electoral democracy among the broader populace.[15] Unfortunately, the legitimacy of the overall political system has not been matched by similar approval ratings for the parties. After a brief honeymoon period in the immediate aftermath of the fall of Suharto, public trust in the parties' ability and willingness to pursue the interests of the people soon plummeted and has remained low ever since, as can be seen from numerous public opinion surveys conducted since 1999. Arguably, the rise of presidentialised parties like PD and, to a lesser extent, Gerindra and Hanura, has been a direct consequence of this widespread anti-party sentiment. With voters looking for ways to express their disappointment with the core parties, they have increasingly turned to personality-based newcomers. There is little evidence to suggest, however, that these new parties are in any way more transparent, effective or inclusive than the increasingly discredited core parties.

OUTLOOK: IS A PARTY SYSTEM WITH WEAK PARTIES SUSTAINABLE?

With the 2009 elections behind them, Indonesia's political parties have quickly turned their attention to the long-term preparations for the next parliamentary and presidential elections in 2014. As Yudhoyono will be unable to seek re-election because of the existing presidential term limit, the electoral landscape of 2014 is certain to look substantially different from the one that marked the 2009 contests. This newly emerging constellation has presented all Indonesian parties with significant challenges. PD, for example, has already begun discussions about how to outlive its patron and become recognised as a political party in its own right. According to Mietzner (2009a: 7), however, PD's institutional and ideological weaknesses dictate that it will only be able to survive in the long term if Yudhoyono remains affiliated with the party in one way or another. Of the other two presidentialised parties, Gerindra is likely to attract more public attention, as Prabowo is tipped to run again for the presidency in 2014. Wiranto, on the other hand, has been widely por-

---

15 Voter turnout dropped from 91 per cent in 1999 to 83 per cent in 2004 and 71 per cent in 2009. As Mietzner (2009a: 17) points out, however, this decline is more indicative of a general normalisation of electoral politics rather than a rejection of democracy as such.

trayed as a spent force after two failed attempts in 2004 and 2009, so his Hanura party may disappear as quickly as it once emerged.

Meanwhile, the core parties have already entered into heated debates on the best strategies to stop the downward spiral and regain some of the votes they have lost over the years. But given the reluctance of their leaders to commit to meaningful reform, these discussions are unlikely to be ground-breaking. Since 1998, all of the core parties except PKS have proven incapable of responding to the challenges of building well-functioning party apparatuses. While Golkar is routinely mentioned as the party with the best organisational network, this infrastructure has not been the result of effective grassroots work since 1998, but rather a legacy of an increasingly distant New Order era. With few resources invested in its maintenance, this party infrastructure has been in constant decline since Suharto's fall. The unpopular tycoon Aburizal Bakrie, elected party chair in the 'battle of the biggest checkbook'[16] in October 2009 and generally better known for his financial prowess than his political astuteness, seems an unlikely candidate to turn Golkar's fortunes around.

Within PDIP, PAN, PKB and PPP, the debates about future strategies have been even more complex and conflict-ridden. In each of these parties, the period after the 2009 elections was dominated by calls for new leadership. But with fewer resources than Golkar and internal problems such as heavy factional infighting, the parties are unlikely to improve their electoral prospects simply by replacing their senior leaders. Against this background, PKS stands out as the only core party with a somewhat positive outlook. While the party has struggled with the task of turning itself into an inclusive mainstream party without forfeiting its Islamic credentials, PKS emerged from the 2009 elections as Indonesia's largest Muslim party and thus seems better positioned than its rivals to compete in the electoral market of 2014. As indicated earlier, however, it is by no means conflict-free; indeed, the internal debates about the party's future course have been highly divisive, undermining the very organisational solidity upon which PKS's previous electoral successes were based. If managed badly, the strategic and ideological discussions within PKS could have an adverse effect on its chances in 2014.

Overall, then, the prospects for Indonesia's party system are rather mixed. On the one hand, the majority of Indonesia's parties are not as short-lived as in Thailand or as corrupt and superficial as in the Philippines. It seems improbable, therefore, that the Indonesian party system will collapse any time soon. But in the medium to long term, the lack of professionally managed and deeply rooted parties has the potential to

---

16 'Cabinet 2009: people's welfare minister Agung Laksono', *Jakarta Globe*, 25 October 2009.

threaten the system's stability, which has so far been guaranteed primarily through institutional engineering. Indeed, the party system could undergo even further concentration after the next election, as a result of the expansion of the electoral threshold to the provinces and the likely decline of some core parties. Temporarily, this might further stabilise the system, but it is unlikely to serve as a reliable foundation for its future sustainability. With only one reasonably well-institutionalised party (PKS), a party system such as Indonesia's is destined to remain highly volatile. And yet, as indicated at the beginning of this chapter, under specific circumstances even a party system with very weakly institutionalised parties might operate for significant periods of time. In light of the continued unwillingness of its parties to press for substantive change, Indonesia looks certain to become an important test case for this proposition.

REFERENCES

Ambardi, Kuskridho (2008), 'The making of the Indonesian multiparty system: a cartelized party system and its origin', PhD thesis, Ohio State University, Columbus OH.

Bubalo, Anthony, Greg Fealy and Whit Mason (2008), 'Zealous democrats: Islamism and democracy in Egypt, Indonesia and Turkey', Lowy Institute Paper No. 25, Lowy Institute for International Policy, Sydney.

Buehler, Michael (2009), 'Suicide and progress in modern Nusantara', *Inside Indonesia* 97(July–September), http://insideindonesia.org/.

Carothers, Thomas (2006), *Confronting the Weakest Link: Aiding Political Parties in New Democracies*, Carnegie Endowment for International Peace, Washington DC.

Davidson, Jamie S. (2009), 'Dilemmas of democratic consolidation in Indonesia', *Pacific Review* 22(3): 293–310.

Fealy, Greg (2009), 'Indonesia's Islamic parties in decline', *Inside Story*, 11 May, http://inside.org.au/indonesia%E2%80%99s-islamic-parties-in-decline/.

Freedom House (2009), 'Country report: Indonesia', Freedom House, Washington DC, http://freedomhouse.org/template.cfm?page=22&year=2009&country=7626.

Hadiz, Vedi R. (2004), 'Indonesian local party politics: a site of resistance to neoliberal reform', *Critical Asian Studies* 36(4): 615–36.

Hasan, Noorhaidi (2009), 'Islamist party, electoral politics and *da'wa* mobilization among youth: the Prosperous Justice Party (PKS) in Indonesia', Working Paper No. 184, S. Rajaratnam School of International Studies, Singapore.

Heilmann, Matthias (2008), 'Islamismus in Indonesien: der Erfolg der Gerechtigkeits- und Wohlfahrtspartei und seine möglichen Auswirkungen' [Islamism in Indonesia: the success of the Prosperous Justice Party and its potential consequences], *Austrian Journal of Southeast Asian Studies* 1(1): 18–28.

Hicks, Jacqueline (2009), 'Democratic disconnects in Indonesia', *Asia Times Online*, 14 July, http://www.atimes.com/atimes/Southeast_Asia/KG14Ae01.html.

Johnson Tan, Paige (2002), 'Anti-party reaction in Indonesia: causes and implications', *Contemporary Southeast Asia* 24(3): 484–508.

Johnson Tan, Paige (2006), 'Indonesia seven years after Soeharto: party system institutionalization in a new democracy', *Contemporary Southeast Asia* 28(1): 88–114.

Laakso, Markku and Rein Taagepera (1979), 'The effective number of parties: a measure with application to Western Europe', *Comparative Political Studies* 12(1): 3–27.

LSI (Lembaga Survei Indonesia) (2008), 'Kecenderungan swing voter menjelang pemilu legislatif 2009' [Swing-voter trends in the run-up to the 2009 legislative election], LSI, Jakarta, http://www.lsi.or.id/riset/354/swing-voter.

Mainwaring, Scott P. and Timothy R. Scully (1995), 'Introduction: party systems in Latin America', in S.P. Mainwaring and T.R. Scully (eds), *Building Democratic Institutions: Party Systems in Latin America*, Stanford University Press, Stanford CA, pp. 1–34.

Mietzner, Marcus (2008a), 'Comparing Indonesia's party systems of the 1950s and the post-Suharto era', *Journal of Southeast Asian Studies* 39(3): 431–53.

Mietzner, Marcus (2008b), 'Soldiers, parties and bureaucrats: illicit fundraising in contemporary Indonesia', *South East Asia Research* 16(2): 225–54.

Mietzner, Marcus (2009a), 'Indonesia's 2009 elections: populism, dynasties and the consolidation of the party system', *Analysis*, Lowy Institute for International Policy, Sydney, May.

Mietzner, Marcus (2009b), 'Political opinion polling in post-authoritarian Indonesia: catalyst or obstacle to democratic consolidation', *Bijdragen tot de Taal-, Land- en Volkenkunde* 165(1): 95–126.

Mujani, Saiful and R. William Liddle (2007), 'Leadership, party and religion: explaining voting behavior in Indonesia', *Comparative Political Studies* 40(7): 832–57.

Platzdasch, Bernhard (2009), 'Down but not out: Islamic political parties did not do well, but Islamic politics are going mainstream', *Inside Indonesia* 97(July–September), http://insideindonesia.org.

Randall, Vicky and Lars Svasand (2001), 'Party institutionalisation and the new democracies', in J. Haynes (ed.), *Democracy and Political Change in the 'Third World'*, Routledge, London and New York, pp. 75–96.

Sherlock, Stephen (2009), 'Parties and elections in Indonesia 2009: the consolidation of democracy', research paper, Department of Parliamentary Services, Parliament of Australia, Canberra.

Slater, Dan (2004), 'Indonesia's accountability trap: party cartels and presidential power after democratic transition', *Indonesia* 78(October): 61–92.

Tomsa, Dirk (2008), *Party Politics and Democratization in Indonesia: Golkar in the Post-Suharto Era*, Routledge, London and New York.

Tomsa, Dirk (2009a), 'Electoral democracy in a divided society: the 2008 gubernatorial election in Maluku, Indonesia', *South East Asia Research* 17(2): 229–59.

Tomsa, Dirk (2009b), 'The eagle has crash-landed', *Inside Indonesia* 97(July–September), http://insideindonesia.org/.

Ufen, Andreas (2008a), 'Political party and party system institutionalisation in Southeast Asia: lessons for democratic consolidation in Indonesia, the Philippines and Thailand', *Pacific Review* 21(3): 327–50.

Ufen, Andreas (2008b), 'From *aliran* to dealignment: political parties in post-Suharto Indonesia', *South East Asia Research* 16(1): 5–41.

Wolinetz, Stephen B. (2006), 'Party system institutionalization: bringing the system back in', paper prepared for the annual meeting of the Canadian Political Science Association, Saskatoon, 29 May–1 June, http://www.cpsa-acsp.ca/papers-2007/Wolinetz.pdf.

8 THE PARLIAMENT IN INDONESIA'S DECADE OF DEMOCRACY: PEOPLE'S FORUM OR CHAMBER OF CRONIES?

Stephen Sherlock

The parliament (Dewan Perwakilan Rakyat, DPR) has been at the centre of the political transformation of Indonesia since 1998. The rise in the importance of the parliament is one of the two biggest shifts in institutional power experienced in Indonesia since the fall of Suharto; the other is the empowerment of regional government. More than any other state institution, the parliament has been the major site of competition between the residual forces of the New Order elite (Robison and Hadiz 2004), the previously excluded groups who want a seat at the high table and those who simply want to influence the decisions that affect their lives. This dynamic power constellation has been the result of fundamental changes instituted since 1998, most notably the introduction of genuinely democratic elections. These highly competitive ballots have shifted the rules of the game and vastly increased the range of voices heard in the parliament. Whereas in Suharto's DPR one could hear only an occasional faint echo of real disputes within the elite (Datta 2002), the post-1998 institution is a lively chamber full of the clamorous noise of debate. In this sense, the new parliament has become the kind of representative legislature that is considered 'normal' in a capitalist democracy.

This chapter discusses the role of Indonesia's parliament in the post-Suharto polity in four steps. The first section argues that democratic elections and constitutional reform have greatly enhanced the role of the parliament, but that its power is limited by the fact that it must share the power to make laws with the executive arm of government. Consequently, concerns about an excessive shift of authority to the parliament are not justified.

In the second section, I contend that certain features of the parliamentary decision-making process inherently favour exclusive elite politics over popular and inclusive deliberations, whether wittingly or unwittingly. Parliaments around the world are, of course, weighted towards the interests of the powerful, but the Indonesian parliament's specific institutional set-up and political culture seem to be particularly supportive of cabalistic or oligarchic control. Of special concern in this regard is the compartmentalisation of decision making within the committee structure and the avoidance of open votes. These practices limit political competition and facilitate a division of political spoils among an elite group of insiders.

Yet, at the same time, the parliament has acquired substantial democratic qualities. The third section of the chapter illustrates how the need to be re-elected and hence to relate to the concerns of the electorate has forced legislators to act in ways that bring important issues to public attention and make the parliament a genuine voice of accountability. However opportunistic the actions of parliamentary committees and individual members may be in many cases, overall they have contributed to the DPR's development into a more representative institution.

The final section discusses the dynamic pluralism of views in the legislature as the result of an apparent institutional paradox: party discipline is weak, but nevertheless the executive does not exercise monopolistic control over the processes of government. In other words, the parliament's fragmentation, usually decried as a weakness, has been one of its greatest assets in its ongoing competition with the executive arm of government.

THE RISE OF THE PARLIAMENT SINCE 1998

The Indonesian constitution was adopted in 1945 but was amended substantially after Suharto's fall. The amended constitution gives three chambers a role in the legislative process: the DPR, the Regional Representative Council (Dewan Perwakilan Daerah, DPD) and the Peoples' Consultative Assembly (Majelis Permusyawaratan Rakyat, MPR). This does not mean, however, that Indonesia has a tricameral system of government: only the DPR has the crucial power to pass laws that defines a legislature (Patterson and Mughan 1999; Baldwin and Shell 2001). The DPD is able to draft bills and provide opinions on bills being deliberated by the DPR, but it cannot pass, reject or amend legislation (Sherlock 2005). The powers of the MPR—theoretically the highest organ of state under Sukarno and Suharto—have been reduced to amending the constitution, inaugurating the president and overseeing impeachment proceedings against a president deemed in violation of certain laws. Because Indonesia has a unicameral system of government, in fact if not in theory, this chapter deals mainly with the DPR.

In accordance with legislation passed in 2008, the DPR is composed of 560 members and is elected through a proportional representation system with multi-member electoral districts. The number of members in each district is roughly proportionate to population, and seats are allocated within the framework of an open party list mechanism. All candidates standing for the DPR must be on a party ticket, but voters may vote either for an individual candidate or for a party. The DPD is composed of 132 members — four from each of Indonesia's 33 provinces regardless of provincial population. A single non-transferable vote system is used to elect the four candidates with the highest number of votes in each province. Members of the DPD are elected as individuals rather than as members of political parties, although candidates running for the DPD are not banned from holding party membership (Sherlock 2005). The MPR is composed of all members of the DPR and DPD.

In part, the rising prominence of the parliament in political affairs since 1998 has simply been the result of the introduction of basic elements of democracy: free and fair elections; the end of restrictions on civic freedoms; and the agreement of all political players to accept the result of open political competition. Elections have conferred legitimacy on a previously hand-picked institution and encouraged its members to assert the powers that in the past had existed only in theory (Ziegenhain 2008, 2009). But there has also been a major institutional shift in power away from the executive branch of government towards the legislature as a consequence of the constitutional reforms carried out between 1999 and 2002 (Ellis and Yudhini 2002; Scheier 2005; Indrayana 2008). The first important change was to explicitly name the DPR as Indonesia's law-making institution. Article 20A(1) of the amended constitution states that 'the DPR holds the authority to make laws'. Previously, the constitution of 1945 had given the power to legislate to the president, with the role of the DPR limited to giving its 'consent' to laws drafted by the executive.

But not all of these constitutional amendments strengthened the parliament, and some actually took powers away from the legislature. Most notably, the DPR lost its power to choose the president, inherited from the original draft of the constitution through its control of the majority of seats in the MPR. Under the Sukarno and Suharto regimes, in practice neither the DPR nor the MPR had been able to exercise their constitutional powers, but after the fall of Suharto in 1998 the letter of the constitution mattered, and the president was elected by the MPR in a highly competitive contest. However, the president elected in 1999, Abdurrahman Wahid, soon clashed with the legislators who had put him into office, and began to assert his powers under what he argued was a purely presidential system of governance. Not surprisingly, the relationship between the executive and the legislature deteriorated, culminating in Wahid being voted out of office by the MPR in 2001. To avoid further crises of this type, the elite decided it was necessary to give the president a stronger mandate and protect him or her from removal from office by the legislature. While supporting this move, Indonesia's NGOs initiated a popular campaign upholding the principle that the president should be elected directly by the Indonesian people. Legislation mandating direct presidential elections was passed in 2002, with the first direct elections held in 2004. The constitution was amended to include provisions for the impeachment of the president, subject to very complex conditions, including verification of the president's wrongdoing by the newly established Constitutional Court.

The reconfiguring of the relative powers of the executive and the parliament thus led to the loss of the DPR's role in the formation of the government, but to an increase in its legislative authority. To this was added a range of powers that boosted the DPR's ability to scrutinise the activities of the executive and appoint senior state officials. Under the amended constitution, the DPR would receive all reports of the State Audit Agency (Badan Pemeriksaan Keuangan, BPK) and appoint BPK members. In addition, it was given a role in selecting members of the Supreme Court, the Constitutional Court and the Judicial Commission. More controversially, the DPR was given the power to approve the appointment of Indonesian ambassadors, and to veto the acceptance of ambassadors from foreign countries. It was also given the authority under various pieces of legislation to approve the appointment of the commander of the armed forces, the chief of police, members of the Corruption Eradication Commission, members of the Ombudsman's Commission and other officials.

The growing power and assertiveness of the DPR has given birth to a discourse about Indonesia's parliament becoming too powerful *vis-à-vis* the executive branch of government. According to this theory, commonly espoused by NGOs and journalists but gaining some credence in scholarly circles as well, the dominance of the president during the Suharto era represented an 'executive-heavy' political system in which the government wielded excessive power. Today, it is contended, the balance has shifted too far in the other direction, upsetting the normal 'checks and balances' of government (Formappi 2005; Susanti 2007) and encouraging corruption. According to Agus Purnomo, a former member of the DPR's Committee III on legal affairs, 'Power tends to corrupt—during the time of [Suharto] it was executive heavy, now it's legislative heavy'.[1]

---

1 'Era legislative heavy, DPR cenderung korupsi' [Legislative-heavy era, DPR prone to corruption], *detikNews*, 25 April 2008.

Such statements need to be qualified in two ways. First, they are an indication that Indonesian political culture is still adapting to the full reality of the kind of political system that was adopted as a result of the constitutional amendments. Partisans of the idea of a problematic, 'parliament-heavy' system usually argue that since Indonesia has a presidential (as opposed to purely parliamentary) system of government, the parliament should not be playing such an assertive role. But they overlook the fact that, in most presidential systems, the separation of powers makes the parliament very strong. A cursory examination of the immense power of the US Congress would illustrate this point. Second, the legislative power conferred on the parliament in the constitutional reforms was partial and ambiguous. The 2002 reforms moved only halfway towards transferring the locus of power from the president to the DPR. Most importantly, the constitution states that laws are to be made by 'joint agreement' between the president and the DPR. In other words, the executive branch of government has veto power over all legislation.

Some observers have pointed out that the president does *not* have power of veto, because bills become law within 30 days of their passage through the DPR regardless of whether or not they have been signed by the president (Laksmana 2009). But in practice the provision for 'joint agreement' to legislation is a strong effective veto, because the government can delay the passage of bills initiated by the DPR simply by not naming a minister to participate in the discussions between its representatives and the relevant DPR committee. Such obstruction of the passage of bills or proposed amendments occurs mainly out of public sight, greatly reducing the political risk for a president who refuses to pass, or delays, legislation. Thus, despite the post-1998 rise of the parliament from a rubber-stamp body to a truly influential institution, the executive largely remains in the driving seat.

DECISION MAKING IN THE DPR

The regulations for the conduct of business in the DPR are set out in a document called *Peraturan Tata Tertib* [Rules of Procedure], commonly known as the *Tatib*.[2] The rules describe the roles of each of the organs of the DPR, such as committees; the types of meetings that can be held; and the procedures for conducting meetings and making decisions. Compared to similar documents in other parliaments, the DPR's rules of procedure contain very little detail. As a result, much of the conduct of DPR

2 See http://www.dpr.go.id/id/tentang-dpr/tata-tertib.

proceedings is not subject to standards or regulations, leaving a great deal of latitude to members to behave as they wish.

The legislative process

The procedural rules provide a basic outline of the official process by which laws are passed. The process varies according to whether the bill is introduced by the government or is initiated by the DPR itself.[3] Government bills (which make up a large majority of all bills) are drafted in the relevant ministry and/or the Ministry of Law and Human Rights. A bill will usually be accompanied by an academic document (*naskah akademis*) containing — in theory at least — a detailed explanation of the matters to be dealt with by the bill, including a clause-by-clause elucidation of the bill's intention. The bill is received by the House leadership (speaker and deputy speakers) and passed to a steering committee (*badan musyawarah*, or *bamus*), which decides which standing committee (*komisi*) or special committee (*panitia khusus*, or *pansus*) will be responsible for overseeing its passage through the House.

Subsequently, the bill enters the first stage (*tingkat I*) of the legislative process, which takes the form of discussions between the relevant DPR standing or special committee and government representatives. The minister usually attends the initial meeting and is then represented by ministry officials in subsequent meetings. At the first meetings, the general views of each party caucus (*fraksi*) are presented. This is followed by the government's formal response to the positions of the caucuses. The main part of the discussion then concerns the compilation of a list of issues (*daftar inventarisasi masalah*, or DIM) identifying potentially controversial clauses of the bill. This list — which may contain hundreds of items — forms the basis for the negotiations between the government and the DPR members. The formulation and discussion of a DIM usually takes place in a working committee (*panitia kerja*, or *panja*), which is essentially a subcommittee of the standing or special committee appointed to deal with the bill. Agreement on the final draft of the bill is reached when all issues in the DIM have been resolved. The bill is then sent back to the steering committee, where it is scheduled for presentation to a plenary session of the DPR.

The second stage (*tingkat II*) of the legislative process features the formal acceptance and passage of the bill through a plenary session. That session hears a report on the results of the deliberations in the first stage, presentations of the final views of the caucuses and the government's response. This is an entirely ceremonial procedure: in most cases, the bill

---

3 The legislative process is described in more detail in Sherlock (2007).

will not go to the plenary until it has been agreed to by all caucuses in the committees and by the government. The bill is then passed to the president to be signed.

DPR-initiated bills face more hurdles than those submitted by the government. A bill initiated by the DPR may be proposed by one or more committees or by the legislation coordination body, and it must be signed by at least 10 DPR members. The bill is then submitted to the DPR leadership, which passes it to a steering committee. From there, it is sent to a plenary session for formal acceptance as a DPR initiative. The leadership then submits the bill to the president with a request that a minister be assigned to represent the government in deliberations. The bill then enters the first stage, and from there on follows the procedures outlined above for government-sponsored bills.

Committees: the centre of decision making

To capture the special character of Indonesia's legislative procedures, it is critical to highlight the dominant role of committees. Essentially, decision making in the DPR takes place in the committees, not in the plenary sessions. Substantive debates during plenary sessions are rare, and when they do occur, they almost never relate to bills. Instead, plenary sessions are a forum for parties or individual members to publicly raise some issue of the day in order to put pressure on the government. Prominent examples include the debates on oil subsidies, on the importation of foreign rice and on the mudflow disaster in Sidoarjo in East Java.

It is in the committees that most of the functions of the DPR are carried out. Their role extends beyond legislative issues to matters of government oversight, with individual committees having considerable power. If an issue of public concern is raised, discussion will usually be confined to the particular committee with responsibility for that policy area and the ministry or agency concerned. When state officials are to be appointed, only members of the responsible committee will be involved in the process of screening and interviewing candidates for the vacant positions. Thus, although it is officially the DPR as an institution that appoints the members of the BPK and examines the president's candidates for commander of the armed forces, in practice it is only Committee XI (on finance and banking) and Committee I (on foreign affairs, defence and information) respectively that would actually decide these appointments.

A major effect of the concentration of decision-making power in the committees has been a 'balkanised' institution. DPR members know what their own committee is doing, but often have little interest in or knowledge about the issues being considered by other committees, unless they are particularly controversial ones. This can lead to a situation in which committee-based solidarity prevails over loyalty to the party or caucus. When committees are in dispute with each other—for example, over the right to take carriage of a particular bill—it is not uncommon for the members of one committee to line up against their colleagues from the same party in an opposing committee. Significantly, this compartmentalisation of DPR activities has contributed to the cabalistic and collusive nature of the institution, with the political elite viewing government in terms of the division of spoils between 'insiders' rather than as a contest of policies. In the same vein, the pressure to produce a united committee position on any particular bill or issue has exacerbated the existing problem of weak policy differences between the parties. Moreover, the huge differences in how the various committees operate have made it difficult for outsiders to seek information or get involved in debates, raising serious questions about the level of transparency and accountability of the DPR.

Empty chairs: the problem of the plenary

The dominance of the committees over decision making in the DPR has left plenary sessions with a relatively minor role. These sessions are a cumbersome and resource-intensive way of fulfilling what, in most cases, is a purely procedural function. Nevertheless, plenary sessions are the public face of the DPR, and in popular imagination the plenary *is* the parliament. Accordingly, media outlets focus obsessively on the issue of non-attendance of plenary sessions by DPR members. Virtually every time the DPR is in session, national newspapers publish photos of empty rows of seats accompanied by an indignant story about the alleged laziness of members, with the stated or implicit inference that members are off pursuing their own personal interests rather than their parliamentary duties. With the public predominantly regarding post-Suharto legislators as lazy, corrupt and self-interested, such stories are an easy way for the media to pander to popular attitudes.

Given the disastrous public image of parliamentarians, developing a wider, non-ceremonial role for the plenary should be an urgent item for reform of DPR procedures. Beyond public relations-related reasons, however, the plenary is in need of revitalisation so that the DPR as a whole—rather than just individual committees—is involved in the scrutiny of bills. In most parliaments, there are several forums in which legislation can be reviewed, with the possibility of a 'second opinion' generally regarded as important for boosting the quality and completeness of laws (Baldwin and Shell 2001). In a bicameral parliament, this would occur in the second chamber. As Indonesia does not possess such a chamber, a second debate on bills in the main or plenary chamber could offer a means of improving the quality of laws. So far, however, the predominance of the committees over the plenary has remained unchallenged.

Closed and unaccountable: decision making by 'consensus'

Another exceptional feature of the DPR is its tendency to make decisions not by majority vote, but through a system of so-called 'deliberation to reach consensus' (*musyawarah untuk mencapai mufakat*). This process, unique among democratic parliaments in the world, is probably the most important instrument for oligarchic control and avoidance of transparency and public accountability. Under this mechanism, which is laid down in the *Tatib* as the official system for all organs of the DPR, decisions are not considered final until there is unanimous agreement. Only if consensus repeatedly fails will a matter be put to a vote. This does not mean, however, that every single member must actively give his or her assent to a decision. In practice, it is assumed that agreement has been reached if no further dissent is expressed. Moreover, it is not individual members who express dissent, but rather the caucuses, in the form of caucus leaders. Thus, ultimately, consensus is expressed through a vote by the caucus leaders. Once all caucuses have expressed their agreement or, more precisely, have ceased to register dissent, unanimous agreement is deemed to have been achieved.

Important aspects of this procedure are closed and non-transparent. During meetings of committees or other DPR organs, each caucus will usually present its views on the matter under discussion. If all take the same position, the chair will declare that there is consensus. If not, the caucus leaders will withdraw to closed-door 'lobbying' meetings to hammer out some kind of deal or agreement. The leaders will then emerge to declare that all caucuses are in agreement so that the chair can rule that consensus has been reached. Such practices virtually eliminate the possibility of dissent by individual members. Members are expected to follow the directions of their caucus leaders, not to dissent from the purported universal agreement of consensus, and to be bound by those decisions. In these circumstances, the only option for dissenting members and caucuses is to register their objections to the result of the lobbying process, although this would typically be followed by assurances that they nevertheless 'honour' the decision and consider it binding.[4]

In practical terms, the principle of consensus has led to substantial delays in lawmaking and other DPR activities. If there is a difference

---

4 'Paripurna DPR juga tolak Agus-Pardede' [DPR plenary also rejects Agus-Pardede], *Bali Post*, 19 March 2008.

of opinion, minority caucuses often hold to their positions long after there is any chance of convincing the other side. As a result, symbolic but non-substantive issues consume huge amounts of time, while discussion of critical policy issues may be rushed through in order to meet deadlines. This is precisely what occurred during August and September 2009, when a number of bills were hurriedly completed before the expiry of the 2004–2009 DPR. This naturally raised concerns, with one prominent leader of a legislative NGO saying he was 'worried about the quality of the laws they produced' during this time.[5] But at the other extreme, delays sometimes continue indefinitely and important legislation remains uncompleted for years, frequently being handed on to successive parliaments.

By effectively making every party a veto-player, the consensus-based system has created incentives for committees and other DPR organs to become 'gatekeepers' who are interested only in rent seeking (Braun 2008). Fortunately, the practice in the early post-1998 period of committees unashamedly extorting favours from ministries, state-owned corporations and private companies appears to have declined (Sherlock 2003, 2007). But it is an open secret that large amounts of money continue to change hands over the appointment of state officials and during deliberations on legislation, especially if they concern traditionally lucrative areas such as contracts for infrastructure, housing, health, education and the *hajj* pilgrimage. The scandal about cash payments to members of Committee XI in connection with the appointment of Bank Indonesia officials is just one of many examples that have recently come to light.[6] While it is important to note that such corrupt practices are not directly caused by the practice of consensus-oriented decision making, they are certainly facilitated by it.

ACCOUNTABILITY AND PUBLIC DEBATE

The previous section has argued that important aspects of the internal procedures of the DPR have helped to maintain oligarchic control and minimise the accountability of the parliament to its electors. Yet, other, more inclusive forces are at play as well. To begin with, strong electoral pressures are forcing the parliament to be more open and accessible to the public. In their various districts, politicians face extensive (and expensive) demands from their constituents for improvements to local

---

5   Sebastian Salang, quoted in 'Closing House rushes bills, falls short of target', *Jakarta Post*, 29 September 2009.
6   'Exposing the BI–DPR money-go-round', *Tempo*, 16 June 2009.

community infrastructure and other forms of development assistance. Moreover, DPR members are regularly approached by individual citizens seeking solutions to their personal problems, often culminating in demands for money or other forms of material assistance. With the introduction of an open list electoral system in the 2009 elections, there is even greater pressure on individual DPR members to build a strong local profile in their districts in order to be re-elected.

In addition to the increased bargaining power of the electorate, other reformist trends have been visible in the DPR. For instance, the DPR has been able to break the executive's stranglehold on policy making, forcing greater accountability on the government and helping to invigorate other institutions of accountability such as the BPK. In addition, despite the continued culture of closed-door decision making in the DPR, a decade of democracy has slowly turned parliament into a conduit for ideas and information. Public hearings by DPR committees, which are sometimes broadcast live on television, are a valuable source of information on the activities of both government and private corporations that would never have been available before. To this extent at least, the DPR has begun to take on the character of a people's forum. As a recent study of the role of the DPR in democratisation has said: 'Despite all weaknesses and an ambiguous performance ... parliament adds to the routinization of democracy' (Ziegenhain 2008: 206).

There is an increasing number of examples of this trend. Following the mudflow disaster in Sidoarjo, East Java, possibly caused by the drilling activities of a company owned by the Golkar-affiliated minister and tycoon Aburizal Bakrie, many of the facts of the case emerged as a result of DPR investigations. The special committee set up to pursue the matter allowed NGOs and victims of the incident to speak out, bringing the incident to wider public attention. Given the powerful forces with an interest in suppressing discussion, the involvement of the DPR was important in maintaining pressure on those involved. All this disregards, of course, the short-term political calculations that may have been behind the committee hearings and the fact that the committee eventually declared Bakrie's company Lapindo to be free of blame for the disaster.[7]

The DPR has also begun to take on the ombudsman role that is a feature of any genuinely representative parliament. One example concerns the case of Prita Mulyasari. She was imprisoned in May 2009 after sending emails to friends complaining about the quality of the treatment she had received at a private hospital in the Jakarta satellite city of Tangerang. Prita was initially charged with defamation under the Criminal

---

7 'Sidoarjo mudflow is a natural disaster, House declares', *Jakarta Globe*, 30 September 2009.

Code, but more serious charges were then added under the Electronic Transactions Law because she had circulated her complaint by email. The media sarcastically described the legal action against Prita as an act of judicial 'creativity', with some suggesting that the hospital had bribed judges.[8] The DPR became involved when public outrage over the case led to an avalanche of blogs and text messages. As a result, Prita was released from custody while her trial continued. The fact that the matter was taken up by the DPR shows that sensitivity to public concerns has become a political necessity for legislators seeking re-election. The case became a *cause célèbre*, illustrating the emerging culture of assertiveness among blogosphere-savvy Indonesians, and demonstrating that the parliament is being pulled along in its wake.

The role of the DPR in bringing to light concerns about the government bail-out of the insolvent Bank Century in November 2008 is a textbook example of effective parliamentary oversight of the executive. In 2008 the government took over Bank Century at the height of the international financial crisis, arguing that the fall of the bank at such a sensitive time could precipitate the collapse of the whole banking system. The DPR's Committee XI on finance and banking subsequently endorsed a government decision to inject Rp 1.3 trillion into the bank, but by mid-2009 the amount had escalated to Rp 6.8 trillion.[9] In August 2009, at a meeting attended by finance minister Sri Mulyani Indrawati, Committee XI members questioned the government's handling of the case. Bank Indonesia was criticised for its failure to detect certain transactions carried out by Bank Century, offences that had led to one of the bank's owners being sentenced to four years' imprisonment. These criticisms were notable in that they involved not only Yudhoyono's newly elected vice-president, former Bank Indonesia governor Boediono, but also one of his key cabinet members, Sri Mulyani. The attacks on Boediono and Sri Mulyani were supported by all major parties in the DPR except Yudhoyono's Democratic Party (Partai Demokrat, PD).

The DPR stepped up its efforts to investigate the case in September 2009, when Committee XI asked the BPK to carry out an audit of the funds used to prop up Bank Century. During the course of the audit, the chair of BPK, Anwar Nasution, reported that Sri Mulyani had expressed doubts about the quality of the data gathered by Bank Indonesia when monitoring Bank Century transactions.[10] Overall, Committee XI's activities succeeded in focusing public attention on the problems in the gov-

---

8   'Prita's nightmare', *Tempo*, 10 June 2009.
9   'House wants investigation of $669m Bank Century bailout', *Jakarta Globe*, 27 August 2009.
10 'Mulyani doubts BI data: BPK', *Jakarta Post*, 25 September 2009.

ernment's oversight of the banking system, particularly the apparent failings in the operations of Bank Indonesia. Moreover, the DPR's support for a BPK audit gave weight and impetus to the agency's operations and may strengthen its effectiveness in the longer term.

Public consultation: a mixed record

Despite signs of improvement, the DPR's record with regard to public consultation has been mixed. Given the parliament's compartmentalised structure, the quality of consultation tends to vary from one committee to another. On the one hand, there have been examples of increasingly inclusive deliberations. After Law No. 27/2009 on the MPR, DPR, DPD and DPRD was passed in August 2009, a legal NGO that had often been critical of the DPR and its proceedings actually commended the committee for its openness to public input and its willingness to experiment with new methods of conducting deliberations (PSHK 2009).

But other cases point to the continued reluctance of some DPR committees to carry out their legislative functions in an open and consultative manner. Some of the worst features of DPR processes were exhibited during the passage of the infamous anti-pornography bill (Sherlock 2008). The initial draft of the bill was compiled without public consultation in the 1999–2004 DPR. It then sat untouched in the DPR secretariat for several years before suddenly being revived by a special committee in 2005. This committee added controversial clauses criminalising public expressions of affection, tight clothing, dances deemed to be sexually provocative and other so-called pornographic activities (*pornoaksi*). Once again the deliberations occurred without any public input, leading to a rancorous debate in the DPR that shook the country during 2006 and 2007. After some token consultations with regions potentially affected by the bill (such as Bali and Papua), a slightly watered-down version was eventually passed into law in October 2008.

The patchy record of the DPR in relation to public accountability is also illustrated by the issue of public access to documentation of DPR debates. In recent years, committees have begun to produce verbatim transcripts of their debates on legislation. One particular motivation for this measure was that committee members were 'frightened of the Constitutional Court' and thus felt the need to have a record of the committee's discussion in order to defend newly passed laws against a possible Constitutional Court challenge.[11] This can be considered a step towards making the DPR a more transparent institution. Internationally, the avail-

---

11 Interview with Alvin Lie, former member of Committee VII, Jakarta, February 2007.

ability of published and accessible transcripts of parliamentary proceedings is regarded as standard good practice for democratic legislatures. Increasingly, there is an expectation that such transcripts will be made available online within a short period of being produced (IPU 2006: 43–68). But in the DPR, transcripts are produced only at the discretion of the committee concerned and for the committee's own internal use. They are not normally accessible to the general public. In other words, the DPR has developed neither the procedures nor the infrastructure to produce accurate, timely and accessible transcripts of proceedings as a routine matter.

CABINET AND PARLIAMENT: THE PARADOX OF INDISCIPLINE

Much of the existing commentary on the DPR focuses on the relationship between the representation of political parties in cabinet on the one hand and their representation in parliament on the other. The basic assumption of these analyses is that there is a close connection between the two: namely that the solidarity of an alliance of parties in cabinet will automatically translate into a solid block of votes from the same parties in the DPR. As a consequence, the outcome of the 2009 elections—which gave the parties supporting Yudhoyono a majority in parliament and handed him a second presidential term—raised concerns that the DPR would cease to be a 'check and balance' on the power of the presidency. With the cabinet containing representatives of all major parties except the Indonesian Democratic Party of Struggle (Partai Demokrasi Indonesia Perjuangan, PDIP), critics argued that the DPR lacked an effective opposition and thus would no longer be able to critically scrutinise government legislation and oversee its policies. Some commentators even expressed fears that the DPR might return to being a 'rubber-stamp' parliament.[12]

Ironically, the opposite concern had been expressed after the 2004 elections. At that time, many observers predicted that Yudhoyono would find it difficult to govern effectively because of his lack of a parliamentary majority.[13] Apparently guided by conventional wisdom, these analysts suggested that the mismatch between a directly elected president and a parliament dominated by opposition parties was a formula for legislative deadlock and possible political instability. Although the early

---

12 'Growing Indonesia coalition may hurt democracy, say activists', *Jakarta Globe*, 2 September 2009; 'Next cabinet could go wild without proper checks and balances: Indonesian experts', *Jakarta Post*, 6 September 2009.

13 'Political coalition could end reforms', *Jakarta Post*, 18 August 2004; 'Indonesia's Yudhyono tells parliament to be nice', *Reuters*, 1 October 2004.

period of the post-2004 DPR initially seemed to provide some evidence for this theory, these alarmist forecasts ultimately did not come to pass. This was because they were based on misconceptions about the way the DPR works, its relations with cabinet and the nature of the connection between ministers and their fellow party members in parliament. For the same reason, the post-2009 concerns will most likely not come to fruition either.

The dynamics of a 'conventional' parliament are usually determined by the balance between the seats held by each party. In Indonesia's DPR, however, decision making is a much more complex and opaque process. The balance of the numbers from each party assembled in a plenary session is relatively unimportant, because decisions are made, not by voting, but rather by consensus-oriented negotiations in the DPR's committees, each of which has its own internal mode of operation. The deliberations and lobbying required to obtain the agreement of all caucuses take place in private meetings and are generally not recorded. Given this dominance of committees over caucuses, 'coalitions' in the DPR have not been solid alliances that vote strictly either for the government or for the opposition. At best, they have been arrangements of convenience about cabinet seats. Such arrangements 'begin with discussion about seats ... and not at all about the platform or direction of the coalition' (Pamungkas 2009). And just as cabinet solidarity has been very weak — with each party interested mainly in supporting and defending 'its' minister rather than the administration as a whole — there has also been no real sense of a 'government party' in parliament.

In the DPR inaugurated in 2009, members of Yudhoyono's PD can be relied on to support the government line on issues of importance, particularly if it is under attack over a sensitive matter. But the behaviour of other parties — in this and previous parliaments — suggests that they will feel little reluctance to criticise the actions of the government even though they may be part of the administration themselves. In the Bank Century case discussed above, for instance, all major parties in the DPR except PD criticised the government for its handling of the issue even though all except PDIP occupied seats in cabinet. Had Boediono and Sri Mulyani been affiliated with a particular party, they probably would have been defended by their respective parties. As independent technocrats, however, they were fair game for all parties except PD.

In the scholarly discussion on political parties in Indonesia, the fact that party leaders exercise little day-to-day control over ordinary members of their caucuses in the DPR has often been overlooked. The dominant view has been that the top leaders of central party boards exercise monopoly power over their parties. While such an interpretation may be true in relation to control of party resources and appointments, it rarely translates into enforcement of a party line on policy in the parliament. Since policy development in most parties is rudimentary at best, leaders rarely have a predetermined view on the issues related to individual bills, particularly if they entail complex technical detail. Thus, committee caucuses commonly express opinions in relation to the clauses of a particular bill without reference to the party leadership. Moreover, the position adopted by members of one committee frequently conflicts with the position adopted by members of the same party in another committee discussing a related bill. At public hearings, it is not uncommon to witness caucus members advocating views that clearly contradict those of their colleagues or that exhibit total ignorance of basic facts. But since members are unable to register a personal vote under the requirement for consensus, it has not really mattered what position they take personally.

This lack of consistency and discipline often escapes public attention, especially if the issue under discussion is a non-controversial one. However, when the topic of debate *is* controversial, the absence of clear party lines and the confusing pluralism of personal opinions become strikingly evident. During the intense arguments about the anti-pornography bill in 2006 and 2007, for example, organisations lobbying the parliament found it extremely difficult to determine the views of the various parties. Members of the same caucus often expressed contradictory opinions during committee meetings. This was the case even with the Prosperous Justice Party (Partai Keadilan Sejahtera, PKS), a party with a reputation for discipline (Sherlock 2008: 172; Sherlock 2009: 28–31).

Interestingly, central party boards have largely been indifferent to the chaotic pluralism of views within their parliamentary caucuses. Some have 'recalled' DPR members (that is, removed them from their seats), but none of these cases has involved the contravention of party policy. Caucus members have been removed for embarrassing personal behaviour, after an internal party split or for switching parties, but never because they failed to toe the party line on policy (Djadijono 2007). On the few occasions when an open vote on a policy issue has been allowed during a plenary session, the parties have found it difficult to discipline their members. During the vote in 2006 on whether or not to allow the importation of foreign rice, for example, some caucuses were split and others had large numbers of members absent themselves.

The paradox of this situation is that the lack of discipline and coordination within parties seems to act as an unintended mechanism of accountability. The individualism of DPR members and parliamentary committees has undermined the executive's attempts to enforce the loyalty of legislators towards the presidency, resulting in continual criticism of the government despite the governing coalition's nominal majority in parliament. Larry Diamond has argued that 'relying for accountability on the *incoherence* of political parties — that is, the fracture between their executive and legislative wings — is hardly a good strategy for democratic development' (Diamond 2009: 335). This is a pertinent observation, but a system in which the executive finds it impossible to establish a monopoly over government — together with confused and inconsistent policy debate — is nevertheless one of the consequences of the complex set of interactions between government ministers and the committee-based DPR. Consequently, a nuanced analysis of the activities of the DPR cannot be based on a count of seats but must identify the interplay of interests among the parties, committees and individuals involved in any particular issue or piece of legislation.

CONCLUSION

The study of parliaments focuses on both the formal institutions of power and the people who exercise power within them, making political parties and their leaders major elements of the analysis. Accordingly, the starting point of this chapter was the DPR as an institution. It subsequently examined key features of the DPR's interaction with the process of democratisation since 1998. Most significantly, constitutional reforms undertaken between 1999 and 2002 have led to a shift in the balance of power between executive and legislature, coinciding with the advent of free elections and the rise of a more assertive civil society. As a result, the post-Suharto parliaments have seen a complex and contradictory interplay between socio-political reforms and pre-existing practices within the DPR.

The dynamic evolution of the parliament has produced a chamber that even the existing political class finds difficult to predict and control. The culture of the Indonesian political elite is still one that is most comfortable when there is a manageable status quo, that is, a collusive division of power among those who are on the 'inside'. But much to the dismay of politicians and their associated patrons and lobbyists, getting inside the chambers of power now depends on appealing to an electorate that is growing in scepticism and choosiness. This, in turn, has created the necessity for them to respond to an increasing range of demanding social interests.

The tension between reform and continued oligarchic power is reflected in the rapidly changing composition of the parliamentary elite. While the elite has not been completely replaced or transformed since 1998, it has been thoroughly shaken up. This trend is manifest in the rise and fall of political parties — and the dramatic changes to their bases — during the course of three elections. Golkar has experienced an erosion of political capital as its hold over the military and bureaucracy has weakened; PDIP's exclusive claim to represent populist nationalism and egalitarianism has faded; and parties relying on the support of Muslim organisations such as Nahdlatul Ulama and Muhammadiyah have declined in influence. On the other hand, newly founded parties such as PD and PKS have grown quickly.

These developments have put pressure on the DPR as well. While the current collusive structures of committee-based, consensus-oriented decision making remain strong, they do not operate as smoothly and complacently as they once did. The DPR may still be seen as a chamber of cronies. But these cronies and the parties from whence they come increasingly have no choice but to be effective representatives of the people if they want to stay in the political game.

REFERENCES

Baldwin, Nicholas and Donald Shell (2001), *Second Chambers*, Frank Cass, London.

Braun, Sebastian (2008), 'Indonesia's presidential democracy: a factor of stability or instability?', PhD dissertation, Humboldt University, Berlin.

Datta, Indraneel (2002), 'Parliamentary politics in Soeharto's Indonesia 1987–98', PhD thesis, School of Oriental and African Studies, University of London, London.

Diamond, Larry (2009), 'Is a "rainbow coalition" a good way to govern?', *Bulletin of Indonesian Economic Studies* 45(3): 333–6.

Djadijono, M. (2007), 'Fraksi, recalling dan performance wakil rakyat' [The party caucus: recall and performance of the people's representatives], *Analisis CSIS*, 36(2): 182–98.

Ellis, Andrew and Etsi Yudhini (2002), 'Indonesia's new state institutions: the constitution completed, now for the detail ... a commentary on the MPR Annual Session 1–10 August 2002', National Democratic Institute, Jakarta, November.

Formappi (Forum Masyarakat Peduli Parlemen Indonesia) (2005), *Lembaga Perwakilan Rakyat di Indonesia: Studi dan Analisis Sebelum dan Setelah Perubahan UUD 1945* [People's Representative Institutions in Indonesia: Studies and Analysis before and after the Amendments to the 1945 Constitution], Formappi, Jakarta.

Indrayana, Denny (2008), *Indonesian Constitutional Reform 1999–2002*, Kompas Book Publishing, Jakarta.

IPU (Inter-Parliamentary Union) (2006), *Parliament and Democracy in the Twenty-first Century: A Guide to Good Practice*, IPU, Geneva.

Laksmana, Evan A. (2009), 'New house, new rules', Centre for Strategic and International Studies, Jakarta, 24 October.

Pamungkas, Sigit (2009), 'Koalisi minus loyalitas' [Coalition minus loyalty], *Kompas*, 26 October.

Patterson, Samuel and Anthony Mughan (1999), *Senates: Bicameralism in the Contemporary World*, Ohio State University Press, Columbus OH.

PSHK (Pusat Studi Hukum dan Kebijakan) (2009), *Penyempurnaan Paket UU Politik terhadap Pengesahan RUU Susduk* [Finalisation of the Packet of Political Laws for Passage of the Bill on Legislative Institutions], PSHK, Jakarta.

Robison, Richard and Vedi Hadiz (2004), *Reorganising Power in Indonesia: The Politics of Oligarchy in an Age of Markets*, RoutledgeCurzon, London and New York.

Scheier, Edward (2005), *The Role of Constitution-building Processes in Democratization: Case Study Indonesia*, International IDEA, Stockholm.

Sherlock, Stephen (2003), 'Struggling to change: the Indonesian parliament in an era of *reformasi'*, Centre for Democratic Institutions, Canberra, January.

Sherlock, Stephen (2005), 'Indonesia's regional assembly: democracy, representation and the regions', CDI Policy Papers 2005/1, Centre for Democratic Institutions, Canberra.

Sherlock, Stephen (2007), 'The Indonesian parliament after two elections: what has really changed?', CDI Policy Papers 2007/1, Centre for Democratic Institutions, Canberra.

Sherlock, Stephen (2008), 'Parties and decision-making in the Indonesian parliament: a case study of the pornography bill', *Australian Journal of Asian Law* 10(2): 159–83.

Sherlock, Stephen (2009), 'Indonesia's 2009 elections: the new electoral system and the competing parties', CDI Policy Papers on Political Governance 2009/01, Centre for Democratic Institutions, Canberra, March.

Susanti, Bivitri (2007) *Menyoal Kompetisi Politik dalam Proses Legislasi di Indonesia* [The Question of Political Competition in the Legislative Process in Indonesia], PSHK, Jakarta.

Ziegenhain, Patrick (2008), *The Indonesian Parliament and Democratization*, Institute of Southeast Asian Studies, Singapore.

Ziegenhain, Patrick (2009), 'The Indonesian parliament and its impact on democratic consolidation', in M. Bünte and A. Ufen (eds), *Democratization in Post-Suharto Indonesia*, Routledge, London and New York, pp. 33–52.

PART II

Society and Democratic Contestation

9   ENTERTAINMENT, DOMESTICATION AND DISPERSAL: STREET POLITICS AS POPULAR CULTURE

Ariel Heryanto

'Clearly, elections are important but perhaps for reasons
different from those asserted in formal democratic theory'
(Taylor 1996: 5)

In an afterword to Robert Taylor's *The Politics of Elections in Southeast Asia* (1996), the late political scientist Daniel Lev expressed relief at discovering that 'culture' had been entirely ignored in the collection of essays. Lev was obviously dissatisfied with the previous efforts of some of his contemporaries who had analysed elections in Southeast Asia in general – and Indonesian electoral politics in particular – from a 'culturalist' standpoint. However, both Lev and those he criticised appeared to recognise only some outdated conception of 'culture'. In their view, 'culture' was something static, unique or essential to a particular society. Presumably Lev and his counterparts were unfamiliar with the growing body of literature in anthropology, gender and cultural studies where culture – as a concept and practice – is critically problematised, instead of being essentialised or avoided. To this day, many political analysts continue to ignore, overlook or underestimate the cultural aspects of electoral processes, leading to a serious gap in the scholarship on elections and their meaning for citizens' daily lives. This chapter attempts to fill this gap by offering an alternative perspective on elections in Indonesia, highlighting key trends since the downfall of the New Order government in 1998.

My discussion focuses on the street politics of non-elite groups – often conveniently referred to as 'the masses' – during the election campaign period. The political and electoral dynamics of the post-Suharto period have produced a new kind of disempowerment – one that is marked by the dominance over the electorate of the entertainment industry and its values. In addition to the rise of the politics of entertainment, the populace has been seriously fragmented by the heightened political competition among its members. As a result, Indonesia's contemporary masses appear to have voluntarily become dispersed and domesticated. Ironically, this is a situation that the New Order strongly desired but was incapable of achieving. Under Suharto, the masses often engaged in rowdy activities when elections were held, eventually worrying the authoritarian government. The regime's attempts to curtail the actions of unruly male youths during election campaigns largely failed. This trend points to an interesting paradox of power relations: systematic state repression does not necessarily generate total powerlessness, passivity or docility among the masses; and conversely, greater political liberalisation does not automatically increase the power of the masses.

The chapter is divided into four main parts. In the first section, I introduce the notion of Indonesia as an orality-oriented society, in which personal interactions and a collective predilection for interactive media predispose citizens towards a different concept of elections than in more literacy-dependent nations. Second, I demonstrate how the new rules in the 2009 elections have both empowered and dispersed the masses, with an unprecedented level of competition among candidates eroding the sense of a 'unified' mass at the grassroots level. By way of contrast, the third part describes the role of the masses during New Order election campaigns, when macho motorcyclists celebrated the violation of traffic rules as a form of subversive act of hyper-obedience to the regime (see more on page 189). Fourth, I analyse the role of the entertainment industry in the 2009 elections, with campaigns copying the formats of television shows and the masses exchanging political participation for the ultimate domestication of politics by entertainment. I conclude by emphasising the irony that the subversive power of the masses has been dissipating at a time of deepening democratic consolidation in Indonesia.

INDONESIA: AN ORALITY-ORIENTED SOCIETY

It is not within the scope of this chapter to discuss this body of literature in detail, but a few of its core features in relation to Indonesia need to be highlighted. Indonesia has a high official literacy rate (92 per cent in 2009, with the country ranked 61st in the world).[1] Statistics aside, however, the official literacy rate refers primarily to the ability to recognise,

---

1   Figures based on the UN's 2009 Human Development Index. See 'RI still propping up Asian list on UN's quality-of-life gauge', *Jakarta Post*, 6 October 2009.

rather than a preference for maximum use of, the alphabet and mathematical figures. In this chapter, the reference to Indonesia as a primarily orality-oriented society implies a fairly low rate of *functional* literacy, as opposed to the *nominal* literacy indicated by the statistics.

Compared to their counterparts in more literacy-dependent societies, people in Indonesia, including the literati and graduates of higher education, prefer to share important information and messages through face-to-face communication. This involves the physical presence of the interlocutors, expressing themselves through words, clothing and body language, in the immediate spatial and temporal ambience of 'real-time' interactions. In such a society, everyday life tends to be communally oriented, with little or no space for privacy.[2] In contrast, in more literacy-dependent societies, separation between author and audience as two separate, autonomous beings is widely celebrated, and accuracy together with a great reliance on objectified text is highly valued. A sacred oath is commonly used to formalise an agreement in an orality-oriented society, whereas a written contract is used in a literacy-dependent society. Silent reading in a busy public space is normal in the latter, while conversations with strangers about family matters are standard practice in the former.

Obviously, no society is in reality either purely orality-oriented or literacy-dependent. Rather, in any given society the different modes of communication are in competition with each other, with certain historical periods more marked by one than the other. The rapid development of digital media technology was more confronting to the older generation in the highly literate societies that produced them (Fernback 2003) than to the rest of the population. The same technology easily finds a warm reception in orality-oriented societies like Indonesia, as it fits better with existing norms and social practices (Heryanto 2007).

Like the modern nation-state itself, elections as we know them today are the product of a highly literate social order. This does not mean, however, that elections or democracy are essentially incompatible with non-Western societies. Among the orality-oriented and formerly colonised peoples in Asia and Africa, elections have been held with varying degrees of success. Regardless of whether or not coercion was involved in their introduction to these orality-oriented societies, elections have often encountered difficulties beyond technical or logistical issues. To date, the standard administration of elections has involved legislation written in the highly analytical language of the literati; a procession

---

2 Strictly speaking there is as yet no word for 'privacy' in Indonesian. With the relentless march of capitalism in Indonesia from the 1980s, there has been a serious struggle to introduce and legitimise the notion of 'private property', with limited and partial success.

whereby voters go to the voting booth as individuals and read and mark the voting paper in solitude; and bureaucratically organised vote counting. Elections may, of course, take on a very different shape and process in the future with the expansion of digital technology, in ways already anticipated by, for instance, the voting procedures used in reality television shows (see more below). Against this background, the following sections will discuss the specific features of the 2009 elections in Indonesia and point to their historical differences to their predecessors.

THE 2009 ELECTIONS: POPULAR EMPOWERMENT AND DISPERSAL[3]

As in most previous Indonesian elections, the outcome of the 2009 national parliamentary ballot was highly predictable, although the precise degree of the winning party's triumph was a subject of speculation prior to voting day.[4] The victory of the Democratic Party (Partai Demokrat, PD) — and the subsequent re-election of incumbent president Susilo Bambang Yudhoyono — also meant a continuation and indeed a strengthening of the political status quo.[5] One important innovation that did distinguish the 2009 elections from their predecessors, however, was a new regulation that allocated seats won by parties to the nominees with the highest number of votes, not those ranked highest on the party list. This open party list system was the result of a decision by the Constitutional Court in December 2008 to declare party list rankings unconstitutional. The new rules had two contradictory effects on the general population: in a very complex way, they were both empowering and disempowering at the same time.

Popular empowerment

Despite a host of logistical problems (see Schmidt in this volume), the 2009 elections had an empowering effect in that they extended or reinforced the political education of all citizens. Through a wide range of

---

3   I gratefully acknowledge the generous assistance of Ahmad Faisol and his team from Institut Studi Arus Informasi (ISAI), Jakarta, in collecting a large amount of empirical material on the 2009 elections on my behalf, which I use in this section.

4   The outcomes of the 1955 and 1999 elections, which both took place at moments of crisis, were less predictable.

5   Taylor (1996: 4) observes that this is the general outcome of elections in Southeast Asia. It should probably be added that the same is true of many other countries outside the region.

means, Indonesians—especially the socially disadvantaged—were informed about the basic principles and values of elections as an essential component of a democracy. This was not a particularly new experience, however. Even at the height of the New Order's politics of depoliticisation, some information on the practical skills and knowledge required to participate in elections had been made available. From 1999, in the absence of state authoritarianism and the former top-down style of propaganda and indoctrination, political education—particularly regarding elections—took on a more democratically conscious character. Most significantly, this change was accompanied by a high degree of voluntarism and bottom-up participation.

Before the 2009 elections, officials from the General Elections Commission (Komisi Pemilihan Umum, KPU) and the political parties travelled to remote areas to explain the new rules and procedures. Many of these activities were designed specifically for targeted audiences from a wide variety of geographical, ethnic and linguistic backgrounds, and most were highly orality-oriented. Consequently, the information sessions relied heavily on face-to-face interactions, including the use of traditional performing arts (with human actors or other visual aids), modern music concerts and ceremonies in the vernacular language, mostly within the framework of casual gatherings. Some KPU and party instructors travelled on foot to traditional markets so that they could communicate with locals face-to-face.

In several places, vans fitted with loudspeakers travelled slowly through the villages, broadcasting important information over their speakers. The attempts to educate the masses even reached people who were too young to vote. In Central Jakarta, for example, teachers from six elementary schools spent many hours training hundreds of pupils in the basic concepts of political elections. The training involved not just lectures and discussions, but also simulation activities in which pupils in grades 5 and 6 experimented with mock elections. The students delivered campaign speeches from lecterns in the school yard, designed posters, engaged in open debates about policy, cast votes by secret ballot and assessed the validity of ballot papers. Activities such as these took place across the archipelago, making the 2009 elections a remarkably instructive and inclusive experience for many.

Popular dispersal

While the elections had energising and empowering effects on ordinary Indonesians, these were counterbalanced by the centrifugal tendencies triggered by the new electoral laws. Most importantly, the new regulations pitted candidates from the same party against each other. One of the most obvious effects of the new laws was to eliminate the longstanding convention of party leaders putting themselves at the top of the party rankings and thus securing their (re-)election. Under the new rules, these politicians had no choice but to invest in new and extensive campaign efforts in order to maintain their positions. As a side-effect of this more competitive electoral system, a new type of candidate emerged to challenge the dominance of old party functionaries: the 'celebrities', referring to television and film actors, musicians and comedians.

Overall, 61 celebrities ran for parliamentary seats at the national level,[6] and 18 of them were successful. In some cases they did much better in the elections than senior politicians. For instance, television drama actor Rieke Dyah Pitaloka obtained the single largest number of votes for PDIP in the West Java II electoral district, leaving party leader Taufiq Kiemas behind. Similarly, former film star Nurul Arifin ranked first in West Java VII district, defeating senior politician Ade Komarudin from the same party, Golkar.[7] Not to be outdone, comedian Mandra came in ahead of the incumbent House speaker Agung Laksono (Bayuni 2009). In 2008, actors Rano Karno and Dede Yusuf had respectively been elected deputy district head of Tangerang and vice-governor of the province of West Java.[8] The considerable success of celebrities was only partly related to the new electoral laws and regulations, however. Other factors were at play as well, as will be discussed later.

An equally significant effect of the amended electoral law was to encourage an upsurge in the desire among ordinary citizens to run in the regional elections. One observer has described Indonesia's 2009 parliamentary elections, which were held from the central down to the provincial, district and municipal levels, as 'the world's largest single-day election':[9] 11,219 candidates competed for the 560 seats in the national parliament; 32,263 nominees tried to obtain one of the 1,998 parliamentary seats at the provincial level; and 246,588 candidates contested 16,270 seats at the district/municipality level.[10] On the one hand, these figures seemed to contradict widespread reports about the prevailing apathy among the general population. On the other hand, the same figures confirmed people's cynical suspicion that something other than genuine

---

6   'Music meets politics', *Jakarta Post*, 8 April 2009.
7   'Dari panggung hiburan ke senayan' [From entertainment stage to parliament], *Koran Tempo*, 26 April 2009.
8   'Pencitraan masih tanpa isi' [Image building still lacks substance], *Kompas*, 1 June 2009.
9   'Successful election marks a decade of democracy', *Jakarta Post*, 9 April 2009.
10 'Selamat berpesta demokrasi Indonesia!' [Enjoy the Indonesian festival of democracy!], *Kompas*, 9 April 2009.

interest in a political or moral cause must have been driving so many people to join the contest.

Entry to electoral politics by citizens with little or no political experience in formal state administration is not new in Indonesia. Especially after the fall of the New Order in 1998, party officials recruited thugs and other underworld figures to act as political fixers or to mobilise voters. In contrast, the 2009 elections saw a significant number of ordinary citizens — including some fragile-looking elderly people — running in the elections. Many of these people did not have any meaningful economic power, political experience or institutional support. Examples abounded across the archipelago: they included *becak* (tricycle) driver Abdul Wahid in Tegal; *ojek* (motorcycle taxi) driver Soleeman Mooi in Kupang; street vendor Erni Wahyuni in Samarinda; vehicle washer Joko Prihatin in Kudus; public parking assistant Sukardji in Ponorogo; and *angkot* (local van) driver Benedictus Adu in Jakarta. Representing the low-income classes of Indonesian society, these candidates claimed to fight not only for themselves, but also for other people in a similar position.

Closely related to the participation of ordinary citizens in the 2009 elections was the emergence of lone campaigners. Apparently, many Indonesians were led to believe that anyone could run in the elections, regardless of their financial and political resources. They also believed, it seems, that campaigning could be done effectively on an individual basis. This did not mean that their election-related gatherings featured a star performer as the focus of the event. Rather, it meant the candidate putting on a one-person show in public, sometimes without the presence of organised supporters. For instance, Enteng Sanjaya, dubbed 'Manusia Contreng' (Man with a Voting Tick), had his whole body painted yellow and white to represent the colours of the ballot paper. He danced alone in the middle of the main street in Pasuruan (East Java) and pushed his bike around the town to spread information on the voting procedure. In the same vein, Sragen-born *ojek* driver Agus Suwarno toured the nation on a bicycle to raise support for his party. In Banten, another lone campaigner, Hudi Yusuf, donned a super-hero costume to gather support for his candidacy. In combination, these individualised activities signified an important shift away from previous campaign practices, which had drawn their strength from impressive displays of mass power.

On the face of it, the increased involvement of commoners and enthusiastic lone performers gave the impression of higher levels of political mass education and more sophisticated campaign strategies. I will argue, however, that this phenomenon has much more consequential external aspects, which are linked to Indonesian politics generally as well as the expansion of the new media and entertainment industry. From this perspective, the competitive individualisation of elections has coincided with the emergence of entertainment and celebrity-driven campaign formats, leading not to the political empowerment but to the dispersal and domestication of the masses. As I will discuss in the next section, this dispersal was something the New Order had tried – but had been unable – to achieve.

THE NEW ORDER: THE MASSES IN THE POLITICS OF APPEARANCE

During much of the New Order, elections were held regularly. However, there was barely anything that resembled a contest of political parties. The outcomes of six successive elections during the New Order were the same and always highly predictable. Nonetheless, the government took the trouble of engineering some rhetorical appearance of popular participation and political contest. It mobilised the masses and attempted to make them appear to be supporters of rival political parties. In reality, however, it transpired that the masses behaved in ways that were very different to what the government wanted – and indeed different to what many urban intellectuals and distant observers have generally understood.

In contrast to the situation since 1999, when scores of contesting parties have fragmented the loyalties of the politically active masses, the masses in post-1971 New Order elections were mobilised behind no more than three officially sanctioned electoral machines. The large concentrations of rival crowds made it possible for members of each group to *imagine* and *act as if* they were part of an overwhelmingly powerful force, even if some crowds were larger than others. This was particularly remarkable since, outside the election period, the regime offered no public space for independent political forces. In an ironic inverse of the post-New Order situation, the masses barely had any power *between* the five-yearly elections, but in the brief moments of the elections they transformed themselves into a gigantic public force. From the perspective of the regime, the elections were intended to be no more than a make-believe spectacle. But in reality, the presence and actions of the masses were real and forceful.

These masses manifested their power not only through their sheer presence in immense numbers in the streets, stadiums and town squares, but more importantly through loud noise and strong colours. This power was not consciously political, ideologically driven or organised along any identifiable structure. It had neither the capacity nor the desire to challenge, let alone replace, the incumbent government. Nonetheless, the effects of this display of power were threatening to the political elite and the politics of appearance ('stability and order') that the government prescribed. The unruly behaviour of the masses took different forms, but one stood out: convoys of motorcycles without mufflers. Macho male motorcyclists in elaborate costumes roamed the streets and flaunted their multiple violations of traffic rules and conventions. More than the allowed maximum of two persons would ride on a single motorcycle, none wearing helmets and some even standing on the seat. They ignored all rules pertaining to traffic direction and lane division. Speeding well above the limit, they performed spectacular moves. Others rode on over-laden trucks, usually playing loud music over their loudspeakers. Pre-dictably, these activities caused traffic jams, accidents, and brawls with non-participants or supporters of other political parties.

It was the down-to-earth, highly masculine festivity and the flaunted illegality of the event that appeared to matter most to the participat-ing masses. The process and results of the election that had provided space for their activities in the first place were simply irrelevant to them. In contrast to the urban intelligentsia and political activists who took the elections seriously and denounced the results as illegal or lacking in credibility, the masses seemed not to care in the least about electoral manipulation or state pretence. What 'these politically alienated and economically exploited masses' cared about was that 'once every five years [they] became the supreme anonymous subjects that dominated the public space for several nights and days' (Heryanto 2006a: 151). To understand these masses, however, we need to go beyond the McLuha-nist conceptual framework of orality-oriented societies. Instead of read-ing their activities as a form of political resistance, perhaps we should understand them — with Jean Baudrillard (1983: 43) — as an unintended subversion on the part of the 'apolitical' masses, who 'accept everything and redirect everything *en bloc* into the spectacular ... without requiring any meaning, ultimately without resistance'.

Cultural politics has been sorely understudied or misunderstood in Indonesian studies. Accordingly, this unintended subversion by a kind of hyper-obedience on the part of the New Order masses has largely gone unnoticed or has been seriously underestimated by the Indonesian intel-ligentsia and distant observers. In contrast, the regime itself was more cognisant of the potential force of the masses. It must be recalled that the New Order state came to power in 1966 on the back of the successful instigation of mass hysteria against and massacres of the left. With sup-port from the world's liberal democracies, Suharto's regime maintained its power for the next three decades with a significant measure of thug-gery. As a result, Suharto knew that:

> ... dictators can go to sleep at night lulled by roars of adulation and support ... only to wake up the next morning to find their golden calves smashed and

their tablets of law overturned. The applauding crowds of yesterday have become today a cursing, abusive mob (Mbembe 1992: 14–15).

Thus, from the 1992 elections onwards, the New Order government attempted to curtail what it had initially sponsored, namely the mobilisation of the urban masses to enliven otherwise dull sham elections. In its place, the government proposed that future election campaigns should be conducted within the confines of a demarcated space (a well-guarded hall or stadium), and preferably through the tightly controlled mass media (particularly television). By keeping the masses at a distance from the campaign venues and turning them into passive spectators of the mass media, the government hoped to maintain 'order and stability'.[11]

As with many other state policies, the proposed restrictions on motorcycle convoys were never fully enforced across the nation. Instead, gradual restrictions were imposed on an ad hoc basis, with uneven results. For instance, in Yogyakarta in 1992 the local government made sporadic and inconsistent attempts to restrict the motorcycle convoys. In hyperobedience, the masses from all parties responded in unison. Not only did they refrain from running the convoys and confronting the security forces, but they went further by removing all signs and appurtenances of the election campaign, thus threatening to destroy the political spectacle the regime liked to call the 'festival of democracy'.

Until the New Order was formally ousted in 1998, the motorcycle convoys were never totally absent from street politics, and during the first post-New Order elections in 1999, the urban masses unleashed some of the greatest convoys ever. Ironically, it was not until 2009 – when the elections had become more liberalised – that the massive crowds dispersed voluntarily, the convoys thinned and became few and far between, and the underclasses were atomised. Thus, when successive post-New Order governments effectively tried to ban motorcycle convoys, this move was already redundant. Few in the population seemed interested either in opposing the restriction or in revitalising the convoys. While motorcycle convoys could still be observed in the 2009 elections, they were far less frequent, attracted much smaller numbers of participants and had none of the previous exuberance of style. In their place, there was a surge in the use of glossy multi-media electoral campaigning. Inadvertently, this trend fitted precisely with the New Order's proposal in 1992 to curtail the kind of disorderly mass participation that it had failed to control.

---

11 There is another layer of irony: the same government attempted to prohibit the publishing of any reports on election campaign activities in 1977 (van Dijk 1977: 12–13).

ELECTION CAMPAIGNS AS POPULAR CULTURE

Earlier in this chapter, I suggested that the trends in the 2009 elections cannot be attributed solely to the competition-inducing nature of the new electoral laws. There is no direct causal relationship between the new laws and the galvanisation of enthusiasm among the underclasses to run for election. The expansion of the new media and entertainment industry must have played a significant role as well. This section will elaborate this point.

Scholars of media studies have long been aware of the Janus-faced effects of media technology. The new media technology is both socialising and alienating, empowering in some areas and disempowering in others. The 2009 electoral laws made democratic procedures more equal, leading many to the illusion that all citizens are politically equal in elections, regardless of their socio-economic strength and connections. In 2009, many individual villagers ran in the parliamentary elections, splintering their local communities and foreclosing the possibility of meaningful mass support for any one candidate. In a separate but intersecting course of development, the new media technology has transformed the brave new industrial world of the mid-twentieth century into what McLuhan called the 'global village'. What McLuhan did not foresee, however, was the inherent countereffect that comes with the dispersal of digital media gadgets. As more and more people separated by large distances have easier, quicker and more affordable access to intimate communication around the clock, they often remain distant strangers to their next door neighbours.

Recent studies on elections and popular culture in Indonesia have highlighted the role of performers in party politics and the growing interest of professional politicians in singing or dancing in public. Newspapers and magazines as well as scholarly works have documented, for example, the incumbent president's success in attracting potential voters through songs he has written himself. Most writing on the connections between politics/politicians and popular culture/artists focuses on the use one makes of the other, or the involvement of one group of professionals in the domain of the other (see Kartomi 2005; Lindsay 2007, 2009; McGraw 2009). Often these studies focus on prominent artists and politicians, and how they 'manipulate' the masses. However, I wish to consider two distinct yet closely related processes. First, I look at the overwhelming impact of the entertainment industry in facilitating the growth of the spectacle and entertainment aspects of elections. Second, I consider the appeal of the 'do-it-yourself' (DIY) spirit to the general population, a recent trend accelerated by new media developments. Both discussions draw less immediate and less personalised connections between politics

192 Problems of Democratisation in Indonesia

and popular culture than have generally been emphasised in the existing literature. The connections between the two processes are more funda-mental and have more far-reaching implications than most studies have indicated thus far, because they represent a new modality of perspective and outlook. Both focus on disadvantaged groups of people.

From 1998, Indonesia experienced a decade of unprecedented media expansion. Driven by the lifting of restrictions on press freedom, the period saw a quantum leap in many directions. The number of print media tripled, the number of national television networks doubled and 200 local television networks sprouted across the archipelago.[12] The number of officially registered radio stations grew from 700 in 1997 to more than 1,200 a decade later,[13] with unregistered stations adding sev-eral hundred more to that number. From 1998 to 2008, the total number of hours of television broadcasting increased nearly fourfold (from 42,029 to 159,097 hours per year), while the number of households with a televi-sion set nearly tripled to almost 16 million. Given the communal style of television consumption in most households, the number of viewers is probably four times that figure.[14]

At the same time, ownership of mobile telephones jumped more than tenfold to 42 million, and private access to an internet connection increased more than 11 times to well over 14 million.[15] As an estimated 65 per cent of internet users went online without owning a computer, instead using a computer at one of the mushrooming internet cafes, the number of Indonesians *owning and using* a personal computer with an internet connection would have been far smaller than the actual number of Indonesians accessing the internet. In 2008, there was a 645 per cent increase in the number of Indonesian Facebook users, to 8.52 million, making Indonesia the world's seventh-largest nation of Facebook users (Eldon 2009).

All the above developments were matched by equally phenomenal growth in the entertainment industry. For the first time in history, a new generation of Indonesian musicians sold well over a million copies of

---

12 The number of well-established local television networks operating regularly is probably somewhere between 30 and 50. See Heryanto and Adi (2002), Heryanto (2008: 6) and Pradityo, Titiyoga and Khafid (2008).

13 'Radio: a friend of yours?', *Jakarta Post*, 20 June 2009.

14 According to a survey conducted by *Kompas* in 2007, less than 5 per cent of respondents watched television while not in the company of family mem-bers. See 'Rating tak cerminkan mutu sinetron' [TV ratings do not reflect the quality of soap operas], *Kompas*, 30 December 2007.

15 For details of mobile phone and internet access as well as television broad-casting and consumption, I am indebted to the generous assistance of Hellen Katherina of AGB Nielson Media Research (private communication, 2009).

their albums. New Indonesian film titles set new records well beyond the popularity of films from any other country, including top Hollywood blockbusters (Grayling 2002; van Heeren 2002; Heryanto 2008: 6). On television, melodramatic *sinetron* (drama series) and reality shows have become the most popular programs, dominating the total broadcasting hours.[16] Of the various subcategories of reality television, talent shows for singers such as *Indonesian Idol* (RCTI) and *Akademi Fantasi Indosiar* (Indosiar) stand out.[17]

The increased power of the media and entertainment industry in Indonesia's economy and politics has gone hand in hand with a marked process of feminisation of public life. This goes beyond the appearance of women in election campaigns and the election of women to parliament. For too long, the entire corpus of the modern nation, including post-colonial Indonesia, had been focused primarily on the masculine-biased history of nation-state building and modernisation, or the impediments to this: militarism, human rights abuses, rampant corruption, violent ethno-religious conflicts and, latterly, Islamist jihadism (Heryanto 2008: 7). Pop culture, especially in the form of televised entertainment, had been relegated to the secondary 'private' or 'domestic' sphere, mostly for women. From this followed a familiar, if deeply problematic, sense of division between the masculine world of news, scholarship and conferences versus the feminine world of soap operas, gossip magazines and family matters.[18] In 2009, however, as the macho motorcycle convoys faded away, a new set of election festivities was evident in its formative stages.

It is important not to romanticise either the macho convoys of New Order street politics or the more feminised and mass-mediated, entertainment-focused politics. Both have had serious consequences for Indonesian society. The testosterone-driven convoys often prompted violent confrontations between ordinary citizens, sometimes with fatal consequences. The media-based feminisation of social life, on the other hand,

---

16 According to an AGB Nielsen survey conducted in July–September 2007, 72 per cent of all soap opera viewers come from households with monthly incomes of less than Rp 1,500,000 (about $160). The survey also found that 'people with a monthly income of below Rp 500,000 spend the most time watching TV, whereas those who make more than Rp 3 million spend the least'. See 'Middle class prefer information to soaps, says survey', *Jakarta Post*, 24 November 2007.

17 See Penelope Coutas's fascinating analysis of these programs in the 2000s (Coutas 2008).

18 According to the 2007 *Kompas* survey (see footnote 14), almost half of all respondents indicated that the children in the family had charge of the remote control for the television set, and more than 20 per cent said the mother was in charge of it. This was well above the number saying that the father or someone else had charge of the remote control.

has led to a situation in which Indonesians adopt the common parameters of a television show to organise their daily activities, conduct casual and formal conversations, and plan future projects. What is occurring in contemporary Indonesia is, in effect, a reality show in reverse: instead of television programs projecting an image of unscripted events involving non-professional performers as an alleged mirror of real life in real time, ordinary people have begun to mimic television programs in the way they act, speak or sing. One common example is found in the way meetings and social gatherings, including formal ceremonies, are hosted. Two young people, one of either sex and equally smartly dressed, emulate the behaviour of television show presenters when hosting such meetings. Mimicking the kind of patter one hears on TV, they take it in turns to speak and finish each other's sentences. They make light jokes and comments on the event, in an attempt to be as entertaining as a television host. Often without the slightest intention of consciously parodying television programs, they use formulaic expressions popularised by TV anchors to, for instance, announce breaks during the meeting: 'Don't go anywhere. Stay with us after these messages' (Heryanto 2006b).

Against this background, it is not at all surprising that the 2009 election campaign was characterised more by entertainment than by political education and propaganda. Traditional and modern genres of performance were deployed to attract the masses, to a greater extent than in previous elections. The images of national pop musicians (Dewa and Slank) as well as internationally famous figures (Barack Obama, David Beckham, Osama bin Laden and Superman) were hijacked and superimposed on campaign posters. Particularly striking, however, was the use of cheerleaders in Bengkulu and fashion shows in two other cities for election campaign purposes. In one such fashion show sponsored by the Temanggung local electoral commission, young girls posed in their glittering sexy dresses, imitating professional adult models seen on television. In Medan, Golkar candidate Himatul Fadillah sponsored another fashion show featuring 50 older Muslim women (all above 45 years old) modelling Muslim dresses. One would encounter great difficulty in finding any content-related connections between the election campaign goals and these shows. The medium was the message — entertainment reigned unequivocally over the entire campaign.

Of all the entertainment formats derived from television programs, *Indonesian Idol* was the one that appealed most to campaigners in the 2009 elections. The program was highly popular on television because of its 'emphasis on the "democratic" voting system via SMS to "elect" the *Idola*' (Coutas 2008: 113). Just as television shows like *Indonesian Idol* have tended to imitate politics, candidates in the 2009 elections moved to imitate this hit television program. This was more than merely a matter of campaign strategy; such shows gave many candidates from disadvantaged backgrounds the inspiration and hope to run in the elections in the first place. Regardless of the ideologies, platforms or even the empty rhetorical styles of the parties they represented, it was the ideology of *Indonesian Idol* that dictated the course of events. This was an ideology — already nationally and internationally upheld — that persuaded people from all walks of life to believe in both the possibility and the desirability of anyone at all venturing out upon their own rags-to-riches story. This ideology had spread widely together with DIY sentiment, spearheaded especially by the first generation of indie musicians and independent film makers.

Unfortunately, the individualisation, DIY spirit and feminisation that marked the 2009 elections had some tragic consequences that came in rather unexpected forms. As the macho motorcycle convoys and associated violence receded into the past, the increased competition among the swelling number of candidates inevitably led to a new phenomenon. Not only were the masses split and dispersed, but many people who did not win seats in the elections experienced great distress. The mass media reported psychiatric wards being overwhelmed with former candidates who were experiencing mental disorders following their defeat in the polls. Employees in one hospital in the city of Solo had to work double shifts when 200 patients in this category arrived in a single day (Bayuni 2009). Elsewhere, a significant number of failed candidates decided to commit suicide. According to one study, women were overrepresented in these cases (Buehler 2009). As in their favourite show *Indonesian Idol*, it appears that many contestants had been lured by false promises of extraordinary success and paid a high price when reality finally hit home.

CONCLUSION

Myths and irrationality are commonly found in all elections (see, for example, Taylor 1996; Heryanto 2006a: 149–53; Chua 2007). Yet, these costly political rituals are held across the globe as a prerequisite for the almost universal commitment to a modern utopia called 'democracy'. Too many of us imagine democracy to be something real, and zealously promote it as universally desirable (Heryanto and Mandal 2003; Lev 2005; Heryanto 2010). This obsession with ideal types of democracy has often led to misunderstandings about the behaviour of the masses in both democratic and authoritarian regimes. In this chapter, I have shown how, during the series of sham elections under the New Order government, the masses behaved in ways that might at first appear vulgar and unruly. But considered within the specific political context of that time, their behaviour can be regarded as much more rational and subversively powerful than has usually been portrayed, more so indeed than the political activism of the urban intelligentsia. In 2009, however, the political setting had altered significantly, and so had the country's electoral laws and procedures. The subversive power of the masses dissipated, ironically at a moment when Indonesia's democracy had become more liberalised.

This new development should not be taken as an anomaly. Benedict Anderson (1996: 14) has noted that 'under normal circumstances, the logic of electoralism is in the direction of domestication'. As Indonesian politics becomes increasingly 'normalised' (Aspinall 2005), it is only to be expected that the great majority of the people would be further 'domesticated'. How the process of domestication via elections unfolds varies across different socio-historical settings. Contrary to Lev's concerns (cited in the opening paragraph of this chapter), in no way does this chapter suggest that the Indonesian case constitutes something uniquely or essentially Indonesian. Rather, it has identified and analysed three specifically historical factors that appear to have contributed significantly to the serious fragmentation of the masses: the new electoral laws in 2009, which forced candidates of the same party to compete against each other for votes; the engulfing effects of the new media, particularly the televised entertainment industry; and the broader context of orality-oriented modes of interaction in Indonesian society.

In 1992, in an attempt to contain the reckless masses that had taken over its 'festival of democracy', the New Order proposed that all campaign activities be moved to the state-controlled mass media. Neither the masculinist and repressive New Order government nor its more democratic successor governments had the capacity to domesticate the powerful masses, which they initially intended to mobilise for their own purposes. In 2009, however, the soft power of the media industry came to their assistance. Gaining momentum from the new electoral laws in 2009, the media industry extended its entertainment ideology and commercial empire into street politics and into the elections. Ultimately, these media companies have had the last laugh.

REFERENCES

Anderson, Benedict R. (1996), 'Elections and participation in three Southeast Asian countries', in R.H Taylor (ed.), *The Politics of Elections in Southeast Asia*, Woodrow Wilson International Centre for Scholars, Cambridge, pp. 12–33.

Aspinall, Edward (2005), 'Elections and the normalization of politics in Indonesia', *South East Asia Research* 13(2): 117–56.

Baudrillard, Jean (1983), *In the Shadow of the Silent Majorities*, Simotext(e), New York NY.

Bayuni, Endy (2009), 'Indonesia's do-it-yourself campaign', *New York Times*, 3 May.

Buehler, Michael (2009), 'Suicide and progress in modern Nusantara', *Inside Indonesia* 97(July–September), http://insideindonesia.org/.

Chua Beng Huat (ed.) (2007), *Elections as Popular Culture in Asia*, Routledge, London and New York.

Coutas, Penelope (2008), 'Fame, fortune, *fantasi*', in A. Heryanto (ed.), *Popular Culture in Indonesia: Fluid Identities in Post-authoritarian Politics*, Routledge, London and New York, pp. 111–29.

Eldon, Eric (2009), 'Facebook gains more ground in Southeast Asia', *Inside Facebook*, 2 September, http://www.insidefacebook.com/2009/09/02/facebook-gains-more-ground-in-southeast-asia/.

Fernback, Jan (2003), 'Legends on the net: an examination of computer-mediated communication as a locus of oral culture', *New Media and Society* 5(1): 29–45.

Genosko, Gary (1999), *McLuhan and Baudrillard: Masters of Implosion*, Routledge, London and New York.

Grayling, A.C. (2002), 'It started with a kiss', *Guardian*, 1 July.

Heryanto, Ariel (2006a), *State Terrorism and Political Identity in Indonesia: Fatally Belonging*, Routledge, London.

Heryanto, Ariel (2006b), 'TV', *Kompas*, 3 December.

Heryanto, Ariel (2007), 'New media and freedom of expression in Asia', keynote address, Freedom of Expression in Asia Workshop, jointly organised by COMBINE Resource Institution (Indonesia) and Global Partners and Associates (United Kingdom), Yogyakarta, 4 November.

Heryanto, Ariel (2008), 'Pop culture and competing identities', in A. Heryanto (ed.), *Popular Culture in Indonesia: Fluid Identities in Post-authoritarian Politics*, Routledge, London and New York, pp. 1–36.

Heryanto, Ariel (2010), 'The bearable lightness of democracy', in T. Reuter (ed.), *The Return to Constitutional Democracy in Indonesia*, Monash Asia Institute, Clayton, pp. 51–63.

Heryanto, Ariel and Stanley Adi (2002), 'Industrialized media in democratizing Indonesia', in R.H.K. Heng (ed.), *Media Fortunes, Changing Times: ASEAN States in Transition*, Institute of Southeast Asian Studies, Singapore, pp. 47–82.

Heryanto, Ariel and Sumit K. Mandal (2003), 'Challenges to authoritarianism in Indonesia and Malaysia', in A. Heryanto and S.K. Mandal (eds), *Challenging Authoritarianism in Southeast Asia: Comparing Indonesia and Malaysia*, RoutledgeCurzon, London, pp. 1–24.

Kartomi, Margaret (ed.) (2005), *The Year of Voting Frequently: Politics and Artists in Indonesia's 2004 Elections*, Monash Asia Institute, Clayton.

Lev, Daniel (1996), 'Afterword', in R.H Taylor (ed.), *The Politics of Elections in Southeast Asia*, Woodrow Wilson International Centre for Scholars, Cambridge, pp. 243–52.

Lev, Daniel (2005), 'Conceptual filters and obfuscation in the study of Indonesian politics', *Asian Studies Review* 29(December): 345–56.

Lindsay, Jennifer (2007), 'The performance factor in Indonesian elections', in Chua Beng Huat (ed.), *Elections as Popular Culture in Asia*, Routledge, London and New York, pp. 55–71.

Lindsay, Jennifer (2009), 'Pomp, piety and performance: *pilkada* in Yogyakarta, 2005', in M. Erb and P. Sulistiyanto (eds), *Deepening Democracy in Indonesia?*

Direct Elections for Local Leaders, Institute of Southeast Asian Studies, Singapore, pp. 211–28.

Mbembe, Achille (1992), 'The banality of power and the aesthetic of vulgarity in the postcolony', *Public Culture* 4(2): 1–30.

McGraw, Andrew C. (2009), 'The political economy of the performing arts in contemporary Bali', *Indonesia and the Malay World* 37(109): 299–325.

McLuhan, Eric and Frank Zingrone (eds) (1995), *Essential McLuhan,* Routledge, London.

McLuhan, Marshall (1964), *Understanding Media,* second edition, McGraw-Hill Book Company, New York NY.

Pradityo, Sapto, Gabriel Wahyu Titiyoga and Supriyanto Khafid (2008), 'Ki Sudrun di layar beling' [Mr Sudrun on the small screen], *Tempo* 37(15), 2 June, http://majalah.tempointeraktif.com/id/email/2008/06/02/MD/mbm.20080602.MD127340.id.html.

Taylor, R.H. (ed.) (1996), *The Politics of Elections in Southeast Asia,* Woodrow Wilson International Centre for Scholars, Cambridge.

van Dijk, Cees (1977), 'The Indonesian elections', *Review of Indonesian and Malaysian Affairs* 11(2): 1–44.

van Heeren, Katinka (2002), 'Revolution of hope: independent films are young, free and radical', *Inside Indonesia* 70(April–June), http://insideindonesia.org/.

10   THE RISE AND FALL OF POLITICAL GANGSTERS IN INDONESIAN DEMOCRACY

Ian Wilson

Preman, a colloquial term for a thug or gangster, is synonymous in the minds of many Indonesians with some of the worst aspects of the country's political culture: intimidation, coercion, extortion and violence. This equation of *preman* with political thuggery developed during the New Order period (1966–98), during which gangs, youths and local thugs were regularly subcontracted and mobilised to carry out violence on behalf of the interests of the state and political elites. This was done in return for various concessions, such as legal immunity for their underworld activities and in some cases entry into and advancement through the government and administrative hierarchy. The word *preman* itself finds its roots in this confluence of state power and criminality.[1] But to what extent have the *preman* become political and politicised subjects themselves in the new democratic Indonesia and sought to pursue their own social, economic and political interests rather than those of their patrons or clients?

The *preman* are commonly defined by their use of violence and criminality, and come from a social and economic underclass of marginalised youth, slum dwellers and urban poor, what Davis (2004) has described as the growing informal proletariat. Since the demise of the New Order, a plethora of social organisations (*organisasi masyarakat*, or *ormas*) have emerged that draw much of their membership from this *preman* underclass, claiming to represent their interests and, by implication, those of other marginalised and 'wounded' urban communities. As during the

---

1   For more on the origin of the word *preman*, see Ryter (1998).

New Order, these groups are often involved in racketeering and violent entrepreneurship, both as a service to supply a ready market for forms of intimidation and in the form of a coercive relationship imposed on their immediate communities. However, at the same time such *preman* groups are increasingly articulating their social and political demands, engaging in grassroots activism and self-organisation, and pursuing strategies for engagement with the formal political process.[2] This chapter examines the tension between criminality and socio-political engagement by looking at the ways in which some *preman* groups have organised themselves politically and sought to benefit from the electoral process. It also reflects on what this tells us about the nature and dynamics of Indonesian democracy.

The chapter will show that *preman* organisations are engaging with the electoral process in increasingly diverse ways that reproduce but also go beyond their New Order role as subcontracted agents of state repression. In contrast to the elections of 1999 and 2004, the legislative and presidential elections of 2009 were marked by a relative absence of overt acts of political thuggery. The reasons behind this decline in political violence are complex, but can be attributed in part to the perception among political actors, including *preman*, that open forms of intimidation and mass mobilisation are becoming redundant as effective strategies for securing electoral success.[3] Some *preman* have joined or formed their own political parties, while others have moved towards what might more accurately be described as 'street organisations', which Brotherton (2007: 252) defines as 'the transitional stage between a gang and a social movement'. In contrast to commentators such as Hadiz and Robison (2004), who argue that Indonesia's democratic institutions have been 'hijacked' by gangsters, this chapter suggests that political gangsterism is in fact on the decline, largely due to the increasing institutionalisation of the democratic process.

As Dichiara and Chabot (2003: 78) state, 'gang formation, organization, and change are both reactive and proactive to social forces and the

---

2   These two countertrends have been identified as a common characteristic of the relationship between gangs as social institutions and their local communities, which often swings between being oppressive and protective (see Rodgers, Muggah and Stevenson 2009). In Indonesia as elsewhere, social class is another factor determining community perceptions of gangs as political agents. While poor neighbourhoods and urban slums often view gangs in a positive light as protectors and leaders of the community, middle-class neighbourhoods almost universally perceive them to be a criminal menace.

3   As Buehler (2009) has noted, the lower degree of importance attached to legislative elections in Indonesia is a core reason why the country has not witnessed the levels of violence seen in places like the Philippines and Thailand.

gang members' perceptions of social reality'. In Indonesia, gangs vary in terms of their organisation, ideology and levels of criminality, just as members range from bona fide gangsters and hardened criminals to unemployed youth, urban poor, informal sector workers and street activists. In Jakarta, the *ormas* most frequently linked to thuggery and gang life — the Betawi Brotherhood Forum (Forum Betawi Rempug, FBR) and the Children of Betawi Communication Forum (Forum Komunikasi Anak Betawi, Forkabi) — have begun voicing populist notions of economic and political rights and providing social services to their members and immediate communities. As a result, they are attracting larger numbers of members from distinctly 'non-*preman*' backgrounds, such as university students, small business owners and formal sector workers. As the membership of such organisations has become more diversified, so too have their collective and organisational perceptions of the political process, in particular elections, and why and how members should engage with it. Recognition of these changing dynamics is crucial to an understanding of how these organisations can *simultaneously* be violent defenders of reactionary and hegemonic interests *and* proactive vehicles for the social and cultural advancement of politically and socially marginalised communities. It also suggests that the dynamics of Indonesian democracy have had their own 'civilising effect', with even some of those most closely associated with anti-democratic forces now accepting the rules of the new democratic game.

NEW ORDER BEGINNINGS

From the first elections in Indonesia during the 1950s, political parties have used strongmen, thugs and gangsters to mobilise support and intimidate rivals. Even before this, gangsters had been at the forefront of the struggle for independence, with many taking up leadership positions within the military and government of the new republic. The Indonesian Communist Party (Partai Komunis Indonesia, PKI) and the Indonesian National Party (Partai Nasional Indonesia, PNI) were among the first to integrate local strongmen and gangsters into their party structures. The Indonesian military followed suit. In 1954 the head of the armed forces, General Nasution, deployed networks of gangsters and former militias as part of a campaign to pressure Sukarno into suspending parliamentary democracy, eventually ushering in the period known as 'Guided Democracy'. Out of this alliance emerged Pancasila Youth (Pemuda Pancasila), which would become the largest quasi-official 'thug' organisation.

During the 1970s and 1980s the New Order regime used *preman*, or *gali* as they were known at the time (an abbreviation of *gabungan anak liar*,

or 'gangs of wild children'), as an integral part of its repressive strategies, especially when it came to ensuring the 'success' of its tightly engineered elections, or 'festivals of democracy' as they were then known.[4]
Military generals fostered their own networks of *preman*. For example,
Ali Moertopo, the head of Special Operations (Operasi Khusus, Opsus),
fostered an extensive network of gangsters and underworld figures, and
put them to work during the elections of 1971 and 1977 to ensure that
the regime's electoral vehicle, Golkar, received its pre-determined quota
of votes. He also used them as *provocateurs* during the infamous 1974
Malari riots in Jakarta.[5] The 1982 elections coincided with an economic
slump, and many of the gangs that had been mobilised in previous elections now faced hard economic times. The resulting increase in crime
rates, together with Suharto's suspicions regarding Moertopo's apparent
aspirations for the presidency, prompted a brutal response. On Suharto's
orders, throughout 1982 and 1983 thousands of alleged *gali* were sum-
marily executed in what came to be known as the 'mysterious shootings'
campaign (*penembakan misterius*, or *petrus*).[6]

After the *petrus* period, thugs and gangsters were increasingly institutionalised through various nationalist and youth organisations such
as Pemuda Pancasila. Traumatised by the brutality of the killings, many
joined out of fear. Although such organisations operated with a degree of
autonomy, akin to that of a franchise, the *petrus* events had made it clear
that the survival of even state-backed groups was ultimately contingent
upon unquestioning loyalty to Suharto. Those who performed well in
their assigned regime-maintenance chores were offered opportunities for
advancement within the regime's administrative hierarchy, with leaders such as Yapto Soerjosoemarno and Yorries Raweyai of Pemuda Pancasila and Harianto Badjoeri of Pemuda Pancamarga given positions that
suited their specialities.[7] The fate of rank-and-file members, however,
remained precarious and dependent on their continued 'usefulness'.
With the eventual unravelling of the New Order in 1998 and the fractur-

---

4   For a detailed analysis of the role played by *gali* during this period, see Bourchier (1990) and Ryter (1998).

5   In 1974 thugs linked to Moertopo turned peaceful student demonstrations in
Jakarta against the visit of the Japanese prime minister into violent riots. This
has become known as the January Disaster (Malapetaka Januari, or Malari).

6   For a detailed description and analysis of the *petrus* campaign, see van der
Kroef (1985).

7   Yapto served as Jakarta head of the state-approved All Indonesia Workers Union (Serikat Pekerja Seluruh Indonesia, SPSI), whereas Badjoeri was
appointed to the tourism office, where he had authority to issue licences to
pubs and nightclubs. He is currently the head of Jakarta's civil ordinance
police.

ing of patron–client networks, these 'foot soldiers' were forced to seek new places of refuge and opportunity.

PARTY *PREMAN* AND *PREMAN* PARTIES

Satgas

The build-up to the 1999 general elections, the first free, multi-party elections to be held in Indonesia since 1955, witnessed what some commentators have referred to as a party 'arms race'.[8] Copying the militaristic and thuggish tactics of New Order politics, many of the new political parties established large paramilitary units known as 'task forces' (*satuan tugas*, or *satgas*).[9] Dressed in garish camouflage clothing and wearing military paraphernalia, the ostensive role of the *satgas* was to provide security, manage traffic and crowds at rallies and protect party assets. The *satgas* were also, however, the perfect vehicle for the new political forces to establish working links with criminal gangs.

Many *preman* interpreted electoral democracy as a new form of turf war. The numerous physical clashes between rival *satgas* groups throughout the 1999 election period were less about political allegiances and competing visions for Indonesia's future than they were struggles over turf and the economic benefits that came with it, such as access to protection money from small businesses, control of security services at entertainment venues, domination of kerbside parking fee collection and the like.[10] The *satgas* used banners and flags as territorial markers, with entire neighbourhoods claimed as 'belonging' to a particular party. The areas claimed by *satgas* units for particular parties correlated closely with turf divisions between rival *preman* gangs, with elections providing an ideal opportunity for territorial expansion.

The parties, too, regarded the informal leadership exercised by *preman* and local strongmen (often known as *jago*, *jawara* or *jeger*) in the streets and *kampung* as an important form of political capital in mobilising and directing community voting patterns. To this end many *preman* were recruited as local party cadres, and assisted to win leadership positions in neighbourhood associations. The extent to which *preman* were actually able to secure votes for the parties, however, is difficult to ascertain. As

---

8   'Gila tentara di tubuh sipil' [Civil bodies are army crazy], *Panji Masyarakat*, 24 May 2000.

9   *Satgas* were first established during the mid-1980s by the New Order as party-based security units under the control of local military commanders.

10 For an analysis of *satgas*-related violence in the 1999 elections, see King (2001).

we will see, the subsequent decline in the mobilisation of *preman* by the time of the 2004 elections suggests that they may have been far less effective than party leaders had originally thought.

Of all the political parties, it was the Indonesian Democratic Party of Struggle (Partai Demokrasi Indonesia Perjuangan, PDIP) that accommodated the largest number of the *preman* underclass. Its populist approach—including its use of Sukarno and other revolutionary-era symbolism, its pro-'little people' rhetoric and its association with mysticism—had an almost natural appeal to the *preman* demographic: poor, unemployed urban males between 18 and 40 years of age.[11] The party actively targeted this group, conducting *satgas* recruitment drives among high-school dropouts. By late 1999 its *satgas* force numbered around 30,000 nationally, together with a vast array of 'sympathiser groups' of varying size, militancy and levels of organisation that operated outside the formal party structure.

In the lead-up to the 2004 elections, however, both the public and the government had become concerned about the size and unruliness of party *satgas* and the potential they posed for electoral violence, leading to increasing calls for them to be disbanded.[12] Particularly vocal were the military, who objected to their use of military-style uniforms and insignia, considering it a challenge to their authority.[13] Less publicly, the success of the *satgas* in wresting control of protection rackets and rent-seeking opportunities previously monopolised by the military and police had aroused their animosity. The General Elections Commission (Komisi Pemilihan Umum, KPU) responded by introducing regulations severely limiting the deployment and mobilisation of *satgas* during the campaign period, and banning the establishment of *satgas* command posts (*posko satgas*) in neighbourhoods.[14] This significantly reduced the street-level usefulness of *satgas* for the parties. Faced with these restrictions, PDIP in particular found itself with an increasingly unruly beast on its hands.

---

11 Interview with gang leader, Jakarta, August 2007.
12 'Menhan: laskar dan satgas berbau militer sebaiknya bubarkan diri' [Defence minister: military-style militias and security forces should disband themselves], *Sinar Harapan*, 1 April 2003.
13 'Panglima Kodam IV Diponegoro minta parpol tertibkan satgasnya' [Commander of Diponegoro IV Military Command asks political parties to put their *satgas* in order], *Kompas*, 1 March 2003. PDIP bluntly rejected the military chief's call for *satgas* and other militias to be disbanded, stating that the military was no longer able to interfere in party affairs, and that the role of the *satgas* was an internal party issue. See 'PDIP tolak bubarkan satgas' [PDIP refuses to disband its security forces], *Sriwijaya Post*, 9 November 2002.
14 KPU Decision No. 7/2004. Modelled on the territorial command system of the military and the posts (*pos siskamling*, or *posko*) set up to ensure neighbourhood security, *posko satgas* in effect operated as party surveillance posts.

Many local PDIP *satgas* units became embroiled in the party's internal factional disputes, forming loyalist groups around candidates in elections for local heads of government. Initially a tool to be employed in electoral turf wars, the *satgas* had now become a largely redundant force for the party as a whole and, according to one PDIP party official, a significant drain on party resources and a 'constant source of trouble'.[15]

The gradual political redundancy of *satgas* units saw some evolve into private enterprises servicing the market demand for bodyguards, debt collectors and land brokers. Others set up illegal parking and other rackets while still wearing the uniforms and colours of their parties, and some cut all ties with the political party with which they had been affiliated. The Alert One Brigade (Brigade Siaga Satu, or Brigass), for example, distanced itself from PDIP and entered the private sector as a security company and debt collector, before returning to politics under a new patron. In 2009 Brigass 'director' Pius Lustrilanang, a former anti-New Order student activist who had been abducted by Special Forces (Kopassus) troops in 1998, re-emerged on the political stage as a successful parliamentary candidate for the Greater Indonesia Movement Party (Partai Gerakan Indonesia Raya, Gerindra) in East Nusa Tenggara. In a peculiar twist of fate, Gerindra was led by Prabowo Subianto, a former head of Kopassus and the very man who had ordered the kidnapping of Lustrilanang and other activists.

Party *preman*

The symbiotic relationship between PDIP and the criminal underworld has perhaps been most evident in Bali, a long-time stronghold of the party. Here, gangs and criminal figures have been accommodated both formally within the party structure and informally through close links with key party figures. PDIP was instrumental in the reinvigoration and institutionalisation of Bali's so-called 'traditional' civilian security forces, known as *pecalang*. Although claiming to be a traditional body, contemporary *pecalang* go back only as far as the party's 1998 national congress in Sanur, when a group of *satgas* militia dressed themselves in traditional Balinese attire in order to create the impression that they were an integral part of the local community.[16]

Nowhere in Bali has the relationship been PDIP and gangs been more evident than in the district of Tabanan. Since the election of Adi Wiry-

---

15 Interview with PDIP official, Jakarta, April 2006.
16 *Pecalang* were formally recognised as a 'traditional security force' in Bali's Regional Regulation No. 3/2001. For more on the background and controversy surrounding *pecalang*, see Suryawan (2005: 286–97).

atama as district head (*bupati*) in 2000, *preman* groups linked to him have been instrumental in intimidating rivals and working to ensure PDIP's dominance. In 2004, masked attackers driving cars with government number plates terrorised Golkar supporters in the village of Tunjuk. When the attackers were arrested by the police, the district head personally intervened on their behalf, convincing the police to release them into his care.[17] Local journalists critical of the Tabanan government have also been subjected to significant levels of intimidation. The success of this approach can be judged from PDIP's continued strong electoral results in Tabanan, despite numerous corruption allegations, a damning and well-publicised audit of district finances by the State Audit Agency (Badan Pemeriksaan Keuangan, BPK) and persistently high rates of poverty and illiteracy.

PDIP won 90 per cent of the vote in Tabanan in 1999, 75 per cent in 2004 and 73 per cent in 2009.[18] In one subdistrict dominated by *preman* groups close to the district head, voter turnout for the 2009 legislative elections was an implausible 100 per cent with no invalid votes cast, in contrast to the rest of the district, which had a voting error rate of 25 per cent. Even more implausibly, 100 per cent of the votes cast in this subdistrict were for a single PDIP candidate.[19] In return for this almost clinical level of voter mobilisation, the party has provided financial backing for members of *preman* groups such as the Tabanan Communication Forum (Forum Komunikasi Tabanan, Forkot) to be elected as village chiefs, from which positions they are able to dominate the allocation of budgetary funds. Forkot members have also secured lucrative positions as brokers for government-tendered contracts. In 2009 the head of Forkot, Komang Gede Sanjaya, won the highest number of votes of any PDIP candidate in Tabanan, much to the surprise and annoyance of PDIP candidates higher on the party's list of preferred candidates.[20]

PDIP's response to any challenges to its hegemony in Tabanan has been unambiguous. In the lead-up to the 2009 elections, machete-wielding members of the PDIP-affiliated youth group Indonesian Young Bulls (Banteng Muda Indonesia, BMI) attacked unarmed members of the *satgas* of the Democratic Party (Partai Demokrat, PD). According to

---

17 Confidential interviews, Tabanan, May 2009.
18 While lower in 2009 than in previous years, the PDIP result in Tabanan was considerably higher than the overall PDIP vote in Bali of 40.4 per cent.
19 Interview with KPU official, Tabanan, May 2009.
20 'Ketua LSM Forkot Tabanan koleksi suara terbanyak' [Head of Forkot NGO in Tabanan collects largest number of votes], *Bali Post*, 11 April 2009. Sanjaya is also the local director of PT Bali Permata Indah, a developer involved in a controversial luxury villa development, and a long-time broker of shady deals involving government projects.

police, the incident was 'purely criminal' and not linked to pre-election tensions.[21] However, the background to the attack was deeply rooted in the political culture of Tabanan. The head of the PD *satgas* was a former follower of the head of the Tabanan BMI, Eka Putra Nurcahyadi. His defection to PD was seen not only as a personal betrayal of Nurcahyadi, who was later charged over the incident, but as an attempt to challenge PDIP turf, albeit through democratic means.[22] Because BMI was an affiliated group and not part of the official party structure, PDIP was able to disavow its violence, despite Nurcahyadi being a housemate of I Ketut Purnaya, a PDIP parliamentarian.

The close association between PDIP and such local-level thuggery has ultimately led to a public image problem for the party nationally. The public perception of PDIP as a 'party of *preman*' had become so entrenched by 2009 that, prior to the elections, the party's national chairperson, Megawati Sukarnoputri, issued instructions to all levels of the party to increase internal discipline and immediately expel any members who engaged in *premanism*. Invoking the colonial origins of the word *preman* in the Dutch *vrijman* ('free man'), one party functionary refuted claims that PDIP was 'thug-ridden' by insisting that 'we aren't a party of "free men"; we have rules and codes of ethics' (Mulyadi 2009).[23]

The fact that even parties like PDIP are viewing the *satgas* as redundant and no longer see *preman* as an effective political tool suggests two things in relation to the development of democratic institutions and culture. The first is that the institutions governing the conduct of elections have strengthened considerably. While parties initially said they would defy calls to disband their *satgas* units, they nonetheless did mostly adhere to the KPU regulation prohibiting the mobilisation of *satgas*. Second, while political parties continued to cling to the New Order-style symbolism and militarism of the *satgas*, it was apparent that the general public had moved on. Voters in most areas could no longer be herded or coerced into voting in particular ways as they once had, and it was clear that to continue to attempt to do so would result in a voter backlash. In a new media-dominated political age, the large and ambitious parties were becoming more concerned about building and maintaining an attractive and responsible image, making them more reluctant to use the politics of coercion and mass mobilisation, even if many of their grassroots opera-

---

21 'Insiden Tabanan murni kriminal' [Tabanan incident was purely criminal], *Antara*, 16 March 2009.

22 Confidential interviews, Tabanan, April–May 2009.

23 The term *vrijman* was used during the colonial period to refer to people who had been excused from the Dutch program of forced labour, usually due to their role as minders or overseers.

tors still saw advantages in such an approach (see also Heryanto in this volume).

Preman parties

Pemuda Pancasila, the 'granddaddy' of organised *preman* groups in Indonesia, has taken a different path to the one described above of joining a *satgas* and teaming up with established parties. Throughout the New Order, Pemuda Pancasila's members were ardently loyal to Suharto and his Golkar party. This relationship changed dramatically after 1998, when many members left Pemuda Pancasila to join other groups. Despite the drop in membership, in 2003 its chairperson, Yapto Suryosoemarno, established a new party, the Patriotic Pancasila Party (Partai Patriot Pancasila), as the formal political vehicle of Pemuda Pancasila, due to the failure of Golkar to 'adequately repay the loyalty we have shown them'. 'Rather than choose a party who doesn't care about us', he added, 'it's better we form our own party'.[24] In this manner, Pemuda Pancasila articulated a feeling being experienced by *preman* nationwide: the bitterness at being used and then discarded by political elites once those elites' political fortunes had shifted. Marred by the stigma of being regime henchmen, the *preman* had been left to fend for themselves while their former patrons reinvented themselves as born-again democrats and reformists, often winning important government posts in the process. Many *preman* who had violently defended New Order interests were now among the most ferocious critics of the former regime, harbouring deep resentment at their own treatment and a more general animosity and cynicism towards government and state institutions.[25]

The new party's platform, however, failed to reflect this sense of disillusionment, blandly restating Pemuda Pancasila's New Order rhetoric of defending the territorial integrity of the Indonesian republic and upholding the state ideology of Pancasila and the 1945 Constitution.[26] Despite its

---

24 'Merasa tak dipedulikan Golkar Pemuda Pancasila daftar partai baru' [Feeling neglected by Golkar, Pemuda Pancasila registers a new party], *Kompas*, 29 July 2003.

25 This was a sentiment commonly expressed in interviews with *preman* who had at one time been part of state-backed gangs. As one colourfully expressed it: 'To them we were nothing but fucking guard dogs. When I see him now [his former patron, currently a member of the MPR] on the TV I want to smash his face'.

26 The five Pancasila principles are: belief in one God, civilized humanitarianism, a unified Indonesia, popular sovereignty and social justice. During the New Order Pancasila was a central ideological tool through which the state sought to legitimise its authoritarian rule.

well-established national network and claims to have millions of members, Partai Patriot Pancasila failed to achieve electoral success. In the 2004 elections the party managed 1.04 per cent (1,178,738 votes) nationally, far short of its optimistic target of 5 per cent. Failing to gain a single national parliamentary seat, the party had to officially dissolve before being re-registered under the abbreviated name of Partai Patriot in order to be able to contest the 2009 elections. But its lacklustre result actually worsened: this time it gained only 0.53 per cent of the vote (547,351 votes), though the party did win a handful of regional seats in stronghold areas such as East Kalimantan and parts of North Sumatra. Competition from rival groups, the unravelling and splintering of its networks and, most significantly, the lingering stigma of New Order thuggery all worked against Pemuda Pancasila's attempted 'democratic' transition. With the votes for Partai Patriot well below Pemuda Pancasila's claimed membership nationally, the question arises as to whether the party has repeated the mistake made by Pemuda Pancasila's former patron, Golkar—that is, whether it has lost grassroots support among its *preman* constituents by failing to articulate and accommodate their aspirations, instead using them as a vehicle for personal gain.[27]

Despite the poor electoral showing of Partai Patriot, another group renowned for its reliance on thuggery and extortion has stated an intention to follow suit. In its 2008 national congress, the Defenders of Islam Front (Front Pembela Islam, FPI), an Islamic group infamous for its violent vigilantism, reached a consensus that it would form its own political party to contest the 2014 elections. Like Yapto, who had expressed disillusionment with Golkar, FPI leader Habib Rizieq claimed that the organisation felt 'betrayed' by the current crop of Islamic parties:

> Because the multi-dimensional crisis affecting the nation is both complex and chronic, it can no longer be fixed with the *reformasi* pill, but must be given the injection of revolution. And not just any old revolution, but an Islamic revolution built upon a foundation of piety and faith in Allah. So the conclusion is, not that FPI becomes a party as some media have reported, but that FPI will form a party.[28]

27　Some former members have suggested that Yapto's primary motive in establishing Partai Patriot was simply to create a niche for himself within the new political system (confidential interviews, Jakarta, August 2007). Other Pemuda Pancasila leaders have found positions within Golkar. Muhammad Nurlif, a former national secretary, is now a Golkar member of the national parliament representing Aceh, while Yorries Raweyai, a former deputy, is currently serving on Golkar's national board.

28　'Pro & kontra "partai FPI"' [For and against an 'FPI party'], http://www.fpi.or.id/artikel.asp?oy=pro-27, 27 December 2008.

The 'Islamic revolution' proposed by FPI, then, is heading in a decidedly unrevolutionary direction, towards formal entry into the world of politics it has long decried. In previous elections FPI called on its supporters to abstain from voting as a protest against the failure of candidates and political parties to 'fulfil the aspirations of the Islamic community', and against the inherently corrupt nature of secular politics (Fasabeni 2004). A fatwa issued by the Council of Islamic Scholars (Majelis Ulama Indonesia, MUI) before the 2009 elections stating that it was forbidden (*haram*) to abstain from voting appeared at first glance to present a theological challenge to this position, especially as FPI has been an aggressive and outspoken defender of MUI decrees.[29] However, a closer reading of the fatwa showed that the prohibition applied only if there were candidates who fulfilled the MUI's morally prescriptive criteria.[30] Initially FPI maintained that there was no candidate who displayed the qualities of piety, honesty and capability stipulated by the MUI; hence it was a religious duty to abstain. However, in a dramatic about-face, FPI changed its stance two months before the presidential election and declared its support for presidential hopeful Jusuf Kalla and his running mate, former armed forces chief Wiranto (Muharrami 2009). Whether this shift was a case of pragmatic alliance building with 2014 in mind remains unclear.

Despite obvious concerns in some quarters about the potential impact of 'thugs in robes' (*preman berjubah*) entering parliament, the plan to establish a party poses more risks for FPI itself. Failure to secure votes and seats will severely undermine its claims to have a huge support base, weakening its political bargaining power.[31] It may also act as a deterrent to new members since, as one member explained, many youth have been attracted to FPI 'because it focuses upon "action" rather than just endless talking'. FPI's symbolic radicalism and anti-state rhetoric would potentially lose credibility if it willingly joined a world it has described as being infected with *sepilis*, an acronym for secularism, pluralism and lib-

---

29 For more on FPI's relationship with MUI, see Wilson (2008).

30 The MUI fatwa states that 'it is obligatory to choose a leader who is pious and honest (*siddiq*), who is trustworthy (*amanah*), active and has aspirations (*tabligh*), who is capable (*fathonah*) and who struggles for the interests of the Islamic community ... Choosing a candidate who does not fulfil these four conditions, or not to vote when there is a candidate who does fulfil these conditions, is *haram*'. See 'Fatwa MUI: Golput wajib! Golput haram!' [MUI fatwa: non-voting is obligatory! Non-voting is forbidden!], 10 February 2009, http://fpionline.multiply.com/journal/item/70/Sikap_FPI_-_Fatwa_MUI_GOLPUT_WAJIB_GOLPUT_HARAM_.

31 FPI has claimed at different times to have anywhere between 2 and 8 million members. A more realistic estimate is probably closer to 200,000 nationally.

eralism.[32] The organisation's ambiguous relationship with figures within the police and military, the reason many suspect it has been allowed to get away with its violent vigilantism for so long, would also be subject to far closer scrutiny. FPI's entry into party politics could be a far more effective strategy for curtailing FPI's 11-year history of religious and political thuggery, violence and extortion than the numerous calls for it to be forcibly disbanded.

A look at the unremarkable electoral performance of Partai Patriot, as well as the unimpressive political careers of lesser-known parliamentarians of *preman* pedigree such as Moses Tambunan and Bangkit Sitepu in North Sumatra, seems to underscore this assessment. While their path to formal political power was facilitated by criminality and informal street power, once in parliament their political performance hardly reflected their origins. These gangster politicians have not so much 'captured' democratic institutions, as Hadiz and Robison (2004: 16) argued, as they have been absorbed, rather uneventfully, by them. As Buehler (2009) has stated, 'gangster figures, should they find their way into politics, have been unable to escape the new democratic dynamics', including the possibility of electoral defeat.

Preman advocates

Satgas, '*preman* parties' and 'gangster politicians' are a few manifestations of the ways in which members of the *preman* underclass and former New Order henchmen have sought to establish a niche for themselves within the democratic political system. Other groups associated with the *preman* world have adopted more complex strategies, attempting to retain organisational independence and utilise a combination of grassroots organisation, advocacy and shrewd political manoeuvring to push their agendas on the political stage.

The Betawi Brotherhood Forum (FBR), for example, is an ethnic organisation that claims to represent the interests of the 'downtrodden' and marginalised indigenous Betawi population of Jakarta. Emerging out of interethnic gang conflict in East Jakarta, the group, which now has a membership of around 200,000, operates protection rackets and pressures businesses to make donations to it under the rationale of empowering the Betawi. It has also controversially courted favour with a number of political figures, including Jakarta's former governor Sutiyoso and current governor Fauzi Bowo.[33] Dogged by accusations that it is little more than a front for criminal extortion, its recently deceased leader Fadloli

---

32 Interview with Habib Rizieq, Jakarta, May 2006.
33 For a more detailed account of FBR and its activities, see Wilson (2006).

el-Muhir defended the transgressions of its members, saying 'We don't deny there are "rough elements" within FBR, but put it in perspective, it's nothing like on the scale of what you see in state institutions such as the military and parliament'.[34]

In 2008 Fadloli declared his intention to run as a candidate for the Regional Representative Council (Dewan Perwakilan Daerah, DPD). Campaigning on a platform of 'defending the interests of the poor' and combating corruption within state institutions and the police, he was expected to do well. Fadloli had already unsuccessfully contested a seat in the DPD in 2004, coming seventh, with the not unsubstantial tally of 224,299 votes.[35] This result sent a powerful message to political parties regarding the organisation's vote-getting potential. Fadloli's decision to run for the DPD, which does not require nomination by a political party, was also a strategic one determined by the view that long-term affiliation with a party would ultimately compromise and be detrimental to the development of FBR. Previous short-lived associations with Golkar, PDIP and the Prosperous Justice Party (Partai Keadilan Sejahtera, PKS) had left the group wary of 'playing party politics'.[36]

Fadloli's unexpected death due to heart failure at the age of 48 in March 2009, just weeks before the election, threw FBR into disarray. It issued a press release stating that, in a final act of respect towards their leader, members would still vote for Fadloli. As the elections were only days away, there was insufficient time to remove his name from the ballot papers. Coupled with scant media coverage of his death, Fadloli managed to win several thousand votes, more than those obtained by the five FBR members contesting the Jakarta legislative elections as candidates for the National Mandate Party (Partai Amanat Nasional, PAN). PAN already had a long-term relationship with another Betawi organisation, Forkabi, and one month before the elections it offered to nominate several FBR members in return for the group's public support. With six seats in Jakarta after the 2004 elections, PAN was convinced that the support of the city's two largest Betawi mass organisations would help it win more seats (Amri and Adam 2009). This was not to be the case: although one FBR candidate narrowly won a seat in Tangerang, overall the number of PAN seats in the capital dropped from six to four.

FBR took the pre-election agreement literally, publicly campaigning for PAN while privately directing members in districts without an FBR–PAN candidate to vote according to their own personal preference. As one senior FBR official explained: 'Ordering members to vote for a par-

---

34 Interview with Fadloli el-Muhir, Jakarta, 26 August 2005.
35 Votes for the top four successful candidates ranged from 316,528 to 457,996.
36 Interview with Fadloli el-Muhir, Jakarta, 14 August 2007.

ticular party risks a backlash. We can present arguments why it could be beneficial to the group, but ultimately members must decide for themselves'.[37] Such leaders assume that the bonds of loyalty to the organisation transcend party affiliation. Political parties are considered, at best, temporary vehicles for the pursuit of the group's goals.

Fadloli was replaced as leader by his deputy, Lufti Hakim, a 33-year-old former Islamic student activist with a fondness for the political philosopher Jürgen Habermas. The tangible excitement among members at having a young, entrepreneurial, educated leader went some way towards dampening the deep loss felt by many at Fadloli's death. Since his appointment, Hakim has taken steps to play down FBR's previous flirtations with hardline Islam and softened its ethnic rhetoric.[38] Building on existing programs such as its legal aid foundation, free ambulance service and cooperatives, he has instigated a micro-enterprise scheme and a university student division.[39] Hakim makes a candid assessment of the nature of party politics:

> Effectively there is no real political opposition in Indonesia such as we see in Europe or the US. The parties are solely concerned with securing power, and not in representing a constituency. What we want is direct participation and representation, not simply to be mobilised on behalf of such-and-such a party.[40]

To this end, Hakim supports the introduction of provisions permitting the formation of local political parties, as in post-peace agreement Aceh. As he explains:

> National parties only show lip service to local issues during the campaign period. Essentially for them it's a numbers game. Local parties would by their nature have to be more responsive to local issues and can be held more directly accountable when they fail to deliver on promises.[41]

---

37   Interview with FBR official, Jakarta, February 2009.
38   In contrast to FBRs previous intransigent stance on 'places of vice', Hakim has taken a more accommodating view: 'It is human nature that we need to relieve ourselves. The important thing is that we do it in the appropriate place'.
39   FBR's legal aid division is staffed by postgraduate law students from the University of Indonesia. Hakim believes it is crucial to encourage university students to join FBR in order to help develop the 'critical consciousness' of the organisation's members (interview with Lufti Hakim, Jakarta, 16 August 2009).
40   Interview with Lufti Hakim, Jakarta, 16 August 2009.
41   Interview with Lufti Hakim, Jakarta, 16 August 2009.

Preman as a campaign issue

In November 2008, Indonesia's new police chief, Bambang Hendarso Danuri, announced a nationwide 'anti-*preman*' campaign. It has become something of a tradition for new police chiefs to begin their tenure with a tough-on-crime approach. However, in this instance the campaign was on a far wider scale than previously. Ordered directly by President Yudhoyono and with a budget of around Rp 20 billion for Jakarta alone, the campaign was framed as a necessary crackdown on 'street criminals' in preparation for the legislative and presidential elections.[42] According to the Bekasi chief of police, the presence of *preman* in the streets could increase the possibility of election-related 'horizontal conflict' through voter intimidation and bribes (Cipta 2009).

Local police were placed under considerable political pressure to make arrests, with threats that those who did not would be demoted or sacked (Wirakusuma 2008). In a period of just two weeks the police claimed to have arrested 10,850 *preman* nationally (Septian 2009). By the end of December 2008 this figure had reached 16,000. After this initial wave, another series of raids was conducted just weeks before the campaign period, resulting in several thousand more arrests. The initial enthusiasm of the press quickly turned to scepticism as more information emerged regarding exactly who had been arrested (Ferdiant 2009). Due to lack of evidence, fewer than 8 per cent of those detained were formally charged with a criminal offence.[43] With no clear operational or legal criteria for identifying exactly who was and was not a *preman*, and a reluctance to confront the larger, better-organised groups, the police rounded up an array of 'likely suspects' such as tattooed punks, street kids, beggars, buskers, shoe shiners, informal traffic wardens and various other informal sector workers.[44]

Fadloli publicly admonished the police, stating that:

> The target of these raids should be those *preman* in ties [*preman berdasi*] sitting in government institutions. Most of those arrested weren't criminals,

---

42 '32 hoodlums freed for lack of evidence', *Jakarta Post*, 22 December 2008.

43 Many others were charged with violating Jakarta Regional Regulation No. 8/2007 on Public Order. This regulation is regularly used to evict street vendors and squatter communities.

44 The Surabaya Legal Aid Foundation reported that children as young as 12 had been arrested and detained by the police as part of the campaigns. See 'Razia preman dapat anjal, pengamen, jukir, dan tukang semir juga kena' [In anti-*preman* raids, buskers, parking wardens and shoe shiners are also nabbed], LBH Surabaya, 18 November 2008, http://www.lbhsurabaya. org/2008/11/razia-preman-dapat-anjal-pengamen-jukir.html.

but simply citizens who due to difficult economic circumstances have been forced to live in the streets.[45]

According to Fadloli, they were not a criminal menace but victims of 'the real *preman*, the ones in ties ... who commit crimes to get richer' (Priyonggo and Pri 2008). Fadloli met with Jakarta's vice-governor, lobbying unsuccessfully for those who had been arrested to be given job training and sent to religious schools rather than jail. The end result was a public relations failure for the police, and by implication Yudhoyono, with some even suggesting it had been little more than an elaborate and expensive 'political project', an electoral campaign by stealth.[46] This episode may have had little direct impact on the election results in Jakarta, but among the thousands affected, the anger and resentment felt towards not just the police, but also the national and regional governments, was intense. As one Tanah Abang traffic warden who had been arrested quipped, 'Anti-*preman* is just another way of saying war against the poor'.[47] So when some political parties that had supported the campaign asked *preman* groups in Tanah Abang to provide 'rent-a-crowds' for election rallies — paying people to attend public rallies and demonstrations is a common practice in Indonesia — it is hardly surprising that their requests were rebuffed.

In FBR, we see the existence of an intriguing set of contradictions. The group has provided hired goons in an attempt to secure patrons — for instance, assaulting poor urban activists on behalf of former governor Sutiyoso — and flirted with participation in formal electoral politics, while at the same time remaining suspicious of and rhetorically hostile towards political elites. It has forged alliances with political parties, but has not felt bound by those agreements. By engaging in a degree of self-organisation and providing tangible services in the communities in which it is based, and by defending the *preman* as a social and economic underclass as opposed to a bunch of criminal thugs, the group has expanded its constituency well beyond its beginnings in the street gangs of East Jakarta. It is premature to suggest that groups such as FBR are heading in the direction of the 'gang as social movement' hypothesised by Brotherton, in which gangs are 'politicised subjects' engaging the 'structures of power that keep them in a state of subjugation' (Brotherton 2007: 251). By the same token, however, they can no longer be adequately characterised

---

45 Interview with Fadloli el-Muhir, Jakarta, November 2008.
46 'Razia preman jangan jadi proyek politik' [Don't let anti-thug raids become a political project], *Republika Online*, 27 November 2009, http://www.republika.co.id/.
47 Interview, Tanah Abang, January 2009.

as merely reactionary and predatory elements of civil society. The reality seems to sit somewhere between the two.

CONCLUSIONS

We can see from the examples discussed in this chapter that *preman*, or at least the people commonly identified as such, are engaging with electoral politics in a variety of ways that go beyond the traditional role of hired thugs and self-serving criminals. While unhealthy coalitions of criminal and political interests continue to present challenges to electoral democracy, as in Tabanan, such phenomena need to be placed in a broader perspective. In the 2007 elections in the Philippines, 34 candidates and another 121 people were murdered, while in Cambodia and Thailand political assassinations and kidnapping have been a regular feature of political life from the 1980s to the present (Boudreau 2009; Buehler 2009). Indonesia has not experienced, and is unlikely to experience, equivalent levels of political thuggery and violence associated with elections. Similarly, despite allegations of vote buying, there is little evidence in Indonesia of the kinds of sophisticated vote-fixing methods used by organised crime in places such as Italy, Bulgaria or India.

Corruption, nepotism and money politics are of course still rampant, but when compared to the electoral gangsterism in neighbouring countries, the intersection of criminality and electoral politics in Indonesia appears relatively insignificant. Despite some residual political thuggery created by demand from political parties and elites as well as small-scale local turf wars, overt forms of intimidation and violence have declined substantially since the first post-New Order elections in 1999. The institutionalisation of Indonesia's democratic electoral system and processes has undermined the effectiveness of political gangsterism as a means of contesting, winning and maintaining political power.

Pemuda Pancasila members' desertion of their 'official' political vehicle and the bitterness towards the state displayed by many henchmen of the former regime hint at the emergence of a different kind of '*preman* politics', one that is oppositional and proactive rather than reactionary and hegemonic. No longer content to serve merely as the disposable foot soldiers of the elites, including their own leaders, some members of the *preman* underclass are turning their backs on thuggery and seeking legitimate democratic political avenues to represent their own interests and find resolutions to the structural problems in which they and their communities are immersed.

REFERENCES

Amri, Arfi Bambani and Mohammad Adam (2009), 'Kampanye PAN di blok S: didukung FBR, PAN pasti menang di Jakarta' [PAN campaign in S block: with FBR's support PAN is certain to win in Jakarta], *Vivanews*, 3 March, http://politik.vivanews.com/news/read/45275-_didukung_fbr__pan_pasti_menang_di_jakarta_.

Boudreau, Vincent (2009), 'Elections, repression and authoritarian survival in post-transition Indonesia and the Philippines', *Pacific Review* 22(2): 233–53.

Bourchier, David (1990), 'Crime, law and state authority in Indonesia', in A. Budiman (ed.), *State and Civil Society in Indonesia*, Centre of Southeast Asian Studies, Monash University, Clayton, pp. 177–214.

Brotherton, David (2007), 'Towards the gang as a social movement', in J.M. Hagedorn (ed.), *Gangs in the Global City: Alternatives to Traditional Criminology*, University of Illinois Press, Chicago IL, pp. 251–72.

Buehler, Michael (2009), 'Suicide and progress in modern Nusantara', *Inside Indonesia* 97(July–September), http://www.insideindonesia.org/.

Cipta, Ayu (2009), 'Jelang pemilihan presiden, 100 preman jalanan disidang' [In lead-up to presidential election 100 street thugs put on trial], *Tempo interaktif*, 30 June, http://www.tempointeraktif.com/hg/kriminal/2009/06/30/brk,20090630-184502,id.html.

Davis, Mike (2004), 'Planet of slums: urban involution and the informal proletariat', *New Left Review* 26: 5–34.

Dichiara, Albert and Russell Chabot (2003), 'Gangs and contemporary urban struggle: an unappreciated aspect of gangs', in L. Kontos, D. Brotherton and L. Barrios (eds), *Gangs and Society: Alternative Perspectives*, Colombia University Press, New York NY, pp. 77–94.

Fasabeni, Muhammad (2004), 'FPI serukan Golput' [FPI calls for vote abstention], *Tempointeraktif*, 22 August, http://www.tempointeraktif.com/hg/jakarta/2004/08/22/brk,20040822-06,id.html.

Ferdiant, Riky (2009), 'Polisi dituduh salah tangkap preman' [Police accused of wrongfully arresting *preman*], *Tempointeraktif*, 5 February, http://www.tempointeraktif.com/hg/kriminal/2009/02/05/brk,20090205-158659,id.html.

Hadiz, Vedi R. and Richard Robison (2004), 'Neo-liberal reforms and illiberal consolidations: the Indonesian paradox', Southeast Asia Research Centre Working Paper Series No. 52, Hong Kong.

King, Philip (2001), 'Securing the 1999 Indonesian elections: *satgas, parpol* and the state', Centre for Asia Pacific Social Transformation Studies Working Paper Series, University of Wollongong, Wollongong.

Muharrami, Novi (2009), 'JK–Wiranto apresiasi dukungan FPI' [JK–Wiranto appreciate the support of FPI], 27 June, *Okezone*, http://pemilu.okezone.com/index.php/read/2009/06/27/268/233403/jk-wiranto-apresiasi-dukungan-fpi.

Mulyadi, Riza (2009), 'Fungsionaris: PDI Perjuangan bukan partai preman' [Functionary: PDIP is not a thug party], *Antara Sumatera Utara*, 7 May, http://www.antarasumut.com/berita-sumut/politik/fungsionaris-pdi-perjuangan-bukan-partai-preman/.

Priyonggo, Ambang and Sally Pri (2008), 'Religion, not jail for street thugs, FBR says', *Jakarta Globe*, 13 November, http://thejakartaglobe.com/news/religion-not-jail-for-street-thugs-fbr-says/300141.

Rodgers, Dennis Robert Muggah and Chris Stevenson (2009), 'Gangs of Central America: causes, costs and interventions', Small Arms Survey Occasional Paper No. 23, Graduate Institute of International and Development Studies, Geneva.

Ryter, Loren (1998), 'Pemuda Pancasila: the last loyalist free men of Suharto's order?', *Indonesia* 66(October): 45–74.

Septian, Anton (2009), 'Sepuluhan ribu preman diciduk' [Around 10,000 thugs arrested], *Tempointeraktif*, 6 February, http://www.tempointeraktif.com/hg/nasional/2009/02/06/brk,20090206-158849,id.html.

Suryawan, Ngurah (2005), *Bali Narasi dalam Kuasa: Politik dan Kekerasan di Bali* [Bali in Narratives of Power: Politics and Violence in Bali], Penerbit Ombak, Yogyakarta.

van der Kroef, Justus M. (1985), '*Petrus*: patterns of prophylactic murder in Indonesia', *Asian Survey* 7(July): 745–59.

Wilson, Ian Douglas (2006), 'Continuity and change: the changing contours of organized violence in post-New Order Indonesia', *Critical Asian Studies* 38(2): 265–97.

Wilson, Ian Douglas (2008), 'As long as it's *halal*: Islamic *preman* in Jakarta', in G. Fealy and S. White (eds), *Expressing Islam*, Institute of Southeast Asian Studies, Singapore, pp. 192–210.

Wirakusuma, Yudha (2008), 'Gagal berantas preman, Kapolres akan dicopot' [After failing to eradicate thugs, local police chief will be sacked], *Okezone*, 25 November, http://news.okezone.com/read/2008/11/25/1/167695/1/gagal-berantas-preman-kapolres-akan-dicopot.

11 INCREASING THE PROPORTION OF WOMEN IN THE NATIONAL PARLIAMENT: OPPORTUNITIES, BARRIERS AND CHALLENGES

*Sharon Bessell**

Throughout Indonesia's history, women have made up only a small proportion of the national parliament. During the New Order period (1966–98), the proportion of women in parliament averaged about 9 per cent, peaking at just over 13 per cent in 1987. The first general election in the post-Suharto period was declared free and fair, yet it produced a worrying result for those who had hoped that democracy would bring greater gender justice: the percentage of women elected to the national parliament fell from 10.8 per cent to 8.8 per cent. In 2004 the proportion of women parliamentarians increased to 11.3 per cent, but the magnitude of the increase fell far short of that hoped for by women's groups. In 2009, 17.8 per cent of those elected to the national parliament were female. This represented a historic high for Indonesia, falling just short of the (very low) global average of 18.8 per cent.

Over the past decade, women's groups have actively called for measures to correct the gender imbalance in parliament. In 2003 parliament introduced Indonesia's first gender quota, with stronger quota provisions included in the 2008 laws on political parties and elections. In 2004 and 2009 Indonesia had in place two measures widely associated with greater numbers of women in parliament—proportional representation and a quota. These had positive effects, but the parliamentary representation of women nevertheless remained low.

* My thanks to Kevin Evans and Hana Satriyo for providing valuable data on the 2009 elections. Any errors in the interpretation of those data are my own.

This chapter explores the reasons for the low number of women in Indonesia's national parliament. In the first section I examine three key factors that have been shown internationally to have a significant influence on the number of women elected to parliament. Next, I examine how each has played out in Indonesia. Finally, I ask whether the historically high number of women elected to the national parliament in 2009 can be considered a success for gender equality.

THE INTERNATIONAL EXPERIENCE: WHAT WORKS?

The proportion of women in parliament is influenced by a range of political, economic, cultural and structural factors. In particular, there are three factors that international experience suggests are important determinants of the number of women in parliament: the broad policy and legislative framework, the electoral system and the use of quotas.

The experience of the Nordic countries indicates the importance of policy and legislative settings. In 2009, when the global average for the proportion of women in parliament was 18.8 per cent, the average for the Nordic countries stood at 42 per cent. In explaining how these countries have achieved such success, researchers have pointed to a range of social and structural factors (Dahlerup 2002). The existence of a welfare state that provided the public facilities necessary to enable women to pursue educational opportunities and enter the labour market has been credited with creating the context for women's engagement in politics (Yuval-Davis 1997: 14). Policies such as paid parental leave and public care services for children and the elderly created an environment in which women's engagement in the public sphere was not only possible but actively encouraged and supported. Hernes (1987) has referred to such policies as 'state feminism'. While the record of the Nordic countries on gender equity is far from perfect (Hernes 1987; Siim 2000), they do perform better on almost all gender indicators than other countries. The Nordic model has been subjected to criticism (Borchorst and Siim 2008) and is clearly not the only path towards gender equality (Pfau-Effinger 1998). Moreover, extensive public care services are likely to be beyond the reach of less wealthy countries, including emerging middle-income countries like Indonesia. The Nordic experience does, however, demonstrate the role of policy and legislative frameworks in establishing a social and structural context conducive to women's parliamentary representation.

In terms of the policy framework, there is also strong empirical evidence to suggest that electoral systems matter. Systems based on proportional representation tend to result in greater numbers of women being elected than majoritarian systems (Norris 1997; Jones 1998; Dahlerup and Freidenvall 2005: 36; Davidson-Schmich 2006). Multi-member electorates with proportional representation allow for the election of both female and male representatives, whereas single-member electorates force voters or parties to decide between male and female candidates, generally to the disadvantage of women (Rule and Zimmerman 1994). Of the 15 democratic countries in which women make up at least 30 per cent of the national parliament, 13 use proportional representation (Dahlerup and Freidenvall 2005: 36). Systems of proportional representation using a closed list[1] are particularly effective when political parties are committed to gender equality or are required by law to adopt affirmative action measures (Larserud and Taphorn 2007). Thus, while electoral systems are important, political parties are still the gatekeepers (Caul 1999: 80). Incentives or sanctions are generally needed to persuade parties to actively promote gender equality.

In addition to electoral systems, quotas for women's representation are a key strategy to enhance numerical gender equality in parliaments. They, too, are hotly debated. Dahlerup (2002) argues that the Nordic path to equal (or near-equal) parliamentary representation for women through welfare provisions and equal opportunity strategies should no longer be considered the preferred model. While the Nordic countries have been successful, the journey has taken several decades. With a faster track needed, quotas by which parties nominate, or parliaments contain, a minimum percentage of women have emerged as 'an expression of growing impatience among the supporters of equal political and social citizenship for women' (Dahlerup 2002: 3).

Empirical evidence points to the effectiveness of quotas in increasing the number of women in national parliaments. Thirteen of the 15 democratic countries with the highest levels of female representation have some form of quota. Drawing on experience in countries as diverse as South Africa, France, Argentina and Costa Rica, Dahlerup and Nordlund (2004) argue that gender quotas make possible — but do not guarantee — historic leaps in women's political representation, potentially within one

---

1 Under a closed list variant of proportional representation, each political party ranks their candidates in advance to determine who will enter parliament if the party wins seats in the election. The candidates placed highest on the list tend to win seats, while those in lower positions are unlikely to gain seats. Under an open list variant, voters have some influence over which candidates are elected. While there are a variety of open list systems, in general seats are allocated according to the number of votes each candidate wins rather than the preferences of the party. A candidate's ranking on the ballot is therefore less important in an open list system than in a closed list system — but it is still significant.

election. For example, in Costa Rica the introduction of a requirement for 40 per cent of candidates to be women and for them to be placed in winnable positions saw the proportion of women in parliament jump from 19 per cent to 35 per cent. In South Africa, the adoption by the African National Congress of a 30 per cent quota for women lifted women's representation in South Africa's first democratically elected parliament to 30 per cent (Dahlerup and Freidenvall 2005).

Quotas take a variety of forms, ranging from voluntary party quotas to those required by law or mandated by a national constitution. Quotas may be applied to the preselection by parties of female candidates for parliamentary seats or they may require a minimum number of parliamentary seats to be reserved for women, which are then filled either by appointment or by election. Quotas on preselection place significant discretion in the hands of parties, which have been known to nominate female candidates but then give them minimal campaign support, place them in electorates where they have little chance of winning or locate them low on the ballot's list of candidates.

Placement on ballots is important, regardless of whether the winning candidates are decided by the party (as in a closed list proportional representation system) or by the electorate (as in an open list system). Either way, preselection is less likely to translate into election if a candidate's name appears very low on the ballot. In response to the problem of ballot placement, advocates of numerical gender equality in parliament have argued in favour of the 'zipper' system. Under a zipper system, male and female candidates' names are placed alternately on the list so that the winnable positions are occupied by both men and women. Zipper systems have been effective in increasing the number of women elected in several countries (Freidenvall 2003).

International experience has shown that gender quotas can ensure that women are elected to parliament. They are, however, highly controversial. Condemned by opponents as undemocratic and counter to principles of merit, quotas have been resisted by many political actors — including in Indonesia. In response, supporters of quotas argue that they are a necessary correction to the structural barriers that exclude women from political, and especially parliamentary, processes.

THE INDONESIAN EXPERIENCE: HISTORICAL LEGACIES AND POLICY FRAMEWORKS

International experience suggests that policy options and strategies exist to increase the proportion of women in parliaments. How has Indonesia fared? Is the policy and legislative framework conducive to increasing the number of women in the national parliament? In answering this question, it is necessary to consider recent developments, the historical legacy of the New Order and what might be described as traditional attitudes towards gender.

Indonesia's transformation since the fall of the Suharto regime has been remarkable. In terms of gender roles and relations, however, the legacy of the New Order remains strong and is central to understanding the barriers to greater gender equality in the national parliament. The stratified gender relations that existed historically in some parts of Indonesia were actively reinforced and 'nationalised' by New Order ideology and institutionalised in law and policy. While the Nordic countries have been described as pursuing 'state feminism', during the three decades of the New Order Indonesia pursued what Suryakusuma (1996) has described as 'state ibuism'. She argues that the New Order state co-opted the term *ibu* (mother) and used it in a narrow way that emphasised the biological meaning, seeking to present motherhood as the primary, predetermined and natural role for women (Suryakusuma 1996: 101). Women were expected to contribute actively to national development, but through their domestic and community roles, not the male preserve of political power and decision making.

In the post-New Order era, Khofifah Indar Parawansa (2005: 87), the former Indonesian minister for women's empowerment, has argued that

> [the] cultural context in Indonesia is still heavily patriarchal. The common perception is that the political arena is for men, and that it is less preferable for women to become members of parliament.

The view that women are not suited to high office is manifest in the very low numbers of women in key political institutions outside parliament (Figure 11.1). The continuing hold of stereotypical and discriminatory views on the appropriate role of women is repeatedly demonstrated in public life, for example in the comments in October 2009 of an advisor to President Susilo Bambang Yudhoyono as the president was considering his new cabinet. The advisor argued that women could be given the leadership of ministries such as social affairs or women's affairs, but were 'not yet' ready for more 'strategic' roles.[2] As Masruchah, secretary-general of the Indonesian Women's Coalition (Koalisi Perempuan Indonesia, KPI), stated in the wake of the 2009 elections:

> There are a lot of questions as to women's capability in legislative, administrative and even judicial bodies. The public is still learning about female

---

2 'Not now, says senior Dem of top female ministers', *Jakarta Post*, 19 October 2009.

Figure 11.1   Proportions of women and men in key institutions, 2005 (%)

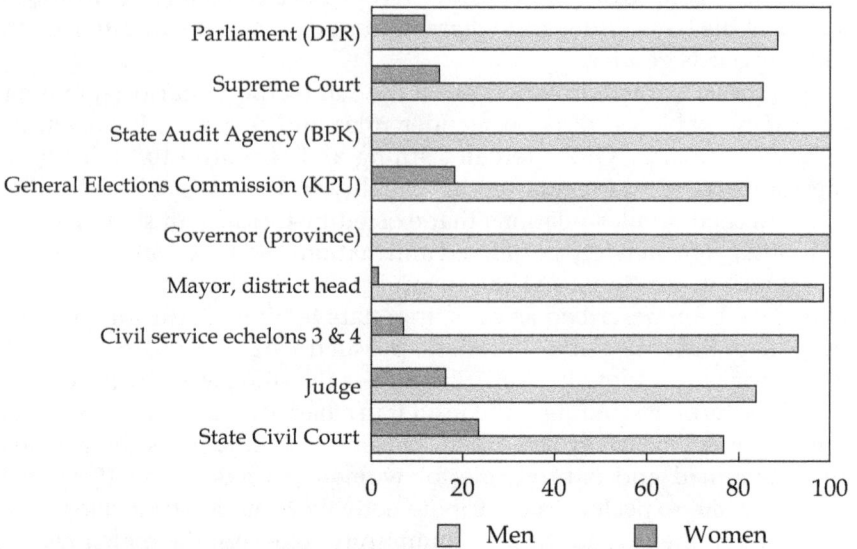

Source: Calculated from Statistics Indonesia data.

leadership because it is still unusual. Largely, they — men — view women as only able to serve in a domestic role.[3]

Rather than fostering greater gender equality, democratisation and — in particular — decentralisation have at times been accompanied by a resurgence of patriarchal attitudes, especially in regional Indonesia. Noerdin (2002: 182) argues that the opportunity for the formation of village councils and customary institutions provided under Law No. 22/1999 on Regional Government was deleterious for women because it lacked an accompanying regulation to 'prevent the revitalisation of feudal and patriarchal values embedded in many of these customary institutions'. She identifies the Nagari system of West Sumatra, which excludes women from formal decision-making processes by restricting participation to (male) clan chiefs, and the revival of *syari'ah* law in some areas, as examples of re-emerging structural barriers to women's representation in local decision-making bodies (Noerdin 2002: 182–4). Another powerful example is the imposition in a few districts of evening curfews on women, which depict women as less than full citizens and undermine their economic, social *and* political roles and rights. Indeed, the propor-

---

3 'Women on the front row', *Jakarta Post*, 8 February 2009.

tion of women in leadership positions in local government is even lower than the proportion in the national parliament (see Satriyo, this volume).

There are, however, important countertrends in contemporary policy, including greater recognition of women in national development planning, the adoption of a 2004 law against domestic violence and, as discussed below, the adoption of gender quotas in national politics (Katjasungkana 2008). Many of these policy changes have resulted from a better-organised women's movement and its attempts to take advantage of the greater political space created by democratisation. In recent years there has been more recognition of principles of gender equality at the national policy level. The obstacles to women's equality nevertheless remain significant and are of a systemic and deeply entrenched character. One certainly sees no systematic attempts to promote women's social and political status, such as those adopted in the Nordic countries. In summary, despite some important progress, the answer to the question of whether Indonesia has a policy and legislative framework conducive to increasing the number of women in the national parliament must be a resounding 'no'.

Indonesia's electoral system until 2004: the power of parties

Indonesia has used a system of proportional representation since its first national election in 1955. The detail of the system has changed markedly over the six decades of independence, reflecting the ebb and flow of political change as the nation has moved from fledgling democracy to authoritarianism and back to democracy. Yet despite the persistence of proportional representation, a consistent feature of the People's Representative Council (Dewan Perwakilan Rakyat, DPR) has been the very low proportion of women, as illustrated in Figure 11.2.

During the New Order, a closed list proportional representation system was used. With voters choosing among parties rather than individual candidates, the party was supreme (Masters 1999: 8). Yet ultimate supremacy among the parties was carefully controlled: only three parties were allowed to contest elections and, of those, the government's electoral vehicle, Golkar, was the only serious contender for electoral power. In the New Order's heavily patriarchal landscape, women were largely excluded from public power and decision making (Bessell 2005). Women won a small minority of seats at each election, with their presence in parliament peaking at just 13 per cent after the 1987 elections. The few women who gained parliamentary representation often did so as a result of strong familial connections (Blackburn 1999: 199).

Given the highly orchestrated nature of elections, the regime would have been able to determine the proportion of women in parliament.

Figure 11.2   Proportions of men and women elected to parliament, 1955–2009 (%)

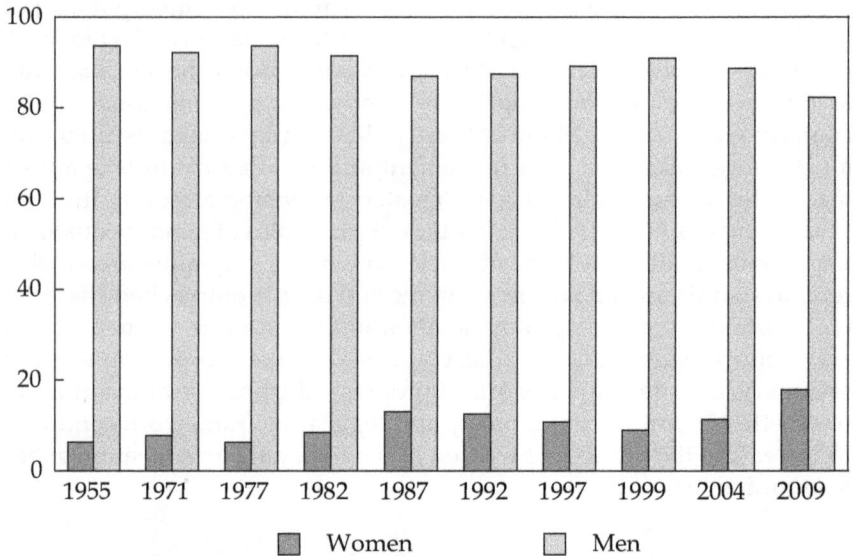

Source: Calculated from electoral data.

Engineering of electoral outcomes to increase the representation of women has been employed in a number of authoritarian socialist states, largely to demonstrate the egalitarian nature of socialism (Jacquette and Wolchik 1998). The New Order government made no such gesture, symbolic or otherwise. Doing so would have run counter to its construction of the ideal woman, who was expected — first and foremost — to be a mother and a wife. In this environment of clearly prescribed gender roles and wider political authoritarianism, proportional representation had very little impact in terms of increasing women's parliamentary representation.

Upon the demise of the New Order, Indonesia's electoral designers had an opportunity to correct the overwhelmingly male nature of the parliament. In the lead-up to the 1999 general elections, this opportunity was not taken up — and as a result women made up only 8.8 per cent of the national parliament elected in that year, the first to be chosen by democratic methods since 1955. The electoral system used in 1999 was based on proportional representation but adopted a modified list variously described as unusual, unique and innovative. Voters cast a single vote for a party. Each party was required to list its candidates in each province prior to the election, so that voters would know beforehand which candidates they were effectively voting for.

This system was designed to strengthen the parties as a core component of the new democracy and discourage individuals from running on personal or issue-based platforms. At the same time, it rewarded well-established, popular candidates with a high profile — most of whom were male. Yet many elements of the system were poorly thought-through and badly implemented, leading the General Elections Commission (Komisi Pemilihan Umum, KPU) to allow parties to determine retrospectively who would occupy the party's seats in parliament (Hicken and Kasuya 2003: 24). This decision greatly enhanced the power of the parties to determine the success of individual candidates, essentially shifting to a closed list. Siregar (2006) has argued that female candidates were seriously disadvantaged by this process because of the patriarchal norms and structures within Indonesia's political parties. When it came to allocating seats, the parties generally favoured men.

Again in the 2004 elections, parties played a crucial role. Under the new electoral laws adopted in late 2003, the list was semi-open, meaning that voters could choose to vote for a party *and* candidates or for a party only. Siregar (2006: 25) has suggested that for women's groups this provided 'hope that an individual candidate could be elected to parliament' as long as she achieved the minimum number of votes required to gain a seat. But in reality, two factors prevented women from being elected. First, because 24 parties contested the election, and because many voters chose to vote for a party alone, it was difficult for individual candidates to secure the minimum number of votes required to be elected. Second, parties placed most female candidates at the bottom of the ballot. Although in theory voters could have chosen to select candidates placed at the bottom of the lists, in effect these positions were unwinnable. Generally, only those candidates placed in the first or second positions on the ballot stood a good chance of winning a seat. A tiny percentage of female candidates were placed in these positions.

Moving towards a quota

Following the 1999 elections, those who argued that Indonesia's new democratic system must foster gender equality actively promoted gender quotas. The fact that the first post-Suharto democratic elections had delivered a decline in the proportion of women elected to parliament galvanized women's groups into action, often with the support of international organisations promoting democracy or women's rights. Several organisations, including the Indonesian Women's Coalition (KPI), the Centre for Electoral Reform (CETRO) and the Indonesian Women's Political Caucus (Kaukus Perempuan Politik Indonesia, KPPI), argued that any new electoral laws needed to address the parliamentary gender imbalance as a matter of urgency. These groups considered gender quotas to be the key strategy for increasing the numbers of women in the national, provincial and district legislatures.

The proposal to adopt a quota proved controversial. During 2000 and 2001, the Ministry for Women's Empowerment supported the campaign, with then minister Khofifah Indar Parawansa lending strong personal support. Since being appointed to the ministry by President Abdurrahman Wahid in 1999 she had actively pursued an agenda for advancing gender equality. Megawati Sukarnoputri, who replaced Wahid as president in 2001, did not share Khofifah's ideas and replaced her with a less proactive minister. Megawati herself openly opposed quotas, describing them in her 2002 Kartini Day speech as bringing about the 'pseudo-advancement' of women.[4] She argued that quotas were counterproductive and undermined the dignity of women, because any advancement secured as a result of them would be neither genuine nor sustainable.[5] Most political parties also exhibited little enthusiasm for quotas, which would have limited their ability to control the selection of candidates and challenged the patriarchal ideology that permeated many of them. Some parties did adopt their own form of internal quotas, with the Indonesian Democratic Party of Struggle (Partai Demokrasi Indonesia Perjuangan, PDIP) — somewhat ironically, Megawati's party — requiring one woman representative for every five men sitting on local executive boards. Overall, however, such internal quotas were weak and ineffectual.

Despite intense lobbying, the DPR in Law No. 31/2002 on Political Parties failed to adopt the 30 per cent quota for women in the preselection of candidates that women's groups had advocated. The debate surrounding the drafting of this law did, however, put the issue of women's parliamentary representation and the idea of quotas firmly on the political and public agenda (Seda 2003: 31). Women's groups continued to lobby for a quota in late 2002 and early 2003, this time with some success. Article 65(1) of Law No. 12/2003 on General Elections, passed by the parliament in February 2003, states that:

> Each political party contesting the General Elections may nominate candidates for each electoral district in the National Parliament [DPR], Provincial Parliaments [DPRD Propinsi] and District/Municipal Parliaments [DPRD Kabupaten/Kota] with consideration of a minimum 30 per cent representation for women.

---

4 Kartini Day celebrates the birth on 21 April 1879 of Raden Ayu Kartini, a Javanese woman remembered for pioneering women's rights in Indonesia.

5 'Megawati tells women to stop seeking pseudo-advancement', *Jakarta Post*, 22 April 2002.

The wording of the article was very weak, with parties merely asked to 'consider' preselecting a certain proportion of women rather than being required to do so. In effect, the article was little more than a gentle reminder to political parties that they might wish to consider achieving greater gender balance.

Here the distinction between types of gender quotas is important. Legal quotas are encoded in a nation's constitution or in legislation, are not voluntary and are enforceable. Party quotas are adopted internally by political parties. While legal quotas do not automatically bring about higher representation for women, they are stronger than party quotas, which are voluntary and subject to the discretion of the party in terms of implementation. The 2003 law did not legislate for a quota per se, but merely suggested the voluntary adoption of party quotas.

In the absence of both incentives and sanctions, political parties were free to determine whether and how they would implement the recommendation. Significantly, Law No. 12/2003 did not address the issue of candidate ranking within the list. This meant that even if parties did as they were urged and preselected female candidates at a rate of 30 per cent, there was no requirement for them to place those candidates sufficiently high on their lists to give them a serious chance of being elected.

Despite the ineffectual wording and lack of any enforcement mechanism, the law's reference to increasing the number of women nominated by parties proved controversial. In the debates on the relevant provisions of the law, four of the nine political groupings (*fraksi*) represented in the national parliament opposed the inclusion of any reference to the nomination of women. Thus, while the bill passed into law, support was by no means widespread. Some parties, and some factions within parties, remained openly hostile to the concept of quotas for women. Yet, the fact that a reference to women's representation was included in the law was a significant step forward. Many women's activists hailed the provision as a major breakthrough. Seda (2003: 31) argued that:

> For the first time in the history of Indonesian political legislation, a legal basis is provided for increasing women's political representation with a specific percentage stated within the article of the law.

How did political parties respond to the suggestion that 30 per cent of candidates for the 2004 election should be female? Sixteen parties won seats in the 2004 election, and seven of them won 45 seats or more. Of these seven major parties, all but one (PDIP) fielded more than 20 per cent female candidates. Three of the major parties — the People's Awakening Party (Partai Kebangkitan Bangsa, PKB), the National Mandate Party (Partai Amanat Nasional, PAN) and the Prosperous Justice Party (Partai Keadilan Sejahtera, PKS) — achieved the 30 per cent quota nationally (see

Figure 11.3   Proportions of male and female candidates nominated nationally by the major parties, 2004 (%)

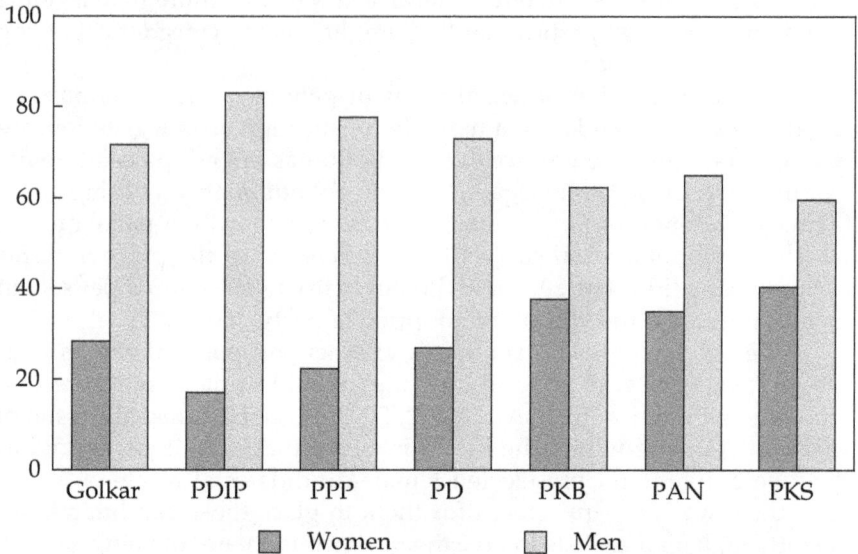

Source: Calculated from International Foundation for Electoral Systems (IFES) data.

Figure 11.3). However, no party met the 30 per cent quota in all electorates. Overall, the major parties nominated more women than previously, but the 30 per cent recommendation was not met.

As the 2004 general elections drew near, media reports indicated that women candidates were dropping down the party lists. Given the large number of votes required by individuals to secure an electoral win, placement on the party list was critical. But as Figure 11.4 demonstrates, all seven major parties failed to place their female candidates in winnable positions on the ballot. The percentage placing their female candidates first or second on the lists ranged from a low of 2.6 per cent for Golkar to a 'high' of 5.3 per cent for PKB. The low positions allocated to most female candidates, combined with the lack of support given to them by their parties (Siregar 2006), accounts for women's poor electoral performance in 2004. While a significant number of women candidates were on the ballot papers, most were not ranked in winnable positions. The gulf between preselection and election was clearly exposed, as were the shortcomings of the election law.

In summary, article 65(1) of the 2003 General Elections Law did not impose a quota in any genuine sense of the term. The percentage of women in parliament following the 2004 election increased from 8.8 per cent to 11.3 per cent, but the commitment of political parties to sig-

Figure 11.4   Proportions of male and female candidates given the top two
positions by the major parties, 2004 (%)

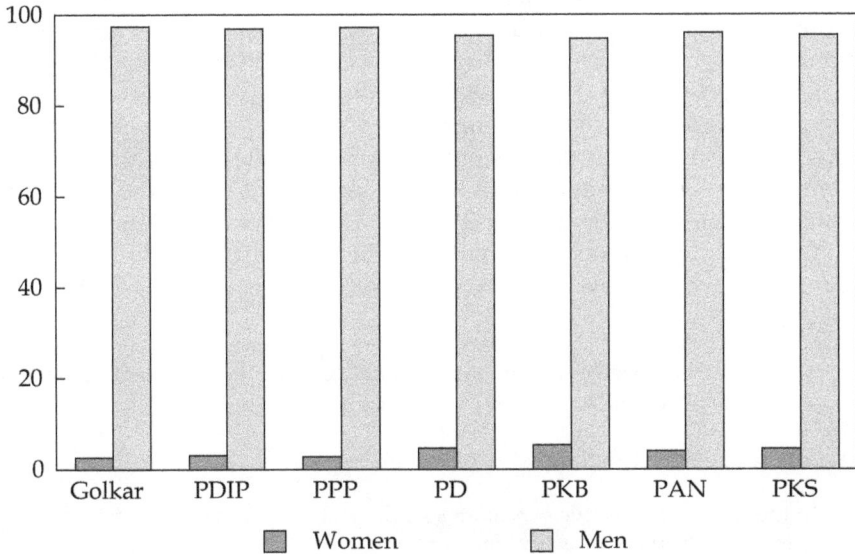

Source: Calculated from International Foundation for Electoral Systems (IFES) data.

nificantly increasing women's representation appeared limited. Nevertheless, the scene was set for supporters of numerical gender equality
in parliament to lobby for more significant reforms in the lead-up to the
2009 elections.

Reforms and debates in the lead-up to the 2009 election

Following the 2004 elections, women's groups continued to lobby for a
quota that would require political parties to nominate female candidates
in larger numbers, place them in winnable positions on the candidate
lists and put them in winnable electorates.

Significantly, political rhetoric had begun to shift and by 2007 all major
political parties indicated support—to varying degrees—for increasing
the number of female members of parliament, although rhetorical support was not necessarily matched by action.[6]

In 2008 two new laws were passed in preparation for the 2009 general elections. Each contained articles on women's representation that

---

6 'Parties unwilling to include women, say analysts', *Jakarta Post*, 5 September
2007.

moved significantly beyond the existing provisions. Law No. 2/2008 on Political Parties required the membership of any new political party to be at least 30 per cent female (article 2, paragraph 2). It also stated that women should occupy at least 30 per cent of the party's executive positions (article 2, paragraph 5). Articles 8 and 15 of Law No. 10/2008 on General Elections stipulated that, for a political party to qualify to contest the general elections, 30 per cent of the positions on its regional executive boards and in the central party leadership should be occupied by women. These requirements were very significant given the power of boards to determine the preselection and ranking of candidates.

In terms of parliamentary gender quotas, articles 53 and 55 of the 2008 General Elections Law were particularly significant. Article 53 stated that:

> The list of prospective candidates ... shall contain the representation of at least 30 per cent women.

Article 55(2) stated that:

> In the list of prospective candidates ... there shall be at least one female prospective candidate for every three prospective candidates.

Article 55 did not unambiguously require political parties to adopt a zipper system, whereby male and female candidates would be placed alternately on the candidate list. However, the KPU's interpretation of the article did require parties to place a female candidate in third place or higher on the list.

Articles 53 and 55 placed a legislative requirement on political parties to preselect women and ensure that one-third of their candidates were female. Unlike the 2004 legislation, the 2008 law included a clear quota for the nomination of women. The support given to female candidates by political parties remained outside the law, but there now existed a clear legal requirement for parties to at least nominate women.

As in the past, however, the issues of women's political rights and parliamentary representation remained controversial. In late 2008, two petitions were lodged with the Constitutional Court, each arguing that several articles of the election law — including those referring to the nomination of women — were unconstitutional. One of the petitioners, himself a candidate for a regional legislature, argued that the requirement for one in three candidates to be female contradicted the constitutional guarantee that 'all citizens shall have an equal position before the law and government' (article 27(1)).

The petitions also challenged article 214 of the 2008 General Elections Law, which set out the minimum share of votes required by a candidate in order to win a seat. It allowed political parties to determine the successful candidate — based on the candidate lists — in the event that no candidate achieved the stipulated minimum number of votes (30 per cent of a full electoral quota) or where two or more candidates achieved an equal number of votes. Article 214(d) also allowed parties to transfer votes to other candidates — based on the candidate lists — if the number of candidates receiving the minimum number of votes was less than the number of seats won by the party. In other words, article 214 gave political parties a significant role in determining a candidate's chances of electoral success, with position on the candidate list being crucial. Article 214 did not refer to gender, but was interpreted by some as allowing parties to improve the prospects of female candidates should they choose to do so. It was also a means for parties to pursue the gender quota contained in articles 53 and 55.

In coming to its decision, the members of the Constitutional Court considered statements from several stakeholders, including the National Commission on Violence Against Women (Komisi Nasional Anti Kekerasan Terhadap Perempuan, or Komnas Perempuan). Komnas Perempuan argued persuasively that special treatment was necessary — and guaranteed under the constitution — where citizens suffered inequality or discrimination. Rather than being contrary to the constitution, it argued, articles 55 and 214 of the election law constituted the practical application of a constitutional commitment to equality.[7]

The Constitutional Court dismissed the petition relating to article 55 of the law (requiring one in three candidates to be a woman), finding that the state had an obligation to foster substantive equality. In explaining its finding, the court stated that affirmative action for women in politics was in keeping with the intent of the constitution. The court also referred to the UN Convention on the Elimination of All Forms of Discrimination against Women (CEDAW), which Indonesia had ratified in 1984, and other international commitments. CEDAW is the primary international treaty on gender equality. It allows for special measures or affirmative action strategies to be adopted to overcome discrimination against women. Such measures are considered corrective rather than a form of reverse discrimination. The Constitutional Court ruling noted Indonesia's 'commitment to human rights instruments relating to the elimination of all forms of discrimination against women as well as the commitment to promote women in the political arena'. The court further stated that its decision to uphold article 55 of the election law was in support of a 'policy of affirmative action which is provisional in nature, in order to promote women's involvement in decision making [and] the

---

7   Constitutional Court Decision No. 22-24/PUU-VI/2008, section 3.15.1, p. 27.

formulation of law'.[8] This decision must be seen as a major victory for those advocating greater numerical equality for women in parliament generally, and for gender quotas specifically.

On the other hand, the court upheld the petition relating to article 214, finding that it contradicted articles in the constitution placing sovereignty in the hands of the people and guaranteeing equality. This decision was significant for Indonesia's electoral system. Sherlock (2009: 6–7) has argued that, as a result of the ruling, a 'tentative move towards a semi-open list system became a leap towards a fully open list system', with parties now being required to allocate their seats to the individual candidates who had won the most votes. Interestingly, the verdict was not unanimous, with one (female) judge dissenting from the ruling. Maria Farida Indrati argued that there was a constitutional requirement to guarantee equality for all citizens, including women. Article 214, she argued, was a legitimate means of doing this. She suggested that there was a contradiction in the decision to overrule article 214 but maintain article 55 (see Suryakusuma 2009).

The Constitutional Court's ruling preserved the 30 per cent quota and the requirement for one in three candidates to be female. However, by invalidating article 214, the court effectively removed the ability of political parties to transfer votes between candidates — whether to strengthen female candidates or not — and greatly reduced the significance of the candidate list, and hence of the one-in-three requirement introduced by article 55(2) of the 2008 General Elections Law.

In considering the relative merits of open and closed list proportional representation systems in facilitating women's access to parliament, Matland (2005) has observed that the key issue is whether it is easier to convince voters or the political parties of women's right to full political participation. In keeping with this observation, in Indonesia the mixed views on the likely impact of the Constitutional Court's ruling on women's electoral chances were determined largely by whether the commentator placed more faith in political parties or in voters. Adhiati (2009: 2) noted that 'the successful outcome for a candidate is no longer based on the ranking system established by the candidate's party, but on the candidate winning the largest number of votes'. In this context, she observed the 'pessimism felt by women's groups and women activists right across the political spectrum' (Adhiati 2009: 3). This pessimism is clearly evident in the comments of KPI head Masruchah when she stated that the court's ruling had 'destroyed all our efforts to campaign for more seats for women ...'.[9] The KPI and other women's groups viewed politi-

---

8 Constitutional Court Decision No. 22-24/PUU-VI/2008, section 3.15.1, p. 41.
9 'Women urge pressure for more seats', *Jakarta Post*, 2 March 2009.

cal parties as potentially delivering on the spirit of the quota, despite their patriarchal structure and historically low commitment to increasing the number of women in parliament. In contrast, Hadar Gumay, executive director of CETRO, offered a more positive interpretation, suggesting that

> Under this ruling, legislative seats are now awarded to the candidates who win the most votes. ... Under this revised system, the authority of political parties is limited to selecting ... candidates to compete in the legislative elections. They have no right to handpick its representatives at the legislative bodies.[10]

2009: A SUCCESS FOR GENDER EQUALITY?

Women gained more seats in the national parliament in 2009 than in any election in Indonesia's history. Women now make up 17.8 per cent of the parliament, an increase of 6.5 per cent over the 11.3 per cent achieved in 2004 and a rise of 4.8 per cent over the previous high of 13 per cent in 1987. This is a notable success, if not the historic leap witnessed in some countries.

The performance of individual parties varied markedly. As Figure 11.5 shows, among the nine parties that gained seats, PKB recorded the highest proportion of seats won by women as a proportion of all its seats (25.9 per cent), and the Democratic Party (Partai Democrat, PD) the second highest (24.7 per cent). Among the other successful parties, the proportion ranged from 14.0 per cent (PAN) to 21 per cent (PDIP). PKS is an interesting anomaly. It did particularly well in nominating female candidates, having reached the 30 per cent quota in 96 per cent of electorates. Yet female PKS candidates won only three (5 per cent) of the 57 seats obtained by the party. Whether the poor results for its female candidates were due to a lack of support from the party or a lack of support from voters is not clear, although PKS's support base does tend to be quite conservative. In October 2009, its deputy secretary general, Zulkieflimansyah, observed that the public considered PKS to be 'an Islamic-based party, not open to pluralism, and turning women into second-class citizens', and proclaimed the need for the party to change its image in order to attract a wider range of voters.[11]

---

10 'Political parties' commitment to women's interests put to the test', *Jakarta Post*, 19 January 2009.

11 'PKS to be more business friendly, open and pluralist', *Jakarta Post*, 26 October 2009.

Figure 11.5   Seats won by women as a proportion of a party's total seats, 2009 (%)

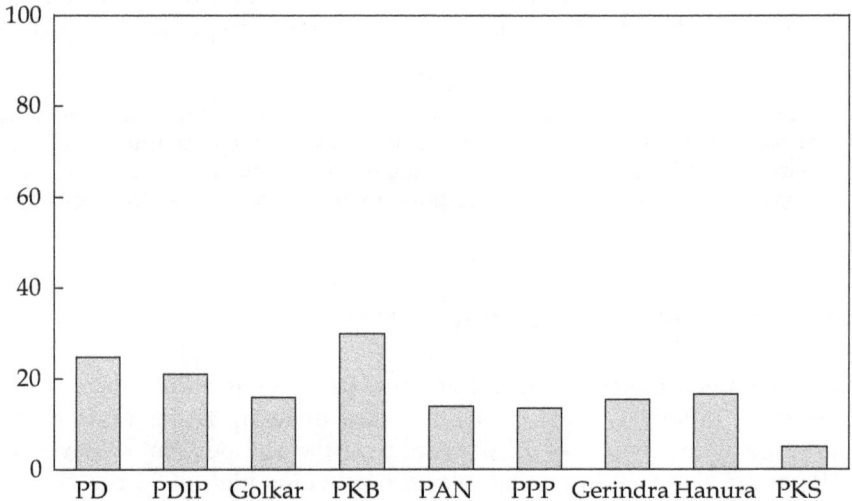

Source: Based on data provided by Kevin Evans, www.pemilu.asia.

Overall, the results of the 2009 national election are mixed from a gender perspective. The Constitutional Court ruling placed limits on the role of political parties in determining electoral success. The way in which parties responded to the quota provisions of the electoral law, however, reveals something of party powerbrokers' attitudes towards women's political representation. Of the 38 parties contesting the 2009 national parliamentary elections, only five nominated at least 30 per cent women and placed a woman in the top three places on candidate lists in all electorates. Each of these was a small party that failed to win seats in the national parliament.

Of the nine parties that won seats in the national parliament, none met the 30 per cent quota in all electoral districts. PDIP and PKS did best, with women making up 30 per cent of candidates in 97 per cent and 96 per cent of electorates respectively.[12] Of the nine winning parties, four — PAN, the United Development Party (Partai Persatuan Pembangunan, PPP), the People's Conscience Party (Partai Hati Nurani Rakyat, Hanura) and the Greater Indonesia Movement Party (Partai Gerakan Indonesia Raya, Gerindra) — failed to meet the quota in more than 50 per cent of electorates. The practical consequence of the failure to attach sanctions or effective incentives to the quota provision became clear. The KPU

---

12   Based on KPU data and data available at www.pemilu.asia.

Figure 11.6   *Placement of women and men on candidate lists, 2009
(positions 1–12)*

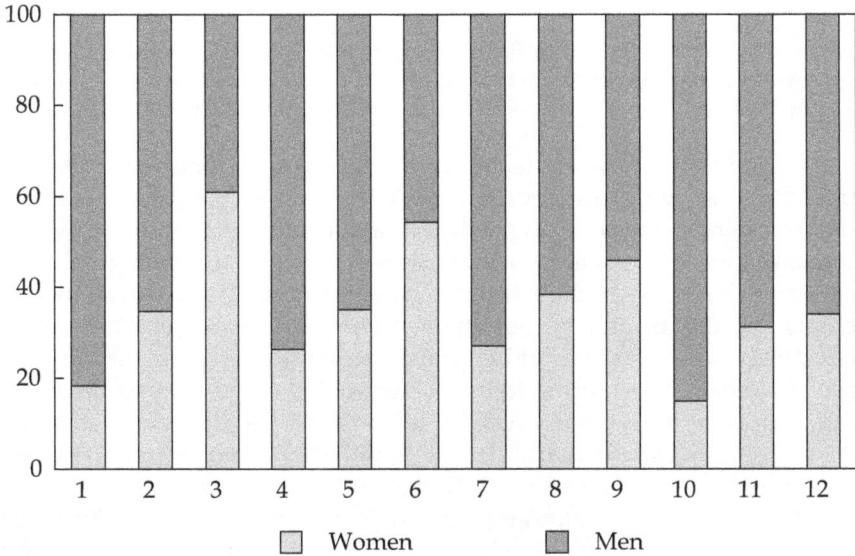

Source: Based on data provided by Kevin Evans, www.pemilu.asia.

announced publicly which parties had failed to meet the quota, but no action was—or could be—taken. As discussed, article 55 of the election law required parties to nominate one woman among every three candidates. As Figure 11.6 indicates, while there was reasonable compliance with this provision, most parties tended to place women in third, rather than first or second, position on the candidate list. While the ruling of the Constitutional Court made candidate lists far less significant than in the past, placement still provided an indication of the attitudes of party powerbrokers towards female candidates.

While the shift to an open list system in the 2009 elections limited the power of parties to determine outcomes, they remained powerful political actors, particularly in terms of the support provided to candidates. During the campaign and in the wake of the elections, media reports suggested that many female candidates had been placed in electoral districts where they were unknown or where the party had little support. There were also reports of female candidates being moved from an electorate where they had popular support to another electoral area, often very late in the campaign. A smaller number of reports suggested that female candidates had been subjected to intimidation and discrimination from within their own parties. In March 2009, just weeks before the election, Komnas Perempuan presented the findings of a survey that indicated continual intimidation and gender-based discrimination against female voters and legislative candidates. Chairperson Neng Dara Affiah was quoted as saying:

> In this election it is still difficult for women, and this vulnerable group has often suffered from intimidation and has been more discriminated against in the lead-up to the 2009 election than in the 2004 general election.[13]

An additional obstacle facing many female candidates in 2009 was the strengthening of money politics. Mietzner (2009: 19) has observed that in recent years political participation has become both more expensive and more complicated, with parties and candidates hiring pollsters and consultants to run their advertising campaigns. This trend was exacerbated by the introduction of an open party list system in 2009, which effectively meant that individual candidates from the same party had to compete against each other to try to ensure that they achieved the highest number of individual votes. More so than in any previous election, it became important for candidates to build — and fund — their own campaigns and campaign teams, which was often a costly exercise.

The high costs of running for office had particularly deleterious effects on female candidates, given their weaker financial support bases. Several high-profile female candidates suggested that their parties had failed to fully support them. Dita Sari, a long-time labour rights activist, failed to gain a seat in the 2009–2014 national parliament despite her high profile. In assessing the reasons for her defeat, Sari identified two factors, each associated with money politics. First, she noted the expectation among voters that candidates would offer financial incentives in return for their votes. Second, she observed that, as the election neared, parties failed to provide financial and other support to female candidates. As she observed, 'We were very much on our own, without financial assistance or facilities … from political parties' (Langit-Dursin 2009).

CONCLUSION: WHERE TO FROM HERE?

Larserud and Taphorn (2007) have observed that women are guaranteed to win seats in parliament when a system of proportional representation with a closed list is combined with a legislative requirement for the nomination of a stated percentage of women and a zipper system. Legislation must include sanctions for non-compliance and these must be enforced. Thus, there exists a formula for success if governments, political parties

---

13 'Discrimination against women in poll rampant', *Jakarta Post*, 24 March 2009.

and societies are serious about creating numerical gender equality in parliament.

Indonesia has proportional representation, and it has moved tentatively but progressively towards gender quotas in recent years. The quota provisions adopted in 2003 were weak and poorly institutionalised. The 2008 provisions were far stronger but still lacked an enforcement mechanism. Other key elements of the successful formula identified by Larserud and Taphorn are also missing. First, there are no sanctions for non-compliance with the quota. Second, the ruling of the Constitutional Court shifted Indonesia's system of proportional representation to an open list system, letting parties 'off the hook' in terms of maximising the electoral prospects of women. It should be noted, however, that there was never any guarantee that parties would use the provisions of article 214 to ensure the electoral success of female candidates. Interpretations that it would be used in such a way may well have been overly optimistic. Third, the law does not clearly and unequivocally require a zipper system. In 2009, when parties did place a female candidate among the top three candidates in a particular electoral district, it was most common for her to be given the third spot. While this may provide an insight into party attitudes, it is less electorally significant under an open list system. If Indonesia continues to use an open list, the challenges will be to convince parties to support female candidates and to convince voters to elect them. These are not easy tasks given the role of money in politics and continuing patriarchal attitudes both within and beyond political parties.

That the national parliament elected in 2009 includes more women than at any other time in Indonesia's history is a cause for some celebration and optimism. Also significant is the Constitutional Court's defence of the election law's quota provisions. However, an analysis of the barriers to women gaining seats in parliament leads to a less sanguine conclusion. The policy and legislative framework, overall, does not foster an environment conducive to women seeking or winning political office. Progress in the development of gender-sensitive policies at the national level is countered in some areas of the country by new discriminatory regulations – such as local-level restrictions on women's freedom of movement – that reinforce the inequitable legacy of the New Order. The resistance of Indonesia's patriarchal political parties and an overall lack of political will to act decisively to promote women's parliamentary representation remain serious obstacles to greater numerical equality in the national parliament. These factors are compounded by the increasingly expensive nature of politics, which acts as a practical barrier to many potential candidates, but has particularly adverse consequences for women. The 2009 election results, the accompanying debates and the adoption of a stronger quota provision suggest, however, that this may be set to change — at least at the national level.

Experience around the globe suggests that there are policy options and affirmative action strategies capable of increasing the number of women in parliament. For Indonesia, the challenge is twofold. The first is to determine how policies and strategies can be adapted successfully to the unique context of Indonesia. This challenge is by no means insurmountable, as demonstrated in recent years in countries as diverse as South Africa, Costa Rica and Rwanda, all of which have achieved much better women's representation in parliament than has Indonesia. The second challenge, on which all else depends, is to garner the political will to move beyond the patriarchal values and attitudes that have long shaped the political landscape in Indonesia. This is a challenge of major proportions. Yet, for organisations and individuals within Indonesia who are committed to both gender justice and democracy, it is a challenge that must be overcome.

REFERENCES

Adhiati, Adriana (2009) 'Women in parliament: quotas and beyond', *Tapol Election Update*, 4, February.

Bessell, Sharon (2005), 'Indonesia', in Y. Galligan and M. Tremblay (eds), *Sharing Power: Women, Parliament, Democracy*, Ashgate, Aldershot, pp. 7–24.

Blackburn, Susan (1999) 'Women and citizenship in Indonesia', *Australian Journal of Political Science* 34(2): 198–204.

Borchorst, Anette and Birte Siim (2008), 'Women-friendly policies and state feminism: theorising Scandinavian gender equality', *Feminist Theory* 9(2): 207–24.

Caul, Miki (1999), 'Women's representation in parliament: the role of political parties', *Party Politics* 5(1): 79–98.

Dahlerup, Drude (2002), 'Quotas — a jump to equality? The need for international comparisons for the use of electoral quotas to obtain equal political citizenship for women', paper prepared for a workshop hosted by the International Institute for Democracy and Electoral Assistance (International IDEA), Jakarta, 25 September.

Dahlerup, Drude and Lenita Freidenvall (2005), 'Quotas as a "fast track" to equal representation for women', *International Journal of Feminist Politics* 7(12): 26–48.

Dahlerup, Drude and Anja Taarup Nordlund (2004), 'Gender quotas: a key to equality? A case study of Iraq and Afghanistan', *European Political Science*, 3(3): 91–8.

Davidson-Schmich, Louise K. (2006), 'Implementation of political party gender quotas: evidence from the German Länder 1990–2000', *Party Politics* 12(2): 211–32.

Freidenvall, Lenita (2003), 'Women's political representation and gender quotas: the Swedish case', Working Paper 2003:2, Research Program on Gender Quotas, Stockholm University, Stockholm.

Hernes, H. (1987), *Welfare State and Woman Power: Essays in State Feminism*, Norwegian University Press, London.

Hicken, Allen and Yuko Kasuya (2003), 'A guide to the constitutional structures and electoral systems of East, South and Southeast Asia', *Electoral Studies* 22(1): 121–51.

Jacquette, Jane and Sharon Wolchik (eds) (1998), *Women and Democracy: Latin America and Central and Eastern Europe*, Johns Hopkins University Press, Baltimore MD.

Jones, Mark P. (1998), 'Gender quotas, electoral laws and the election of women: lessons from the Argentine provinces', *Comparative Political Studies* 31(1): 3–21.

Katjasungkana, Nursyahbani (2008), 'Gender and law reform in Indonesia: overcoming entrenched barriers', in T. Lindsey (ed.), *Indonesia: Law and Society*, second edition, Federation Press, Sydney, pp. 483–98.

Langit-Dursin, Richel (2009), 'Indonesia: women activists draw lessons from failed election bids', Jakarta, 20 August, http://tapol.gn.apc.org/elections/digest20.htm.

Larserud, Stina and Rita Taphorn (2007), *Designing for Equality: Best-fit, Medium-fit and Non-favourable Combinations of Electoral Systems and Gender Quotas*, International IDEA, Stockholm.

Masters, Edward (1999), 'Indonesia's 1999 elections: a second chance for democracy', Asia Society, Jakarta, http://www.asiasociety.org/publications/update_indonesia.html.

Matland, Richard, (2005), 'The effect of development and culture on women's representation', in A. Karam (ed.), *Women in Parliament: Beyond Numbers*, revised edition, International IDEA, Stockholm, pp. 93–111.

Mietzner, Marcus (2009), 'Indonesia's 2009 elections: populism, dynasties and the consolidation of the party system', *Analysis*, Lowy Institute for International Policy, Sydney, May.

Noerdin, Edriana (2002), 'Customary institutions: *syariah* law and the marginalisation of Indonesian women', in K. Robinson and S. Bessell (eds), *Women in Indonesia: Gender, Equity and Diversity*, Institute of Southeast Asian Studies, Singapore, pp. 179–86.

Norris, Pippa (1997), 'Choosing electoral systems: proportional, majoritarian and mixed systems', *International Political Science Review* 18(3): 297–312.

Parawansa, Khofifah Indar (2005), 'Enhancing women's political participation in Indonesia', in A. Karam (ed.), *Women in Parliament: Beyond Numbers*, revised edition, International IDEA, Stockholm, pp. 82–90.

Pfau-Effinger, B. (1998), 'Gender cultures and the gender arrangements: a theoretical framework for cross national gender research', *Innovation* 11(2): 147–66.

Rule, Wilma and Michael Zimmerman (eds) (1994), *Electoral Systems in Comparative Perspective: Their Impact on Women and Minorities*, Greenwood Press, Westport CT.

Seda, Francisia (2003), 'Beyond numbers: strengthening women's political participation', in International Institute for Democracy and Electoral Assistance (International IDEA) (ed.), *Strengthening Women's Political Participation in Indonesia: Conference Report*, International IDEA, Stockholm, pp. 19–23, http://www.idea.int/publications/swppi/index.cfm.

Sherlock, Stephen (2009), 'Indonesia's 2009 elections: the new electoral system and the competing parties', CDI Policy Papers on Political Governance 2009/01, Centre for Democratic Institutions, Canberra.

Siim, Birte (2000), *Gender and Citizenship: Politics and Agency in France, Britain and Denmark*, Cambridge University Press, Cambridge.

Siregar, Wahidah Zein Br (2006), 'Political parties, electoral system and women's representation in the 2004–2009 Indonesian parliaments', CDI Policy Papers on Political Governance 2006/02, Centre for Democratic Institutions, Canberra.

Suryakusuma, Julia I. (2006), 'The state and sexuality in New Order Indonesia', in L.J. Sears (ed.), *Fantasizing the Feminine in Indonesia*, Duke University Press, Durham, pp. 92–119.

Suryakusuma, Julia I. (2009), 'Women's political misrepresentation', *Jakarta Post*, 4 January.

Yuval-Davis, Nira (1997), *Gender and Nation*, Sage, London and New York.

12 PUSHING THE BOUNDARIES: WOMEN IN DIRECT LOCAL ELECTIONS AND LOCAL GOVERNMENT

Hana A. Satriyo

Since 2004, Indonesia has conducted more than 490 elections for heads of local government at both the provincial and district levels. Although the introduction of direct elections for local government heads (*pemilihan kepala daerah,* or *pilkada*) has created opportunities for women to run as candidates, their level of participation has been extremely low. By the end of 2009 only nine women had been elected head of a regional government in direct elections: seven as district head (*bupati*); one as mayor (*walikota*) of an urban municipality; and one as the governor of a province. Indonesia also had one female deputy governor and 14 women serving as deputy mayors or deputy district heads. These very low numbers are far from ideal for a country that says it is serious about promoting gender equality in political life.

There have been some genuine efforts to increase women's political participation in Indonesia since the beginning of the democratic transition in 1998. At the national level, these have included the introduction of a 30 per cent quota for female legislative candidates in 2004 and the adoption of a 'zipper' system for candidacy lists in 2009. Under the zipper system, political parties had to include at least one woman among the three candidates they placed at the top of their lists, thus giving women candidates a real chance of being elected. These efforts have produced a slight improvement in women's representation in the national legislature, the People's Representative Council (Dewan Perwakilan Rakyat, DPR). In elections for local government heads, however, even weak affirmative action measures have been conspicuously absent, and there has been no serious policy consideration of how to reduce the gender gap in local government leadership positions.

244 Problems of Democratisation in Indonesia

In this chapter I examine the factors confronting women who want to be nominated as candidates in local executive elections. Beyond the absence of positive discrimination measures, one key challenge for women is that they still have difficulty convincing party leaders and other political elites of their electability. Women also tend to lack the financial resources and political networks necessary to achieve political success in regional Indonesia. While local political and religious leaders are often hostile towards women candidates, there are indications that voters will support capable women candidates if given the opportunity. Moreover, women who have jumped all the hurdles necessary to become regional government heads have generally performed well, giving them a good chance of being re-elected. But despite some positive signs of changing public attitudes and the examples of successful female regional government leaders, the overall picture is one of considerable gender inequality, with little immediate prospect of improvement.

The chapter is divided into four sections. The first provides an overview of data and trends concerning women's participation in direct local elections. The second focuses on the barriers women face in seeking to become candidates, especially the role played by political parties in the nomination process. The third section contrasts the views of local political, religious and social elites with those of ordinary voters, pointing to both the opportunities and the challenges for women who aspire to political leadership positions at the local level. Finally, I describe the backgrounds of the nine women who won local government elections between 2005 and 2008, seeking to identify common sources of strength. Although a diverse group, many of these women drew on the same sorts of powerful political networks that have propelled successful male candidates into office. One message that arises from this section is that women who have been given the opportunity to lead a regional government have generally performed well, with the result that they have been re-elected at higher rates than their male counterparts.

WOMEN IN LOCAL GOVERNMENT ELECTIONS: THE BIG PICTURE

With no central government body systematically collecting information on *pilkada*, it is not easy to count the exact number of local elections held between 2005 and 2008, let alone compile comprehensive data on the candidates (Nalenan 2008). The fact that there is no legal requirement to collect gender-disaggregated data on candidates running in direct local elections (unlike in legislative elections) further complicates the task of identifying precisely how many women have run for local executive gov-

Table 12.1   *Numbers of female and male candidates in direct local elections,*
2005–2008

Position	Number of female candidates	Number of male candidates	Female candidates as a % of all candidates
Province			
Governor	3	129	2.3
Deputy governor	4	128	3.1
District/municipality			
District head/mayor	35	1,659	2.1
Deputy district head/ deputy mayor	92	1,602	5.7
Total	**134**	**3,518**	**3.8**

Source: JPPR database.

ernment office. It has been left to non-government organisations like the People's Voter Education Network (Jaringan Pendidikan Pemilih untuk Rakyat, JPPR) to compile figures on parties and candidates running in Indonesia's direct local elections. JPPR has documented 466 *pilkada* at the district/municipality level and 33 at the provincial level between 2005 and 2008. It has counted a total of 3,652 candidates competing for the positions of head or deputy head in those elections. Of that number, a mere 134 (4 per cent) were women (Table 12.1).

One reason for the small number of women candidates needs to be highlighted from the outset: the absence of a supportive legal framework. Despite appeals from women's groups for affirmative action to encourage more women to run, *pilkada* are arguably among the least gender sensitive of all Indonesia's democratic institutions.[1] There are no provisions in the relevant law to encourage the Regional General Election Commissions (Komisi Pemilihan Umum Daerah, KPUD), political parties or other relevant bodies to promote women as candidates. Nor is there any requirement for the KPUDs or other agencies to prevent gender-based discrimination or attacks against women candidates.

Given women's poor participation rate as candidates in direct local elections and the absence of serious efforts to address the problem, it is

---

1 'Kaum perempuan usulkan perubahan UU Pilkada' [Women propose changes to the Law on the Election of Local Government Heads], *KapanLagi.com*, 12 January 2007, http://www.kapanlagi.com/h/0000152651.html.

Table 12.2   Numbers of women and men elected in direct local elections, 2005–2008

Position	Number of women elected	Number of men elected	Women as a % of all those elected
Province			
Governor	1	32	3.0
Deputy governor	1	32	3.0
District/municipality			
District head/mayor	8	459	1.7
Deputy district head/ deputy mayor	14	453	3.0
Total	**24**	**976**	**2.4**

Source: JPPR database.

not surprising that the number of women actually elected to lead local governments is also very low (Table 12.2). Across the country, only 2.4 per cent of those occupying the positions of head or deputy head at the local level are women. Although the small absolute numbers make it hard to draw any grand conclusions, this suggests that when women do run for office, they are less likely to be elected than men.

The trends are not encouraging either. After direct elections for local government heads were introduced in 2005, the share of women elected increased slightly until 2007 but then declined sharply in 2008 (Table 12.3). Overall, the period did not see an increase in women's involvement in local government, in sharp contrast to the results of the 2009 national election, where women's representation in the DPR increased from 11.3 per cent to 17.8 per cent (see Bessell's chapter in this volume).

In explaining the reasons for these poor outcomes, it is important to examine both the obstacles that stand in the way of women who want to stand for executive government positions as well as the underlying attitudes and structures that account for those obstacles. I turn to these issues in the next two sections.

BARRIERS TO ENTRY

Political parties are the dominant players when it comes to deciding who can run as a candidate in a direct local election. When the Regional Government Law was amended in 2004 to allow for the direct election of local government heads, it stipulated that only political parties, or coa-

Table 12.3   Number of direct local elections, and number and percentage of women elected, 2005–2008

	2005	2006	2007	2008
Number of direct local elections	224	81	38	151
Total number of women elected	13	6	3	2
Governor	1	0	0	0
Deputy governor	0	0	0	1
District head/mayor	3	3	1	1
Deputy district head/ deputy mayor	9	3	2	0
Successful female candidates as a % of all successful candidates	5.8	7.4	7.8	1.3

Source: JPPR database and other sources.

litions of parties, that held at least 15 per cent of the seats or had won at least 15 per cent of the vote in the region concerned could nominate candidates. In 2007 the Constitutional Court handed down a decision that allowed independent candidates to run in direct local elections. However, the candidacy requirements remain onerous and in practice political parties still dominate the nomination process. Affiliation with a major party such as Golkar, the Indonesian Democratic Party of Struggle (Partai Demokrasi Indonesia Perjuangan, PDIP) or the People's Awakening Party (Partai Kebangkitan Bangsa, PKB) therefore remains the most practical route to nomination, although party coalitions also nominate large numbers of candidates (Pratikno 2009).

The problem for women who aspire to leadership positions in local government is that most of Indonesia's political parties are still dominated by men. Internal party leadership bodies often contain few or even no women, especially at the local level. It is not surprising, then, that when parties look internally for candidates, they usually pick males who are already entrenched in party structures. But parties also look outside their own ranks for candidates, especially to find people with high electability as demonstrated by opinion polls, and the resources to fund their own campaigns and subsidise the party.

Some parties choose their candidates at local party conventions; others use closed internal mechanisms. In both cases, the final selection of *pilkada* candidates depends almost entirely on the preferences and decisions of party elites. In order to win over party elites, candidates need strong campaign teams who can design strategies, lobby local and sometimes national party leaders, and mobilise resources. People with these

Table 12.4   Political parties and coalitions nominating women candidates in direct local elections, 2005–2007[a]

Nominating party or coalition	Number of female candidates	Total number of candidates	Female candidates as a % of all candidates
Independent	5	9	55.6
Golkar	24	176	13.6
Golkar without coalition	*15*	*51*	*29.4*
Coalition of Golkar & smaller parties	*5*	*64*	*7.8*
Coalition of Golkar and PDIP	*4*	*61*	*6.6*
PDIP	15	152	9.9
PDIP without coalition	*8*	*27*	*29.6*
Coalition of PDIP & smaller parties	*3*	*64*	*4.7*
Coalition of PDIP & Golkar	*4*	*61*	*6.6*
Coalition of PD & other parties	6	46	13.0
Coalition of PPP & other parties	6	60	10.0
Coalition of small parties	21	289	7.3
Coalition of PAN & other parties	5	72	6.9
Coalition of PKS & other parties	3	50	6.0
Coalition of PKB & other parties	3	55	5.5

a   The table covers the direct local elections held between June 2005 and November 2007. It includes only women candidates whose party of nomination could be identified.

Source: JPPR database; Lingkaran Survei Indonesia data.

kinds of skills and resources tend to be established members of the local elite: politically well-connected businesspeople, bureaucrats, incumbent politicians and the like. Women are poorly represented in this group. As a result, very few have the political networks, experience or wealth to successfully navigate party nomination processes.

Table 12.4 summarises what is known about the parties that nominated women in the direct local elections held between 2005 and 2007. The party that nominated the most women was Golkar, the largest party at the national level after the 2004 elections and a very influential political force in many regions. Golkar participated in almost all *pilkada* across Indonesia, and it is likely that its sheer weight of numbers allowed it to take chances with female candidates. Structurally, Golkar has a number of women's organisations that have been affiliated with the party for over three decades. It therefore already had a large pool of potential women candidates, and established channels for nominating women. However, Golkar's record in winning *pilkada* has not been as good, partly because it has had a tendency to support unpopular incumbents (Haris 2008). This also helps to explain why it did not support even more women candidates: because most incumbents were men, women were not in a position to take advantage of this particular strategy of Golkar.

The party to support the second-largest number of women candidates was PDIP. Its secular nationalist outlook has meant that religious arguments against women candidates carry little influence, but patriarchal structures and patterns of behaviour nevertheless remain entrenched within the party. PDIP's mechanisms give the party's central board the authority to override the nominations of its regional conventions (Asydhad 2006). Even though the party's national chairperson, Megawati Sukarnoputri, is a woman, the central board she leads sometimes used this authority to frustrate women candidates with grassroots support.

One good example is provided by the case of Ratna Ani Lestari, a longstanding PDIP member. She managed to gain the endorsement of her local party branch to run for the position of district head in Banyuwangi, East Java, in 2005, gaining 17 out of the 21 available votes. The party's central board was not confident that Ratna could win, however, and endorsed a rival, Ali Sya'roni (Lingkaran Survei Indonesia 2007a). He was a high-ranking official in the East Java provincial government who was close to the party's central board. Ratna went on to stand for the position anyway as the nominee of a coalition of small parties, and won. PDIP then acknowledged Ratna as a party member and has since defended her against attacks from other political parties and local community leaders (see below).

Also disappointing some female members of PDIP was the party's decision to nominate Rustriningsih, the head of Kebumen district in Central Java, as deputy governor rather than governor in the 2008 *pilkada*. Rustriningsih was a popular district head who stood a good chance of winning the governship had she been allowed to stand. The party itself acknowledged that adding her to the ticket would increase its chances of victory because of her popularity among women and young voters in particular.[2] Nevertheless, it decided to nominate Bibit Waluyo, a retired general, as its gubernatorial candidate because, in the words of the party's secretary general:

> Bibit's former experience as the regional commander of Central Java provides him with the 'firm and solid leadership' needed for the position of governor.

---

2 'Bibit–Rustri pimpin Jateng' [Bibit–Rustri lead in Central Java], *Radar Bogor*, 23 June 2008.

He will be supported by Rustriningsih's competence and capability in running local government.[3]

As Table 12.4 shows, among the large parties, it was the religious parties that nominated the fewest female candidates. Some of these parties do not formally oppose the notion of women in leadership roles in local government, giving them a certain degree of flexibility. Thus, the United Development Party (Partai Persatuan Pembangunan, PPP), a major Islamist party, was willing to support Khofifah Indar Parawansa in the East Java gubernatorial election in August 2008. On the other hand, the Prosperous Justice Party (Partai Keadilan Sejahtera, PKS), since 2009 the best-represented Islamist party in the national parliament, has a relatively clear policy of not supporting women candidates for the top positions in *pilkada*[4] but is willing to nominate them for the position of deputy at both the provincial and district levels.[5] The approaches of the National Mandate Party (Partai Amanat Nasional, PAN) and PKB have been rather erratic, with no standard policies or instructions for party members regarding the nomination of female candidates. However, surveys show that PKB voters have been the most supportive of female candidates, with only 18 per cent disapproving of women as leaders, while PAN and PKS voters have been the least supportive, with 35 per cent and 45 per cent respectively disapproving of women in leadership positions (Indo Barometer 2009).

With limited access to leadership positions and little support from power brokers in the big parties, some women who seek election have turned to coalitions of political parties, especially the smaller parties, to obtain nominations (Table 12.3). Stitching together a coalition of small parties gives *pilkada* candidates the room to manoeuvre around the obstructive party elites in particular parties. It is hard to discern general patterns here, because most such coalitions are formed on an ad hoc basis rather than on the basis of a shared platform. In fact, some small parties simply nominate the would-be candidate who has given them the largest cash payment. Once again women face major hurdles in this respect, because they tend to lack the political networks to pull together a coalition of minor parties and the financial resources to pay them. And even when a female candidate does succeed in being nominated by such a

---

3 'DPP PDIP usung Bibit–Sri di pilkada Jateng' [PDIP supports Bibit–Sri in Central Java elections], *detikNews*, 21 February 2008.

4 'Dewan Syariah PKS Jatim keberatan cagub perempuan' [East Java Syariah Council of PKS objects to female candidates for governor], *Gatra*, 28 March 2008.

5 'PKS pilih perempuan jadi calon wakil bupati' [PKS selects woman as its candidate for deputy district head], *Kompas*, 26 July 2007.

coalition, it is rare for the parties to rally behind her during the campaign (Soetjipto 2006).

Since mid-2007 it has been possible for women to stand in direct local elections as independents, thereby avoiding the need to seek political party support at all.[6] However, the conditions are onerous: independent candidates must submit evidence of support in the form of signed letters from supporters and, to avoid fraud, these must be accompanied by verified photocopies of identity cards. The number of supporters required at the district level ranges from 16,250 to 210,000 depending on the population of the district.[7] Few women have the resources to undertake such a costly exercise. But in addition, independent candidates have to finance their own campaigns without help from a party machine. One woman candidate I interviewed had to abandon her plans to run in West Java because of the expense and difficulty of collecting at least 180,000 ID cards and having them verified (confidential interview, 16 September 2009).

In summary, women who seek to run as candidates in *pilkada* face serious obstacles even before they begin to campaign. It is difficult for them to get their foot in the door during the nomination process. The nomination procedures used by parties are generally not accessible to women, who tend to lack the political connections and financial clout to win over party forums. It is usually only core members of the established — mostly male — political elite in a region who possess such connections and resources. Running as an independent is an alternative, but here too the high financial barriers discourage most women.

ELITE VERSUS PUBLIC PERCEPTIONS OF WOMEN IN POLITICS

An even more fundamental problem confronting women candidates is the still widespread perception that women are not fit for political leadership. However, there is evidence that this view is stronger among members of the political elite than among the public at large.

When asked about the small numbers of women they have nominated for local government positions, party leaders typically claim that they do not reject women as a matter of principle but rather because they lack suitably qualified women candidates. Men, they add, are just as able as women to represent women's interests. Party leaders emphasise that women who want to win party endorsement need to demonstrate their qualities as strong candidates, just as their male counterparts do. Never-

---

6 Constitutional Court Decision No. 5/PUU-V/2007, dated 24 July 2007.
7 Law No. 12/2008 on Regional Government.

theless, it is clear that cultural and religious filters do influence the views of party leaders on just what sort of person counts as a 'strong' candidate.

When explaining why the women who have put themselves forward for nomination are not suitable, party leaders often reveal their patriarchal values. PKB, for instance, decided against nominating Poppy Darsono as its gubernatorial candidate for Central Java in 2008, opting instead for a 'strong and decisive' candidate—implying that she was not (Purwanto 2005). PDIP gave a similar reason for nominating Bibit Waluyo rather than Rustriningsih in the same race, as noted above. A few party leaders have been even more blunt, simply rejecting point blank the idea that a woman can be a leader. As one local leader of a major national political party in Aceh told me:

> Women are not meant to be leaders. For one week a month, during their menstrual period, they cannot make any decisions. They are emotional and irrational. So, how can they be leaders?[8]

In East Java, where conservative religious leaders have considerable influence, the religious arguments against women's leadership featured strongly during the 2008 gubernatorial election. PPP fielded a strong female candidate, Khofifah Indar Parawansa. She had been minister for women's empowerment in Abdurrahman Wahid's cabinet (1999–2001) and was the chair of Muslimat, the women's wing of the traditionalist Islamic organisation Nahdlatul Ulama (NU). Many NU leaders opposed her nomination, putting the view, widely held in conservative Islamic circles, that a woman cannot be elected leader of a community if a man capable of doing the job is available. They argued that local political leaders were required to play a prominent role in religious ceremonies as imams or prayer leaders in addition to their political and administrative duties. Because women were traditionally not permitted to lead prayers, they could not lead a local government (Ida 2008).

Unfortunately, Indonesia's local election commissions typically did not make serious attempts to contain campaigns that promoted such negative views of women candidates. During the 2008 election in the district of Karanganyar, Central Java, for example, a local religious group circulated fliers outlining the religious arguments against women leaders and advising voters not to vote for a woman. As the only woman running for the position of district head, Rina Iriani Sri Ratnaningsih complained to the local election committee that the flier obviously targeted her, and therefore should be prohibited as part of a negative, or 'black', campaign. She condemned the leaflet for

---

8 Interview with political party leader, Banda Aceh, July 2009.

... insulting not only myself, but all women. ... It says that people who vote for women are lost and will go to hell. It's ridiculous to suggest that a person can go to hell just because of an election.[9]

The committee did not take action, stating that the flier did not qualify as a 'black' campaign because it did not mention Ratnaningsih by name. Worse still, it asked local religious leaders to rule on the question of whether the leaflet constituted a 'black' campaign, even though the law clearly states that campaign materials should not

... insult any individual, religion, ethnicity, race, group, regional head/deputy head, candidates and/or political parties, or provoke or pit individuals and/or social groups against each other.[10]

Political leaders like to tell the public and the media that they do not discriminate against women when selecting candidates, and that the law applies equally to all citizens, men and women alike. Almost all party platforms state that parties aim to prepare all their cadres for leadership positions and will consider gender equality during that process. However, there is a major gap between the parties' formal commitment to gender equality and their actual practices at the grassroots level. Local party leaders frequently claim that their party members—their 'people'—are 'not ready' for women leaders. However, many of them are unable even to identify the discriminatory social attitudes that stand in the way of women's leadership aspirations, let alone the deeper structural obstacles.[11]

In fact, it appears that the general public is more ready to support women candidates than are party leaders. In an opinion poll conducted in March 2009, a month before the general election, 84.5 per cent of those surveyed supported equal rights for women in elections. A large majority supported women's right to run for parliament and 75.8 per cent supported their right to run for the presidency. A sizeable 64.3 per cent supported the inclusion of affirmative action measures in the country's election laws. The same survey showed that conservative religious interpretations of women's role in politics were not popular among voters, with a majority of Muslim respondents, around 62.2 per cent, agreeing that Islam teaches equality, and that capability, not gender, should

9   'Pilkada Karanganyar memanas, muncul selebaran gelap' [Karanganyar election heats up, anonymous pamphlets appear], *Jakartapress.com*, 11 September 2008.

10 Law No. 32/2004 on Regional Government, article 78.

11 For instance, the chair of PPP, Suryadarma Ali, insists that the party does not discriminate against women, despite its poor record of fielding women candidates in both local and national elections. See 'PPP tak diskriminasi perempuan' [PPP does not discriminate against women], *Republika*, 31 March 2008.

determine whether a person becomes president. Around 63 per cent of respondents stated that they would ignore the instructions of religious leaders not to vote for a woman (Indo Barometer 2009).

Other opinion polls, however, show that there is still some distance to go. When asked in January 2009 who they would vote for in a local election if there was a female and a male candidate with similar qualifications, 44 per cent of respondents said they would vote for the man and only 12 per cent said they would vote for the woman. On the other hand, 48 per cent agreed that more women were needed in government to make it more responsive to the needs of all citizens (IRI and USAID 2009).

WOMEN WHO WIN: EXPLAINING VICTORIES BY FEMALE CANDIDATES

The tiny numbers of women who are elected to the position of local government head makes it hard to draw general lessons from their victories. Successful women candidates who have been elected governor, district head or mayor all talk about their campaigns as challenging experiences. Some say that being a woman was a liability, but interestingly, others see it as an asset that helped them to reach out to women voters. What is striking about these women, however, is the extent to which they had to draw on all the established mechanisms for securing political victory in regional Indonesia: distribution of political patronage, long-time party loyalty, mobilisation of financial resources and promises of better government performance. The following discussion describes all nine women who were elected regional heads between 2005 and 2008.

The only woman to be elected to the position of governor was Ratu Atut Chosiyah. She was elected governor of Banten, a new province carved out of the western end of West Java province in 2000. Ratu Atut's victory was exceptional in several ways. She was already the acting governor of Banten when the election was held in 2006, after her predecessor was charged with corruption and removed from office. As an incumbent, she had no trouble securing the nomination.

Ratu Atut's campaign team made sure that billboards, banners and posters promoting her achievements and those of her government were plastered across Banten.[12] She also had the advantage of being a prominent member of Banten's most important political family. Her father, Chasan Sochib, had 'exercised a strong political and economic influence in Banten for over three decades' owing to his business and criminal

---

12 'Birokrat diduga pengaruhi pilkada Banten' [Bureaucrats suspected of influencing the Banten election], *Republika*, 6 December 2006.

underworld connections, and had been a key leader in the movement to make Banten a province (Okamoto 2008). According to Okamoto, Chasan 'used a combination of coercion and pay-offs to secure the vice-governor-ship' for his daughter in December 2001. There were rumours of bribes paid to parliamentarians — this was in the days before the introduction of direct elections — and considerable intimidation, with thugs (*jawara*) 'dressed in black and armed with machetes' securing the parliamentary building and 'guarding' parliamentarians' cars.

Despite such backing, and that of two big parties (Golkar and PDIP), conservative religious groups in Banten resisted Ratu Atut's nomination for the governorship in 2006 on the grounds that a woman could not be a political leader. She responded by emphasising her religious credentials:

> Not all *ulama* hold such opinions. There are *pesantren* [Islamic boarding school] leaders who support me even though they are very traditional. This shows that Islam does not reject women as leaders.[13]

In the end Ratu Atut gained 40 per cent of the vote, while her nearest rival, Zulkieflimansyah of PKS (a male candidate whose running mate was a woman, Marrisa Haque), gained 33 per cent. But rather than being seen as a woman candidate's triumph against the odds to defeat gender-based discrimination, her victory should be seen as that of a powerful clan and political machine struggling to maintain its regional dominance by means of patronage and intimidation.

A better-known and perhaps more inspiring story is that of Rus-triningsih. In 2000 she was elected district head of Kebumen district in Central Java, the first woman in the country to be elected, rather than appointed, district head. In June 2005, as the candidate for PDIP, she won the first direct election for the same position in a landslide victory, capturing 78 per cent of the vote. Such a wide margin of victory is rare in direct local elections. Her career continued to blossom: in 2008 she became the first woman to be elected deputy governor in a direct local election, winning that post in Central Java.

The origins of her political success lay in her strong connections with PDIP. Her family had been supporters of the Indonesian National Party (Partai Nasional Indonesia, PNI), the now defunct party established by Sukarno, former president Megawati Sukarnoputri's father. This family history helped Rustriningsih secure support among local party leaders, and she initially received strong backing from Megawati herself. Above all, she developed a reputation as a capable leader who had pioneered various 'open government' approaches and improved government serv-

---

13 The statement appears on Ratu Atut's website: http://ratuatutchosiyah.com/profil/69-satu-satunya-gubernur-perempuan-di-indonesia.html.

ices and development outcomes in the district. She also managed to attract support from international organisations and the media for her attempts to develop Kebumen, building a public image as someone who 'symbolized the emergence of women in politics' in post-Suharto Indonesia (Ratnawati 2009: 175).

The experience of Ratna Ani Lestari in Banyuwangi, East Java, suggests a different route to success. Initially a PDIP member of the district parliament in Jembrana, Bali, she too was a member of a prominent local political family. Her husband was a leading member of PDIP and the district head of Jembrana. He was best known for establishing an innovative free health-care program in his district. As described earlier, Ratna failed to win the support of the central board of PDIP to run as its candidate for district head of Banyuwangi (located at the eastern tip of Java, and separated from Jembrana only by a narrow strait). However, she managed to pull together support from 18 small political parties, playing on the resentments of parties that had little or no representation in the local parliament, and offering herself as a weapon to strike back at the big parties (Lingkaran Survei Indonesia 2007b).

Ratna showed considerable political astuteness in choosing as her running mate a popular young leader of NU, which enjoys strong support in the district. Rival politicians and religious leaders nevertheless criticised her throughout the campaign, targeting her especially for her religious convictions. Ratna was vulnerable on this score because her husband was a Balinese Hindu. Her opponents accused her of blasphemy, alleging that she practised a different religion from the one stated on her ID card. Yet these accusations failed to have an effect and Ratna was elected district head with 39 per cent of the vote.

Ratna faced stiff opposition after being elected as well. The Banyuwangi legislature refused to swear her in and voted to oust her from office on the grounds of election fraud, although most political observers believed this move was illegal. She was eventually sworn in on 20 October 2006, at the office of the district head rather than at the local parliament as is usually the case. The local legislature has made repeated moves to remove or frustrate her throughout her period in office (Asydhad 2006) and she has faced constant allegations of corruption. In August 2008, for example, the attorney general officially declared Ratna a suspect in a shady land deal related to the purchase of land for a planned airport in Banyuwangi. Despite failing to support her nomination in 2006, PDIP has helped her fight off these accusations and attacks, and at a party convention held in December 2009, the party endorsed her as its candidate for the 2010 elections.[14]

---

14 'Melalui persaingan sengit, Ratna Ani Lestari menang' [Ratna Ani Lestari wins in a bitter contest], *Antara*, 27 December 2009.

Haeny Relawati Rini Widyastuti became head of Tuban district in East Java in 2001, the first district head to be elected by the local parliament in the reform era. Haeny was a seasoned politician who had been building a political career within Golkar since the early 1990s. She was elected deputy chair of the party's Tuban branch in 1992 when she was only 28 years old and became its chair in 1999. She was made speaker of the local parliament in the same year and then decided to run for the position of district head. At a time when the position of district head was still decided by votes in the local parliament, she demonstrated considerable skill in securing PDIP's support and defeating a strong PKB candidate. In April 2006 she won re-election in the first direct election in the district, gaining 52 per cent of the vote.

Haeny's position as incumbent gave her an opportunity to promote her achievements as district head, with voters apparently seeing her as having made significant progress in the development of Tuban's rural areas (Fata 2006: 4). She intensified road-building projects to reach remote and isolated villages, giving the villagers much needed access to markets and public facilities in the nearest towns. However, Haeny's development programs were not without problems, with accusations of collusion and corruption accompanying the awarding of construction contracts. She was also accused of using government networks and facilities to support her 2006 re-election campaign. In fact, many local people rejected the election results as fraudulent. This led to rioting in the city of Tuban and the imposition of a curfew, making the *pilkada* one of the most violent Indonesia has seen.[15]

Another female incumbent who was rewarded for good performance was Suryatati A. Manan, the mayor of Tanjung Pinang in the Riau Islands. She was popular locally, being regarded as both a capable administrator and relatively 'clean'. Suryatati and her deputy stormed to victory with 84 per cent of the vote in the election held in December 2007.[16] This was her third term as mayor. Unusually for a regional government head in Indonesia, her incumbency dated back to the end of the New Order period: she was first appointed mayor in 1997. Before that she had been a career civil servant, an appointed subdistrict head and the head of the Tanjung Pinang revenue office. During the *pilkada*, opponents attacked her for being of Chinese rather than Malay descent. (In fact, she was adopted and raised by a Muslim Malay family and has promoted Malay symbols during her term in office, commonly reciting traditional

---

15 'Tuban rusuh, jam malam diberlakukan' [Riot in Tuban, curfew is imposed] *Suara Merdeka*, 30 April 2006.

16 The local media welcomed Suryatati A. Manan's victory. Various news and blog postings acknowledging her strengths as a politician can be found at http://www.forum-politisi.org/arsip/article.php?id=565.

Malay *pantun* poems at official functions, for instance; see Sirait 2009.) In the Indonesian context, such political attacks can easily backfire. This is what appears to have happened in Tanjung Pinang, with Suryatati quickly gaining public sympathy.

Another seasoned local female politician who was elected for a second time was Rina Iriani Sri Ratnaningsih, the head of Karanganyar district in Central Java. Her father was a member of the local parliament who had taught her how to handle herself in tough political times. Shortly after local parliamentarians first elected her to the position of district head in 2003, she was accused of engaging in 'money politics' to secure her victory. Members of the local parliament brought a case to the minister of home affairs asking for the election results to be annulled but their suit was eventually dismissed.[17] In the October 2008 direct election she won a handsome victory with 61 per cent of the vote, and this time the results were not disputed.

During her first term in office, Rina Iriani had generated popular support by cutting red tape to give constituents greater access to various government services. In particular, she greatly simplified the process for having land measured, registered and certified, in the face of stiff resistance from bureaucrats in the land office and subdistrict offices who did not want to forgo the corrupt payments they had been able to reap from this process.[18] Rina Iriani herself has admitted that 'people initially looked down on me just because I'm a woman and because of my background as an elementary school teacher'. Later, however, they admired her for her economic achievements: 'I was able to increase [the district's] locally generated revenue from Rp 18 billion in 2002 to Rp 62 billion in 2007'.[19]

The remaining three women heads were Vonny Anneke Panamunan, the district head of North Minahasa (North Sulawesi); Marlina Moha Siahaan, the district head of Bolaang Mongondow (North Sulawesi); and Asmah Gani, the district head of Nunukan (East Kalimantan).

Vonny Anneke Panamunan was the only non-incumbent among these three women. A businesswoman, she was supported by the Democratic Party (Partai Demokrat, PD) and secured 40.6 per cent of the vote

---

17 'Rina Iriani S Ratnaningsih: tirakat sebagai penyeimbang hidup' [Rina Iriani S. Ratnaningsih: spiritual guidance as a balance in life], *Suara Karya*, 11 December 2005.

18 'Larasita, otonomi daerah yang sesungguhnya' [Larasita, the real regional autonomy], *Suara Merdeka*, 21 January 2008.

19 'Daftar perempuan "penguasa" pemerintahan' [List of women 'rulers' in government], http://jakarta.wartaegov.com/index.php?option=com_conte nt&view=article&id=710:daftar-perempuan-penguasa-pemerintahan&catid =34:wartautama&Itemid=54, 1 June 2008.

in the June 2005 election. However, she was unable to complete her term in office after being sentenced to 18 months in prison for corruption. She was released from jail in September 2008. Despite the legal obstacles to her candidacy, Vonny says she plans to run for the governorship of North Sulawesi.

Marlina Moha Siahaan was re-elected district head of Bolaang Mongondow in the direct elections in March 2006. Using the services of pollster and electoral consultant Indonesian Survey Circle (Lingkaran Survei Indonesia), her campaign emphasised the scholarship and life insurance programs Marlina had promoted while in office.[20] She won with 47.2 per cent of the vote.

Asmah Gani was the head of the Social Affairs Office in Nunukan before being elected head of the district in April 2006. As a senior public servant, she understood the local government machinery. She was backed by Golkar and obtained 55 per cent of the vote.

So what lessons can be learned from the set of women who were elected regional heads between 2005 and 2008? First, a striking fact is that all but two of the nine women were already incumbents when they were elected in *pilkada*, having previously won their positions through ballots in their local parliaments. Winning re-election as an incumbent is far from automatic in Indonesia, where voters are quite capable of punishing non-performing office holders. Throughout Indonesia, around 40 per cent of incumbents were voted out of office in local executive elections between 2005 and 2008, one of the highest such rates in the world. In 2005, of 124 incumbents who participated in *pilkada*, 87 (40.9 per cent) lost their positions. In 2007, only 15 of the incumbents who ran for re-election were successful (JPPR 2008). The number of women incumbents who were re-elected was much higher. In 2005, when direct elections were introduced, a total of seven women held positions as regional government heads.[21] Six of the seven have since been re-elected, the exception being Siti Nurhayati, the head of Nganjuk district, East Java. The success rate of female incumbents is therefore 86 per cent, suggesting that, on average, women heads of government have been much more effective and popular than their male counterparts.

It is certainly the case that most of the women who were re-elected as local government heads in direct elections had notched up considerable achievements in office that helped to ensure their victories. Some have even been singled out for praise by national and international agen-

---

20 'Pasangan Marlina–Sehan optimis menang' [Marlina–Sehan pair optimistic about winning], *Suara Karya*, 19 January 2006.

21 Data gathered from the Gender Division of the Centre for Electoral Reform (CETRO) and the JPPR database.

cies for introducing innovative approaches that helped improve government services for the benefit of local people. In Kebumen, Rustriningsih became famous for pioneering the use of the local media as a channel to open up new avenues of communication between the government and the people. She appeared every morning on a live talk show hosted by local television station Ratih TV, where she listened and responded directly to the comments and complaints of the public.[22] In Karanganyar, Rina Iriani's land certification program, Larasati, was recognised with an award from the minister for bureaucratic reform as the first e-government program for land certification.

But the high proportion of women incumbents who have been re-elected in *pilkada* also points to another sobering reality: the very poor success rate of women who are *not* incumbents. Of the nine women elected regional government heads in 2005–2008, only two, Ratna Ani Lestari and Vonny Anneke Panambunan, were not already in office. This outcome suggests that it is very difficult for new women players to become local government heads.

A second important lesson is that women have to be well endowed with the usual attributes that contribute to political success for male politicians in regional Indonesia. All nine of the women who were elected to local government positions had managed to build strong political networks among parties and reach out to broader social constituencies, such as religious organisations and business networks. Each was able to secure strong financial backing, a key ingredient for success given the importance of money for securing the nomination of a political party and organising an effective election campaign.[23] This points to another key factor: at least some of these women succeeded because they were as deeply embedded in the politics of patronage as their male counterparts. This was most obvious in the case of Ratu Atut Chosiyah, whose victory must be viewed above all as the victory of a particularly influential and predatory local political clan. But she was by no means the only woman candidate to be accused of engaging in money politics or financial irregularities while in office; nor was she the only one whose political success relied at least partly on family connections.

A third point is that these women did not use their gender to mobilise voters. In Indonesia, candidates for local executive positions often appeal to ethnic and religious identities to attract votes. Gender identity cannot be used in the same way. Women candidates cannot rely on women voters to vote for them automatically, nor can they highlight gender issues

---

22 'Mengapresiasi program "Selamat Pagi Bupati"' [Appreciating the *Good Morning Bupati* program], *Suara Merdeka*, 6 March 2004.

23 On money politics in local politics see, for example, Hidayat (2009).

in their campaigns, except peripherally by mentioning the importance to women in particular of their education and health care policies. In this regard, Indonesia is not so different from other democracies, where gender-based solidarity is rarely a significant factor in elections (Hooks 2000: 44). In Indonesia, women do not appear to be more likely than men to vote for women candidates.

CONCLUSION

Women who succeed in being elected to local government face many challenges. Not only do they have to deal with the normal problems of crafting effective policies, maintaining political support and improving government services, but they typically lack strategic allies who, like them, are women. They therefore have to negotiate with male-dominated local parliaments and political parties. Sometimes, local (male) religious leaders are hostile to women leaders and do not respect their authority.

They cannot expect to find female allies in the local civil service either. Very few women are in senior decision-making positions in local bureaucracies: only 8 per cent of upper-level (echelons 3 and 4) civil servants with policy and budgetary authority are women (BKN 2009). Often, the local government head is the only female face in an inner circle of local government decision makers. Even so, the high rate of re-election of women heads of regions suggests that those women who do make it past all the barriers to reach office tend to be effective once they get there. Accordingly, they are rewarded by voters on the basis of their performance, rather than being punished by them for being a woman.

Despite the indications that voters are willing to support strong women candidates when given the choice, the picture presented in this chapter is overall a sobering one. Perhaps the most striking figure of all those presented above is this: only 2.4 per cent of those holding the top local government positions in Indonesia are women. This tiny figure, and all the underlying structural obstacles, social prejudices and ingrained discrimination it points to, indicates a tremendous waste of human resources. Women make up more than 50 per cent of the Indonesian population. They should constitute at least that proportion of leaders in Indonesia's new democracy.

The fact that the introduction of direct elections in 2005 did not see a significant increase in the number of women heads of regions is also not encouraging. There is a need for Indonesia's policy makers, party leaders and civil society to examine seriously the reasons for both women's poor rate of participation in *pilkada* as well as the lack of progress in increasing the numbers of women in public office over time. In this respect, institutions where there *have* been improvements in the representation of women can provide important lessons. In the Regional Representative Council (Dewan Perwakilan Daerah, DPD) — whose members are all elected as independents — women's representation currently stands at 28 per cent. This relatively high level of representation is proof that the public will support women candidates who stand as independents. Relaxing the registration requirements for independent candidates in *pilkada*, for instance by significantly reducing the number of letters of support needed from constituents (to, say, 5,000), would open up the process to more women candidates. Improvements in the level of women's representation in the DPR, where the quota and the zipper system have had a positive effect (despite their shortcomings), similarly point to a need to introduce affirmative action measures for political parties when they nominate candidates for local government positions. It should be possible, for example, to legislate to require parties to include a minimum number of women among the potential candidates they consider at the 'fit and proper' stage of testing candidates. Without bold initiatives to revisit the rules of the game that govern *pilkada*, it is difficult to hope for significant improvements for women in the next round of direct local elections to be held between 2010 and 2013.

REFERENCES

Asydhad, Arifin (2006), 'Lika-liku hubungan bupati Ratna dengan PDIP' [The ins and outs of district head Ratna's relationship with PDIP], *detikNews*, 8 May, http://www.detiknews.com/read/2006/05/08/100902/590075/10/lika-liku-hubungan-bupati-ratna-dengan-pdip.

BKN (Badan Kepegawaian Nasional) (2009), 'Jumlah pegawai negeri sipil menurut golongan and jenis kelamin Juni 2009' [Number of civil servants according to echelon and gender, June 2009], Jakarta, http://www.bkn.go.id/stat_indo/tabel8a2009.php.

Fata, Ahmad Khoirul (2006), 'Kesaksian dan refleksi seorang warga Tuban' [Testimony and reflections of a Tubanese citizen], *Jawa Pos*, 1 May.

Haris, Syamsuddin (2008), 'Nasib Golkar dalam pilkada' [Golkar's bad luck in the direct local elections], *Kompas*, 16 July.

Hidayat, Syarif (2009), '*Pilkada*, money politics and the danger of "informal governance" practices', in M. Erb and P. Sulistiyanto (eds), *Deepening Democracy in Indonesia? Direct Elections for Local Leaders (Pilkada)*, Institute of Southeast Asian Studies, Singapore, pp. 125–46.

Hooks, Bell (2000), *Feminist Theory: From Margin to Center*, second edition, South End Press Classics, Cambridge MA.

Ida, Laode (2008), 'Pertarungan kultural dan kepentingan pemilu 2009' [Cultural competition and vested interests in the 2009 elections], *Okezone*, 15 August, http://news.okezone.com/index.php/ReadStory/2008/08/15/58/137056/pertarungan-kultural-dan-kepentingan-pemilu-2009.

Indo Barometer (2009), 'Keterwakilan perempuan dan pemilu 2009' [Women's representation and the 2009 elections], national survey data, 2–11 March.

IRI and USAID (International Republican Institute and United States Agency for International Development) (2009), 'Public opinion survey', IRI and USAID, Jakarta, 12–22 January.

JPPR (Jaringan Pendidikan Pemilih untuk Rakyat) (2008), 'Fenomena kekalahan incumbent dalam pilkada' [The phenomenon of incumbents losing in elections of local government heads], press release, Jakarta, 23 January.

Lingkaran Survei Indonesia (2007a), 'Perempuan dan pilkada' [Women and elections of local government heads], Kajian Bulanan Edisi 01, May, http://www.lsi.co.id/media/ kajian_bulanan_01.pdf.

Lingkaran Survei Indonesia (2007b), 'Pilkada dan pemerintahan yang terbelah' [Elections of local government heads and divided government], Kajian Bulanan Edisi 07, November, http://www.lsi.co.id/media/KAJIAN_BULANAN_EDISI_NOMOR_7_(NOVEMBER_2007).pdf.

Nalenan, Josef Christofel (2008), 'Misteri jumlah pilkada' [The mystery of the number of elections of local government heads], 25 February, http://www.jppr.or.id/index2.php?option=com_content&do_pdf=1&id=764.

Okamoto, Masaaki (2008), 'An unholy alliance: political thugs and political Islam work together in Banten', *Inside Indonesia* 93, http://www.insideindonesia.org/content/view/1101/47/.

Pratikno (2009), 'Political parties in *pilkada*: some problems for democratic consolidation', in M. Erb and P. Sulistiyanto (eds), *Deepening Democracy in Indonesia? Direct Elections for Local Leaders (Pilkada)*, Institute of Southeast Asian Studies, Singapore, pp. 53–73.

Purwanto, Herie (2005), 'Perjuangan dalam pilkada' [Struggle in elections of local government heads], *Suara Merdeka*, 9 April.

Ratnawati, Tri (2009), 'Gender and reform in Indonesian politics: the case of a Javanese woman *bupati*', in M. Erb and P. Sulistiyanto (eds), *Deepening Democracy in Indonesia? Direct Elections for Local Leaders (Pilkada)*, Institute of Southeast Asian Studies, Singapore, pp. 174–89.

Sirait, Bunga (2009), 'Suryatati A. Manan: the poetic mayor', *Jakarta Post*, 7 October.

Soetjipto, Ani (2006), 'Perempuan dan demokrasi' [Women and democracy], *Kompas*, 4 December.

PART III

Local Democracy

13 DECENTRALISATION AND LOCAL DEMOCRACY IN INDONESIA: THE MARGINALISATION OF THE PUBLIC SPHERE

Michael Buehler

In 1999, Indonesia embarked on an ambitious decentralisation program that initiated a restructuring of the country's political institutions on a scale unprecedented since the 1960s.[1] Only a year after Suharto's New Order regime was overthrown, two new laws were adopted that shifted political and economic power from the centre to the subnational level of government. Law No. 22/1999 on Regional Government spelled out the conditions for the devolution of political authority, while Law No. 25/1999 on Revenue Sharing outlined a new system of fiscal arrangements between Indonesia's national and subnational political entities (Aspinall and Fealy 2003: 9). With the implementation of these laws in 2001, a considerable amount of political authority was handed to the district (*kabupaten*) and municipality (*kota*) level of government, leaving the centre with just a few key responsibilities, namely security and defence, foreign policy, justice and religious affairs (Usman 2001: iii).[2] At the same

---

1 In the immediate years after the transfer of sovereignty in 1949, the central government was fairly weak and did not have much influence in the regions. The institutional setting of this early period of the Indonesian republic has thus been described as a decentralisation by default (Mackie 1980: 675).

2 The Indonesian state has five tiers of government, namely national, provincial, district/municipality, subdistrict and village. Assemblies exist at all but the subdistrict and village levels (USAID 2008: 2). This chapter focuses on provinces, districts and municipalities. Districts are rural jurisdictions with an elected head and municipalities are urban jurisdictions with an elected mayor.

time, much of the executive's fiscal authority was shifted from the centre to the district and municipal governments. The new regulatory framework required the central government to transfer a minimum of 25 per cent of domestic revenues to subnational governments, of which 90 per cent had to be allocated to districts and municipalities.[3] In short, Indonesia has been transformed from a highly centralised state into one of the most decentralised in the world.

There were various reasons for the government's decision to shift power away from the national level after 1999. Several active secessionist movements, some of which had been lingering for decades, had raised fears among the political elite in Jakarta that the collapse of the oppressive New Order regime would reinvigorate demands for independence in such areas.[4] Consequently, the government believed that transferring some power to the regions would meet their mounting demands for more authority and thereby forestall secessionist aspirations (Hadiz 2003: 12; Turner and Podger 2003: 25). It was this consideration that motivated the government to shift most power to the district level, with the national elite harbouring concerns that excessively empowered provinces could push for secession. While the central government was anxious to avoid the disintegration of Indonesia, it also faced tremendous pressure to reform the kleptocratic institutions the New Order government had left behind. President B.J. Habibie, who originated from the outer island of South Sulawesi, publicly blamed the rigid, Java-focused centralisation of the state apparatus under the New Order for the failure of democracy in Indonesia. According to him, the highly hierarchical structures of the state had allowed a small number of national politicians to exploit their political authority. (Of course, he had been a key member of that elite himself.) Only the decentralisation of political authority would prevent similar developments in the future, said Habibie.[5]

In a similar vein, reformist elements within the national elite, cheered on by international development agencies, argued that the devolution

---

Districts and municipalities are located in the same tier of government. Provinces are headed by an elected governor, whose exact powers have become somewhat unclear as a result of the decentralisation process (Schulte Nordholt and van Klinken 2007: 13).

3   The own-source revenues of a region (*pendapatan asli daerah*) have increased gradually since decentralisation. Up to 93 per cent of district expenditures, however, continue to be covered by transfers from the central government (von Luebke 2009: 203).

4   For an overview of violent and non-violent secessionist movements in Indonesia at the time of the regime collapse in 1998, see Bertrand (2004: 135–219).

5   'Indonesia: Habibie says a centralistic gov't sparks birth of authoritarian attitude', *Antara*, 10 July 1999.

of political authority to the local level would make it easier to identify and address local needs. In their view, 'bringing government closer to the people' would improve service delivery, as local governments were certain to be more exposed to public scrutiny. In addition, they believed that decentralisation would create opportunities for local communities to participate in decision-making processes, increasing the transparency and accountability of local governments (World Bank 2000: 3; Colongan 2003: 93; Asia Foundation 2004) and providing 'the impetus for the growth of a public sphere at the local level' (Hidayat and Antlöv 2004: 281). In short, decentralisation was aimed at fostering democracy and introducing legitimacy in a political system that had just overcome more than four decades of authoritarian rule.[6]

This chapter evaluates the extent to which the expectations placed on decentralisation in the early post-Suharto period have materialised. In particular, the analysis focuses on the political aspects of decentralisation, namely the impact devolution has had on government accountability and effectiveness at the local level. The chapter discusses this subject in four separate segments. The first reviews the attempts since 1999 to increase the vertical accountability between local governments and the electorate at the grassroots level. The discussion will show that institutional reforms have formally strengthened vertical accountability, with the competitiveness of elections steadily increasing over time. The second section, however, demonstrates that the continued dominance of oligarchic elites has substantially undermined the effectiveness of the new institutional accountability mechanisms. While voters have been given more power to throw out corrupt officials, their replacements have often been recruited from the same pool of elite politicians. The third segment concentrates on post-1999 systems of horizontal accountability, especially the checks and balances between local parliaments and local executive governments. These mechanisms remain weak, with local executives gradually strengthened at the expense of their legislative counterparts. The fourth section of the chapter analyses the effectiveness of local governance since 1999, arguing that while public services have not deteriorated, there have been no great improvements either. The conclusion weighs the various findings of the chapter against each other, issuing a mixed report card for the post-Suharto decentralisation process.

---

6 A recent article argues that decentralisation took place in 1999 despite the interests of powerful actors rather than because of them. New Order-era elites gambled on the advice of a team of experts without being aware of the actual consequences (Smith 2008).

VERTICAL ACCOUNTABILITY: LOCAL ELECTIONS SINCE 1999

Various reforms implemented since 1999 have strengthened vertical accountability mechanisms in Indonesian local politics. Most importantly, democratic subnational elections for both executive and legislative posts have become a regular affair in the archipelago. Since 2005, direct gubernatorial ballots have been held in all 33 provinces in Indonesia (JPPR 2009), and the 500 or so districts and municipalities have conducted direct elections for their heads of government. Likewise, local legislative elections have taken place every five years since 1999, held concurrently with the polls for the national parliament. In April 2009, 32,263 candidates competed for a total of 1,998 seats in provincial parliaments across the state, and 246,588 parliamentary hopefuls tried to seize one of the 16,270 seats available in district and municipal parliaments.[7] On average, over 100 subnational elections have been run annually, with the ordinary Indonesian voting in seven or eight separate ballots between 2004 and 2009 alone (Gunawan and Siregar 2009: 10). This is in stark contrast to the New Order era, when subnational executive chiefs were hand-picked by the centre and local legislative elections were rigged in favour of the regime.

Since 1999, a comprehensive regulatory framework for both executive and legislative local elections has been established and continually revised. Law No. 22/1999 on Regional Government initially stipulated that district heads (*bupati*), mayors (*walikota*) and governors (*gubernur*) were to be elected by local parliaments, with each party caucus allowed to nominate one candidate. However, it soon became apparent that local assemblies across the archipelago were using their newly acquired powers for rent-seeking purposes. In exchange for their vote on election day, many local assembly members demanded money and favours from candidates aspiring to run for executive positions. As a result, parties found it difficult to convince their legislators to support nominees endorsed by the central party leadership; instead, the majority of parliamentarians voted for whoever offered them the most money, leading to the election of local government heads with no or weak ties to parties or to the assemblies dominated by those parties. As the flaws in the election framework became obvious and 'tensions in the relations between the district head and the [local] parliament in ... almost all districts' mounted,[8] it became clear that changes in the electoral framework were inevitable.

---

7 'Selamat berpesta demokrasi Indonesia!' [Enjoy the Indonesian festival of democracy!], *Kompas*, 9 April 2009.

8 'Kemelut soal kepala daerah: antara pemilihan langsung dan cari keseimbangan baru' [The problems with local government heads: between direct elections and the search for a new balance], *Kompas*, 11 May 2002.

In response to growing public pressure, new regulations on local executive elections were adopted through Law No. 32/2004 on Regional Government. The law introduced direct, popular elections for district heads, mayors and governors. Proponents of the new law argued that direct elections for subnational executive posts would minimise 'money politics' in these elections, as local assemblies would no longer be able to blackmail candidates. At the same time, they hoped that the popular mandate of local government heads would be stronger if it was granted directly by the electorate.[9] Despite these changes, however, parties still played a large role in the local contests. The revised regulatory framework required local candidates to be nominated by a party or a coalition of parties that had earned at least 15 per cent of the vote in the most recent local assembly election, or that controlled at least 15 per cent of the seats in the local legislature. In other words, considerable power continued to be concentrated in the local parties. Consequently, money politics and political corruption did not disappear; they simply shifted from the local assemblies to parties and their subnational branches. In order to participate in local elections, candidates for district head, mayor or governor now had to pay off party ward bosses and local party cadres to secure a nomination.

To break the parties' monopoly on nominations, the Constitutional Court ruled in 2007 that candidacy for local government posts should be open to all eligible citizens, not just candidates supported by political parties. Consequently, yet another set of rules for subnational executive elections was introduced in April 2008 to accommodate the verdict. Law No. 12/2008 on Regional Government amended Law No. 32/2004 to allow independent candidates to participate in subnational executive government elections.[10] Nomination by a party, in other words, was no longer the only avenue to run for district head, mayor or governor. This innovation was the climax of an overall trend towards greater competitiveness and inclusiveness in local executive elections. By gradually expanding the importance of the popular vote in selecting local leaders, the new electoral regime has introduced a level of vertical accountability in subnational executive government that goes well beyond that offered by any previous political system in Indonesia, including parliamentary democracy in the 1950s and the polity of the early post-Suharto period.

---

9   'Prof Dr Miftah Thoha MPA: otonomi belum sepenuhnya dipahami' [Prof. Dr Miftah Thoha MPA: local autonomy is not yet completely understood], *Kompas*, 11 September 2000.

10 The new rules became valid only in districts, municipalities and provinces in which regional election commissions had not yet registered candidates under the old system. Therefore, independent candidates were not able to participate in subnational elections held before July 2008.

Electoral reforms were not limited to the executive realm, however. Changes to the framework of elections for local legislatures (Dewan Perwakilan Rakyat Daerah, DPRD) strengthened institutional accountability mechanisms as well. While local executive elections have been regulated under the regional government laws, subnational parliamentary ballots have been anchored in national election laws. Initially, Law No. 3/1999 on General Elections stipulated that voters could vote only for a party and not for individual candidates. In other words, the law introduced a closed party list system for local legislative elections. Based on this system, seats were allocated to those nominees ranked highest on the list submitted by parties prior to the election, with some loopholes in the law giving parties the flexibility to shift candidates around after the polls (Sherlock 2004). Not surprisingly, the nomination of candidates was thus determined largely by backroom deals and internal party horse-trading. There was little transparency, and it was difficult for the electorate to hold individual politicians accountable through the ballot box.

Following public pressure to increase the accountability and transparency of legislative elections, revisions to the election law in 2003 introduced a partially open party list system. Law No. 12/2003 on General Elections allowed voters to select a party on the ballot and then also select one of the legislative candidates listed for each party. However, the provisions outlined in the law set a very high bar for candidates to win a seat directly based on the number of individual votes they received. As a consequence, the vast majority of candidates still won their seats in assemblies based on their position on the party list. With the composition of party list rankings fraught with political corruption and intra-party dynamics continuing to determine the outcome of local elections, activists and the media demanded further changes. Against this backdrop, Law No. 10/2008 on General Elections reduced the importance of party list rankings.[11] Ultimately, a decision by the Constitutional Court in December 2008 abolished party list rankings altogether. In the 2009 elections, therefore, seats won by parties in local parliaments were handed to those nominees who had gathered the largest number of personal votes, regardless of their ranking on the party list.

Thus, as with local executive elections, subnational legislative ballots have become increasingly competitive since Suharto's fall. Not only has

---

11 In the 2004 legislative elections, a candidate was allocated a seat regardless of his or her ranking on the party list if the individual had received enough votes to surpass 100 per cent of a predefined divisor. The divisor was calculated by dividing the total number of votes in a district by its number of seats, and therefore varied between electoral districts. Article 214 of Law No. 10/2008 greatly reduced the proportion a candidate had to exceed, from 100 per cent to 30 per cent of the divisor.

the authoritarian, election-rigging regime of the New Order been swept away, but the institutional authority of parties to hand their leaders seats in parliament without any real electoral contest has steadily been reduced. Voters are now more powerful than at any other time in Indonesian history, leading to significant improvements in the formal structures of vertical accountability at the local level. The following section will demonstrate, however, that the effectiveness of these institutional reforms has been undermined by structural hurdles privileging the elite and by strong socio-economic countercurrents on the ground.

ACCOUNTABILITY REVISITED: THE PERSISTENCE OF ELITE POLITICS

Despite the generally positive trends outlined above, Indonesian local politics since 1999 has remained elitist in nature. While the new electoral regulations have increased opportunities for popular participation in politics at the local level, the elite has managed to ensure that significant restrictions persist. For instance, some sections of the election and regional autonomy laws effectively exclude large parts of the Indonesian population from running in electoral contests. Both the 2004 and 2008 regional government laws, for example, stipulate that candidates must have at least a senior high school degree in order to stand in local executive elections.[12] In many Indonesian districts, a majority of local citizens would be unable to meet this requirement. For example, in South Sulawesi — one of the biggest provinces in Indonesia — 35 per cent of the local population was without a primary school education in 2004, and only 10 per cent of the population had finished senior high school (BPS Sulawesi Selatan 2004: 38–9). Obviously, this combination of educational thresholds for nomination and Indonesia's social realities has created a situation in which many underprivileged Indonesians — peasants, factory workers, domestic helpers and others — are unable to run for office.

Other regulations for local executive polls also work in favour of the rich and powerful. For instance, independent candidates keen to run for district head, mayor or governor without the nomination of a party or coalition of parties are obliged to post an election bond and garner a certain number of signatures from voters. They have to prove that they enjoy the support of between 3 and 6.5 per cent of the residents in their territory, with the exact figure depending on population size. The fulfilment of this regulation requires candidates to build up large logistical

---

12 Law No. 32/2004 on Regional Government, article 58c; Law No. 12/2008 on Regional Government, article 58c.

networks, the mobilisation of which creates substantial costs. An additional institutional hurdle is created by the fact that independent candidates must pay a fine of Rp 20 billion (approximately $2 million) if they withdraw their nomination after it has been approved by a regional elections commission (Law No. 12/2008, article 62). Candidates nominated by parties face no such fines. Given these administrative obstacles and the high costs associated with overcoming them, only very few independent candidates have run in subnational executive elections since the new regulations were adopted in 2008.

But it is not just ordinary citizens who find it prohibitively expensive to seek top posts in local government. Party officials, too, are often unable to raise sufficient funds to finance their electoral campaigns. In addition to the compensation paid to party organisations for a nomination and campaign support, candidates are forced to finance media advertisements, opinion surveys, staff and witnesses at the polling stations (Mietzner 2007). A 2005 sampling of Indonesia's district and municipal races found that the campaign expenses for winning candidates averaged $1.6 million (Rinakit 2005). Confronted with such cost estimates, most parties have resorted to selling nominations for executive posts to non-party candidates. These nominees usually do not enjoy the support of a certain political constituency or party, but are sufficiently well off simply to buy enough party endorsements to reach the necessary nomination threshold. Not coincidentally, the relationship between such candidates and 'their' parties has often collapsed immediately after election day (Buehler and Tan 2007).

The escalating campaign costs have affected the dynamics of local legislative elections as well, albeit to a lesser extent. Many parties in the post-Suharto polity have experienced serious funding problems, especially at the local level, because membership dues have declined and state subsidies are low (Mietzner 2007). This has meant that candidates have had to foot the bill for their political activities themselves. Ironically, this trend has been accelerated by the gradual opening up of the electoral system, which activists had demanded in order to increase vertical accountability. The introduction of an open party list system has essentially created an environment of fierce competition not only between candidates of rival parties but between nominees of the same party as well. With candidates trying to achieve the highest number of personal votes to beat their fellow party members in the fight for a seat, the costs of local legislative elections have sky-rocketed. In some cases, this race to outspend each other has led to tragic results. Many ordinary citizens who were foolish enough to think that they stood a real chance of winning a seat in a local parliament found themselves so heavily indebted after the 2009 election that they committed suicide or suffered a mental breakdown (Buehler 2009a).

Table 13.1   Background of all candidates in gubernatorial elections,
*   2005–2008*

	Candidate for governor		Candidate for deputy governor		Total	
	(no.)	(%)	(no.)	(%)	(no.)	(%)
Bureaucrat	21	15.9	40	30.3	61	23.3
Parliamentarian (all levels of government)	27	20.4	35	26.5	62	23.3
District head / mayor	33	25.0	11	8.3	44	16.7
Military/police	15	11.4	6	4.5	21	7.9
Businessperson	8	6.0	13	9.9	21	7.9
Incumbent deputy governor	10	7.6	5	3.8	15	5.7
Incumbent governor	14	10.6	0	0.0	14	5.3
Academic	3	2.3	11	8.3	14	5.3
Party cadre	0	0.0	7	5.3	7	2.7
Lawyer	1	0.7	0	0.0	1	0.4
Other	0	0.0	4	3.0	4	1.5
Total	**132**	**100.0**	**132**	**100.0**	**264**	**100.0**

Source: Author's own data; JPPR (2009).

Evidently, the institutional and socio-economic conditions surrounding local politics have been such that they work in favour of a confined
number of local elites. These elites are well entrenched in the political
ecologies of their respective regions and therefore command the necessary means or contacts to obtain enough financial contributions to run in
the subnational elections. At the same time, the likelihood that an ordinary Indonesian will penetrate the political system in a district or municipality is marginal. A background analysis of all candidates who ran in
the 33 gubernatorial elections between 2005 and 2008 reveals that such
races were contested mostly by figures from within the traditional political system. Almost 50 per cent of the candidates were either bureaucrats
or parliamentarians (many of whom had formerly been bureaucrats), as
is shown in Table 13.1. A close examination of the careers of these figures
reveals that many of them were involved in local politics for years, if not
decades, throughout the New Order. Overall, very few fresh faces have
been elected to office through subnational elections in recent years.[13]

---

13 The relative insignificance of civil society representatives in Indonesian
     local politics is congruent with their marginalisation from post-New Order
     national affairs (Boudreau 2009: 237).

Only a tiny number of women have participated in such contests, as is shown in Hana Satriyo's chapter in this volume (see especially Table 12.1). The figures are only marginally different from those during the New Order. For instance, there was not a single female governor during the entire New Order, while in 2010 there was one. At the district level, two women became district heads in the 32 years under dictatorial rule (Malley 1999: 162, note 82), while by 2010 – after more than a decade of democratic reform – there were only five more.

The absence of a comprehensive overhaul of the *class politique* at the local level has severely undermined the effectiveness of elections as a means for increased vertical accountability. On the surface, the turnover rate of 40 per cent among incumbents in local executive elections seems to be comparatively high, suggesting that Indonesian voters do now have a choice between different candidates and that there has been real electoral competition. However, the options for ordinary citizens hoping to choose someone from their midst remain severely limited. With the majority of candidates competing in local elections deeply entrenched in their respective constituencies and closely affiliated with New Order networks, those politicians voted out of office have largely been replaced by representatives of the same old elite. Accordingly, the high rate of incumbency turnover does not have as much meaning as initially thought.

There are many cases illustrating the circumstance that the increased competitiveness of local elections has not necessarily produced more qualified and less corrupt leaders. To begin with, the district elections in Kutai Kartanegara in East Kalimantan in 2005 were won in a landslide by Syaukani Hassan Rais, a well-connected and seemingly popular politician. But Syaukani was arrested and jailed for corruption only two years later.[14] His replacement, Samsuri Aspar, was also held for corruption in 2008.[15] Similarly, the former governor of South Sulawesi, Amin Syam, was replaced in 2007 by Syahrul Yasin Limpo, a larger-than-life figure who had been arrested for drug consumption and involvement in prostitution a few years earlier. Syahrul's younger brother, Ichsan Yasin Limpo, won the first direct elections for district head in Gowa, South Sulawesi, in 2005, replacing Hasbullah Djabbar, a corrupt politician who had been jailed for embezzling state money during his term of office. However, Ichsan Yasin Limpo himself had previously been charged with misappropriating $1.9 million, together with 13 other politicians, dur-

---

14 In September 2009, the Supreme Court in Jakarta rejected Syaukani's appeal against a six-year sentence for corruption. See 'Court rejects former regent's appeal', *Jakarta Post*, 16 September 2009.

15 'Pemerintahan: DPRD Kutai Kartanegera minta bupati "pengganti"' [Government affairs: Kutai Kartanegera parliament asks for replacement district government head], *Kompas*, 26 July 2008.

ing his time as a member of the provincial parliament of South Sulawesi (Buehler 2007).

These examples reflect larger patterns in subnational politics. In 2008 alone, more than 20 governors, former governors, district heads and mayors were detained or declared suspects in corruption cases.[16] Similarly, more than 1,000 local parliamentarians across the country were under investigation for corruption-related charges in 2006, according to data published by Indonesia Corruption Watch, an independent NGO (USAID 2008: 3). In October 2009, only two weeks after their inauguration, 10 parliamentarians from the North Sulawesi provincial assembly were arrested for embezzlement of state money during their first term in parliament between 2004 and 2009.[17]

The continued success of corrupt and otherwise questionable politicians in local elections has been assisted by weak legal and social sanctions against their behaviour. Both the 2004 and 2008 regional government laws as well as the 2008 legislative elections law stipulate that criminal suspects and persons who have served sentences on charges punishable by less than five years' imprisonment can contest local executive and legislative elections. In addition to these legal loopholes, the ability of Indonesians to sanction corruptors at the ballot box has been greatly reduced by the fact that there are simply not enough 'clean' candidates running in many of these local competitions. Perfectly aware of the powerlessness of voters in this regard, political parties have largely been indifferent in the rare cases when Indonesian voters have actually protested against a party's nomination of a corrupt candidate.[18] Thus, despite the creation of a regulatory framework that has formally increased vertical accountability, the larger institutional and socio-economic context within which these accountability mechanisms are embedded has made it very difficult for ordinary citizens to kick the rascals out of office. Instead, they are merely rotated from one post to another.

HORIZONTAL ACCOUNTABILITY AND EXECUTIVE DOMINANCE

While vertical accountability at the local level is working inefficiently at best, the horizontal accountability between local parliaments and local

---

16 'Graftbuster's uphill battle in Indonesia', *Straits Times*, 6 September 2008.
17 'Perjalanan dinas fiktif: polisi akan periksa 10 anggota DPRD Sulawesi Utara periode 2009–2014' [Fictitious official travel: police arrest 10 members of the North Sulawesi parliament 2009–2014], *Kompas*, 22 October 2009.
18 'Political parties brush off public complaints about nominees', *Jakarta Post*, 21 October 2008.

executive governments has gradually been weakened. Whereas the 1999 Regional Government Law gave local assemblies extensive powers *vis-à-vis* subnational governments, Law No. 32/2004 on Regional Government tilted the balance of power in favour of the latter. It strengthened, for example, the fiscal authorities of district heads, who were empowered to control the financial management of their respective territories, to authorise expenditure and to set priorities as well as the ceiling of the budget (articles 156 and 192). While the budget theoretically needed to be approved jointly with the local parliament (article 180), evidence suggests that the participation of subnational parliaments in the budget process has been limited and fraught with problems. Local assemblies report difficulties in engaging in budget formulation processes due to their weak capacity, but also because the (already passed) local budget has to be 'evaluated' by the central government for final approval. Many local parliaments complain that this vetting process undercuts their independence.

The 2004 Regional Government Law also expanded the power of subnational executive governments through a clause that allowed district heads to issue local regulations together with the local parliament (article 140). As in the case of legislative budgeting, the experience of the past decade shows that local parliaments rarely initiate such regulations and that district heads are usually the dominant force in these deliberations (Kristiansen et al. 2008: 70).[19] Between 2001 and 2006, the local parliaments of four subnational governments initiated just 1.6 per cent of all local regulations, as is shown in Table 13.2. This would be typical of most local governments (Ibrahim et al. 2009: 1–42). According to Robert Endi Jaweng, external relations officer at the non-governmental Regional Autonomy Watch (Komite Pemantauan Pelaksanaan Otonomi Daerah, KPPOD):

> In the drafting process for local regulations ... members of local parliaments usually ... simply copy and paste similar regulations from other districts. [They do this] despite the fact that the circumstances are different in every region.[20]

Once again, limited resources and a lack of drafting expertise among committees and council secretariats have mainly been responsible for this development (USAID 2006: 30).

---

19   The executive has also dominated the public policy process at the national level (Boudreau 2009: 242).

20   'Pembatalan perda: kemampuan legislasi DPRD lemah' [Annulment of local bylaws: legislative capacity of local parliaments is weak], *Kompas*, 28 June 2008.

Table 13.2 *Initiators of local government regulations in four districts and municipalities, 2001–2006*

Initiator	Probolinggo, East Java		Madiun, East Java		Sidaoarjo, East Java		Blitar, East Java		Total	
	(no.)	(%)	(no.)	(%)	(no.)	(%)	(no.)	(%)	(no.)	(%)
Local parliament (DPRD)	1	1.3	1	1.1	1	1.3	2	2.8	5	1.6
District head/ mayor	77	98.7	87	98.9	74	98.7	69	97.2	307	98.4
Total	**78**	**100.0**	**88**	**100.0**	**75**	**100.0**	**71**	**100.0**	**312**	**100.0**

Source: Ibrahim et al. (2009: 27).

Finally, Law No. 32/2004 on Regional Government allowed district heads to intervene in the work of the parliament. The appointment and control of civil servants in the local parliament secretariat now fall under the authority of the district head. This has reduced the autonomy of local assemblies and weakened their ability to scrutinise the executive, given that it is conventionally the secretariat that is supposed to prepare the material necessary for legislators to hold the head of the regional government accountable.

The strengthening of local executive power described above has been accompanied by cuts to the institutional authority of local parliaments. Law No. 22/1999 gave local assemblies the authority to request an annual accountability report from the district head. If that report was rejected, local parliaments could proceed to impeach the district head and propose his or her dismissal to the Ministry of Home Affairs. However, local assemblies across the archipelago misused their leverage to demand bribes and favours from heads of subnational governments in return for passing their accountability reports. As a result of this obvious abuse of power, Law No. 32/2004 abolished the requirement for local assemblies to approve such reports. While it is still possible to impeach a district head, in practice this has become much more difficult. Most significantly, the Ministry of Home Affairs has regularly emphasised its unwillingness to remove a local government chief simply because the person has become engulfed in a dispute with an assembly.

The most recent addendum to the regional government laws, adopted through Law No. 12/2008, reduces the duties and authorities of the local parliament yet further. Based on this revision, a local parliament no longer has the power to establish a supervisory committee to oversee district head elections.[21] The local assembly is also no longer responsible for screening candidates prior to district head elections.[22] While these powers had become redundant anyway with the introduction of direct elections and the consequent empowerment of regional election commissions to run these ballots, the formal cancellation of rights held by local parliaments nevertheless symbolises their decline. In short, the effectiveness of local oversight mechanisms through which subnational assemblies supervise their executive counterparts has continued to erode slowly but steadily.

The fierce criticism of the local assemblies has led to wide-ranging proposals for reform. For example, in the context of the planned revision of Law No. 32/2004, it has been suggested that well-resourced local assembly secretariats should be established that are free of any influence by the district or provincial government head (USAID 2009a: 65). While certainly well meaning, such ideas do little to reduce the ability of local government heads to buy off parliamentarians with financial inducements — an ability that governors and district heads alike do not hesitate to expose publicly. During a workshop on local governance organised by the Organisation for Economic Co-operation and Development (OECD) and other donor agencies in Jakarta in June 2009, Fadel Muhammad, then governor of Gorontalo province, explained the 'secret' behind his 'success' in getting reform policies approved in his home province. Hailed as a reform figure by the foreign development industry, Fadel Muhammad boasted in front of more than 100 donor representatives that he regularly sent provincial parliamentarians on 'pleasure cruises' disguised as 'study tours' (*studi banding*) to Australia, Thailand or Singapore. Upon their return, the parliamentarians usually approved his 'reform' initiatives swiftly and without much opposition.[23]

LOCAL GOVERNMENT EFFECTIVENESS

The inability of local populations to put pressure on their leaders has had serious consequences for the effectiveness of local government. While there are differences between individual districts and municipalities, with some being more effective than others, 'Both nation-wide snapshots and case study results indicate that overall performance levels remain

---

21   Article 42, paragraph 1, section I of Law No. 32/2004, which regulated the role of the local parliament in establishing supervisory committees in district head elections, was deleted in Law No. 12/2008.

22   Article 59, paragraph 3 of Law No. 32/2004 was deleted in Law No. 12/2008.

23   Fadel Muhammad speaking at a seminar organised by the OECD/Korea Policy Centre in Jakarta, 9–11 June 2009; personal notes by the author.

relatively low' (von Luebke 2009: 225). For example, administrative performance as measured by the quality of public service delivery has not improved significantly at the local level since 1999, despite decentralisation initiatives and the introduction of local elections. According to a report by one of the largest international development agencies, 'service delivery did not suffer significant declines after decentralization ... but it also did not get much better' (USAID 2009b: 47). The few successful reform efforts at the local level have largely been driven by a handful of exceptionally well-performing administrators (von Luebke 2009) and are therefore not a reflection of broader trends.

Often, reform initiatives crumble shortly after a reform-minded politician leaves office. In Solok, a district in West Sumatra, a 10-year bureaucratic reform initiative started to fall apart shortly after the popular and reformist district head, Gamawan Fauzi, left office to take up his new position as governor in 2005. According to Sofjan Wanandi, chair of the Association of Indonesian Entrepreneurs (Asosiasi Pengusaha Indonesia, Apindo), 'Gamawan could not fire the bureaucrats as they were well protected by the civil service law. So all the corrupt officials remained, waiting for the right time to regain control'.[24] In October 2009 Gamawan Fauzi was appointed minister of home affairs. While he may now be able to implement some of his ideas for structural change at the centre, there are widespread fears that after his departure, the reforms in West Sumatra province initiated during his governorship may soon collapse in the same way they did in Solok several years earlier.

In the same vein, the regulatory frameworks developed by subnational governments and assemblies have suffered from poor preparation, lack of clarity and inherent self-contradictions. Not only have the regulations issued by local governments been of consistently low quality, but they have often obstructed local economic activity and undermined the rule of law. Predatory taxes, for example, have been widespread at the subnational level. Based on a survey conducted in 2008, Regional Autonomy Watch estimated that around 30 per cent of all local regulations were predatory in nature and an impediment to investment (KPPOD 2008). Responding to this development, the national parliament adopted a new regional taxation law in August 2009 that aimed to eradicate such harmful practices. It listed the taxes subnational governments were allowed to implement, and it set minimum and maximum rates for each type of local tax (Buehler 2009b).

While a recent study on local policy reforms in Indonesia shows that the absence of a coherent set of formal regulations does not necessarily preclude reform initiatives per se (von Luebke, McCulloch and Patunru

---

24 'Bureaucrats rule supreme as reform falters', *Jakarta Post*, 28 April 2009.

2009: 270), there is much evidence that chaotic regulatory frameworks have been an impediment to effective local governance. According to USAID (2009b: 12):

> The avalanche of regulations (some replacing rather new regulations) in recent years has not been coordinated or properly developed and vetted. The results are largely poor quality products that are not workable—that waste valuable time and resources of local governments.

Local bureaucracies often take advantage of such contradictions and ambiguities in laws and regulations to reduce their accountability, both vertically and horizontally, and to 'enhance their discretionary authority in financial matters' (Kristiansen et al. 2008: 76).

The effectiveness of local governance and public service delivery has also been undermined by widespread corruption and rent seeking. This is reflected not only in the aforementioned predatory tax regimes established in hundreds of districts and municipalities across the country, but also in the prevalence of illegal fees and other forms of bribes. The 2008 KPPOD study estimated that up to 80 per cent of local businesses continue to pay bribes. In addition, there are indications that the levels of transparency may actually have decreased since decentralisation, with one study suggesting that 'detailed annual budgets are mostly unavailable to the public [and] only general information and overall figures are made available' (Kristiansen et al. 2008: 77).

Finally, the weaknesses in local government capacity in Indonesia are apparent in subnational spending patterns. For example, local administrations find it difficult to spend all of their allocated funds, largely due to their inability to develop coherent and effective projects. Since 1999, unspent local government reserves have been rising rapidly (World Bank 2007: xxi). By July 2008, for example, the province of Jakarta had spent only 17 per cent of its annual budget. Similarly, the majority of local governments are routinely late in submitting their budgets to the central government, despite this being a prerequisite to receive fiscal equalisation funds. In January 2009, only two-thirds of all regional governments had handed in their 2009 budgets to the central government (Gunawan and Siregar 2009: 33). While budgeting delays and low levels of budget realisation affect the central government as well, they are much more common at the local level, with severe consequences for ordinary Indonesians seeking satisfactory public services.

CONCLUSION

This chapter's evaluation of the decentralisation process since 1999 has produced a mixed picture. On the one hand, extensive reforms to Indonesia's political framework have led to real electoral competition at the local level, with the hundreds of ballots held so far widely regarded as free and fair. In executive elections, voters have thrown out many corrupt or underperforming local officials, while the introduction of an open party list system for parliamentary polls has intensified the links between the electorate and legislators. Thus, from an institutional perspective, mechanisms of vertical accountability have been put in place that — in combination with a free press and a vibrant civil society — have led to an unprecedented level of public scrutiny being imposed on Indonesian local governments and legislatures.

Beyond casting their votes, however, ordinary citizens are not able to actively influence and shape local politics as much as had initially been hoped following decentralisation and the introduction of direct local elections. Both institutional and socio-economic factors have limited the pool of people who can run in elections to a small group of local elites, most of them rooted in the New Order regime. While the electorate can vote people in and out of office, the lack of horizontal accountability mechanisms and the weakness of political parties make it difficult for any political force — whether institutional or societal — to monitor the activities of district heads, mayors and governors. After a rapid expansion in the beginning, the much anticipated 'growth of the public sphere' at the local level has yet to occur.

REFERENCES

Asia Foundation (2004), 'Final synopsis report of the 5th Indonesia rapid decentralisation appraisal 2004', November, http://asiafoundation.org/publications/pdf/397.

Aspinall, Edward and Greg Fealy (2003), 'Introduction: decentralisation, democratisation and the rise of the local', in E. Aspinall and G. Fealy (eds), *Local Power and Politics in Indonesia: Decentralisation and Democratisation*, Institute of Southeast Asian Studies, Singapore, pp. 1–11.

Bertrand, Jacques (2004), *Nationalism and Ethnic Conflict in Indonesia*, Cambridge University Press, Cambridge.

Boudreau, Vincent (2009), 'Elections, repression and authoritarian survival in post-transition Indonesia and the Philippines', *Pacific Review* 22(2): 233–53.

BPS (Badan Pusat Statistik) Sulawesi Selatan (2004), *Sulawesi Selatan dalam Angka 2004* [South Sulawesi in Figures 2004], BPS, Makassar.

Buehler, Michael (2007), 'Rise of the clans: direct elections in South Sulawesi show that a new breed of political godfathers is coming to power in Indonesia's regions', *Inside Indonesia* 90(October–December), http://www.inside indonesia.org/.

Buehler, Michael (2009a), 'Suicide and progress in modern Nusantara', *Inside Indonesia* 97(July–September), http://insideindonesia.org/.

Buehler, Michael (2009b), 'The new regional taxation law: an end to predatory taxation?', *Van Zorge Report on Indonesia: Behind the Headlines*, 11(8): 9–11.

Buehler, Michael and Paige Johnson Tan (2007), 'Party–candidate relationships in Indonesian local politics: a case study of the 2005 regional elections in Gowa, South Sulawesi province', *Indonesia* 84(October): 41–69.

Colongan, A. (2003), 'What is happening on the ground? The progress of decentralisation', in E. Aspinall and G. Fealy (eds), *Local Power and Politics in Indonesia: Decentralisation and Democratisation*, Institute of Southeast Asian Studies, Singapore, pp. 87–101.

Gunawan, Anton H. and Reza Y. Siregar (2009), 'Survey of recent developments', *Bulletin of Indonesian Economic Studies* 45(1): 9–39.

Hadiz, Vedi R. (2003), 'Power and politics in North Sumatra: the uncompleted *reformasi*', in E. Aspinall and G. Fealy (eds), *Local Power and Politics in Indonesia: Decentralisation and Democratisation*, Institute of Southeast Asian Studies, Singapore, pp. 119–31.

Hidayat, Syarif and Hans Antlöv (2004), 'Decentralisation and regional autonomy in Indonesia', in P. Oxhorn, J.T. Tulchin and A.D. Seele (eds), *Decentralisation, Democratic Governance, and Civil Society in Comparative Perspective: Africa, Asia, and Latin America*, Woodrow Wilson Center Press, Washington DC.

Ibrahim, Anis, Sirajuddin, Nuruddin Hady and Umar Sholahuddin (2009), *Parlemen Lokal DPRD: Peran dan Fungsi dalam Dinamika Otonomi Daerah* [Local Parliament DPRD: Role and Function in the Dynamics of Regional Autonomy], Setara Press, Malang.

JPPR (Jaringan Pendidikan Pemilih untuk Rakyat) (2009), 'Data pasangan calon gubernur dan wakil gubernur pilkada 2005 s/d 2008: diolah oleh Jaringan Pendidikan Pemilih untuk Rakyat [Data on pairs of candidates in elections for governor and deputy governor between 2005 and 2008: collected by People's Voter Education Network], unpublished spreadsheet, JPPR, Jakarta.

KPPOD (Komite Pemantauan Pelaksanaan Otonomi Daerah) (2008), 'Provinsi terbaik bagi penanaman modal: survei pemeringkatan iklim usaha di 33 provinsi, 2008' [Best provinces for investment: business climate ranking in 33 provinces, 2008], January, http://kppod.org/ind/datapdf/rating/2008/Survei%2033%20Propinsi.pdf.

Kristiansen, Stein, Agus Dwiyanto, Agus Pramusinto and Erwan Agus Putranto (2008), 'Public sector reforms and financial transparency: experiences from Indonesian districts', *Contemporary Southeast Asia* 31(1): 64–87.

Mackie, J.A. (ed.) (1980), *Indonesia: The Making of a Nation*, Research School of Pacific Studies, Canberra.

Malley, Michael (1999), 'Resource distribution, state coherence, and political centralization in Indonesia, 1950–1997', PhD thesis, University of Wisconsin, Madison WI.

Mietzner, Marcus (2007), 'Party financing in post-Soeharto Indonesia: between state subsidies and political corruption', *Contemporary Southeast Asia: A Journal of International and Strategic Affairs* 29(2): 238–63.

Rinakit, Sukardi (2005), 'Indonesian regional elections in praxis', IDSS Commentaries No. 65/2005, September, http://www.rsis.edu.sg/publications/Perspective/IDSS652005.pdf.

Schulte Nordholt, Henk and Gerry van Klinken (eds) (2007), *Renegotiating Boundaries: Local Politics in Post-Suharto Indonesia*, KITLV Press, Leiden.

Sherlock, Stephen (2004), 'The 2004 Indonesian elections: how the system works and what parties stand for', Centre for Democratic Institutions, Australian National University, Canberra, February, http://aceproject.org/ero-en/regions/asia/ID/Sherlock.pdf/view.

Smith, Benjamin (2008), 'The origins of regional autonomy in Indonesia: experts and the marketing of political interests', *Journal of East Asian Studies* 8(2): 211–34.

Turner, Mark and Owen Podger (eds) (2003), *Decentralisation in Indonesia: Redesigning the State*, Asia Pacific Press, Canberra.

USAID (United States Agency for International Development) (2006), 'Decentralization 2006: stock taking on Indonesia's recent decentralization reforms', August, http://pdf.usaid.gov/pdf_docs/PNADH312.pdf.

USAID (United States Agency for International Development) (2008), 'The role of DPRDs in promoting regional autonomy and good governance: framework, challenges and new approaches', March, http://pdf.usaid.gov/pdf_docs/PNADQ130.pdf.

USAID (United States Agency for International Development) (2009a), 'Decentralization 2009: stock taking on Indonesia's recent decentralization reforms: main report', July, http://www.drsp-usaid.org/publications/index.cfm?fuseaction=pubdetail&ID=238.

USAID (United States Agency for International Development) (2009b), 'Decentralization 2009: stock taking on Indonesia's recent decentralization reforms: summary report', July, http://www.drsp-usaid.org/publications/index.cfm?fuseaction=pubdetail&ID=239.

Usman, Syaikhu (2001), *Indonesia's Decentralisation Policy: Initial Experiences and Emerging Problems*, SMERU Research Institute, Jakarta.

von Luebke, Christian (2009), 'The political economy of local governance: findings from an Indonesian field study', *Bulletin of Indonesian Economic Studies* 45(2): pp. 201–30.

von Luebke, Christian, Neil McCulloch and Arianto A. Patunru (2009), 'Heterodox reform symbiosis: the political economy of investment climate reforms in Solo, Indonesia', *Asian Economic Journal* 23(3): 269–96.

World Bank (2000), *Working Together: The World Bank's Partnership with Civil Society*, World Bank, Washington DC.

World Bank (2007), *Spending for Development: Making the Most of Indonesia's New Opportunities*, World Bank, Jakarta.

14 SERVICES RENDERED: PEACE, PATRONAGE AND POST-CONFLICT ELECTIONS IN ACEH

Blair Palmer *

Indonesia's April 2009 legislative elections had special significance for the province of Aceh, where the Helsinki Memorandum of Understanding (MOU) of 2005 had marked an end to the 30-year separatist conflict between the Free Aceh Movement (Gerakan Aceh Merdeka, GAM) and the Indonesian government. The 2009 elections were an important part of the peace process, as former GAM members were contesting power (in the form of provincial and district-level legislative seats) through democratic means. The MOU enabled the formation of local parties, and the Aceh Party (Partai Aceh, PA), the party formed to represent former GAM members, achieved a strong win in both the provincial and district-level elections.

The first goal of this chapter is to examine how PA achieved its impressive win, and the implications of its victory for peace in Aceh. Election implementation suffered from many problems and tensions but I argue that PA's win was legitimate and bodes well for continued peace. In its campaign efforts, PA benefited from the far-reaching and well-organised structure left behind by GAM. In addition, it managed to attract the votes

---

* This chapter is based on a study called 'Citizens, leaders, and conflict' carried out by the Center for Peace and Conflict Resolution Studies (CPCRS) at Syiah Kuala University, Banda Aceh, with assistance from the author and Adrian Morel. Fieldwork for the study was undertaken in 10 districts in February–June 2009 and the final report was published in 2010. The views expressed in this paper are those of the author, not the institutions supporting the research. The author wishes to thank the CPCRS research team for their hard work and Adrian Morel and Jesse Grayman for comments on an earlier draft.

Map 14.1   Aceh

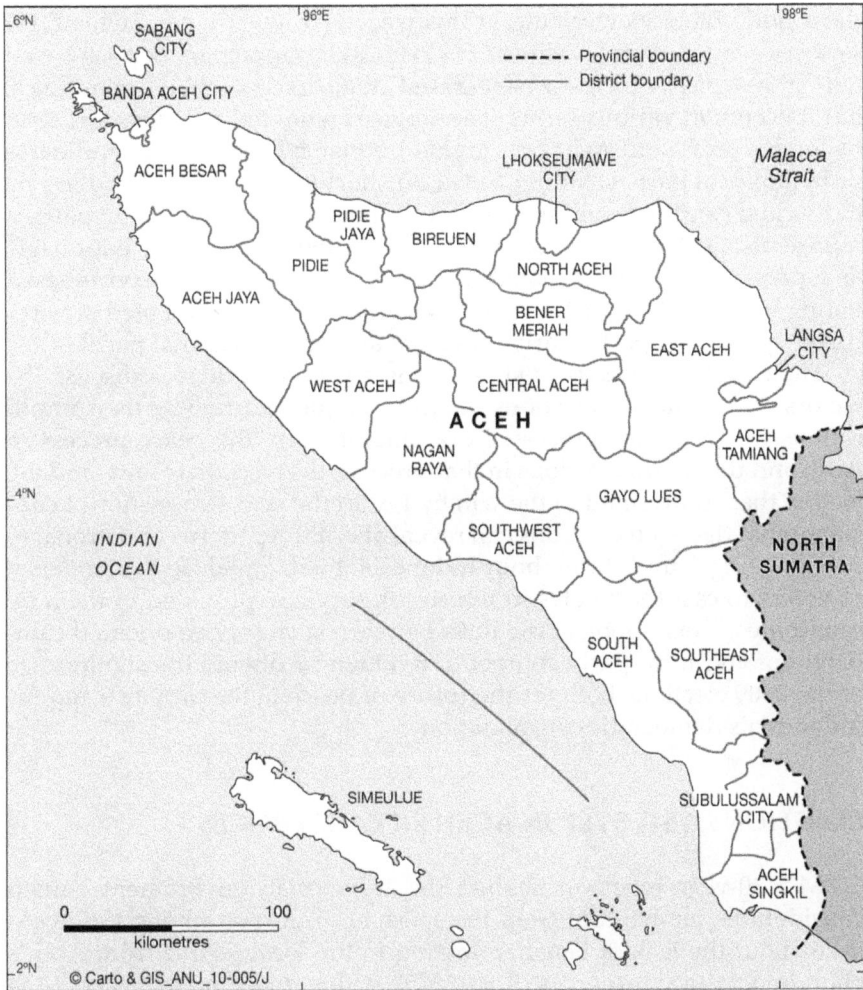

of many people who had not previously supported GAM, primarily those who hoped that a win for PA would help sustain the peace in Aceh.

A second goal of the chapter is to treat the Aceh elections as a prism through which to view wider political processes in Indonesia. The participation of local parties and former rebels in the elections marked Aceh as different to the rest of Indonesia. However, in terms of the political dynamics that were influential in the province during the elections, Aceh had much in common with the rest of the country. One common phenomenon in Indonesian politics is a 'service-based' candidate–voter relationship whereby votes are cast as a reward for services rendered by a party or candidate. There is considerable evidence that many candidates and voters view voting in this way: as a reward, or payment, for services rendered, in an almost business-like transaction. Service-based voting is typical of a patronage-based democracy such as Indonesia's, but it occurs in various forms. The services rendered may be short term or longer term, and may be provided either by individual candidates or by political parties. Voting based on short-term services provided by individual candidates, rather than collective goods provided by parties, represents a subverting of democratic principles in favour of patronage, and presages poor governance to follow. Party-oriented service-based voting was a factor in PA's victory, whereas candidate-oriented service-based voting was particularly prevalent among the national parties.

The chapter proceeds in six sections. In the first three, I discuss the factors that made the elections in Aceh unique and review their implications for the peace process. I examine, in turn, the peace process in Aceh and the role of elections in that process; the election results; and the factors that contributed to the win by PA. In the next two sections I consider what the Aceh elections can reveal about the patterns of patronage-based voting found throughout Indonesia. First, I analyse the tendency of voters to cast their votes in return for 'services' provided to them by candidates. Next, I look at the links between such service-oriented campaigning and intra-party competition. Finally, I discuss the significance of the 2009 elections both for the future of peace in the province and for Indonesia's democratic consolidation.

ELECTIONS AS A STEP IN ACEH'S PEACE PROCESS

GAM's 30-year rebellion against the Indonesian government gained considerable momentum from the sense of grievance among the Acehnese about the lack of benefits flowing to the local people from Aceh's abundant natural resources (Ross 2005). Although for many years GAM did not enjoy a mass following, the brutal human rights abuses committed by the military during operations in the province galvanised additional support for the movement (Aspinall 2009a). After the fall of Suharto in 1998, the student-led Aceh Referendum Information Centre (Sentral Informasi Referendum Aceh, SIRA) organised demonstrations attended by hundreds of thousands of people demanding a referendum on independence for the province. Eventually, however, the euphoria of this period was met with a renewed military campaign to end separatist sentiment in Aceh, beginning in 2003. The Indian Ocean tsunami that hit Aceh in December 2004 gave momentum to the peace talks already under way between the Indonesian government and GAM. The talks led to the signing in August 2005 of the Helsinki MOU, which officially ended the conflict with a promise of autonomy for Aceh within the state of Indonesia.

The Helsinki MOU contained two important stipulations that would enable former combatants to contest political power in Aceh through democratic means. Clause 1.2.2 stated that 'the people of Aceh will have the right to nominate candidates for the positions of all elected officials to contest the elections in Aceh in April 2006 and thereafter'. This was understood to mean that independent candidates (including former combatants) would be allowed to contest the elections for provincial and district heads to be held in 2006–2007. Clause 1.2.1 stated that local parties could be formed to contest legislative elections. This was important, as otherwise GAM would have been unable to form a party: to preclude parties focused on narrow regional interests, Indonesian law states that all political parties must be 'national', that is, have significant branch structures in at least 60 per cent of all provinces. These were key provisions in the MOU, without which GAM may not have been willing to give up its calls for independence.

The first stage of GAM's political integration occurred with the 2006–2007 direct elections for heads of local government in Aceh. The transition from armed movement to political body was symbolised by the formation of the Aceh Transitional Committee (Komite Peralihan Aceh, KPA), an organisation representing the interests of former GAM combatants. In these elections, a GAM/KPA-affiliated candidate was elected provincial governor and GAM/KPA-affiliated candidates were elected district head in 10 of Aceh's 23 districts. Although the elections proceeded smoothly, with little violence, patronage-based relationships between candidates and voters were common, and in the post-election period conflict arose over government construction projects, bureaucratic appointments and other benefits of office (Clark and Palmer 2008).[1] Reintegration programs aimed at former combatants were of minimal efficacy (Palmer 2007), but many former combatants sought and obtained work as contractors or used their connections and 'street power' to obtain construction contracts from local governments (Aspinall 2009b).

The MOU provision permitting the formation of local parties was duly included in Law No. 11/2006 on the Government of Aceh. Local parties were only allowed, however, to contest seats in the local — that is, provincial and district — legislatures; they were not allowed to compete for seats in the national parliament, for which the law on national parties applied in Aceh as in the rest of Indonesia. Former GAM supporters,

---

1 Government construction contracts are one of the primary methods of distributing patronage in Indonesia, especially at the local level (Hidayat 2009).

along with many other Acehnese, were not troubled by this limitation, because they were primarily interested in gaining power in Aceh, not in representing Aceh in Jakarta. Six local parties succeeded in satisfying the conditions for registration, but by far the most important was PA, formed by former GAM members.

The elections thus played an important role in the peace process, marking a new stage in the implementation of the Helsinki MOU and giving the former armed rebels of GAM an opportunity to become more deeply engaged with peaceful political participation and local government.

Of course, elections by themselves are not sufficient to establish peace; other factors such as economic development and security are equally important (Collier, Hoeffler and Söderbom 2008). Aceh has considerable potential for economic development given the extensive resources now at the local government's disposal, but great improvements in governance will be necessary if these resources are to be utilised effectively (Barron and Clark 2006). The current state of democracy in Indonesia can be described as patrimonial (Webber 2006), in so far as the distribution of patronage infuses the electoral system and legislatures, as it does other state institutions. If Aceh's democracy proves to conform to the Indonesian standard, with the same reliance on elite-level patronage networks fuelled by massive corruption, then it seems likely that local governance will not improve. In this case, corruption, poverty and a sense of grievance will remain and could threaten the peace, at least in the long term (Clark and Palmer 2008).

THE ELECTION RESULTS

At first it seemed as if the 2009 parliamentary elections would trigger more violence, not consolidate peace. In the months leading up to the elections, there were 32 arson or grenade attacks on party offices, with PA the target of 27 of them, and five people associated with the party or KPA were murdered. Some of the murders were probably related more to business than politics, but in Aceh, as elsewhere in Indonesia, business and politics are inextricably linked through networks of patronage. Former GAM combatants have entered these networks aggressively since the MOU in 2005. Thus, the violence against PA figures could indicate struggles over business deals and patronage, involving either former combatants and established elites, or different factions of former combatants. Nevertheless, many PA leaders suspected a campaign of intimidation was being waged against them, engineered by elements of the security forces. Tensions between PA and the armed forces were high.

Many political parties reported widespread intimidation in the former GAM strongholds along the east coast, and in these cases supporters of

Table 14.1   Distribution of seats in the Aceh provincial parliament, 2009

Party	No. of seats
Partai Aceh (PA)	33
Partai Demokrat (PD)	10
Golkar	8
Partai Amanat Nasional (PAN)	5
Partai Keadilan Sejahtera (PKS)	4
Partai Persatuan Pembangunan (PPP)	4
Partai Kebangkitan Bangsa (PKB)	1
Partai Bulan Bintang (PBB)	1
Partai Daulat Aceh (PDA)	1
Partai Keadilan dan Persatuan Indonesia (PKPI)	1
Partai Patriot	1
Total	**69**

Source: Aceh's Independent Elections Commission (Komisi Independen Pemilu).

the former insurgent organisation seemed mostly to be responsible. But local parties also reported intimidation in the central highlands, where GAM had historically been weak.[2]

Nevertheless, election day passed peacefully, and rates of voter turn-out were even slightly higher than those recorded elsewhere in Indonesia (78 per cent for the provincial-level election). After the results were announced, allegations of fraud emerged, and some losing candidates launched court cases to challenge the results. Although a few seats changed hands as a result, the overall results stood, none of the protests turned violent, and all parties seemed to accept the final result, even though it was clear that election implementation was far from perfect, as in the rest of Indonesia (see Schmidt's chapter in this volume).

PA emerged as the clear winner in both the provincial elections (where it won 33 of 69 seats) and the district-level elections (where it won 237 of 645 seats). It emerged as the largest party in 16 of Aceh's 23 districts, with an outright majority in seven of those. This was an extraordinary outcome for a party whose leaders had been fighting the Indonesian state by force of arms just five years earlier. Indeed, PA achieved a level of representation in local parliaments that has rarely been achieved by any Indonesian political party since the country embraced democracy. The results are presented in Tables 14.1 and 14.2.

---

2   For details, see CPCRS (2009) and World Bank (2009).

Table 14.2   Seats won by Partai Aceh in Aceh's 23 district parliaments, 2009

District	Seats in parliament (no.)	Seats held by PA (no.)	Seats held by PA (%)	Position of PA
1 Pidie	45	34	76	Holds majority of seats
2 North Aceh	45	32	71	Holds majority of seats
3 East Aceh	35	25	71	Holds majority of seats
4 Bireuen	35	25	71	Holds majority of seats
5 Aceh Jaya	20	14	70	Holds majority of seats
6 Pidie Jaya	25	16	64	Holds majority of seats
7 Lhokseumawe	25	14	56	Holds majority of seats
8 Southwest Aceh	25	9	36	Minority but largest party
9 South Aceh	30	10	33	Minority but largest party
10 Sabang	20	6	30	Minority but largest party
11 Aceh Besar	35	10	29	Minority but largest party
12 Aceh Tamiang	30	8	27	Minority but largest party
13 Langsa	25	6	24	Minority but largest party
14 West Aceh	30	7	23	Minority but largest party
15 Banda Aceh	30	6	20	Second-largest party
16 Nagan Raya	25	5	20	Minority but largest party
17 Bener Meriah	25	3	12	Second-largest party (tied)
18 Central Aceh	30	3	10	Second-largest party (tied)
19 Simeulue	20	2	10	Minority but largest party (tied)
20 Gayo Lues	20	1	5	
21 Southeast Aceh	25	1	4	
22 Aceh Singkil	25	0	0	
23 Subulussalam	20	0	0	
Total	**645**	**237**	**37**	

Source: Author's calculations using data from Aceh's Independent Elections Commission (Komisi Independen Pemilu).

In the election for seats in the national parliament, President Susilo Bambang Yudhoyono's Democratic Party (Partai Demokrat, PD) was the clear victor, winning six of the 13 seats available for Aceh. PD also did well in the provincial and district elections, obtaining 10 seats in the provincial parliament and 76 seats in the district parliaments, and narrowly beating PA to become the largest party in two districts. The high levels of approval for the president, especially for his role in achieving peace in Aceh, seemed to be the main factor driving PD's electoral success. A further sign of this came in July 2009, when Yudhoyono won 93 per cent of Aceh's vote in the presidential election, by far the highest proportion recorded for the president across all of Indonesia.

Golkar, the former party of the Suharto regime, obtained eight provincial seats and 59 district seats, making it the third-largest party in both levels of government. It gained the most seats in five districts in the central highlands and on the southwest coast, areas with large minorities of non-Acehnese ethnicity where the GAM insurgency had always been weak. But although national parties like PD and Golkar gained the most seats in a few districts, none achieved an outright majority. In general the districts not won by PA were extremely fragmented, with no party winning as much as 25 per cent of the seats, and with the average number of seats per party under two. This was the case for seven districts.

The success of PA in the provincial and district elections did not come as a big surprise, given the success of GAM-affiliated candidates in the 2006–2007 local executive elections. Less anticipated, however, was the almost total failure of the five other local parties to win seats. Only one obtained a seat in the provincial parliament, all fell short of 2 per cent of the vote, and none will be able to contest the 2014 elections. (To be eligible to contest the 2014 elections, local parties had to obtain at least 5 per cent of the seats in the provincial parliament, or 5 per cent of the seats in half of the district parliaments.) Local parties, it seemed, had not had enough time and were not sufficiently well funded to develop a significant support base, and never managed to convince voters that local parties meant more than just PA.

EXPLAINING PARTAI ACEH'S WIN

PA's victory was related to a number of factors, the most important being the strength of KPA's operational structure, which stretched down to the village level right across the province. Acting as a powerful resource for the mobilisation of campaign efforts, this gave PA an advantage not enjoyed by any other party in the rest of Indonesia.

PA also largely managed to avoid divisive intra-party competition, with PA candidates campaigning together in their electoral districts rather than competing against each other as happened with most of the other parties. In the election, voters could vote either for a party or for an individual candidate from one of the parties. Under the open party list system, seats won by parties were allocated to the candidates with the most votes, regardless of their position on the party list.[3] This led

---

3 In the 2004 elections as well, voters were allowed to select either a party or an individual candidate. However, under the partial open list system used in the

*Table 14.3   Votes for parties (versus votes for individual candidates) in the
district legislative elections, selected parties (%)*

Party	Party votes versus candidate votes
Partai Aceh (PA)	53
Partai Demokrat (PD)	44
Golkar	15
Partai Amanat Nasional (PAN)	18
Partai Keadilan Sejahtera (PKS)	32
Partai Persatuan Pembangunan (PPP)	20

Source: Author's calculations using data from Aceh's Independent Elections Commission (Komisi Independen Pemilu).

to much divisive competition between candidates from the same party, demonstrated by a high percentage of voters who picked individual candidates instead of the party symbol. Among the top vote-getting parties in the district-level elections, however, PA had the highest percentage of party votes as opposed to votes for candidates (see Table 14.3). Again, PA's unity of purpose was probably a result of the strength of GAM's ex-military command structure.

PA candidates kept their campaign message clear and simple, and generally avoided making unrealistic promises, which Aceh's cynical voters seemed to appreciate. They simply pointed out that their struggle had led to the MOU and peace in Aceh, and promised that they would continue to fight for full implementation of the MOU.

In interviews conducted by the author and other researchers in 2009, voters identified a number of quite different reasons for voting for PA. Consequently, PA's vote tally cannot be considered a measure of ideological commitment to GAM and the independence struggle. Certainly some PA voters were longstanding and loyal supporters of GAM. Others, however, voted for PA from pro-Aceh sentiment. Many Acehnese expressed a high degree of cynicism towards the national parties, which were seen as not having Aceh's best interests at heart.

2004 elections, candidates had to obtain a certain quota of votes before they could win a seat based on those votes rather than the party list. Only two of the 550 members sitting in the national parliament actually earned their seats in this manner, with all others determined by the party lists (Sherlock 2009: 5). In the lead-up to the 2009 elections, the Constitutional Court decided that, regardless of whether candidates met the quota, seats won by parties would go to the candidates with the most votes, not those highest on the party list.

There are several explanations as to why PA managed to obtain most of the 'pro-Aceh' votes at the expense of the other local parties. Many voters said they had voted for PA out of gratitude for GAM's struggle. They said that GAM had obtained a strong autonomy deal for Aceh, and that PA should be rewarded for GAM's service to the Acehnese people. Others said they had voted for PA out of concern that PA cadres might become 'disappointed and angry' if the party lost, leading to renewed conflict. These responses indicate that sustaining the peace was a primary concern among voters, with many feeling that it was wisest to vote for PA in order to achieve that. These votes can be called 'votes for peace'. As one citizen in West Aceh said, 'let's give it to [PA] now, and they can do what they want'. This strategy of appeasement was fairly common among voters.

Still others voted for PA because they could see that it was likely to win. In Aceh it is seen as a wise and safe strategy to vote for whoever is predicted to be the winner, in the hope of gaining patronage-related benefits later as payment for that political support. This voting style can be called 'picking the winner'.[4]

Of course, voters often had multiple considerations in their decision to vote for PA. The point here is that many who did vote for PA acknowledged that they had no allegiance to GAM, and did not even expect that PA would govern particularly well, but still chose to vote for the party for reasons such as those listed above.

PA may also have benefited from votes cast under duress. First, PA supporters were present at some polling booths in former GAM strongholds along the east coast, sometimes even working as polling booth supervisors, and may have 'guided' some elderly or confused voters to vote for PA. However, the fact that support for PA was already extremely high in those areas suggests that this sort of illicit influence was not responsible for a large number of additional votes. Second, some people undoubtedly voted for PA from fear that there might be violent consequences for themselves or their villages if they did not do so. In a Javanese transmigrant village in North Aceh, for example, voters expressed concerns about retribution if the results for the village showed a low vote for PA. Again, such fears appear to have influenced votes in only a few ethnically distinct enclaves in highly pro-PA regions, and thus provided only a few additional votes for PA.

Indirect forms of intimidation seem to have had a greater effect on the results than direct forms of intimidation. Much of this was directed

---

4   For more on this style of voting in the context of Aceh's 2006–2007 local elections, see Clark and Palmer (2008); see also Muhammad Qodari's chapter in this volume on the 'bandwagon effect' of published opinion polls in Indonesia.

not at voters but at party officials and candidates, restricting their ability to campaign effectively. In addition, supporters sometimes encountered roadblocks set up by their political opponents as they attempted to attend party rallies in the towns. PA and the other five local parties were the primary victims of such intimidation in the central highlands, but in the former GAM strongholds along the east coast, many parties reported intimidation—much of it by PA supporters, but also some directed towards PA.

Many of PA's competitors chose to keep their campaigns low-profile in the east and to avoid large patches of territory that were considered highly pro-PA, for their own safety. This meant that voters did not receive as much information about those parties as they otherwise might have. In many of these areas only PA banners could be seen, because people removed the banners of other parties within days of them being raised. Although many of the voters would not have been swayed away from PA in any case, it is fair to say that this situation may have had some impact on the results. The destruction of other parties' campaign materials signalled an intolerance of democratic competition that may have worried voters (increasing the number of 'votes for peace' going to PA), and acted as a sign that PA was strong and likely to win (increasing the number of votes for PA by those attempting to 'pick the winner').

Also evident throughout the campaign period was the use of slander and scare tactics to drive voters away from particular parties.[5] The targets differed according to locality: in the central highlands it was the local parties who were targeted the most, whereas on the east coast all parties were targeted. Some supporters of national parties portrayed local parties as traitors to Indonesia, while some PA supporters portrayed all other parties as standing against Aceh's interests. The threat of a return to conflict was often present, with stories spreading in some areas that if PA won there would be conflict, and in other areas that if PA *lost* there would be conflict.

In text messages, pamphlets and banners, PA and other local parties were referred to as 'separatists', 'rebels' and 'communists'. A banner on a main road in East Aceh proclaimed: 'Choosing separatists means you are anti-peace'. One of the pamphlets circulating in the central highlands declared that anyone who voted for PA was a communist and would be killed, together with their children and grandchildren. In Bener Meriah in the central highlands, an anti-GAM stronghold during the conflict years, the local government hosted an event ostensibly to 'remember the

---

5   Obviously, such tactics were not unique to Aceh. See Smith (2009) for an example of negative branding in the 2005 mayoral elections in Ternate, North Maluku.

victims of the GAM separatist conflict'. A representative of a local party who attended claimed that government and military officials warned the public not to vote for PA, saying 'If PA wins Aceh will return to conflict. … Let's make war on [*perangi*] local parties'.

PA supporters, on the other hand, sometimes portrayed the national parties as 'Java parties' — where 'Java' signified the enemy during the conflict years — and claimed that Aceh would return to a state of conflict if the national parties won. Villagers reported PA campaign officials saying things like 'If you want it to be like 2003 [an intense period of conflict] then pick a different party'. But the main targets of PA supporters were the other local parties, which they sometimes portrayed as 'Indonesian agents' and traitors to Aceh's cause, or as 'opportunists' who had not participated in the struggle that had led to the MOU but were trying to steal the fruits of the agreement from PA.

These 'black campaigns', as they are called in Indonesia, could be seen as attempts to obtain the 'peace vote' by convincing voters that a particular party was best placed to secure the peace. Overall, PA probably benefited most from such scare tactics, even though it may have lost some votes in the central highlands.

Taken together, the political dynamics surrounding PA's win have several implications. First, the role of direct physical intimidation and fraud seems to have been small, and thus the win by PA should not be seen as illegitimate. Nevertheless, the prevalence of indirect intimidation shows that law enforcement officials and election supervisors failed to guarantee a level playing field for all parties in Aceh, with infractions presumably tolerated either in the name of peace or out of simple incompetence. The five local parties other than PA suffered disproportionately from this indirect intimidation, and their opportunity to contest the elections was unfairly restricted. Second, in addition to its core of loyal supporters, PA was endorsed by many voters who did not necessarily support its policies or believe it would govern well, but wanted to compensate PA for its long struggle and wanted to keep the peace (among other considerations). Voters are likely to cast their votes based on different considerations next time — such as PA's performance in government. Or perhaps they will judge individual PA candidates in much the same way as they judge candidates from other parties, a topic I turn to now.

SERVICE-BASED VOTING

In consolidated democracies, parties will ideally develop campaign platforms and communicate their policies to voters, who will then select the party whose policies best accord with their own view of how the region (or country) should be governed. This form of party–citizen relationship did not characterise the elections in Aceh. Most of the parties had only very vague policy platforms, and votes were generally not endorsements of particular policy directions. As one Acehnese voter put it, 'platforms don't sell here'.

Parties and candidates did not engage seriously with issues such as the implementation of Islamic law (*syari'ah*), a major issue in the province since the granting of special autonomy in 2001; the state of the local economy; or the best way to use Aceh's considerable oil and gas revenues. Nor did voters ask them to do so. As one community leader explained, 'None of us know anything about party platforms ... maybe [candidates] said something but none of us remember any of it'. PA was a partial exception in that candidates made it clear that they would struggle for fuller implementation of the MOU. A few other parties, such as the Islamist Prosperous Justice Party (Partai Keadilan Sejahtera, PKS) and the Aceh People's Party (Partai Rakyat Aceh, PRA — a left-wing local party formed by former student activists), also expressed some clear policy priorities, but on the whole the election was not decided by a contest of policy platforms.

Instead, voters based their decisions on other factors, such as the desire for peace mentioned above.[6] Personal relationships were of great importance in the elections, with candidates appealing to their family networks for support, leading some Acehnese to dub them 'family elections'. This is similar to what happens in elections in many other parts of provincial Indonesia (see Buehler and Tan 2007). Another prominent style of voting is what I call 'service-based voting': casting one's vote as a reward for services rendered by a party or candidate. This style of voting has important implications for Indonesia's democratic development as a whole, and is explored in more detail here.

In Indonesia, many ordinary people, especially in rural villages, view a good leader as someone who takes care of the people's immediate material needs. In the Aceh elections, candidates commonly attempted to highlight how they had assisted communities in the past, and engaged in further distribution of such 'assistance' as part of their campaign strategies.[7] Voters often discussed which candidates or parties had provided them with the best 'service' (*jasa*) in the past, and considered this seri-

---

6 One could argue that the people who voted for peace were making a policy choice. However, all parties in Aceh were in favour of peace, not just PA. And when people voted for PA from fear that PA supporters would run amuck if they lost, they were not basing their decision on policy considerations.

7 Similarly, Antlöv (2004: 123) found that the Javanese believe that 'good leaders, and those they represent, should distribute goods and prove themselves to be service-minded'.

ously when deciding how to vote. The services rendered could range from gifts such as donations of food and clothing to more enduring services such as employment. Coffee farmers were loaned fertilizer; voters were offered employment on pineapple and cassava plantations; and villages received donations of building materials for the village mosque as well as sports uniforms and copies of the Koran.

It was individual candidates, rather than the parties, who provided most of these services. Voting for services rendered thus led to a higher number of votes being cast for individual candidates than for that candidate's party. As indicated in Table 14.3, votes for candidates accounted for 70–85 per cent of the votes received by the major parties, with the exception of PA and PD (the two winners), which had a much higher percentage of party votes than the other parties. The service-based style of campaigning was much more prevalent among established elites – incumbent legislators, local businesspeople, civil servants and the like – who were candidates for national parties than among candidates for local parties. Many of the latter came from activist backgrounds and lacked access to state office and the patronage resources this provided, while most PA candidates also lacked the financial resources to run service-based campaigns.

However, parties could also benefit from service-based voting, especially when voters thought of services in depersonalised terms. As described earlier, PA received some service-based votes in gratitude for GAM's role in achieving regional autonomy for Aceh, and PD received many votes in gratitude for the president's role in the peace process.[8] Golkar gained some votes from Javanese transmigrants in gratitude for the government program that had brought them to Aceh decades earlier, and from civil servants grateful for their privileges during the years Golkar was in power. PKS reminded voters in the district of West Aceh of the assistance the party had rendered after the tsunami, and managed to win four district parliament seats through this strategy. When referring to a party's past performance, voters often used exactly the same word – *jasa* – as they did when referring to the more personal gifts or donations provided by individual candidates.

Thus, both parties and individual candidates could offer services; the services could be either material gifts or longer-term assistance; and they could benefit individuals, a particular community such as a village, or

---

8 Although then vice-president Jusuf Kalla had been instrumental in achieving the peace deal, this did not translate into a high number of service-based votes for his party, Golkar, possibly because Golkar continues to be associated with the Suharto government and the military abuses perpetrated in Aceh during the conflict years.

Aceh as a whole. Service-based voting is partly explained by the high degree of cynicism towards politicians and their promises found among Aceh's population. In a strongly worded but not exceptional expression of this outlook, one voter told me, 'There are thousands of candidates. ... They are all liars, all thieves!' Voters were highly sceptical of candidates' promises, and more inclined to consider their past actions. They sometimes viewed statements of policy positions as merely 'making promises' in contrast to actually doing something to help. They also likened policy presentations to 'selling medicine' — best viewed with scepticism due to its uncertain efficacy. Many voters expressed the opinion that nothing would change no matter who won, so rather than vote in the hope of change, it made more sense to cast one's vote as an expression of gratitude for past assistance or to get what one could in the present. By rewarding a candidate for past service, voters may also have been hoping to keep such services coming, creating a kind of reciprocal gift-giving relationship.

In their campaigns, candidates actively reminded voters of services rendered in the past. For the many candidates with a civil service or legislative background, this often included attempting to take credit for government programs that had directly improved people's lives at the local level. Some of these officials and legislators designed their campaigns around events at which government goods were to be distributed, taking credit for the delivery and telling recipients to 'remember me when it comes to voting time'. This sometimes involved cutting corrupt deals with officials from a government department, for instance, persuading Ministry of Agriculture staff to let them deliver, and take the credit for furnishing, government-provided seed to villagers.

Besides reminding voters of services rendered in the past, candidates actively provided services during their campaigns, paid for out of their (personal) campaign funds. This approach was risky, however, as other candidates were doing exactly the same thing. Candidates complained about being 'deceived' by voters who had agreed to vote for them, and accepted goods or cash for doing so, but had then voted differently. 'Voters are cunning these days', said one candidate, 'If you're not careful they will trick you'. One way of dealing with the problem was to postpone full payment until after the election, by agreeing, for instance, to repair a village road in return for votes, but carrying out only half the work before the election, with the remainder to be completed if the result went the candidate's way.

Seen in this light, what is referred to in Indonesia as 'money politics' — direct gifts of cash and/or goods to voters in order to influence their votes — is just another form of service, and many Acehnese voters viewed it as such. Both candidates and voters to some degree saw money politics as a legitimate form of campaigning. Many of them did not understand the legal definition of 'money politics', assuming that the term referred to cash bribes only, not the donation of goods. Local people did not see making such donations as a crime, but as a form of *jasa*, and indeed, they sometimes felt it was merely polite for a powerful figure to bring gifts when visiting a poor village. Candidates, too, described feeling socially negligent if they did not bring gifts for the villagers when visiting a village to 'ask for votes'. Some voters spoke in offended tones about the 'improper' behaviour of candidates who had come asking for their votes while offering nothing in return. Many villagers actively solicited gifts, asking candidates who turned up in their villages, 'What did you bring?' or 'What are you going to give us so that we remember you?', and reminding candidates that 'If you want fruit, you have to plant something first'.

In fact, though, voters displayed a variety of reactions towards money politics. Probably most commonly, they accepted whatever a candidate offered but did not feel honour-bound to vote for the donor. Some said that candidates who paid bribes were not fit for office and should be avoided. Others said they *did* feel bound to vote for the candidate, and would feel embarrassed if it became known that they had accepted a payment but not delivered their vote.[9] And some refused to accept the goods in the first place, saying they had already decided who to vote for. Some candidates, in turn, assumed that the acceptance of payment implied agreement to vote accordingly, as became evident when a number of them asked for their donations to be returned after they failed to win a seat.[10] Overall, money politics on its own was rarely enough to secure an election victory, as voters were aware of the opportunistic nature of those handing out the gifts. On the other hand, voters often viewed donations

---

9   One humorous example recounted by a villager hints at the overt nature, and efficacy, of money politics. In a village in West Aceh, a district-level PD candidate had allegedly made significant donations of Ramos-brand noodles. When the votes were being counted, at each vote for PD the polling booth officials called out 'Ramos!' instead of the party name.

10 It is often claimed that, in a secret ballot, money politics tends to fail because candidates cannot know whether or not those who accepted their gifts voted for them. However, in Aceh, this was not always the case. Because the vote tally for each polling booth was made public, candidates did know how many votes they had received at each booth, and therefore whether a significant number of people had reneged on their promises. Moreover, one candidate claimed to know how particular people had cast their votes, because an election official had 'assisted' by making an identifying mark on the ballot papers handed out to certain people so that it would be possible to check later how they had voted.

of cash and goods by candidates who already enjoyed a good reputation in the community as an additional reason to vote for them.

It is likely that service-style voting was more prevalent in the elections for district legislatures than in the elections for the provincial or national-level bodies, due to the closer connection between voters and local politicians at the district level. The fact that PA won 48 per cent of the seats at the provincial level but only 37 per cent at the district level (see Tables 14.1 and 14.2) may be because the many service-based votes at the district level mostly went to individual candidates from parties other than PA.

SERVICE-BASED CAMPAIGNING AND INTRA-PARTY COMPETITION

The prevalence of service-based campaigns by individual candidates was partly due to the Constitutional Court decision in December 2008 to allocate seats won by a party to the candidates who received the most votes rather than those highest on the party list. Before this decision, candidates with the highest position on the party list were the most active, often funding the campaigns of candidates beneath them on the list, who were referred to as 'vote-getters' rather than serious candidates because they were unlikely to win seats themselves. After the decision, any candidate who could obtain more votes than his or her colleagues stood a chance of winning a seat, leading to a high level of intra-party competition. In practice, this translated into an increase in service-based campaigns, with more donations of goods, and more allegations of fraud in the vote-counting process.

Candidates for most of the parties — again, PA and PD were the main exceptions — generally eschewed campaigning in groups or by way of large rallies, instead campaigning alone for personal rather than party votes. Candidates largely funded their own campaigns, with the party providing only some campaign materials, such as party banners, stickers, name cards and T-shirts. In some cases the increased competition between candidates in the same party led to bitter conflict. For example, in March 2009 a Golkar office in Nagan Raya district was broken into and campaign materials stolen. A party official alleged that Golkar candidates themselves were involved in the robbery, as they were eager to distribute the materials personally in order to increase their personal votes (*Serambi Indonesia*, 8 March 2009).

The new electoral system also led to an increase in money politics by individual candidates. In the past, party officials acting on behalf of the candidate at the top of the party list might have handed out money or goods in order to secure votes. Now, all candidates had an incentive to engage in money politics, in competition with each other. The increased competition in the 'vote-buying' market allegedly led to a rise in the price of a single vote from approximately Rp 50,000 ($5) to somewhere in the range of Rp 75,000–100,000 ($8–10). Campaign teams distributed cash in envelopes to voters when they visited villages. This meant there was a lot of money flowing to villagers, who received a windfall in 'donations' from candidates. However, as explained above, not all voters felt compelled to vote for the individuals who had made the gifts, and many candidates incurred large debts, meaning that both winners and losers would need to recoup the losses later.

Intra-party competition also led to allegations of fraud in the vote-counting process, specifically in the tallying of personal votes within parties. Many candidates believed that some votes for them were fraudulently counted as party-only votes (remembering that voters had a choice to vote either for a party or for a particular candidate) or for a rival candidate. During vote counting at the polling booths, party witnesses were on hand to verify their own party's vote count, but paid little attention to the breakdown of personal votes for other parties. A party's witness may have been the only person to record the personal votes of the various candidates within that party, and may have been under pressure from particular candidates to reduce the vote count of other candidates. Candidates thus needed to establish relationships of trust with witnesses (usually facilitated by payments), or hire their own witnesses to 'protect' their votes at each of the booths where they anticipated doing well. One losing candidate explained his loss in this way: 'I could only pay witnesses at 20 out of 116 polling booths, whereas [my rival] had witnesses at every polling booth'. Election officials reported being offered money to increase the personal vote tallies of candidates so that they could beat a rival for a seat. Candidates, in turn, reported being approached by district election officials, who offered to convert party votes into individual votes for them, at a price.

Parties were weakened by such tactics. Winning candidates felt they owed little to their party for their victory, since they had funded their own campaigns and did not depend on the party platform to attract votes. Competition between candidates and underhanded tactics soured relationships within parties.

Service-based voting can be positive when it rewards parties for their past achievements, but when it is oriented towards individual candidates and short-term material benefits it leads to negative outcomes for citizens. Service-based voting is backward-looking. One of the functions of democratic elections is to allow voters to signal their policy priorities for the future. When legislators are elected through service-based campaigns by individual candidates, no such signalling occurs, and elected deputies may be unresponsive to voters whose votes have been 'pre-paid' with services. Also, the candidates who win are likely to be those with deep pockets and an effective strategy for service-based campaigning based on the distribution of patronage, not those who would be the most competent at governing. Candidates incur large debts to pay for their campaigns, meaning that those who win may seek to recoup their expenses later through corruption.

CONCLUSION: SUSTAINABLE PEACE IN ACEH AND INDONESIA'S DEMOCRATIC CONSOLIDATION

In many ways, the 2009 election in Aceh was a tale of two very different elections. On the one hand, especially when it came to voting for the national and provincial legislatures, many citizens made the choice to reward parties they thought had contributed to Aceh's peace process, or whose victory they thought would secure the peace in the future. PD and PA were the main beneficiaries of this pattern of voting, and they also stood out from almost all of the other parties in their united campaigning style. On the other hand, especially when it came to district elections in rural areas, many voters voted in a way that reflected and reinforced the patrimonial style of politics infusing Indonesia's new democracy: they chose to support individuals rather than parties, judging them on the basis of the personal services they had rendered in the past rather than in terms of the policy choices they offered for the future.

In terms of their contribution to sustaining peace, the 2009 elections in Aceh must be seen as a success, despite all the problems. Violence was present, but at low levels compared to other post-conflict elections; there were many allegations of fraud, but not enough to threaten the overall legitimacy of the election; and the results were largely accepted as representing the will of the people. PA's win means that disappointment among ex-combatants is unlikely to threaten the peace in the short term, as their leaders have the opportunity to govern the province.

Perhaps the central issue for both peace and democratisation in Aceh is whether the PA representatives who have won positions in parliament and government will use the opportunity to promote an agenda of democratic consolidation and governance reform, or merely seek to benefit from holding positions of power within a patrimonial democracy without changing the system itself. New legislators will be under intense pressure to distribute benefits to loyal followers, as were the victorious GAM-affiliated district heads after the 2006–2007 local executive elections (see Clark and Palmer 2008). If legislators deliver on those expectations, it will likely lead to poor governance as well as conflicts over who gets these benefits. It will also reinforce old patterns of service-based voting, exposing PA candidates in the future to the kind of cynicism reserved thus far for candidates from the national parties and the established elite. But if they do not distribute the benefits of office, the result may be conflict instigated by large numbers of dissatisfied supporters. This is a delicate balance, but it must tip in the direction of better governance if real change, and the hope of long-term sustainable peace, is to come to Aceh.

For now, the success of the 2009 elections means that the challenge facing Aceh in its progress towards sustainable peace is the same as that facing the rest of Indonesia in its process of democratic consolidation: to move away from patrimonial democracy.

REFERENCES

Antlöv, Hans (2004), 'National elections, local issues: the 1997 and 1999 national elections in a village on Java', in H. Antlöv and S. Cederroth (eds), *Elections in Indonesia: The New Order and Beyond*, RoutledgeCurzon, New York, pp. 111–37.

Aspinall, Edward (2009a), *Islam and Nation: Separatist Rebellion in Aceh, Indonesia*, Stanford University Press, Stanford CA.

Aspinall, Edward (2009b), 'Combatants to contractors: the political economy of peace in Aceh', *Indonesia* 87(April): 1–34.

Barron, Patrick and Samuel Clark (2006), 'Decentralizing inequality? Center–periphery relations, local governance and conflict', Conflict Prevention and Reconstruction Paper No. 39, World Bank, Washington DC.

Buehler, Michael and Paige Johnson Tan (2007), 'Party–candidate relationships in Indonesian local politics: a case study of the 2005 regional elections in Gowa, South Sulawesi province', *Indonesia* 84(October): 1–30.

Clark, Samuel and Blair Palmer (2008),'Peaceful *pilkada*, dubious democracy: Aceh's post-conflict elections and their implications', Indonesian Social Development Paper No. 11, World Bank, Jakarta.

Collier, Paul, Anke Hoeffler and Måns Söderbom (2008), 'Post-conflict risks', *Journal of Peace Research* 45: 461–78.

CPCRS (Center for Peace and Conflict Resolution Studies) (2009), 'Aceh peace monitoring update March–June 2009', CPCRS, Syiah Kuala University, Banda Aceh, http://www.conflictanddevelopment.org/data/CPCRS/eng/Aceh%20Peace%20Monitoring%20Update%20March%20-%20June%202009.pdf.

Hidayat, Syarif (2009), '*Pilkada*, money politics and the dangers of "informal governance" practices', in M. Erb and P. Sulistiyanto (eds), *Deepening Democracy in Indonesia? Direct Elections for Local Leaders (Pilkada)*, Institute of Southeast Asian Studies, Singapore, pp. 125–46.

Palmer, Blair (2007), 'The price of peace', *Inside Indonesia* 90(October–December), http://www.insideindonesia.org/.

Ross, Michael L. (2005), 'Resources and rebellion in Aceh, Indonesia', in P. Collier and N. Sambanis (eds), *Understanding Civil War: Evidence and Analysis*, World Bank, Washington DC, pp. 35–58.

Sherlock, Stephen (2009), 'Indonesia's 2009 elections: the new electoral system and the competing parties', CDI Policy Papers on Political Governance 2009/01, Centre for Democratic Institutions, Canberra, March.

Smith, Claire Q. (2009), 'The return of the sultan? Patronage, power, and political machines in "post"-conflict North Maluku', in M. Erb and P. Sulistiyanto (eds), *Deepening Democracy in Indonesia? Direct Elections for Local Leaders (Pilkada)*, Institute of Southeast Asian Studies, Singapore, pp. 303–26.

Webber, Douglas (2006), 'A consolidated patrimonial democracy? Democratization in Post-Suharto Indonesia', *Democratization* 13(3): 396–420.

World Bank (2009), 'Aceh conflict monitoring update December 2008–February 2009', World Bank, Jakarta, http://www.conflictanddevelopment.org/data/doc/en/regCaseStudy/aceh/mon/Aceh%20Conflict%20Monitoring%20Update%20Dec08%20Feb09.pdf.

15 ELECTORAL POLITICS AND DEMOCRATIC FREEDOMS IN PAPUA

Richard Chauvel *

Indonesia's process of democratisation has been most problematic in those provinces where large parts of the population wanted to be independent of Indonesia. In East Timor, Papua and Aceh, local people took advantage of the democratic space that opened up after the end of the Suharto regime to press their demands for independence, leading in each province to renewed political tensions, violent conflict and government repression. The crises that resulted were resolved by independence for East Timor and a peace deal for Aceh. But no such resolution has taken place in Papua.[1]

Compared with other parts of Indonesia, Papua in some ways is caught in a democratic time warp. Certainly Indonesian security forces exercise a degree of control there that they no longer exercise elsewhere. Human rights abuses remain endemic in Papua and popular aspirations for independence are suppressed. But in other ways, democratisation has proceeded in Papua much as it has in other parts of Indonesia. Indeed, the results of the 2009 parliamentary and presidential elections have provided a reassuring picture of normalcy. The largest political parties — Golkar, the Democratic Party (Partai Demokrat, PD) and the Indonesian Democratic Party of Struggle (Partai Demokrasi Indonesia Perjuangan,

---

* This chapter draws on an earlier version of the article published in *Inside Indonesia* in 2008; see Chauvel (2008).
1 The Indonesian province of Papua was called Irian Jaya until 1999, when it was renamed Papua. In 2003 it was divided into the two provinces of Papua and West Papua (see Map 15.1). In this chapter I refer to the two provinces collectively as 'Papua' but distinguish between them where necessary.

Map 15.1 Papua

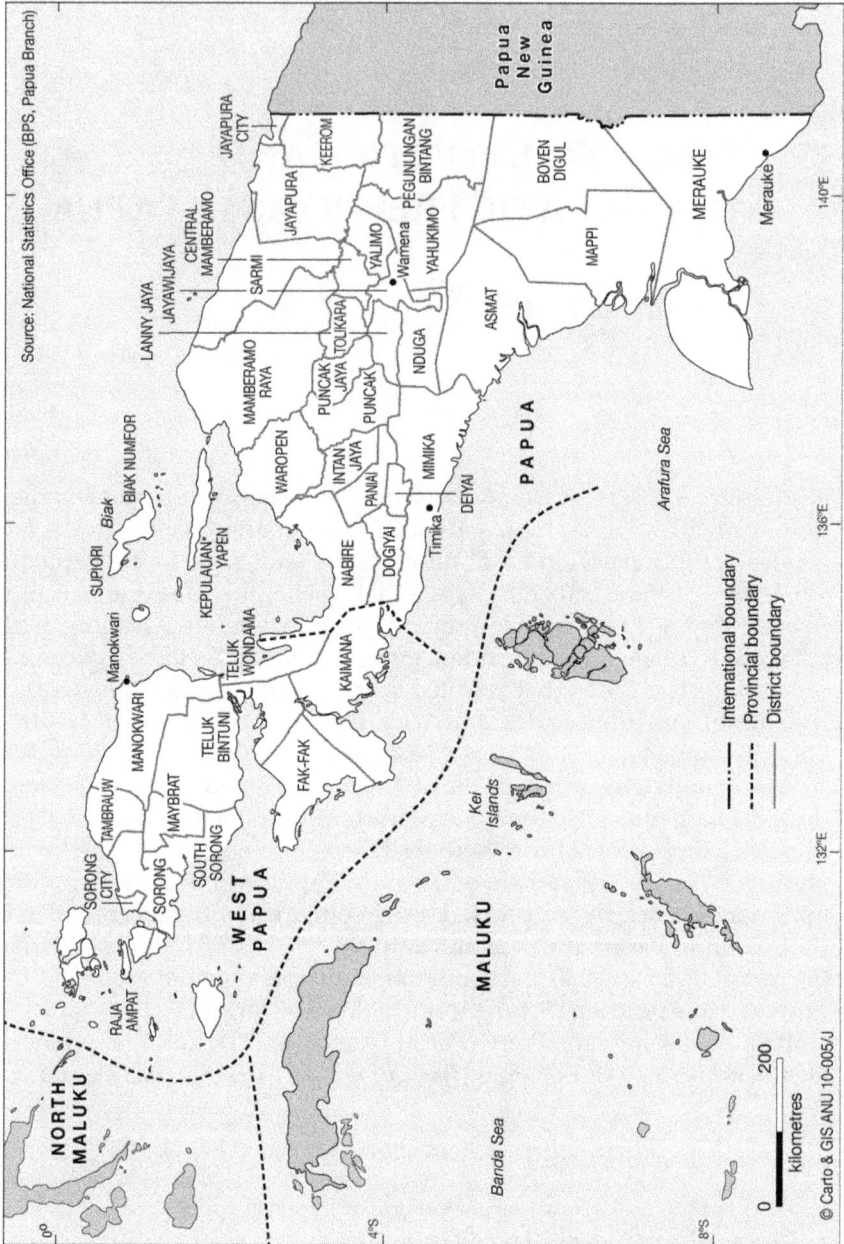

Source: National Statistics Office (BPS, Papua Branch)

© Carto & GIS ANU 10-005/J

308

PDIP) — are all committed to upholding the national integrity of the Indo-nesian state. Yet all did well in Papua in the national elections, and each is represented in Papuan legislatures at every level of government. The pattern of voting in Papua differed somewhat from that for Indonesia as a whole, but not as sharply as did South Sulawesi, Bali or Aceh. In the presidential election, Papuans supported the re-election of the nationally popular incumbent, Susilo Bambang Yudhoyono.

Can these two different pictures of Papua be reconciled? In this chapter I attempt to do so by arguing that there are two distinct realms of politics in Papua. The realm of Papuan nationalist politics is partly clandestine, partly public and tightly controlled. The realm of electoral politics, on the other hand, is open and highly competitive. The former is reminis-cent of the repression of the New Order regime rather than the ideals of Indonesia's reform era. The latter has many of the characteristics of elec-toral competition that have developed throughout Indonesia since the resignation of Suharto. The dynamics of these two political realms are quite different: the politics of Papuan nationalism is constructed within a 'Papua' versus 'Indonesia' dichotomy; electoral politics is about Papuans competing against other Papuans as well as against Indonesian settlers. The continuing existence of these two realms suggests that many of the ideals of the early *reformasi* period have not yet been realised in Papua. Even so, electoral politics and decentralisation have radically changed the nature of politics in Papua.

In this chapter, I develop my argument by way of several steps. In the first section I briefly review the politics of Papuan nationalism, pointing to the continuing suppression of nationalist sentiment and the restric-tions on freedom of expression and organisation that this entails. In the second section, I discuss the institutional arrangements that have shaped the realm of electoral politics in Papua in the *reformasi* era, including spe-cial autonomy and the creation of new districts. Next, I examine the ways in which electoral politics is changing the political landscape in Papua. I discuss, in turn, the direct elections for governors and district heads (sec-tion 3), the 2009 parliamentary and presidential elections (section 4) and the issue of indigenous Papuan representation (section 5).

Although government restrictions and suspicions about Papuan sep-aratism keep the two realms of politics apart, there are also instances of seepage where the concerns that motivate Papuan nationalism find expression in the electoral arena. One such example would be the issue of migration. Even so, elections in Papua have become an arena of demo-cratic competition in the midst of a wider political context that retains significantly undemocratic features.

THE FIRST REALM: PAPUAN NATIONALIST POLITICS

In the first years after Suharto's resignation in 1998, the public space in Papua was dominated by the articulation of demands for independence. In February 1999, a team of 100 Papuan leaders met with President B.J. Habibie to demand independence for the province. In 2000, Papuans focused their hopes for a quick transition to independence on two mass public gatherings. The second of these gatherings, the Papuan Congress (Kongres Papua), was partly funded by President Abdurrahman Wahid, the country's first democratically elected leader. In an expression of good-will towards Papuans, earlier in the year he had issued a decree changing the name of the province from Irian Jaya to Papua. In a highly symbolic gesture, he also gave permission for the Papuan Morning Star flag to be flown alongside the Indonesian flag. An Indonesian intelligence assessment prepared immediately after the Papuan Congress described the atmosphere throughout Papua as one of euphoria and enthusiasm for the idea of *merdeka* (independence).[2]

This 'Papuan Spring' was short-lived. The detention of five leaders of the pro-independence Papua Presidium Council (Presidium Dewan Papua, PDP) in late November 2000, the subsequent occupation of Jayapura by Indonesian troops and the clampdown on celebrations of Papuan 'Independence Day' on 1 December 2000 closed down the public politics of Papuan nationalism. The detention of the PDP leaders marked the culmination of a series of violent incidents created by the Indonesian security forces' determination to stop the public display of the Morning Star flag and other attributes of Papuan nationalism, the president's views on the subject notwithstanding. A year later, PDP leader Theys Eluay was assassinated by Special Forces soldiers. Although the government granted Papua special autonomy in 2001 under Law No. 21/2001 on Special Autonomy for Papua, it made it clear at the same time that it would not tolerate 'separatism'.

There were still occasional public outbursts of Papuan nationalism, such as flag-raising incidents and demonstrations. Yet the Indonesian authorities' heavy-handed responses to such incidents showed how restricted the realm of Papuan nationalist politics had become. In 2007, the national government issued a regulation banning the display of separatist symbols such as the Morning Star flag. This led in January 2008 to the detention of three Papuan women for selling handicrafts incor-

---

2 Nota dinas, Direktur Jenderal Kesbang dan Linmas, Ermaya Suradinata to Menteri dalam Negeri [Official memo, Director General of National Unity and Protection of Society, Ermaya Suradinata, to Minister of Home Affairs], 9 June 2000, 578/CD/Kesbang/D IV/VI/2000.

porating the flag on the streets of central Jayapura.³ Trials for political offenses, particularly rebellion (*makar*), remained relatively common in Papua even though they had almost died out in other parts of Indonesia. In October 2008, for example, Buchtar Tabuni was charged with rebellion after leading a demonstration in Jayapura to support the formation in London of an organisation called the International Parliamentarians for West Papua.⁴ The judges found Tabuni not guilty on this charge, because the demonstration, although anti-Indonesian, had been peaceful. However, he was sentenced to three years in jail on the lesser charge of provocation because he had used the terms 'autonomy' and 'referendum'. The presiding judge determined that:

> Such words can harm the sense of national unity and the unitary state of Indonesia, hamper development, defy laws and disturb peace among the heterogeneous peoples of Papua.⁵

In November 2009, Human Rights Watch (2009) estimated that more than 170 people were 'currently imprisoned throughout Indonesia for peaceful expression, particularly in Papua and the Moluccas, where there are separatist movements'.⁶ And while Buchtar Tabuni would be behind bars for a relatively short period, others received more severe punishments. Filip Karma and Yusak Pakage, for example, were found guilty of rebellion and sentenced to 15 years and 10 years in jail respectively after raising the Morning Star flag in December 2004.

The sloganeering the judges found offensive in the Tabuni case— 'Autonomy NO, Referendum YES'—was echoed in many other protests in Papua in the lead-up to the 2009 elections. For instance, on 10 March 2009, a month before the parliamentary elections, a crowd of several hundred pro-independence activists mobilised by the West Papua National Committee (Komite Nasional Papua Barat, KNPB) gathered in the grounds of the West Papua provincial parliament to listen to speeches under the watchful eyes of the security forces.⁷ The demonstrators' ban-

---

3 'Warga pegunungan tengah diminta patuhi PP No. 77/2007' [Central highlanders asked to obey Government Regulation No. 77/2007], *Cenderawasih Pos,* 21 January 2008.

4 In December 2008, this organisation issued a declaration recognising 'the inalienable right of the indigenous people of West Papua to self-determination'. See http://www.ipwp.org/.

5 'West Papua Indonesia put Buchtar Tabuni 3 years for using word referendum yes and autonomy no', *Suara Baptis Papua,* 8 July 2009.

6 In 2007 Human Rights Watch (2007: 5) found that at least 18 people had been arrested and imprisoned in Papua while campaigning peacefully for self-determination.

7 Estimates of the size of the crowd varied from several hundred to 2,500.

ners carried slogans such as 'Elections are not the solution to Papua's problems' and 'Independence YES, Elections NO'.

The speakers were equally critical of the parties and the candidates competing in the elections. One told the demonstrators:

> Your future will be determined, not by the Papuan People's Assembly [MRP], the provincial parliament [DPRD] or the 2009 elections, but by when Indonesia and its forces leave West Papua. ... Don't let the 2009 elections become an opportunity for the candidates' political rhetoric to deceive the people of West Papua.[8]

Another speaker told the crowd that the politicians elected to the Papuan People's Representative Council (Dewan Perwakilan Rakyat Papua, DPRP) in 2009 would not be able to protect the rights of Papuans to basic services such as education and health so long as large numbers of police and military remained deployed in the province.[9]

Clearly aware that there were two distinct spheres of politics in Papua, the demonstrators opted to reject outright elections and the special autonomy policies that underpinned them. In similar fashion, Papua's internet salons featured remarkably little discussion of the elections and the key issues being fought out between the parties and their candidates. Much of the discussion on the Yahoo site Komunitas Masyarakat Papua (Papuan People's Community), for example, focused on the usual fare of Papuan nationalist politics: human rights abuses, the activities of the Indonesian security forces, the latest stories about the Freeport mine, the prospects for 'dialogue' with Jakarta, and the activities of the Free Papua Movement (Organisasi Papua Merdeka, OPM) and the international pro-independence organisations.

It should be clear from the preceding discussion that, in arguing that the public realm of Papuan nationalist politics has been closed down, I am not suggesting that political sentiment has changed significantly since the heady days of the Papuan Congress. Indeed, the factors that have fuelled Papuan nationalism — mass migration, economic marginalisation and the brutal behaviour of the security forces — remain part of the Papuan experience of Indonesian rule. What *has* changed is that Papuan protestors and nationalists now have more than the central government and the security forces to contend with. There is, in addition, a new stra-

---

8 'Demo KNPB minta referendum: juga serukan boikot pemilu' [KNPB demonstrators demand a referendum: also urge an election boycott], *Cenderawasih Pos*, 11 March 2009.

9 'Ribuan massa KNPB duduki DPRP, tolak pemilu 2009 dan tuntut referendum' [Thousands of KNPB supporters occupy the provincial parliament, reject the 2009 elections and demand a referendum], *WPToday*, 11 March 2009.

tum of Papuan bureaucrats and politicians—some of them with nation-alist aspirations—who have entered the realm of electoral politics to achieve advancement for themselves and their policy agendas. There is a disconnect between the two realms of politics, but they are also related to one another.

THE SECOND REALM: ELECTORAL POLITICS IN PAPUA

The second realm of politics in Papua is defined by elite and bureaucratic competition for control of government positions and resources. In this realm, the 2001 Special Autonomy Law, the establishment of new district governments in a process known as *pemekaran* and the introduction in 2005 of direct elections for local executive positions have all shaped the political and institutional framework.

Special autonomy has been the focus of intense debate since its inception. But widespread Papuan disenchantment notwithstanding, the Special Autonomy Law has profoundly changed Papua and shaped its politics and administration. Indonesia's upper house, the People's Consultative Assembly (Majelis Permusyawaratan Rakyat, MPR), first enshrined special autonomy as a policy goal for some provinces in 1999. The MPR linked the granting of special autonomy to the objective of strengthening Indonesia's national integrity within the unitary state. After the Papuan Congress, the parliament instructed Abdurrahman Wahid to take decisive action against separatism in Papua (and Aceh) and to implement special autonomy. During the brief Papuan Spring, the Papuan advocates of special autonomy found it difficult to compete against those who were promising independence. Few Papuans were interested in such a compromise when full independence seemed achiev-able. However, following the detention of some PDP leaders and the ces-sation of negotiations with those still at liberty, special autonomy became more attractive.

The team of negotiators appointed by Governor J.P. Solossa to talk to Jakarta achieved what appeared to be, by the standards of post-independence Indonesia, a generous autonomy package for Papua. The 2001 Special Autonomy Law gave Papua significantly more govern-ment revenue and decision-making authority than other provinces had received under the nationwide regional autonomy laws of 1999. The law stipulated that the governor and deputy governor of the province should be ethnic Papuans, and provided for an exclusively indigenous upper house—the Papuan People's Assembly (Majelis Rakyat Papua, MRP)—charged with protecting Papuan values and interests. Not every-thing Solossa's team proposed in their various drafts of the law was accepted, but the negotiations with the Indonesian parliament neverthe-less instilled a strong sense of ownership of the law, broadly felt across the bureaucratic and political elites in Jayapura.

Given this history, it is not surprising that the Special Autonomy Law has dominated political discourse among Papuans since it was first proposed. Solossa's successor as governor of Papua, Barnabas Suebu, made special autonomy the basis of his election campaign in 2006. He argued that special autonomy gave Papuans unprecedented authority to develop a 'new Papua'.[10] Arguing in 2007 against the celebration of Papuan Independence Day, he asserted that:

> Under special autonomy within the framework of the Unitary Republic of Indonesia, Papua is able to govern itself. I use 'Papuan freedom' here to mean the freedom of self-government. Papuans have become the rulers of their own country through special autonomy, because it is all contained in the Special Autonomy Law.[11]

Not all Papuans agreed with Suebu's views. In August 2005 the Papuan Customary Law Council (Dewan Adat Papua)[12] delivered a cof-fin to the central government to make the symbolic point that the Special Autonomy Law had not been effective or properly implemented.[13] In April 2007 student protesters in Jayapura argued that:

> Access to education and health services in the interior is still very limited. Employment opportunities are very narrow. Income is low, with many Papuans living in poverty despite the fact that Rp 9 trillion [about $1 billion] has been allocated to Papua under special autonomy. Thus, we conclude that, for the six years special autonomy has operated, it has failed.[14]

Others, such as Socratez Sofyan Yoman of the Baptist Church, have criti-cised the special autonomy arrangements for failing to curb military and intelligence operations in the province.

---

10 'Visi dan misi gubernur provinsi Papua', (Vision and mission of the governor of Papua province) http://web.papua.go.id/content.php/id/9.

11 'Pemerintah larang peringatan 1 Desember di Papua' [Government bans 1 December anniversary], *Suara Pembaruan*, 29 November 2007.

12 The Papuan Customary Law Council (Dewan Adat Papua) represents tra-ditional (*adat*) communities in Papua. It has a strong political dimension because many of its leaders were prominent in the PDP.

13 'Minta perhatian pemerintah pusat: ribuan warga Papua turun ke jalan' [Demanding the attention of the central government: thousands of Papuans take to the streets], *Kompas*, 12 August 2005.

14 'Minta dialog nasional: melihat otsus gagal, ratusan massa demo' [Demand for national dialogue: viewing special autonomy as a failure, hundreds dem-onstrate], *Cenderawasih Pos*, 28 April 2007.

Although special autonomy did not satisfy the supporters of independence, in retrospect the greatest threat to it as a policy framework to resolve the conflict in Papua came from sections of the Indonesian government, not the sceptics in Papua. Figures within the Ministry of Home Affairs, the military and the intelligence agencies considered the law too generous to Papuan interests, fearing that it would empower a Jayapura-based Papuan elite and pose a threat to national unity (Chauvel and Bhakti 2004: 36–40). To break the symbolic nexus between the name of the province ('Papua'), the Morning Star flag and Papuan nationalism, they advocated the partition of Papua into three provinces.

In January 2003, President Megawati Sukarnoputri was persuaded to issue a presidential instruction dividing Papua into three provinces: Papua, West Irian Jaya (later renamed West Papua) and Central Irian Jaya. The new province of West Papua was created in the western part of Papua with its capital in Manokwari, but Megawati's attempts to establish Central Irian Jaya had to be abandoned in the face of riots in its proposed capital, Timika. However, subsequent proposals to establish three new provinces—South Papua, Southwest Papua and Central Papua—have found support in the respective regions as well as in the national parliament. In January 2008, draft legislation was initiated in the parliament to establish these provinces.

Megawati's presidential instruction also created three new districts and one municipality—the districts of Paniai, Mimika and Puncak Jaya and the city of Sorong. Since then 24 more districts have been created, giving a grand total for Papua and West Papua of 40 districts and municipalities, and more than tripling the number of local governments since the Special Autonomy Law was introduced. While the number of district governments throughout Indonesia has also increased in the post-Suharto period, from 344 to approximately 500, the trend has been much more pronounced in Papua and the impact on governance more significant.

Megawati's presidential instruction and the subsequent proposals to create new provinces in Papua have been the focus of conflict between the central government, the provincial government in Jayapura and other Papuan politicians. Much of the debate touches on the nature and extent of autonomy as enacted under the Special Autonomy Law—specifically whether the relevant provisions of the law mean what they say and it is up to Papuans to decide whether they want new districts and provinces; or alternatively, whether the central government retains the power to determine provincial and district government structures in Papua.

Jakarta's unilateral creation of the province of West Papua in 2003 has done much to undermine the goodwill and trust created by the negotiation and enactment of the Special Autonomy Law. However, it would be misleading to suggest that the proliferation of districts and the proposals for new provinces have simply been a consequence of the central government's divide-and-rule policies. Some Papuan politicians also have an interest in territorial fragmentation. The proliferation of local governments has created new arenas of political competition for government positions and access to government resources (which have increased greatly under special autonomy). In the 2009 parliamentary elections there was spirited competition for seats in the 40 district and two provincial legislatures. Thus, while the realm of Papuan nationalist politics is marked by the closure and even suppression of debate, the second realm of official politics has seen considerable competition, participation and even 'Papuanisation'.[15]

DIRECT LOCAL ELECTIONS AND THE 'PAPUANISATION' OF POLITICS

Electoral politics has created a new sphere of political competition in Papua, as elsewhere in Indonesia. This has led in turn to an increase in the number of Papuans in local executive governments and legislatures, although, as will be discussed later, the level of Papuan representation became an issue in the 2009 parliamentary elections. As noted earlier, under the Special Autonomy Law all members of the MRP as well as provincial governors and deputy governors must be indigenous Papuans. At present the heads of all district administrations are also Papuan, although some of their deputies are Indonesian settlers. The governors of the two extant provinces and the district heads of all but the most recently created districts were elected directly. Most are from the districts they govern. Space does not permit detailed consideration of all of the direct elections for local government heads that have been conducted in Papua since 2006. However, analysis of a sample should illustrate some of the main shifts in the political and demographic balance of power that these elections have produced, and give some insight into the interaction between the two realms of Papuan politics.

The 2006 elections for the position of governor in the two Papuan provinces were the most significant in shaping electoral politics in Papua. The decision to hold gubernatorial elections in West Papua — the first for

---

15 In contrast to the 'Papuanisation' and localisation of the *elected* political leadership in district governments, the reverse pattern is evident among government officials. The main reason is that there are insufficient numbers of qualified indigenous Papuans to fill these posts. The International Crisis Group has estimated that about 85 per cent of officials in some new districts are non-Papuans (ICG 2008: 13).

the province — demonstrated the determination of the Yudhoyono government to support the establishment of the province, the opposition of much of the Papuan elite notwithstanding. Megawati had appointed retired marine brigadier general Abraham Atururi as acting governor of the province when it was first established, and he became the candidate of her political party, PDIP. He had also previously served as a deputy governor of Papua. Yorris Raweyai also put his name forward. He has been one of the few PDP leaders to venture into electoral politics. The son of a Chinese doctor and a Papuan woman from Serui, Yorris had a mixed, even contradictory, political heritage. Before becoming involved in the pro-independence movement, he had been a deputy leader of Suharto's infamous youth-cum-gangster group, Pancasila Youth (Pemuda Pancasila). In 2004 he was elected to the national parliament — the People's Representative Council (Dewan Perwakilan Rakyat, DPR) — where he represented Papua (not West Papua) on behalf of Golkar. The third candidate was Dortheis 'Decky' Asmuruf, a former secretary of the provincial government in Jayapura. He was the only candidate from the province itself but had spent many years working as a senior bureaucrat in Jayapura.

Although it was the central government's intention with the establishment of the new province to undermine the power of the Jayapura-based Papuan elite, ironically, in the election for governor of West Papua, it turned out that all three candidates had pursued their political careers in Jayapura. Atururi was elected governor with a substantial majority.[16] The strong electoral support for Atururi gave the province greater legitimacy in the face of opposition from much of the Papuan elite. Subsequently, however, Atururi did little to develop West Papua's administrative capacity and faces a campaign led by 'Decky' Asmuruf to create a breakaway province of Southwest Papua.

In the province of Papua, Barnabas Suebu was the best known of the candidates running in 2006. He ran on the PDIP ticket despite having a long association with Golkar. Suebu had been a governor of Papua during the New Order period and had served as Indonesia's ambassador to Mexico, Honduras and Panama. As noted earlier, he had been a persuasive advocate of special autonomy, and he made the need for more effective implementation of the special autonomy arrangements the basis of his campaign. However, Suebu's candidature posed something of a dilemma for the government in Jakarta. On the one hand, the gov-

---

16 'Bram-Katjong tak terkejar di IJB: Yorrys: ada konspirasi KPUD menangkan kandidat tertentu' [Bram Katjong unassailable in West Irian Jaya: Yorrys: there is a conspiracy against certain candidates in the Regional General Elections Commission], *Cenderawasih Pos*, 13 March 2006.

ernment needed somebody like Suebu as governor if special autonomy was to have any credibility in Papuan eyes. But on the other hand, he was just the sort of politician that some in the government did not want to empower, because he was suspected of harbouring pro-independence sentiments. In an intelligence document produced in mid-2000 following the Papuan Congress, then-ambassador Suebu was listed alongside public advocates of independence and members of the Papuan elite as a member of the 'overseas elite' who supported Papuan independence.[17]

Although Suebu was a longstanding member of Golkar, the party nominated John Ibo, the head of the provincial parliament, as its candidate. Like Suebu, Ibo was from Sentani on the outskirts of Jayapura, and he too was suspected of harbouring pro-independence sentiments. After the military and police commanders in Papua questioned his loyalty, Ibo was obliged to perform various gymnastics to placate them, such as running full-page advertisements in the Jayapura press proclaiming his loyalty to the Indonesian state (Mietzner 2007: 17). The other candidates were Constant Karma and Henk Wabiser, both from the island of Biak, and Lukas Enembe from the central highlands. Karma had been Solossa's deputy governor and the head of the Committee to Combat AIDS. A veterinary scientist by training, he had previously worked as a senior provincial government official. Wabiser was a former navy commander for Papua and Maluku whose name had been put forward as a possible contender for the position of governor in the proposed new province of Central Irian Jaya.[18]

Most of the candidates were well-established members of the Jayapura political elite. Yet the elections also pointed to an important new development in Papuan politics: the rise of the highlanders. Despite the fact that the majority of the Papuan population lives in the highlands, no highlander has been elected governor. But elections give political meaning to demographic realities, and several highlanders stood for election. Lukas Enembe was the only highland candidate in the first direct elections for governor. He was the deputy head of a remote highland district—Puncak Jaya—and he campaigned as a 'traditional' highland leader (Mietzner 2007: 13). In addition, three of the candidates for deputy governor—Paskalis Kossay, Donatus Mote and Alex Hessegem—

---

17 Nota dinas, Direktur Jenderal Kesbang dan Linmas, Ermaya Suradinata to Menteri dalam Negeri [Official memo, Director General of National Unity and Protection of Society, Ermaya Suradinata, to Minister of Home Affairs], 9 June 2000, 578/CD/kesbang/D IV/VI/2000.

18 'Nyaris terjadi bentrok massal antar kelompok pro pemakaran dan kontra pemekaran provinsi Papua Tengah di Biak' [Conflict close between supporters and opponents of Central Papua province in Baik], *Elsham News Service*, Sabtu, 17 April 2004.

were highlanders. Suebu won the election by a margin of 31.4 per cent to Enembe's 29.6 per cent. That Suebu won was not a surprise, but that he won by such a small margin against a relatively unknown candidate was. Suebu's narrow victory can be attributed to his standing in official politics, his ability to articulate Papuan aspirations and his choice of Alex Hessegem, a well-known highlander, as his running mate.

Placed in a longer historical framework, the election results suggest a shift in the regional composition of political leadership in Papua from the coastal areas and islands to the highlands. In a survey conducted in 1962, Paul van der Veur (1964: 429–30) found that students were best represented in the secondary school population in areas that had had the longest contact with the colonial administration and missionaries — namely the coastal areas and off-shore islands. This pattern continued over subsequent decades. There were no highlanders among the 1950s' and 1960s' generation of Papuan nationalists, nor did many highlanders become public servants or otherwise integrate themselves into the narrow Papuan political elite that worked with the Indonesian government from the 1960s onward. The marginalisation of highlanders from official politics, whether government or opposition, was a trend that lasted to the end of the New Order and beyond. With the exception of Tom Beanal, the pro-independence leaders who emerged after the fall of Suharto were politicians from coastal areas.

Yet not only are the highlands Papua's demographic heartland, but they have also been a site of considerable political discontent. Many of the most enthusiastic supporters of the armed secessionist OPM movement live in remote highland districts, and much of the bitterest violence of the Suharto and post-Suharto periods has taken place there. During the Papuan Spring, highlanders began to make an impact on the public politics of Papuan nationalism. Highlanders, particularly from around Wamena in Jayawijaya district, made a strong impression at the Papuan Congress in mid-2000. One of them told the congress:

> I was born naked and brought up naked. I walked here from the highlands to the coast. Some of you came by planes and boats. I walked on my own two feet. I just want independence (Worth 2003).

The 2006 elections marked the beginning of the entry of the highlanders into official politics. Highlanders like Lukas Enembe, Paskalis Kossay, Donatus Mote and Alex Hessegem came from regions that had experienced their first contact with missionaries and government officials only in the final years of the Dutch administration.

It is not surprising, therefore, that some of the most significant electoral contests for the position of district head were fought out in remote highland areas of Papua where the interplay between Papuan nationalism and electoral politics has been most overt. In 2007, for example, Lukas Enembe was elected district head of Puncak Jaya in the central highlands after defeating Elieser Renmaur, the incumbent district head and a Kei Islander. Renmaur was the last of the non-Papuan district heads to lose his position. The electoral campaign became intertwined with a struggle between the security forces and the OPM when Renmaur attempted to mobilise support from a seemingly unlikely source: Guliat Tabuni, a local OPM leader. A Special Forces report asserts that Renmaur held meetings in early October with OPM members, who pledged their support for his candidature.[19] In June 2006, Guliat Tabuni had also sent a letter to the chair of the MRP in Jayapura asking for Renmaur to be reappointed as district head. Written in formal bureaucratic Indonesian on what purported to be OPM letterhead marked with the insignia of the 'Revolutionary Provisional Government of the Republic of West Papua', the letter stated that the OPM supported Renmaur because Papuan leaders in Puncak Jaya were not committed to serving the people and were corrupt:

> They eat in Mulia [the capital of Puncak Jaya], take their afternoon nap in Jayapura and sleep in Jakarta.[20]

The OPM's support for Renmaur was not sufficient to deny Lukas Enembe victory, however.

The neighbouring district of Jayawijaya, with its capital in Wamena, has been a centre of conflict between pro-independence activists and security forces in the post-Suharto era. In 1999 David Hubi was elected district head of Jayawijaya, marking the first time a local politician had been elected to this position: in the early Indonesian period, two of Jayawijaya's district heads had been from Biak; in the later New Order period, all were non-Papuans. Hubi was later convicted of corruption, and his successor, Nicolas Jigibalom, and members of the Jayawijaya district parliament have also been investigated for corruption. Despite this chequered record, political competition continues to be fought out between local politicians. In the 2008 elections for district head, John Wempi Wetipo defeated Jigibalom. Like his two predecessors, he was a local. However, reflecting local rivalries, each of the three district heads

---

19 Henri Mahyudi, Infantry Captain, Kopassus, Post 7, Mulia, 'Kronologis aksi anarkhis massa penerima bantuan dana kompensasi BBM atau BLT di distrik Mulia kabupaten Puncak Jaya' [Chronology of the anarchist actions of recipients of BBM and BLT compensation payments in Mulia in the district of Puncak Jaya], Special Report, R/01/LAPSUS/X/2006, 15 October 2006: 4.

20 Letter, Gen. Goliath Tabuni and Gen. Negoobet Tabinu to the chair of the MRP, 9 June 2006, 201/TPN-OPM/PB/III/2006.

since 1999 has come from a different ethnic group and region within Jayawijaya.

The examples cited above suggest that special autonomy, the proliferation of new district governments and direct elections have brought about at least three key changes in the pattern of politics in Papua. First, politics is no longer the sole preserve of Jayapura. The devolution of authority and revenue to the districts has made the control of district governments a focus of political contestation. The career of Lukas Enembe shows that even politicians who are not part of the Jayapura elite can build a base in district government from which to launch a provincial political career. There are other examples. John Gluba Gebze, for instance, has used his position as head of the district of Merauke as a base to campaign for the establishment of a new province of South Papua.

Second, unlike in the realm of Papuan nationalist politics, electoral politics involves political competition among Papuans, and between Papuans and Indonesian settlers. The Special Autonomy Law prevents non-indigenous Papuans from running for governor, but no such restrictions apply to district heads. In the direct elections held thus far, only local Papuan politicians have succeeded in being elected district head, although Indonesian settlers and non-local Papuans have been elected to the position of deputy head. In the competitions between indigenous Papuan candidates, it appears that local ethnic and tribal identities have been more important than the policies of the political parties the candidates formally represent. Indeed, the churches in Papua have expressed concerns that direct elections may exacerbate local ethnic and religious tensions.[21]

Third, electoral politics has facilitated a shift in the balance of power from coastal Papuans to highlanders. The rising political power of the highlanders was confirmed by the 2009 local legislative elections, which saw twice as many highlanders as members from coastal areas elected to the provincial parliament in Jayapura. This represented a major shift from the parliament elected in 2004.[22] In the national legislative elections, Paskalis Kossay—a Golkar politician from the Baliem valley in the central highlands, a former deputy head of the provincial parliament and an

---

21 'Forum Persekutuan Gereja di Papua khawatir pilkada berujung konflik' [Forum of the Association of Churches in Papua concerned that direct elections for district heads will incite conflict], *Suara Pembaruan*, 11 June 2005.

22 'Didominasi wajah baru: anggota DPRP terpilih resmi ditetapkan' [Dominated by newcomers: members of Papuan provincial parliament officially determined], Office of National Unity, Ministry of Home Affairs, Papua Office, 10 September 2009; '49 anggota DPRD Papua dilantik hari ini: sementara 7 orang yang bermasalah tak bisa dilantik' [49 members of the Papua provincial parliament installed today: in the meantime, 7 people who face problems can't be installed], *Cenderawasih Pos*, 8 October 2004.

unsuccessful candidate for deputy governor — received more votes than any other member elected to represent Papua, and about three times as many as Yorris Raweyai and former minister Freddy Numberi, both coastal Papuans.[23]

The electoral success of highland Papuans has been all the more notable given highlanders' prominent participation in the post-Suharto renaissance of Papuan nationalism. The central highlands remain a region of conflict between Indonesian security forces and local Papuan communities, and the nature of Indonesian governance has turned many highlanders into nationalists.

THE 2009 LEGISLATIVE AND PRESIDENTIAL ELECTIONS

As noted at the outset, in many respects the results for Papua in the 2009 national elections were similar to Indonesia-wide patterns. Papua strongly supported the re-election of Yudhoyono. In both Papuan provinces the Yudhoyono–Boediono ticket received 74 per cent of the vote, well above the nationwide figure of 61 per cent. Golkar candidate Jusuf Kalla also did better in Papua (20 per cent) and West Papua (16 per cent) than in Indonesia as a whole (12 per cent), perhaps reflecting the presence in both provinces of significant numbers of migrants from Kalla's home province, South Sulawesi. Megawati's divide-and-rule policies as president and the record of human rights abuses in Papua of her running mate, former general Prabowo Subianto, may help explain why the Megawati–Prabowo ticket attracted only 6 per cent of the vote in Papua, less than a quarter of its vote nationwide, and a marginally better 10 per cent in West Papua.

Despite the success of the Yudhoyono–Boediono ticket in the presidential election, Yudhoyono's party, PD, did not attract the same level of support. Voters in the province of Papua elected three members each from Golkar and PD, while the province of West Papua sent two Golkar members and one PD member to Jakarta. The new electoral threshold of 2.5 per cent that was required for parties to be allocated seats in the national parliament functioned to consolidate party representation, with only six parties securing the seats in the DPR reserved for Papua and West Papua, and only Golkar and PD securing more than one seat. The

---

23 KPU, daftar terpilih anggota Dewan Perwakilan Rakyat pemilihan umum tahun 2009, daerah pilihan: Papua [General Elections Commission, list of elected members of the House of Representatives, 2009 general election for the electoral district of Papua].

relative strength of Golkar is a pattern that both Papuan provinces share with many other parts of eastern Indonesia.

By contrast, the pattern of party representation at the provincial and district levels (where there is no electoral threshold) was one of extreme fragmentation. Golkar remained the largest party in the Papuan and West Papuan provincial parliaments, and in most district and municipal legislatures. Only in three districts, Nabire, Boven Digul and Puncak Jaya, did PD secure the largest number of seats.[24] Political party representation was quite fragmented in the provincial parliament in Jayapura, with 14 parties represented in a parliament of 56 members. In some district and municipal legislatures with half that number of seats, an even greater number of parties were represented in parliament, with the result that some legislatures had an average party representation of less than two members. In the district of Biak Numfor, for example, 15 parties were represented in a 25-member parliament, and the largest party, Golkar, had just five members.

A comparison of the provincial-level results for the three elections held between 1999 and 2009 shows a progressive increase in the fragmentation of party representation in the provincial parliament in Jayapura. In 1999 PDIP and Golkar were the dominant parties; by 2004 both had lost support, PDIP more dramatically than Golkar. This trend continued in 2009. Golkar remained the largest party in the provincial legislature but its support had declined significantly since 1999 and even 2004. The fall in support for PDIP in Papua has been more marked than the national decline in support for the party.

The fragmentation of party support at both the provincial and district levels raises the question of what party identity and loyalty mean in Papua. Apart from the contest for government positions, the political issues that most interest Papuans are not the ones that interest and distinguish the national political parties. Moreover, among the most senior Papuan politicians, there is considerable flexibility in party allegiance. The case of Barnabas Suebu has been noted: he was a long-time Golkar politician who became the successful PDIP candidate for the governorship of Papua in 2006. Nevertheless, in the 2009 elections Suebu's authority and popularity as governor did not benefit PDIP, whose support in Papua continued to decline. Lukas Enembe is another Papuan politician whose allegiance to a national political party could be considered flex-

24 By this time the new district head of Puncak Jaya, Lukas Enembe, had also become the head of PD in Papua. He was thus able to deliver his district not only to PD in the legislative elections, but also to the Yudhoyono–Boediono ticket in the presidential vote with an incredible 98 per cent of the vote. See 'Di Puncak Jaya, SYB–Boediono raih 98 persen suara' [In Puncak Jaya, SBY–Boediono get 98 per cent of the vote], *Papua Pos*, 17 July 2009.

ible and pragmatic. In 2006 Enembe was nominated as a gubernatorial candidate by a small Christian party, the Prosperous Peace Party (Partai Damai Sejahtera, PDS). He campaigned for the governorship as a highland leader rather than as a candidate of a national political party. In 2007, he became district head in Puncak Jaya after being nominated by Golkar. By 2009 he was also the head of PD in Papua. The fragmentation of political party representation in Papua's legislatures suggests that, for the candidates, party allegiance is a matter of short-term pragmatism and a product of the legal requirement that candidates must be nominated by a national party.

INDIGENOUS PAPUAN REPRESENTATION

If political party loyalties were only a weak factor in the 2009 elections, one issue that was very important was the level of representation of 'indigenous' Papuans. Papuan nationalists have long decried the high levels of migration from other parts of the Indonesian archipelago, fearing that this would eventually marginalise indigenous Papuans. In the electoral competition of 2009, the key demographic reality that Indonesian settlers now made up about 35 per cent of the Papuan population could not be ignored — and raised difficult political questions. Under the Special Autonomy Law only Papuans could be elected governor or deputy governor,[25] and as we have seen, Papuans have been very successful in the elections for district heads despite the lack of such a provision. However, in the elections for legislatures at all levels of administration, ethnic Papuan politicians faced much stiffer competition from both Indonesian settler candidates and other Papuans.

It was evident from the campaign posters and banners adorning the streetscapes and buildings of Jayapura in February 2009 that many of the candidates were Indonesian settlers. In December 2008, the Constitutional Court had decided that parties that won seats in the legislative elections would be obliged to allocate them to the candidates with the largest number of votes rather than those placed highest on the parties' lists of candidates. This and the superior economic resources of settler candidates raised the prospect that the election would produce Papuan legislatures with greater settler representation.

---

25 For a discussion of the politics surrounding the 'Papuanness' of the candidates for governor, see Mietzner (2007: 9 ff.). It is worth noting that this provision of the Special Autonomy Law did not apply in West Papua. If it had, then of all the candidates running in 2006, only two, Asmuruf and Atururi, would have complied.

Agus Sumule (2009), a Papua-based academic and a key negotiator of the Special Autonomy Law, believed that Papuans might actually become a minority in the provincial parliament, an outcome that he argued would be contrary to the objectives of the Special Autonomy Law to support, protect and empower Papuans. He claimed that the candidate selection processes of the political parties, particularly the larger ones, discriminated against indigenous Papuans: in three of Papua's six electoral districts, a majority of the candidates nominated by the larger parties were Indonesian settlers; in electoral district 3 encompassing Merauke and Mappi in southern Papua, 73 per cent of the large parties' candidates were settlers;[26] and in the province as a whole, the large parties' candidates were nearly evenly split between Papuans and settlers. To address this problem, Sumule suggested reserving an additional 11 seats in the provincial parliament for Papuans, relying on article 28(3) of the Special Autonomy Law. He had the backing of the MRP, which appealed to Papuans to support their own candidates and to party leaders to promote Papuan candidates.[27]

Yet in the event the concerns about declining Papuan representation were not realised. In the elections for the provincial parliament in Jayapura, only one or two fewer Papuan members were elected in 2009 than in 2004. In the DPR, indigenous Papuan representation increased significantly. And in the less significant Regional Representative Council (Dewan Perwakilan Daerah, DPD) in Jakarta, it remained stable.

The pattern of Papuan representation in the district and municipal legislatures was much more diverse. In highland districts with strong majority Papuan populations, the new legislatures were dominated by indigenous Papuans. In Dogiyai and Puncak Jaya, no Indonesian settler candidate was elected; and in Pegunungan Bintang and Paniai only one and two settlers respectively were successful. In the city of Jayapura, where Indonesian settlers constitute over 60 per cent of the population, Papuans obtained a slim majority of seats in the municipal legislature.

---

26 Only one of the seven members elected from electoral district 3 was Papuan. See 'Didominasi wajah baru: anggota DPRP terpilih resmi ditetapkan' [Dominated by newcomers: members of Papuan provincial parliament officially determined], Office of National Unity, Ministry of Home Affairs, Papua Office, 10 September 2009.

27 'MRP rekomendasikan dukung caleg orang asli Papua' [MRP recommends support for indigenous Papuan candidates], *Tabloid Jubi,* 25 March 2009. The military commander in Sorong, Colonel Fransen G. Siahaan, responded by saying that the MRP's recommendation for Papuans to support Papuan candidates (as well as its support for a 30 per cent quota for female candidates) threatened national unity and might cause conflict. See 'Korem 171/PVT deteksi 7 ancaman serius' [Military commander detects 7 serious threats], *Fajar Papua,* 6 April 2009.

With the electoral district of Jayapura voting along similar lines in the provincial election, Jayapura sent John Ibo and Jan Ayoni, two of the most senior Papuan politicians, to the provincial parliament. In many areas, it seems that the change in the electoral rules in favour of individual candidates did not in fact advantage the better-resourced settler candidates, but rather candidates who could present themselves as representatives of the indigenous community.

Nevertheless, in some parts of Papua the level of representation of settlers in local legislatures did grow significantly. In Keerom district, the site of large-scale transmigration between Jayapura and the border with Papua New Guinea, about 70 per cent of the members of the new local legislature were settlers. In 2000 the late Michael Rumbiak, a Papuan demographer, had found that the local community was increasingly dominated by transmigrants, that Papuans were being displaced from their lands and that the local culture was being overwhelmed by Javanese culture (Rumbiak 2000: 7–9). It appears that the socio-economic and cultural changes he identified a decade ago now extend to the political sphere. At the western extremities of Papua in the Raja Ampat Islands and Sorong, longer-established patterns of migration were again reflected in local legislatures with slim Indonesian settler majorities.[28]

The issue of indigenous Papuan representation became a matter of debate and conflict in southern Papua following the parliamentary elections. Particularly in the new districts created from Merauke in 2003, the elections produced local legislatures with a greater preponderance of settler members than the region's demographic profile would suggest. In Merauke itself, a delegation of Papuan candidates lobbied the local election commission when the preliminary vote count indicated that many of the numerous Papuan candidates would not receive significant levels of support and the district legislature was likely to be dominated by settlers. 'We understand that our migrant colleagues have also worked hard to win seats', said the leader of the delegation, 'but it has to be understood that indigenous Papuans need to be given the opportunity to voice the interests of the local society'.[29] In the neighbouring district of Asmat, which split from Merauke in 2003, the response to the preliminary elec-

---

28 'FPCP tuntut pelantikan DPRD dibatalkan' [FPCP demands that the inauguration of the DPRD be cancelled], *Radar Sorong*, 26 September 2009; 'DPRD kabupaten resmi dilantik' [District DPRD officially inaugurated], *Radar Sorong*, 29 September 2009; 'Pelantikan DPRD R4 diwarnai aksi demo' [Inauguration of DPRD in Raja Ampat accompanied by demonstration], *Radar Sorong*, 28 October 2009.

29 'Caleg putra daerah "serbu" KPUD Merauke' [Local indigenous candidates 'attack' the Regional General Elections Commission in Merauke], *Papua Pos*, 16 April 2009. When the membership of the Merauke DPRD was announced

tion results was more violent. The office of the local election commission was damaged by protestors upset by reports that only six of the 20 members would be from the local community in a district where Papuans constituted a majority of the population.[30] In Boven Digul, another new district created from Merauke, it initially appeared that 16 of the 20 members of the new legislature would be settlers, although the official outcome in fact resulted in a smaller settler majority.[31]

Opponents of the proposal to establish a new province of South Papua argue that the creation of new districts from Merauke has already had the effect of marginalising indigenous Papuans and consolidating the dominance of settler communities. Creating a new province, they say, would only further this process.

CONCLUSION: ELECTORAL CHANGE AND LIMITED DEMOCRATIC FREEDOMS

This chapter has argued that there are two distinct realms of politics in Papua, kept apart by the security authorities. Parties and candidates are not permitted to discuss issues of Papuan nationalism during elections. Such issues impinge on the public space during election campaigns only when Papuans hold street demonstrations.

Yet the separation of these two distinct realms of politics has implications for the legitimacy and credibility of the political leadership in Papua. In the early years after Suharto's fall, the unelected pro-independence leadership led by Theys Eluay's PDP usurped the legitimacy of the elected provincial parliament. The PDP claimed that it had a 'mandate' from the Papuan people for its peaceful struggle for independence. But after the imprisonment of its leaders, the assassination of Eluay and the curtailment of the PDP's public activities, the pro-independence movement became fragmented. Of the senior PDP leaders, only Yorris Raweyai has ventured into electoral politics.

The elected Papuan politicians do not have to compete with their unelected pro-independence compatriots as directly as they did in the immediate post-Suharto years, but they are still constrained in how they can develop their credibility as leaders of Papuan society. They cannot

---

in August, there in fact turned out to be equal numbers of Papuan and settler members.

30 'Kota Asmat normal' [Town of Asmat normal], *MetroTVNews*, 27 May 2009.

31 'Tanah Muman jadi kabupaten, orang asli jadi kaum pinggiran!' [If the Land of Muman becomes a district, the indigenous people will be marginalised!], 28 September 2009, http://muman-net.blogspot.com/2009/09/tanah-muman-jadi-kabupaten-orang-asli.html.

engage publicly with their constituents on Papuan nationalist issues. Some, most notably Governor Suebu, have found a language in which to talk about Papuan political aspirations and values without crossing the ever-shifting boundary between the permissible and the proscribed. However, it is a muted and — for a Papuan politician — uncharacteristically indirect language that does not allow Suebu to grapple publicly with the concerns that animate many Papuans.

At the same time, the question of Papuan representation in the 2009 elections illustrates how one of the factors that has fuelled Papuan nationalism — mass migration and the demographic transformation that has engulfed Papua — is informing electoral politics. At the core of the 2001 Special Autonomy Law was the objective of protecting and enhancing Papuan values and interests. At the same time, it is elections that have been giving political meaning to demographic change. Decentralisation and the proliferation of local governments have increased the importance attached to local politics and enabled indigenous Papuan politicians to become local government leaders. But in the urban areas of Papua, in sites of major transmigration like Keerom, in the regions of older Indonesian settlement in western Papua and in the districts of southern Papua, Indonesian settlers are well represented in the local legislatures elected in 2009, and even better represented in the civil administrations of the new district governments.

Electoral politics has turned demographic change and the economic marginalisation of Papuans — matters that have long fuelled nationalist sentiment — into heated issues in the realm of open politics. This has the potential both to galvanise Papuans around issues of representation, the meaning of autonomy and the control of local governments as well as to channel the energies of Papuan politicians away from nationalist issues. The 2009 election results in the regions of Papua discussed in this chapter demonstrate that in many cases local Papuan politicians failed to secure control of their local legislatures. Special autonomy and electoral politics could become a great deal less attractive to members of the Papuan elite if competition with settler politicians becomes tougher and provincial and district boundaries are drawn in such a way as to create settler-dominated constituencies.

Indonesia has made significant progress towards democratisation since the fall of Suharto. With East Timor no longer part of Indonesia and Aceh relatively peaceful, Papua remains Indonesia's last remaining region of separatist conflict. While aspects of healthy electoral political competition have developed in Papua, discussion and political mobilisation around the issues that matter most to Papuans are deemed impermissible and are subject to legal sanctions. The two distinct realms of politics in Papua and the continuing restrictions on freedoms make Papua a singular exception to the Indonesian democratic norm.

REFERENCES

Chauvel, Richard (2008), 'Rulers in their own country?', *Inside Indonesia* 94(October–December), http://www.insideindonesia.org/.
Chauvel, Richard and Ikrar Nusa Bhakti (2004), 'The Papua conflict: Jakarta's perceptions and policies', Policy Studies No. 5, East West Center, Washington DC.
Human Rights Watch (2007), 'Protest and punishment: political prisoners in Papua', 20 February, http://www.hrw.org/en/reports/2007/02/20/protest-and-punishment-0.
Human Rights Watch (2009), 'Indonesia: release Papuan flag-raisers', 18 November, http://www.hrw.org/en/news/2009/11/18/indonesia-release-papuan-flag-raisers.
ICG (International Crisis Group) (2008), 'Indonesia: communal tensions in Papua', Asia Report No. 154, ICG, 16 June.
Mietzner, Marcus (2007), 'Local elections and autonomy in Papua and Aceh: mitigating or fueling secessionism?', *Indonesia* 84(October): 1–39.
Rumbiak, M.C. (2000), 'Migrasi spontan dan transmigrasi' [Spontaneous migration and transmigration], unpublished paper, Faculty of Economics, University of Cenderawasih, Jayapura.
Sumule, Agus (2009), 'Indigenous Papuans could become a minority in the Papuan Regional Representative Assembly (DPRP)', Tapol Election Update No. 6, April, http://tapol.gn.apc.org/elections/updates/Issue%206%20article%20final.pdf.
van der Veur, Paul (1964), 'Questionnaire survey among the potential Papuan elite in 1962 West New Guinea', *Bijdragen tot de Taal-, Land- en Volkenkunde*, 120(4): 424–60.
Worth, Mark (2003), *The Land of the Morning Star*, Film Australia/Australian Broadcasting Corporation production, broadcast on ABC TV on 2 February 2004.

16 THE NORMALISATION OF LOCAL POLITICS? WATCHING THE PRESIDENTIAL ELECTIONS IN MOROTAI, NORTH MALUKU

Sidney Jones

Ever since the introduction of democratic elections in 1999, observers have engaged in intense debate about the factors that motivate Indonesian voters when going to the ballot box. Some analysts believe that Indonesians are still primarily driven by their ethnic, religious, social or regional affiliations, as in the country's first democratic polls in 1955 (King 2003; Baswedan 2007). Others have emphasised the importance of 'money politics' in electoral behaviour. According to this view, Indonesians mostly vote for political patrons who offer them cash or other forms of material inducements, including jobs (Sulistyo 2002). But an increasing number of scholars contend that Indonesian voters are becoming more rational, critically evaluating politicians' leadership qualities, the performance of the incumbent government and the media advertisements presented during the campaign (see, for example, Mietzner 2009 and Mujani and Liddle in this volume). Obviously these highly divergent views on electoral behaviour have led to equally differing assessments of the state of Indonesia's democracy: while those who stress the significance of primordial attachments and material inducements generally see Indonesia as being at a very early stage of democratisation, the proponents of the view that the electorate is becoming more rational maintain that the country has made considerable progress.

Many of the studies mentioned above are based on national survey data or analyses of Jakarta-based newspapers and magazines. While this is a useful (and perhaps inevitable) approach to the regionally frag-

Map 16.1   North Maluku

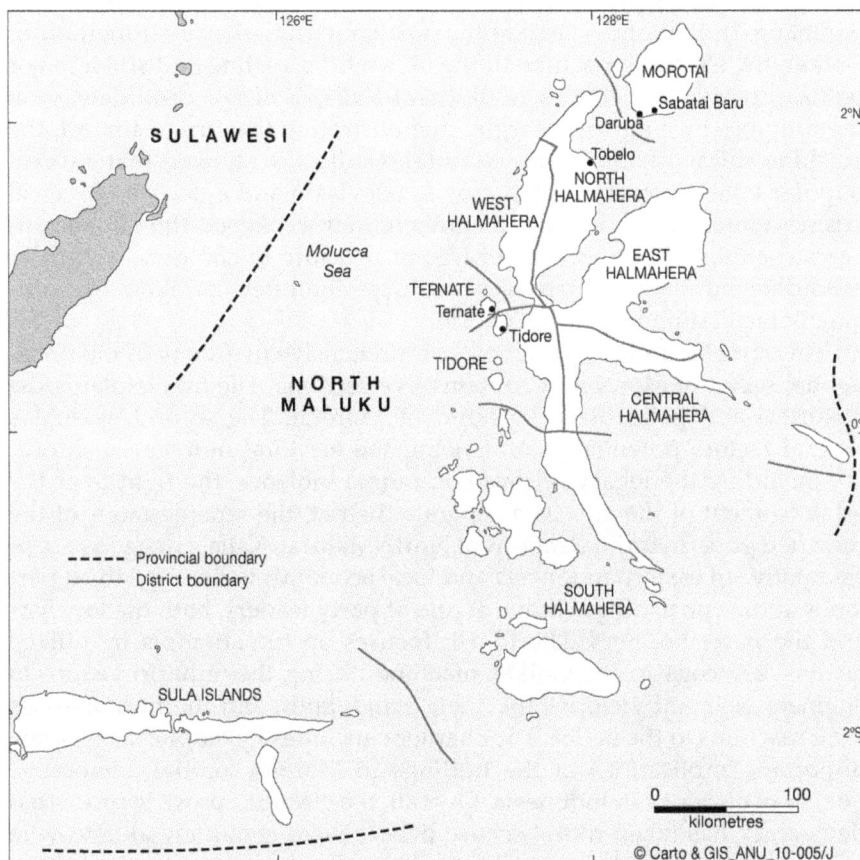

mented landscape of post-Suharto politics, it often misses nuances and details that only grassroots research can capture. Therefore, this chapter offers a local perspective on the 2009 presidential elections, evaluating from a close distance the key drivers of voting behaviour in one of Indonesia's most remote islands. The observations presented here on the elections in Morotai, an island off the north coast of Halmahera in North Maluku province (see Map 16.1), are not meant to establish more generalised claims about electoral patterns in other parts of Indonesia's vast archipelago. They do, however, present important insights into the workings of Indonesia's democracy in an area far off the journalistic and scholarly track.

The presidential elections in the district of Morotai were a quiet, orderly exercise in civic duty, marked more by a quiet cynicism that nothing would change than excitement over the candidates. Contrary to expectation, they produced a victory for incumbent president Susilo Bambang Yudhoyono — despite the area's reputation as a stronghold of Golkar, the electoral machine of the New Order regime and still a major political party since its downfall. Jusuf Kalla, Golkar's candidate, won the province by a narrow margin, demonstrating that, up to a point, the machine still worked. But the Morotai results also showed that a direct popular vote, a secret ballot, access to television and a decision by local business interests to back the incumbent had weakened the old patronage structures.[1] Voters were not free of pressure to choose a particular candidate, but the pressures were multiple and often contradictory, ultimately facilitating individual choice.

This chapter aims to provide a comprehensive overview of the presidential ballot in Morotai. It contains five sections. The first explains the historical and political background of Morotai. The second evaluates several factors potentially influencing the electoral outcome in Morotai, including the legacy of past communal violence, the fight over the establishment of the area as a separate district, the repercussions of the disputed gubernatorial elections of North Maluku, Kalla's image as a representative of eastern Indonesia and local economic issues. The third part looks at the (surprisingly limited) role of party leaders, both the loyalists and the party hoppers. The fourth focuses on the attempts by village heads — key cogs in the Golkar machine during the Suharto years — to engineer electoral victories for 'their' candidates, and the fifth assesses local reactions to the ballot. The chapter concludes by emphasising some important implications of the findings in Morotai for the democratic quality of elections in Indonesia. Overall, the elections provide proof that democracy has taken root, because people were genuinely able to vote in accordance with their conscience. Some locals, however, viewed the national elections as irrelevant; for them, the approaching district head elections of 2010 were much more important.

BACKGROUND: MOROTAI AFTER 1998

The district of Morotai, with a population approaching 60,000, is known chiefly for the role it played as a staging area for General Douglas MacArthur's campaign in the Philippines in 1944. Even in the eyes of its residents, the island's importance has declined ever since. (It was in Morotai that the last Japanese soldier stumbled out of the forest in 1974

---

1   Those structures were still alive and reasonably well in North Maluku in 2005, as described eloquently by Smith (2009).

to learn that the war was over.) Today, the old US airstrip is still used for twice-weekly flights, but most travellers fly into Ternate, take the ferry to the Halmahera mainland, take a three-hour trip overland to Tobelo on the northeast coast, and from there make the three-hour crossing by ferry to Daruba, Morotai's main town (see Map 16.1). Not surprisingly, the island's isolation from both regional and national hubs has had a major impact on how citizens of Morotai view Indonesia and the rest of the world.

In the three years preceding the 2009 elections, local politics in Morotai had been coloured by the island's push for separate status as a district (*kabupaten*). Until March 2009 it was part of the district of North Halmahera, which itself had broken off from Halmahera to become a separate district in 2003. This separation was part of the Indonesia-wide process of *pemekaran*, or administrative fragmentation, which has led to the creation of smaller and smaller units since 1998. While the splitting of territories was undertaken in the name of bringing government closer to the people, it has frequently been driven by a local elite's desire for a greater share of the political and economic pie. A well-financed campaign for Morotai's own district began in 2006, over the objections of the district head (*bupati*) of North Halmahera. Local notables argued that Morotai's potential for tourism — based on World War II nostalgia — and its strategic location facing Mindanao, warranted the division. The Indonesian parliament accepted the argument — as well as the emoluments that went with it — and in October 2008 passed a law making Morotai a district (Law No. 53/2008 on the Formation of the District of Morotai Island in North Maluku Province).[2] The Ministry of Home Affairs formally signed off on the new entity and appointed a caretaker district head in March 2009. However, because it was too late to set up a separate electoral administration for the legislative ballot in April and the presidential poll in July, Morotai participated in the elections as part of North Halmahera.

The politics of the *pemekaran* campaign added one more fault-line to the host of existing ones. The district head of North Halmahera was a Golkar politician of the old school, not afraid to twist arms. But he was also seen as having opposed Morotai's breakaway, and as a result his — and Golkar's — influence over Morotai's voters probably weakened.

---

2 The national parliament initially rejected the proposal to establish a separate district of Morotai on the grounds that a district, in this case North Halmahera, had to be in existence for seven years before undergoing further division (Government Regulation No. 78/2007). The law establishing the district of Morotai was eventually enacted on 31 October 2008 after legislators agreed to overlook this provision. For an archive of news articles pertaining to Morotai's creation, see http://roby-aemba.blogspot.com/.

Before the 2009 elections, the district had been considered a Golkar stronghold like most other places in the province. In the 2004 presidential election, it had voted for the Golkar candidate, General Wiranto, in the first round. Wiranto secured a significant 39.1 per cent of the vote province-wide, and it was only when there was no Golkar candidate in the second round that voters turned to Yudhoyono, giving him a 62.1 per cent victory. Thus, despite Golkar's lack of support for Morotai's establishment as a district, there was a general sense that Jusuf Kalla would win in Morotai in 2009, not only because he could use Golkar's tested campaign network but also because he was the only candidate from eastern Indonesia. Even the head of Yudhoyono's local campaign team suspected that primordial loyalties would remain paramount, negatively affecting the chances of his candidate.[3]

But while the party elites developed strategies to win the elections, many of those interviewed in Daruba and the surrounding subdistrict of South Morotai said they were just tired of voting. 'We're fed up with elections', said the wife of a local leader of the Democratic Party (Partai Demokrat, PD) when her husband was out of the room. 'It doesn't make a difference anyway.' Nevertheless, virtually every adult I encountered with access to a television had watched the presidential debates. In addition, the candidates' slogans were widely known and used, with many conversations punctuated by Yudhoyono's 'Lanjutkan!' (Continue!) or Kalla's 'Lebih cepat, lebih baik' (The faster, the better). On 8 July, most of the citizens of Morotai went to the ballot box because this was what was expected of them, but there was little sense of excitement. The results for Morotai and the subdistrict of South Morotai, as well as the district of North Halmahera and the province of North Maluku, are shown in Figure 16.1.

POTENTIAL FACTORS IN THE ELECTIONS

In the run-up to the elections, observers speculated about several factors that had the potential to influence the election in Morotai: the legacy of the communal conflict between Christians and Muslims across North Halmahera in 1999–2000; the politics surrounding the creation of Morotai as a district; residual bitterness from a provincial election dispute in North Maluku in 2007–2008; the appeal of Jusuf Kalla as the candidate from eastern Indonesia; and the desperate need of Morotai for economic development. In the following, I will evaluate the impact of each of these factors on the elections and their outcome.

---

3   Interview with Richard Samatara, Daruba, Morotai, 7 July 2009.

Figure 16.1   Results of the 2009 presidential election: North Maluku, North Halmahera, Morotai and South Morotai (%)

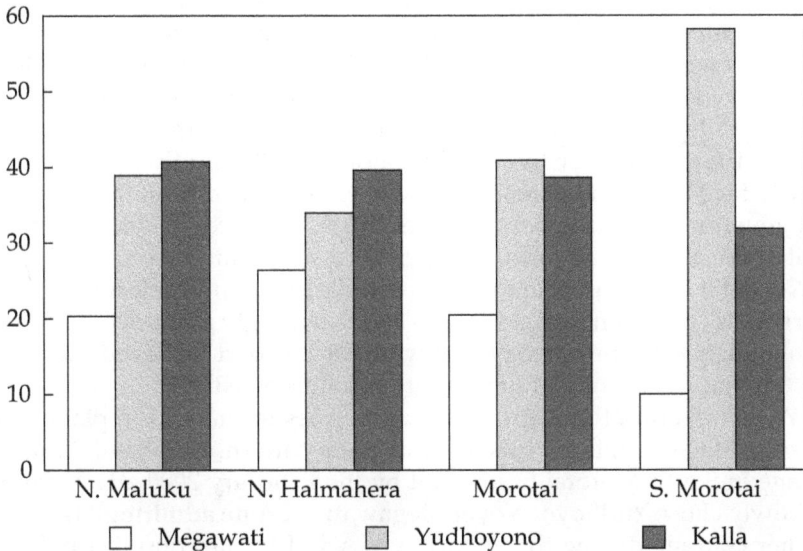

Source: General Elections Commission (Komisi Pemilihan Umum, KPU) website and local press sources.

Legacy of the conflict

On 28 December 1999, the worst single massacre of the Maluku conflict took place in Tobelo, North Maluku, when Christian villagers massacred some 500 Muslims, many of them migrants. The Tobelo massacre became a rallying cry for horrified Muslims both locally and nationally, and a series of attacks took place in retaliation.[4] One of these hit Morotai on 20 February 2000, when a group arriving by boat from Tobelo landed at Daruba and proceeded up the road, burning houses as they went. By that time most Christians had already taken shelter at the local airforce base or had fled to Tobelo; a few of the wealthier ones had made it to Manado. Some 60 homes were burned and in the village of Sabatai Baru 11 people died. One pastor estimated that only 20 per cent of the Christian population of South Morotai had returned by 2009.[5]

---

4   For a full discussion of the conflict in North Maluku and the Tobelo massacre in particular, see Wilson (2008).
5   Interview with Protestant pastor who asked for his/her name to be withheld, South Morotai, 6 July 2009.

The exodus of Christians solidified Muslim domination of Morotai's commercial centre in Daruba and left a legacy of tense relations among neighbours. Although communal relationships in North Maluku are based more on ethnicity than on faith,[6] many inhabitants of Morotai had charged memories of the conflict that influenced their voting behaviour. In Darame village, one extended Christian family whose home had been burned to the ground in 2000 and who had ended up living in a tent at the airforce base for five months alongside 3,000 other people, was solidly for Megawati because she had been the only official from the central government to take notice of their plight. As vice-president, she had visited the airport base once, in April 2004, and had made several visits to North Halmahera.[7] 'She's the only candidate comfortable mixing with Christians', one man said, adding as an afterthought that prices had been stable during her presidency. His wife, for her part, believed that Yudhoyono had surrounded himself with hardline Muslims.[8]

While several other Christian interviewees in the village planned to vote for Megawati, there was no systematic pattern. In Sabatai Baru, the village in South Morotai hardest hit by the February 2000 attack, voters narrowly chose Yudhoyono over Megawati. Despite admiring Megawati for her courage during the Suharto years and for her pluralist politico-ideological orientation, many voters apparently took a pragmatic stance. Megawati's chances of winning the presidency for a second time were seen as slim at best, whereas Yudhoyono's victory seemed all but certain. One pastor, who admitted that his sympathies lay with Megawati, said shortly before the election that he was going to vote for Yudhoyono: 'The train's already moving', he said. 'We might as well get on it.'

Politics of separation

The battle over the establishment of Morotai as a separate district was fresh in everyone's minds and may have influenced the choices of some voters. It had pitted politically ambitious businesspeople on Morotai, most but not all of them Muslim, against the district head of North Hal-

---

6 Many ethnic Galelan Christians are followers of the Islamist PKS. This is attributable to the influence of the Kasuba family, which has strong links to PKS but has both Muslim and Christian members. One member of the family holds the position of deputy governor of North Maluku and another the position of district head of South Halmahera.

7 'Pengungsi Maluku Utara takut minum susu bantuan wapres' [North Maluku's displaced persons afraid to drink milk provided by vice-president], 22 August 2000, http://www.astaga.com/Article/0,2124,29912,00.html.

8 Interviews with Darame villagers who asked for their names to be withheld, 4 July 2009.

mahera, Hein Namotemo, a Christian, who had no desire to see his territory diminished. The arguments for the split had nothing to do with religion and everything to do with what the business community and many others in Morotai saw as Tobelo's systematic neglect of the island's roads and ports. When North Halmahera had sought the approval of Jakarta to become its own district in 2003, it had won the national parliament's support by promising that a duty-free port similar to Batam would be developed on Morotai. This never happened, leading residents to conclude that the only way to improve the economy was for Morotai to break away from North Halmahera. Nevertheless, some Christian leaders on the island were concerned that they would be politically and economically marginalised if and when a new district administration was created, and they felt safer under Hein.[9]

Hein had resisted the separation from the start. The *pemekaran* movement began in August 2006 with five Morotai members of the North Halmahera district legislature, all from Golkar, making a formal request to the district head for separation. They then went to Jakarta to lobby for their cause, with funds they allocated to themselves out of the North Halmahera district budget. Abdul Gafur, the man who was later to be involved in the contested election for governor of North Maluku, was then a Golkar member of the national parliament (Dewan Perwakilan Rakyat, DPR). As a member of Committee II, the committee responsible, among other things, for local government and regional autonomy issues, he was able to help the team make useful contacts in Jakarta. Committee II agreed to Morotai's request, a move that convinced the provincial governor, Thaib Armaiyn, to give his endorsement as well.

On the ground in Morotai, fanatic supporters of the split sealed off subdistrict government offices from late February to April 2007, demanding that the new district be established immediately.[10] By 2008, the only obstacle left was Hein Namotemo, who called in the five legislators and threatened them with dismissal from the party, which would have meant automatic dismissal from the district legislature. Finally, a prominent Morotai businessman chartered five speedboats and a ferry and brought almost 2,000 supporters of the split to Tobelo, the North Halmahera

---

9   One leader of the *pemekaran* campaign confirmed that Christians were not as involved in the movement to establish a separate district as Muslims. However, this was not because they were against the division, he said, but rather because it was not 'the right time'.

10 'Aktivitas pemerintahan di Morotai masih lumpuh' [Government activities in Morotai still paralysed], *MetroTVNews*, 10 April 2007; 'Aktivitas pemerintahan di Pulau Morotai kembali normal' [Government activities return to normal in Morotai], *Antara*, 12 April 2007.

capital.[11] Hein gave in, fearing violence, and produced an official letter of recommendation. There were several more hurdles to be cleared in Jakarta, but once the district head had capitulated, the way was clear for the new district to be approved.[12]

The battle led to some significant political realignments. Because Hein, a Golkar stalwart, had threatened the pro-separation legislators with dismissal, some joined other parties. One such person crossed over to the National Mandate Party (Partai Amanat Nasional, PAN) out of gratitude to a senior member of Committee II who was a cadre of that party and had strongly supported Morotai's separation. Despite Abdul Gafur's early assistance, Golkar was associated with opposition to the new district owing to Hein's rejection of the plan. In contrast, Thaib Armaiyn, who by 2007 was representing PD, had provided early endorsement. Those who were deeply involved in the separation campaign saw PD and Yudhoyono's government as having been helpful, and therefore deserving of support. Said one of the leaders of the Morotai campaign: 'Thaib is head of Yudhoyono's success team, and Thaib supported *pemekaran* — so if I didn't support Yudhoyono, I'd be a traitor'. 'But', he continued, 'in my heart, I'm for Jusuf Kalla'.[13]

Legacy of the contested gubernatorial election

Traces in Morotai of the prolonged conflict over the North Maluku governorship were harder to find, and the impact, if any, was indirect. The election contest between Golkar member Abdul Gafur and PD-backed Thaib Armaiyn, which was held in November 2007 and finally resolved in Thaib's favour in early 2009, probably intensified the competition between the campaign teams of Kalla and Yudhoyono, particularly at the provincial level (ICG 2009).[14]

At the district level, Hein ran a Golkar fiefdom, but he was leaving nothing to chance. In July, other parties complained — with justification — that he was threatening civil servants with consequences if they did not vote for Kalla; the head of the district education office of North Halmahera was said to be meeting with village chiefs, heads of schools and teachers, warning them that if they had not yet received a formal let-

---

11   Interview with Syakir Sandry, 6 July 2009.
12   This account is based on interviews on 7 July 2009 with two of the principal supporters of separation, a member of the North Halmahera district parliament, Ahmad Peklian, and businessman Syakir Sandry.
13   Interview with Syakir Sandry, 7 July 2009.
14   Thaib was actually installed as governor in September 2008 but it took a Constitutional Court decision in early 2009 to finally put an end to Gafur's battle.

ter of assignment for their current jobs, he would ensure they were sent to remote areas if they did not choose Kalla.[15] Some teachers in remote Morotai also felt the pressure, although for them the threat of being sent to another out-of-the-way location was obviously less potent.

Thaib, on the other hand, was seen as having vast financial resources and good connections in Jakarta; he also had the advantage of backing a popular incumbent. Anyone with political ambitions had an incentive to cast their lot with him, despite the deep dislike many of them harboured for Thaib because of the questionable tactics he had used to win the governorship. As one party leader pragmatically said, 'No matter how bad he is, he's still powerful'. Apparently, the political elite in Morotai — including the five or six men with aspirations to be elected district head in 2010 — were caught in a dilemma: all were confronted with Hein and Thaib as the two most important local officials, and it was almost impossible to stay on the good side of both.

Kalla as the candidate of the east

Before the election, many in Morotai believed that Jusuf Kalla — who originated from South Sulawesi — had the local vote sewn up because the people of eastern Indonesia would naturally choose one of their own. Even if they themselves had decided on another candidate, they were convinced that their neighbours would vote for Kalla. One businessman said that when Habibie (another native of South Sulawesi) was president between 1998 and 1999, prices for two of Morotai's main crops, copra and cloves, had been high, and local farmers saw this as evidence that prosperity came when easterners were in charge. The good times had nothing to do with Habibie's policies, he said, but nevertheless many thought that if Kalla was elected, then commodity prices would somehow rise.[16]

An official of the local council of religious scholars (*ulama*) enumerated all the reasons he liked Kalla. First, because he was an easterner, 'like me'. Kalla, he said, came from the business world and therefore mixed easily with everyone, as opposed to Yudhoyono, who came from the military and was used to just taking or giving orders. The official also thought that Kalla's mission statement (*visi dan misi*) as expressed in the television debates was superior to Yudhoyono's; he particularly liked the proposed credit program for high school and university students. But despite all this the man said he was going to vote for Yudhoyono. The

---

15 These allegations were aired in the local press and confirmed by a teacher in Morotai.

16 Interview with Richard Samatara, 7 July 2009.

reason, once again, was highly pragmatic: 'Suharto was good because he had a long time to achieve things'. he said. 'If we give Yudhoyono five more years, maybe he'll be able to do more.'

Local economic issues

Among the voters and political leaders I interviewed, there was universal agreement on what Morotai needed: jobs, improved infrastructure, investment and better education. In 2006, per capita income was around half the national average — about $800, compared with a national average of about $1,500.[17] More and better roads were especially badly needed. A few kilometres outside Daruba the road was barely passable, and there were no paved roads at all in the western part of the island. A ring road was planned, as well as better facilities for air travel. The only transport to the Halmahera mainland that was both reliable and affordable was the ferry from Daruba to Tobelo; while there were some local marine taxis to other towns on the island, they were often out of commission because of high waves.

As noted above, when the district of North Halmahera came into existence in 2003, there were plans for a duty free port in Morotai. That idea has never materialised, although it remains part of the vision for the new district. The local elite continues to believe that Morotai has great potential for tourism. Several interviewees suggested that if only they could erect a monument to General MacArthur (and persuade President Obama to unveil it), then hoards of American tourists would flock to visit the rusting tanks and crumbling bunkers left over from the war. But with the island's electricity service operating for only half of every day at best, transportation poor and youthful backpackers showing little interest in the war relics, there is little to suggest that Morotai will become a tourist Mecca anytime soon. Indeed, its claim to economic viability — ostensibly a prerequisite for becoming a district — is open to serious question.

Very few people on Morotai believed that the outcome of the 2009 presidential elections would have a direct impact on the economic situation in Morotai. As an island at the margins of both the Indonesian state and the province of North Maluku, Morotai was unlikely to be on the radar screen of any of the three presidential candidates. This realisation was to a large extent responsible for the lack of enthusiasm among voters for the presidential ballot on Morotai, and explains why they believed that the upcoming district head election would be much more significant for their personal lives.

---

17   For the Morotai figures, see 'Profil Pulau Morotai' [Profile of Morotai Island], http://www.halmaherautara.com/artikel.php?id=10.

PARTY LEADERS

The legislative elections in April 2009 turned out not to be a particularly good predictor in Morotai of how voters would make their choice in July. This was in part because the old Golkar machine was more relevant for the legislative vote and thus made its presence more felt then. In addition, many of the smaller parties had strongholds in Maluku and recorded results there that were well above their national averages, but they had little influence on the presidential election dominated by Jakarta-based leaders. Most importantly, however, the local party leaders—with a few exceptions—were surprisingly powerless to influence the results, limiting their ability to act as effective power brokers for the presidential polls.

The good showing of the smaller parties produced a highly fragmented electoral landscape in North Halmahera and Morotai. In North Halmahera, Hein Namotemo produced a 16.9 per cent vote for Golkar. This was twice as high as the vote of any other party. PD came a distant second with 8.8 per cent, but other parties were clustered closely around it: the Crescent Moon and Star Party (Partai Bulan Bintang, PBB) gained 8.7 per cent, the Indonesian Democratic Party of Struggle (Partai Demokrasi Indonesia Perjuangan, PDIP) 7.8 per cent and the Christian-affiliated Prosperous Peace Party (Partai Damai Sejahtera, PDS) 7.1 per cent.[18] In the subdistrict of South Morotai, Golkar was again first, with 11 per cent of the vote, while PD came sixth, with 5.5 per cent. It was beaten by four Muslim parties—the United Development Party (Partai Persatuan Pembangunan, PPP), the Prosperous Justice Party (Partai Keadilan Sejahtera, PKS), the Star Reformist Party (Partai Bintang Reformasi, PBR) and PAN—and by the obscure Pioneers' Party (Partai Pelopor). Despite PD's poor performance, however, Yudhoyono won the subdistrict in July with 58.2 per cent of the vote. Coalition politics alone cannot explain the margin: whereas at the national level PD was backed by the four Muslim parties mentioned above, in North Maluku senior politicians of PPP and PAN actively supported Kalla.[19]

---

18 It is worth noting that the support for Islamist parties and PDS may be indicative of the religious polarisation that remains as a consequence of the 2000 conflict.

19 'Golkar Malut optimis menangkan JK–Win' [Golkar in North Maluku is optimistic about creating a Kalla–Wiranto victory], *Antara*, 24 May 2009. The article says that PAN, PBB and the People's Awakening Party (Partai Kebangkitan Bangsa, PKB), but not PPP, backed Kalla, but in Morotai PPP had banners up backing Kalla.

Despite Yudhoyono's success in 2004, Golkar leaders in North Halmahera and Morotai were confident that Kalla would be able to secure victory in 2009. They felt encouraged not only by Golkar's superior results in the local legislative elections, but also by the fact that Yudhoyono had won in 2004 only after the Golkar candidate had dropped out in the first round. In 2009, by contrast, Kalla was not only the official Golkar candidate but the party's chairperson. For his part, district chief Hein Namotemo argued that everything 'the government' had done in the last five years was actually part of Golkar's program, and had been implemented by Golkar's man, Vice-President Kalla. In a backhanded way, this was an implicit acknowledgment of the Yudhoyono administration's popularity and perceived achievements.[20]

While Golkar had high hopes for its candidate and confidence in its own role in facilitating his election, the reality on the ground was strikingly different. The influence of Golkar leaders — and other party functionaries — on the outcome of the election was in fact marginal. Local state officials, from village heads upwards, played a much more important role in mobilising the vote in July, because they had the wherewithal to exert pressure and offer incentives. The negligible role of party leaders was in part a function of the character of the personality-oriented presidential election in which the parties naturally mattered less than in the legislative polls that had preceded it. It was also a result of the neglect of Morotai — and sometimes even of the province — by the central party structures in Jakarta. In Morotai, the campaign teams of the presidential candidates at times seemed to operate independently of and more effectively than the parties, with the clout of local businesspeople being brought to bear.

The party loyalists

In spite of the general ineffectiveness of the parties, many party officials in Morotai were deeply committed to their organisations' broad ideological principles and historical roots. While at times highly critical of their parties, these functionaries shrugged off all suggestions of leaving them and joining rival organisations. Instead, they loyally carried out the orders of their central party boards and supported the presidential candidates nominated by them.[21]

---

20 'Tim JK–Win telah siap menggerakkan mesin politik' [Kalla–Wiranto team ready to mobilise political machine], *Tobelo Pos*, June 2008: 6.

21 All of the party leaders I interviewed were district-level functionaries, covering all of Morotai but operating out of a base in the subdistrict of South Morotai.

The two most striking examples of party loyalists were the leaders of PDIP and PPP. Surprisingly given their positions, they were frank in the extreme about the shortcomings of their parties. The PDIP leader, a man called Marhaen (after a peasant hero Sukarno used to refer to in his speeches), noted that he had received nothing from the party – not a single banner or piece of cloth – for use during the pro-Megawati campaign. Moreover, he complained, the party had no program to develop cadres and no sense of ethics. According to him, PDIP selected unpopular candidates to run for office and left it to the local party structure to promote them. He was not happy, for example, with Megawati's choice of former army Special Forces commander Prabowo Subianto as her vice-presidential candidate. Marhaen said his father had been a member of the Indonesian National Party (Partai Nasional Indonesia, PNI), PDIP's predecessor founded by Sukarno, and he was therefore determined to stay with PDIP no matter what. Given all of the party's problems, he said, the only way to keep yourself going was to have a sense of history.

The head of PPP was a transplanted Javanese businessman named Haji Abdullah M.T. Zain who had married a local woman and had been living in Morotai since 1986. He attributed PPP's disappointing result in the legislative elections to poor party management and poor communication between the executive council and local branches. In his view, the party had focused too much on religion and not enough on people's everyday concerns. He was not happy with PPP joining Yudhoyono's coalition, because the president was inclined to make glib promises on free schools, lower oil prices and so on that were not fulfilled. He also believed that Yudhoyono's government cared only about Java. Eventually, however, the PPP leader voted for Yudhoyono. When asked why he did not just leave PPP, he was shocked: 'To leave would be to allow oppression; the responsible thing to do is to stay and fix it'. But as in the case of his PDIP counterpart, he had a strong family connection to the party: one of his older brothers was Tosari Wijaya, a former secretary general of the party during the late Suharto years.

In addition to these examples from PDIP and PPP, there were many other party functionaries for whom the idea of joining another party – or voting for a candidate other than the one the party supported – was unthinkable. Though dissatisfied with their central party boards, they still felt bound to the institution and its candidates. In Golkar, there was a similar sense of loyalty towards party chair Kalla, although that had less to do with loyalist obedience to the party's headquarters in Jakarta than with Kalla's eastern Indonesian origins. Within PKS, by contrast, such loyalty was the result of the most rigorous and effective cadre training of all Indonesian parties.

The crossovers

While there were many party loyalists, party hopping was also wide-spread. Party politicians who left their old parties to join new ones had a variety of reasons for doing so. However, these reasons were more often related to unhappiness with the original party than to enthusiasm for the new one. Only in the case of the newly established Greater Indonesia Movement Party (Partai Gerakan Indonesia Raya, Gerindra) was attraction to and active support for the party leader, Prabowo Subianto, the determining factor.

One of the most prominent people in Morotai to change parties was a well-known businessman who had been a member of PPP throughout the Suharto years, saying it was the only way he could express his opposition to the regime. After the fall of the New Order, he became a leader of the campaign to establish Morotai as a district. In 2009 he decided to leave PPP after 21 years, saying it was on the decline, and joined a small party called Sun of the Nation Party (Partai Matahari Bangsa, PMB). Among political analysts, PMB was generally thought to stand a good chance in the elections because it was tacitly endorsed by Din Syamsuddin, the head of the mass modernist Muslim organisation Muhammadiyah. Feeling that he had a better chance of getting elected to local parliament with a smaller party, the former PPP cadre complained that 'in a big party, you have to play by other people's rules'. In the April elections, he indeed gained a seat in the district parliament and currently plans to run for district head. In the meantime, his party affiliation had no bearing on his choice for president: he opted to vote for Yudhoyono only because Thaib Armaiyn had supported the creation of the district of Morotai.

The head of Gerindra in Morotai had formerly been a supporter of the Islamist party PBB, and a strong proponent of Islamic law. But noting that public interest in religious parties was declining, he decided there was no longer any point in fighting for *syari'ah*. He saw more opportunities in the national parties, and he liked Prabowo's emphasis on clearing Indonesia's debt. He and his younger brother were recruited into Gerindra by the brother's classmate, who was the provincial party chair. Across Indonesia, the party was then seeking young professionals, and the brother — who had worked for an international non-government organisation helping with post-conflict reconstruction — fitted the bill. However, neither brother was enthusiastic about Megawati, the candidate Gerindra was backing.

Given the ambiguity of the feelings such party leaders expressed towards the candidates, it is not surprising that they had so little impact on the way the parties' followers voted.

VILLAGE HEADS

In contrast to the party leaders, the village heads had a huge amount at stake in the presidential election. They were under pressure both from the district head and the governor to deliver votes for their preferred candidates. If they failed to do so, they faced direct, palpable consequences, either for themselves or for their villages. From the village heads' perspective of power maintenance, the only two candidates worth supporting were Yudhoyono and Kalla; Megawati had no backers among the officials who counted. In the past, and particularly before 1998, village heads had often been a vital part of the Golkar machine. They were expected to fall into line with their superiors and produce a pro-government vote. Village heads today retain some vestiges of that influence, especially in remote areas such as Morotai. But even determined support from a village head could not necessarily deliver the desired result, as two of the following four examples suggest.

One village chief, just finishing up his six-year term, was a politically ambitious Bugis migrant who saw the governor — and therefore support for Yudhoyono — as the way forward for his career. Located not far from a port, his village had been badly affected by the attack in 2000, with churches and Christian houses burned to the ground. The resulting exodus had left a Muslim majority, and the fraction of the original Christian population that remained believed they would be safer with a Muslim head. He made no secret of the fact that he expected a Yudhoyono vote, and some families were afraid of him because of his thuggish behaviour. He frequently got drunk in the evenings and went around intimidating anyone he thought inclined to vote for another party. On election day he stood outside the polling place watching everyone come and go. The village voted overwhelming for Yudhoyono, with 276 votes for the president, 131 for Jusuf Kalla and 87 for Megawati.

The second village head interviewed was a local Golkar stalwart who ran a village in the heart of the urban commercial area of South Morotai. His closest political ties were to the district head. He threw himself fully into the campaign for Kalla, as he would have done for any Golkar candidate. He was also an unabashed political operator and disarmingly open about his methods. When people came to get their identity cards renewed or to obtain other letters or permits, he would talk up the Kalla candidacy and offer to waive document fees if the applicant promised to vote for him. He gave newcomers to the village special attention, suggesting that a vote for Kalla would ensure their security. He acknowledged cheerfully that delivering a win for Kalla would secure construction projects for the village, so there were direct payoffs, presumably for himself as well. On the day before the election he was absolutely convinced that he could

346   *Problems of Democratisation in Indonesia*

deliver a victory—and he did. His village voted 248 for Kalla, 192 for Yudhoyono and 24 for Megawati.

The third case study involved a village head from PDIP. He disclosed that many village chiefs were under enormous pressure because they were being given different directives from the governor and the district head. In his own case, he was more afraid of the district head and had thus agreed to deliver a Kalla victory. However, he failed miserably: the village delivered 237 votes to Yudhoyono, 88 to Kalla and 13 to Megawati. 'It would have been better if it had been close', he said morosely. On the following day, he had to go to Tobelo and face the district head. All those who produced Kalla wins would get an 'envelope', a cash payout. He was not willing to speculate what the consequences of his failure would be, and was at a complete loss to explain the Yudhoyono victory in his village.

The fourth village was the one that had been worst hit by the February 2000 violence. But in the view of villagers, it delivered the perfect outcome: 131 votes for Kalla, 129 for Megawati and 126 for Yudhoyono. The consensus of an impromptu post-poll discussion among the people from all four villages was that such a close and harmonious result was real democracy. The village head had backed Yudhoyono, but he had got a result that would please the district head without offending Yudhoyono's backers.

REACTIONS TO THE RESULTS

As the national results began to come in, several village heads and a few local businessmen gathered under a tree near a popular roadside shop. They were shocked that Kalla had not done better; at the very least they had expected him to perform well enough to keep Yudhoyono beneath the 50 per cent threshold that candidates needed to exceed in order to avoid a run-off. One participant in the discussion tried to explain the strong local vote for Yudhoyono in terms of the women's vote. 'They think he's handsome', he said, to general chuckles. (The shop owner's wife, when she heard this later, said in irritation, 'Does he think we can't choose for other reasons?') But the man then speculated that the vote for Yudhoyono must have been largely spontaneous, because pressure from the village heads could not explain the high margins.

The group came to three general conclusions. First, in the overall picture of the national elections, eastern Indonesia did not matter. 'We can all vote one way, East Java votes another, that's it. ... We don't count', said one. Second, they were convinced that pre-election surveys had influenced the voters. The lesson they drew for the upcoming 2010 election for Morotai district head was that the candidates should conduct surveys and announce the results before the election so that people could vote for the winner. Third, in the next presidential election in five years time, all the old faces would be too old to run, leaving only Prabowo, Megawati's running mate, on the horizon. 'In 2014', one man said to general assent, 'Prabowo will clean up (*Prabowo makan semua*)'. They agreed that there was no chance that a candidate would emerge from among the ranks of local officials such as governors, 'because by the time their terms are up, they're all corrupt'.

CONCLUSION

This case study of the presidential ballot in Morotai provides useful insights into how elections are fought in post-Suharto Indonesia, and what motivates citizens when casting their votes. Most importantly, the findings of the study show that analysis of voting behaviour and other electoral patterns in democratic Indonesia needs to avoid excessive generalisations. Voters make their choices based on a vast range of personal and political considerations, defying theoretical models developed by comparative political scientists. On Morotai, primordial affiliations motivated some voters, but were irrelevant for others; some citizens were susceptible to offers of material or service-based compensation for their votes, but others were not; and some locals had very rational considerations for their choice, while others did not. But for all of the pre-election politicking that went on in Morotai, and for all of the pressure at the provincial, district and village levels, the fact remains that most voters seemed to vote according to their conscience. A few particularly dynamic — or particularly intimidating — village heads may have managed to sway the vote, but the general surprise at the results suggests that outside influence was limited.

While not the main focus of this chapter, the case study also adds an interesting local perspective to the debate about the logistical problems that engulfed the elections across Indonesia (see Schmidt's chapter in this volume). In Morotai, all of the citizens I interviewed took part in the elections, and while there were invalid ballots, I found no cases of blank ones in the villages that I visited. Since everyone knew everyone else, there was no question of people not being registered or not being allowed to vote. If someone's name did not appear on the list but otherwise met the qualifications, he or she was allowed to vote. There were problems with the voter lists in Morotai as elsewhere, but it did not seem to result in any widespread disenfranchisement.

Finally, the findings of this study highlight the complex interplay between local and national politics. No one was foolish enough to believe that Morotai's concerns would be a priority for the newly elected government in Jakarta. But there was a vague sense of connection between national and local politics. Yudhoyono's win redounded to the credit of those members of his local campaign team who planned to contest the 2010 district elections. Overall, there was widespread awareness that the 2010 elections would matter more to the lives of people on Morotai than the presidential ballot, explaining the absence of great enthusiasm for the latter. But the inhabitants of Morotai also accepted the idea that this five-year cycle of choosing a national leader was now routine and no longer a hugely exciting event of historic proportions. In other words, the elections in Morotai provide evidence for the 'normalisation of politics in Indonesia' (Aspinall 2005), with all its appealing — and less appealing — ramifications.

REFERENCES

Aspinall, Edward (2005), 'Elections and the normalization of politics in Indonesia', *South East Asia Research* 13(2): 117–56.

Baswedan, Anies (2007), 'Indonesian politics in 2007: the presidency, local elections and the future of democracy', *Bulletin of Indonesian Economic Studies* 43(3): 323–40.

ICG (International Crisis Group) (2009), 'Local election disputes in Indonesia: the case of North Maluku', Asia Briefing No. 86, ICG, 22 January.

King, Dwight (2003), *Half-hearted Reform: Electoral Institutions and the Struggle for Democracy in Indonesia*, Praeger, New York NY.

Mietzner, Marcus (2009), 'Indonesia and the pitfalls of low-quality democracy: a case study of the gubernatorial elections in North Sulawesi', in A. Ufen and M. Bünte (eds), *Democratization in Post-Suharto Indonesia*, Routledge, London and New York, pp. 124–49.

Smith, Claire Q. (2009), 'The return of the sultan? Patronage, power, and political machines in "post"-conflict North Maluku', in M. Erb and P. Sulistiyanto (eds), *Deepening Democracy in Indonesia: Direct Elections for Local Leaders*, Institute of Southeast Asian Studies, Singapore, pp. 303–26.

Sulistyo, Hermawan (2002), 'Electoral politics in Indonesia: a hard way to democracy?', in A. Croissant (ed.), *Electoral Politics in Southeast and East Asia*, Friedrich Ebert Stiftung, Singapore, pp. 75–99.

Wilson, Chris (2008), *Ethno-religious Violence in Indonesia*, Routledge Contemporary Southeast Asia Series, Routledge, Oxford.

INDEX

B

Bakrie, Aburizal, 69, 70, 111, 157, 170
Bali, 79, 124, 152, 172, 205–6, 256, 309
Bangladesh, 24, 25, 27, 28, 29, 30, 31, 32, 33, 34, 36
Bank Century, 70, 171, 174
Bank Indonesia, 171, 172
Banten, 254–5
Betawi Brotherhood Forum (FBR), 211–12
BMI
    see Indonesian Young Bulls
Boediono, 61, 64, 70, 78, 79, 82, 84, 88, 94, 127, 136, 171, 174, 322, 323n
Bolivia, 25, 27
BPK
    see State Audit Agency
Brazil, 24, 28, 29, 30, 32, 36, 45
breakdown of democracy, 24, 25–6
Brigass, 205
Bulgaria, 216
Burundi, 25

C

Cambodia, 8, 216
candidacy lists, 'zipper system', 222, 232, 238, 239, 243, 262
    see also party list system, open
candidates, electoral
    background of, 275, 300, 325
    celebrity, 12, 15, 59, 186
    competition between, 186, 187, 195, 272–3, 274, 293, 294, 302, 303
    corrupt, 276–7
    direct local elections, 126, 131, 245, 246–51
    educational threshold for nomination, 273
    independent, 247, 251, 262, 271, 271n, 273–4, 289
    number in 2009 elections, 186, 270
    ordinary citizens' participation, 187, 273–4, 275
    proportions of male and female, 230, 245, 247, 248
    role of political consultants, 133–6
    selection of, 126–7, 131, 246–51, 325
    top positions on party list, 231
Central African Republic, 26
Central Asia, 4
Centre for Electoral Reform (CETRO), 55, 227–8, 235, 259n
children
    arrests of, 214n
    child care services, 220
    mortality rate, 28, 30
Children of Betawi Communication Forum (Forkabi), 201, 212

China, 24
civil liberties, 6, 25, 26, 30–35
    trends, 31
civil service, 26, 33, 224, 261
    local, 279, 280–82, 300
civil society, 11–13, 66, 115–16, 176, 261, 275, 283
civil war, 27, 35
clerics, 71
comparativism, 2, 3–5, 23–49
Constitutional Court, 58, 59, 62, 63, 70, 100, 112, 119, 120, 143, 155, 163, 172, 184, 232, 247, 271
    ruling on party lists and quotas, 107, 108, 110, 233–4, 236, 237, 239, 272, 302, 324
constitutional reforms, 6, 10, 161, 162–3, 176
consultants, professional, 64, 122–39
corruption, 2, 5, 7, 9, 27, 34, 48–9, 103, 104, 141, 143, 146, 157, 163, 212, 216, 254, 255, 276–7
    Aceh, 290, 300–302
    control of, comparisons, 26n, 32, 33–4, 35, 36
    elections, 55
    local, 16, 257, 258, 259, 269, 270, 277, 279, 280, 281, 282, 283, 300
    members of the legislature, 9, 11, 98, 148, 163, 170, 277
    political parties, 147–9, 152, 210, 271, 272
Corruption Eradication Commission (KPK), 34, 48, 148, 163
Corruption Perception Index, 9
Costa Rica, 222, 240
Council of Islamic Scholars (MUI), 210
Crescent Moon and Star Party (PBB), 58, 291, 341, 344
cronyism, 15, 177
culture, 181, 189, 326
    political, 16, 72, 96, 161, 164, 170, 176, 199, 207
    popular, 191–5

D

data collection, local elections, 244–5
decentralisation, 15, 16, 224, 267–83, 328
    budgets, 278
    effect on accountability and transparency, 273–80, 282
    reasons for, 268–9
    regulatory framework, 270–73
    revenue sharing, 267–8
Defence Cooperation Agreement, 68
Defenders of Islam Front (FPI), 13, 209–11
    membership, 210n
democracy indexes, 4, 5

INDONESIA UPDATE SERIES

Indonesia Assessment 1988 (Regional Development)
edited by Hal Hill and Jamie Mackie

Indonesia Assessment 1990 (Ownership)
edited by Hal Hill and Terry Hull

Indonesia Assessment 1991 (Education)
edited by Hal Hill

Indonesia Assessment 1992 (Political Perspectives)
edited by Harold Crouch

Indonesia Assessment 1993 (Labour)
edited by Chris Manning and Joan Hardjono

Finance as a Key Sector in Indonesia's Development (1994)
edited by Ross McLeod

Development in Eastern Indonesia (1995)
edited by Colin Barlow and Joan Hardjono

Population and Human Resources (1996)
edited by Gavin W. Jones and Terence H. Hull

Indonesia's Technological Challenge (1997)
edited by Hal Hill and Thee Kian Wie

Post-Soeharto Indonesia: Renewal or Chaos? (1998)
edited by Geoff Forrester

Indonesia in Transition: Social Aspects of Reformasi and Crisis (1999)
edited by Chris Manning and Peter van Diermen

Indonesia Today: Challenges of History (2000)
edited by Grayson J. Lloyd and Shannon L. Smith

Women in Indonesia: Gender, Equity and Development (2001)
edited by Kathryn Robinson and Sharon Bessell

Local Power and Politics in Indonesia: Decentralisation and Democratisation (2002)
edited by Edward Aspinall and Greg Fealy

Business in Indonesia: New Challenges, Old Problems (2003)
edited by M. Chatib Basri and Pierre van der Eng

The Politics and Economics of Indonesia's Natural Resources (2004)
edited by Budy P. Resosudarmo

Different Societies, Shared Futures: Australia, Indonesia and the Region (2005)
edited by John Monfries

Indonesia: Democracy and the Promise of Good Governance (2006)
edited by Ross H. McLeod and Andrew MacIntyre

Expressing Islam: Religious Life and Politics in Indonesia (2007)
edited by Greg Fealy and Sally White

Indonesia beyond the Water's Edge: Managing an Archipelagic State (2008)
edited by Robert Cribb and Michele Ford

Problems of Democratisation in Indonesia: Elections, Institutions and Society (2009)
edited by Edward Aspinall and Marcus Mietzner

www.ingramcontent.com/pod-product-compliance
Lightning Source LLC
Chambersburg PA
CBHW021544260326
41914CB00001B/156